I0047808

Building Dashboards with Microsoft Dynamics GP 2016

Second Edition

Learn to build professional and powerful dashboards with Microsoft Dynamics GP and Excel

Belinda Allen

Mark Polino

Pack<t>

BIRMINGHAM - MUMBAI

Building Dashboards with Microsoft Dynamics GP 2016

Second Edition

Copyright © 2017 Packt Publishing

All rights reserved. No part of this book may be reproduced, stored in a retrieval system, or transmitted in any form or by any means, without the prior written permission of the publisher, except in the case of brief quotations embedded in critical articles or reviews.

Every effort has been made in the preparation of this book to ensure the accuracy of the information presented. However, the information contained in this book is sold without warranty, either express or implied. Neither the authors, nor Packt Publishing, and its dealers and distributors will be held liable for any damages caused or alleged to be caused directly or indirectly by this book.

Packt Publishing has endeavored to provide trademark information about all of the companies and products mentioned in this book by the appropriate use of capitals. However, Packt Publishing cannot guarantee the accuracy of this information.

First published: March 2013

Second edition: March 2017

Production reference: 1030317

Published by Packt Publishing Ltd.
Livery Place
35 Livery Street
Birmingham B3 2PB, UK.

ISBN 978-1-78646-761-4

www.packtpub.com

Credits

Authors
Belinda Allen

Mark Polino

Reviewer
Vaidhyanathan Mohan

Commissioning Editor
Ashwin Nair

Acquisition Editor
Denim Pinto

Content Development Editor
Siddhi Chavan

Technical Editors
Kunal Chaudhari

Abhishek Sharma

Copy Editors
Zainab Bootwala

Karuna Narayanan

Project Coordinator
Izzat Contractor

Proofreader
Safis Editing

Indexer
Aishwarya Gangawane

Graphics
Jason Monteiro

Production Coordinator
Aparna Bhagat

Cover Work
Aparna Bhagat

About the Authors

Belinda Allen is a Microsoft Most Valuable Professional for Dynamics GP (MVP) and a GPUG (GP User Group) All-Star. Belinda is currently the Business Intelligence Program Manager for the new Azure Cloud-based SaaS ERP offering, PowerGP Online. This is an amped-up version of the GP we all love, running in the Microsoft Azure Cloud. In this role, she helps both Partners and Customers design and implement BI methodologies, allowing businesses to make decisions based on timely and accurate information.

Belinda was one of the co-founders of Smith & Allen Consulting, Inc. (SACI), a New York City based firm with over 25 years' experience specializing in business intelligence, analytics and ERP software. On April 1, 2016, SACI joined forces with Njevity, Inc. (www.NjevityToGo.com). Now she gets to spend time in her favorite place, the world of Business Intelligence (BI). NjevityToGo offers solutions for ERP, CRM, BI, and much more in the cloud. Njevity is also the force behind PowerGP Online.

Belinda's first book, Real-world Business Intelligence with Microsoft Dynamics GP was co-written with Mark Polino. It's a dive into where to Implementing a Business Intelligence Methodology with Microsoft Dynamics GP.

Currently a member of the Credentialing Council for the Association of Dynamics Professionals, Belinda was the first Council Chair. In this role, she led a team of community leaders providing guidance and insight in the delivery and development of credentials for both Microsoft Dynamics GP and Microsoft Dynamics NAV.

Belinda is also an inaugural member of the Board of Advisors for PBIUG (Power BI User Group.) In this role she provides her experience to the User Board Members, while they create the foundation for this new organization. The goal is to make Power BI a critical tool in the user's organizations.

Belinda began implementing ERP systems so long ago that Windows was not an operating system but an application. And at that time, larger businesses used main frames with monitors that projected green type on black backgrounds, and smaller business did their accounting by hand. Having seen the evolution that has taken place over the years from sheets of paper to integrated analytics, Belinda still gets excited every time she helps a business improve.

Belinda is also well known for her blog, `www.BelindaTheGPcsi.com`. On her blog, she shares really useful information about the product quickly and succinctly. She has earned the nickname GP CSI because she excels at reviewing GP problems and figuring out what went wrong… and why. With followers from all over the globe, she is able to share knowledge and achieve her mission--"To improve the lives and business success of my followers." Belinda has just started her new blog, `www.BIbelinda.com`, which is devoted to Microsoft Power BI.

When not delving into GP problems and spearheading business success for clients, Belinda enjoys sailing, crochet/knitting, sewing/quilting, reading, and turning wood.

For all the good things in my life, I would like to thank my husband, Richard Allen. He's been my best friend and the love of my life for close to 30 years. He's one of the few people I know who loves learning as much as I do. Besides that, he gets my odd sense of humor.

I'd like to thank Mark Polino for trusting me to update his words and ideas. I'm not only honored by this trust, I'm grateful for the opportunity. Counting you (and Dara) as my friends is something I cherish.

Finally, I'd like to thank my parents. Their support for me has only grown stronger as time goes by. I'm thankful they taught me to think for myself, love to learn new things, and laugh.

Mark Polino is CPA, with additional certifications in financial forensics (CFF) and information technology (CITP). He is a Microsoft MVP for Business Solutions and a GPUG All Star who has worked with Dynamics GP and its predecessors since 1999.

He works as the Director of Client Services for Fastpath, and he runs the `DynamicAccounting.net` website dedicated to all things Dynamics GP. He is a regularly featured speaker at Dynamics GP related events.

This is Mark's tenth book, and his seventh GP related book with Packt Publishing. His work includes eight technology-focused books and two novels.

He is also the author of the best-selling Microsoft Dynamics GP 2010 Cookbook, the spin off Lite edition, and a co-author for updated GP 2013 and 2016 editions, all from Packt Publishing.

First, a huge thank you to Belinda Allen for taking on this project and extending it into places I wouldn't have had the courage to go. You were the driving force behind making this book a reality.

Second, to all my friends in the greater GP community, thank you for putting your trust in me through the website, presentations, and books like this. It is not something I take lightly.

Finally, to my wife, thank you again for your infinite patience as you listen to me blather on about book projects I'm working on.

About the Reviewer

Vaidhyanathan Mohan is a certified Senior Microsoft Dynamics GP/CRM Implementation & Product Consultant, with expertise in Microsoft Dynamics GP and related technologies. He has worked on various challenging Dynamics GP customizations and implementations.

He's an active participant on all Microsoft Community forums. His blog, Dynamics GP - Learn & Discuss (`http://vaidymohan.com/`) has been listed on Microsoft's official Dynamics GP blog space. He has also reviewed several books on Dynamics GP, such as Developing Microsoft Dynamics GP Business Applications, Microsoft Dynamics GP 2013 Cookbook, etc.

He is who he is now because of his devoted parents, his brother, his wife, and his daughter. He is an avid photography enthusiast (`http://500px.com/seshadri`), loves music, lives on coffee, travels to learn different cultures and nature, and is immensely interested in anything related to Microsoft Dynamics GP.

www.PacktPub.com

For support files and downloads related to your book, please visit
www.PacktPub.com.

Did you know that Packt offers eBook versions of every book published, with
PDF and ePub files available? You can upgrade to the eBook version at www.
PacktPub.com and as a print book customer, you are entitled to a discount on the
eBook copy. Get in touch with us at service@packtpub.com for more details.

At www.PacktPub.com, you can also read a collection of free technical articles,
sign up for a range of free newsletters and receive exclusive discounts and offers
on Packt books and eBooks.

Mapt

https://www.packtpub.com/mapt

Get the most in-demand software skills with Mapt. Mapt gives you full access to all
Packt books and video courses, as well as industry-leading tools to help you plan
your personal development and advance your career.

Why subscribe?

- Fully searchable across every book published by Packt
- Copy and paste, print, and bookmark content
- On demand and accessible via a web browser

Customer Feedback

Thanks for purchasing this Packt book. At Packt, quality is at the heart of our editorial process. To help us improve, please leave us an honest review on this book's Amazon page at https://www.amazon.com/dp/1786467615.

If you'd like to join our team of regular reviewers, you can email us at customerreviews@packtpub.com. We award our regular reviewers with free eBooks and videos in exchange for their valuable feedback. Help us be relentless in improving our products!

Table of Contents

Preface

The first edition of *Building Dashboards with Microsoft Dynamics GP 2013 and Excel 2013*, written by Mark Polino, is an amazing tool for building dashboards in Excel. Since the release of this book, Excel has continued to increase its value to the GP Community. With GP having gone through two major updates and Excel having gone through one major update, Mark felt it was time to refresh his book. Luckily, Mark chose me to take the lead on the updating process.

Those of you who know Mark and me know that although we are close friends, we love to challenge each other and ourselves. We prove this year after year in an Excel Deathmatch we call The Excel Shootout. We invite another contestant for the audience, but it's really a duel between Mark and me. The same thing in our souls that force us to challenge ourselves made us think, what if we added some other Excel and dashboarding elements? The result: this second edition, including both the new free Jet Express for GP and Microsoft Power BI. More Excel, more dashboards, and more cow bell. Sorry for the cow bell joke, that was just for Mark.

Can you use this book if you do not have Dynamics GP? Of course! Although, the data samples come directly from GP, the Excel and Power BI sections are generic for any data. The Jet Express for GP section will work only for Dynamics GP and Dynamics NAV.

What this book covers

Chapter 1, *Getting Data from Dynamics GP 2016 to Excel 2016*, covers the first step to building a report or a dashboard and getting data. In this chapter, we discuss the many options of getting GP Data (and in some cases, any SQL data) into Excel.

Chapter 2, *The Ultimate GP to Excel Tool – Refreshable Excel Reports*, walks us through using prebuilt Excel reports in GP. This chapter also covers two other important topics—granting security to the GP (SQL) data and how to refresh the data in the reports once they are built.

Chapter 3, *Pivot Tables – The Basic Building Blocks*, explains the most important element of the dashboard, the Pivot Table. The Pivot Table is such a powerful tool; every Excel user should make it their go-to tool of choice.

Chapter 4, *Making Your Data Visually Appealing and Meaningful with Formatting, Conditional Formatting, and Charts*, guides you through formatting options. Formatting is more than just making a chart pretty. What's more valuable when you are driving in your car, the gas gauge or the number of miles you can drive with the amount of gas you have?

Chapter 5, *Drilling Back to the Source Data and Other Cool Stuff*, helps you add credibility to your report. Being able to look at the data in its source with a single click will make you the office champion. This chapter also covers slicers and timelines, which are essential for creating focus on your data.

Chapter 6, *Introducing Jet Reports Express*, explains not only why you would want to use this report to create basic financial statements inside Excel, but also why they are giving their product away for free. We'll even build an Excel-based General Ledger Trial Balance.

Chapter 7, *Building Financial Reports in Jet Express for GP*, walks us through building a simple Balance Sheet and a simple Profit and Loss report. Using the foundations learned in the chapter, you can become a lean, mean financial report writing machine.

Chapter 8, *Introducing Microsoft Power BI*, acquaints us with Microsoft's new pride and joy, Power BI. This chapter is an overview of the product itself. Understanding where and how the reports are consumed is essential in planning how to build them.

Chapter 9, *Getting Data in Power BI*, reviews (only) some of the options of getting data into Power BI.

Chapter 10, *Creating Power BI Visuals*, will probably be your favorite chapter. In this chapter, we will actually create the charts, cards, tables, and other visuals that display our data.

Chapter 11, *Using the Power BI Service*, is where we learn how to publish and consume our data on the Web and, therefore, our mobile devices. We will even learn how to combine individual visuals on different reports to make a single dashboard.

Chapter 12, *Sharing and Refreshing Data and Dashboards in Power BI*, followed by the summary of this chapter.

Chapter 13, *Using the Power Query Editor*, is probably the most important chapter in the Power BI section. Rarely our data is formatted (or modeled) exactly the way we need for reports. It could be that we just want to combine data from our GP with data from our CRM. This chapter covers how to edit or model our data.

Chapter 14, Bonus Chapter, is kind of the proverbial kitchen sink. We'll see two additional features for Excel—Jet Express for GP and Power BI. This was just for fun!

What you need for this book

The following list is software prerequisites that are required:

- Microsoft Office 2016 Professional Plus or Microsoft Office 365 Business
- Microsoft SQL Server 2012, 2014 or 2016
- Microsoft Dynamics GP 2016 with the Fabrikam sample company deployed
- A web browser for links
- Optional—being a data nut like me!

Who this book is for

This book is for the person that always gets asked questions about their GP data. How much cash do we have? What's the Accounts Payables and/or Receivables balance? Who have we sold our product to? What's in Inventory? You get the point. Basically, if you spend time digging through data for answers, this is for you.

This book is also for the forward-thinking individuals who want to stay ahead of trends and competitors and get the raise they deserve.

Conventions

In this book, you will find a number of text styles that distinguish between different kinds of information. Here are some examples of these styles and an explanation of their meaning.

Code words in text, database table names, folder names, filenames, file extensions, pathnames, dummy URLs, user input, and Twitter handles are shown as follows: "The Dex.ini file is located in the Data folder of the Dynamics GP installation directory."

A block of code is set as follows:

```
=GETPIVOTDATA("Period Balance",Revenue!$A$3,"Year",$E$5,"Period
ID",E$6)
```

New terms and **important words** are shown in bold. Words that you see on the screen, for example, in menus or dialog boxes, appear in the text like this: "We need to turn on **Developer** ribbon in Excel. In Excel 2016, go to **File** | **Options** | **Customize Ribbon**."

> Warnings or important notes appear in a box like this.

> Tips and tricks appear like this.

Reader feedback

Feedback from our readers is always welcome. Let us know what you think about this book—what you liked or disliked. Reader feedback is important for us as it helps us develop titles that you will really get the most out of.

To send us general feedback, simply e-mail feedback@packtpub.com, and mention the book's title in the subject of your message.

If there is a topic that you have expertise in and you are interested in either writing or contributing to a book, see our author guide at www.packtpub.com/authors.

Customer support

Now that you are the proud owner of a Packt book, we have a number of things to help you to get the most from your purchase.

Downloading the color images of this book

We also provide you with a PDF file that has color images of the screenshots/ diagrams used in this book. The color images will help you better understand the changes in the output. You can download this file from

https://www.packtpub.com/sites/default/files/downloads/
BuildingDashboardswithMicrosoftDynamicsGP2016SecondEdition_
ColorImages.pdf

Errata

Although we have taken every care to ensure the accuracy of our content, mistakes do happen. If you find a mistake in one of our books—maybe a mistake in the text or the code—we would be grateful if you could report this to us. By doing so, you can save other readers from frustration and help us improve subsequent versions of this book. If you find any errata, please report them by visiting http://www.packtpub.com/submit-errata, selecting your book, clicking on the **Errata Submission Form** link, and entering the details of your errata. Once your errata are verified, your submission will be accepted and the errata will be uploaded to our website or added to any list of existing errata under the Errata section of that title.

To view the previously submitted errata, go to https://www.packtpub.com/books/content/support and enter the name of the book in the search field. The required information will appear under the **Errata** section.

Piracy

Piracy of copyrighted material on the Internet is an ongoing problem across all media. At Packt, we take the protection of our copyright and licenses very seriously. If you come across any illegal copies of our works in any form on the Internet, please provide us with the location address or website name immediately so that we can pursue a remedy.

Please contact us at copyright@packtpub.com with a link to the suspected pirated material.

We appreciate your help in protecting our authors and our ability to bring you valuable content.

Questions

If you have a problem with any aspect of this book, you can contact us at questions@packtpub.com, and we will do our best to address the problem.

1

Getting Data from Dynamics GP 2016 to Excel 2016

In more than 25 years of experience working in **enterprise resource planning** (**ERP**) consulting, every customer I've worked with put something of importance in Microsoft Excel. Why? The same reason you are reading this book. We all know how to use it, we like using it, and the people we share reports with know how to use it. However, we all want to know more about Excel, we all want to use it better, and (I cannot state this in big enough font) we want to impress someone with how great we are at using it. Yes, this means we want to share files and reports that make our colleagues and managers say, "Wow, how did you do this?," all while creating and managing these reports in less time.

Together, we will explore the power of **Microsoft Excel 2016** and **Microsoft Dynamics GP 2016** where we will build simple dashboards that looks anything but simple. Don't worry; we will not be doing any of the "developer-ish" stuff such as named ranges, macros, or VLOOKUPs. Microsoft has added so many amazing features to Excel that you can create amazing reports and dashboards all using native tools.

Before we can build a great Excel-based dashboard using the data in Dynamics GP 2016, we have to get the data out of GP and into Excel. This chapter covers eight major ways to get data from Dynamics GP into Excel, with a few extra options thrown in at the end.

By the end of this chapter, you should be able to get data into Excel using:

- SmartList exports
- SmartList Export Solutions
- Get and Transform (formerly Microsoft Power Query)

- Office data-connection files
- **SQL Server Reporting Services (SSRS)**
- **SQL Server Management Studio (SSMS)**
- Jet Reports Express for Excel
- Analysis cubes

> Occasionally, we will reference either the Rich Client or the Web Client for Dynamics GP 2016. If you are not sure which option you have, follow the directions for the Rich Client.
>
> - **Dynamics Rich Client**: This is when Dynamics is installed directly on the machine
> - **Dynamics Web Client**: This is when Dynamics is accessed through a browser (Internet Explorer, Chrome, Firefox, Safari, and so on)

SmartList exports

Exporting from a SmartList to Excel is the easiest and most commonly used method in Dynamics GP to get data to Microsoft Excel. We'll practice with an account summary SmartList.

To export from a SmartList to Excel for the Dynamics Rich Client, follow these steps:

1. In Dynamics GP 2016, go to **Microsoft Dynamics GP | SmartList**.
2. Click on the plus sign (**+**) next to Financial and select Accounts.
3. Once the SmartList finishes loading, click on the large, green **Excel** button to export this SmartList to Excel:

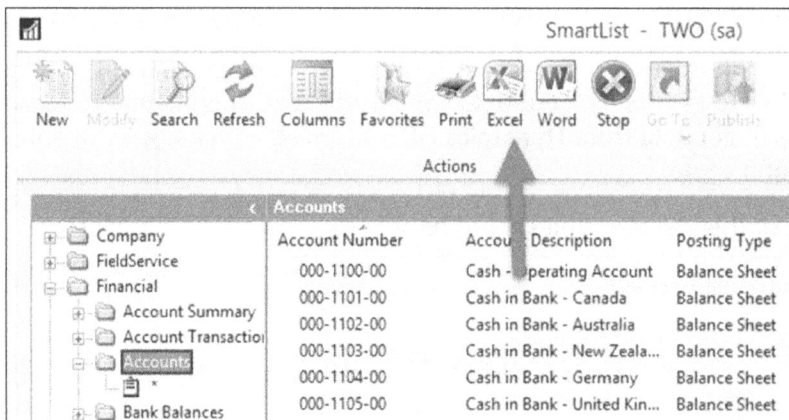

To export from a SmartList to Excel for the Dynamics Web Client, follow these steps:

1. In Dynamics GP 2016, select **Administration** from the navigation panel on the left-hand side.

2. On the area page, go to **Reports | SmartList**.

3. Click on the plus sign (**+**) next to Financial and select Accounts.

4. Once the SmartList finishes loading, click on the large green **Excel** button to export this SmartList to Excel.

In 2010, Microsoft revealed a previously unreleased Dex.ini switch that can dramatically improve the time it takes to export SmartLists to Microsoft Excel. The Dex.ini file is a launch file used to control system behavior, and this switch changes the behavior of an Excel export. Instead of sending data to Excel one line at a time, the switch tells Dynamics GP to bundle the SmartList lines together and send them to Excel as a group.

This switch is unsupported and can render the results differently than the default export process. Test this in your test system before using in production. The Dex.ini file is located in the Data folder of the Dynamics GP installation directory. To use this switch, add the following line to the Dex.ini file and restart Dynamics GP:

```
SmartlistEnhancedExcelExport=TRUE
```

SmartList Export Solutions

While SmartList exports are great for sending Dynamics GP data to Excel for analysis, they aren't an ideal solution for a dashboard. SmartLists sends data to a new Excel file each time. It's a lot of work to export data and rebuild a dashboard every month. An improved option is to use a SmartList Export Solution.

SmartList Export Solutions let you export GP data to a saved Excel workbook. They also provide the option to run an Excel macro before and/or after the data populates in Excel. As an example, we will format the header automatically after exporting financial summary information.

Getting ready

We have a little setup work to do for this one first. Since these exports are typically repetitive, the setup is worth the effort. Here is how it's done:

1. Access SmartList in the same method used for SmartList exports (where you open SmartList depends on whether you are using the Rich Client or the Web Client of GP).

2. Go to `Financial | Account Summary` on the left-hand side to generate a SmartList.

3. Click on the **Excel** button to send the SmartList to Excel.

4. Next, we need to turn on **Developer** ribbon in Excel. In Excel 2016, go to **File | Options | Customize Ribbon**.

5. Select the box next to **Developer** on the right-hand side. Click on **OK**.

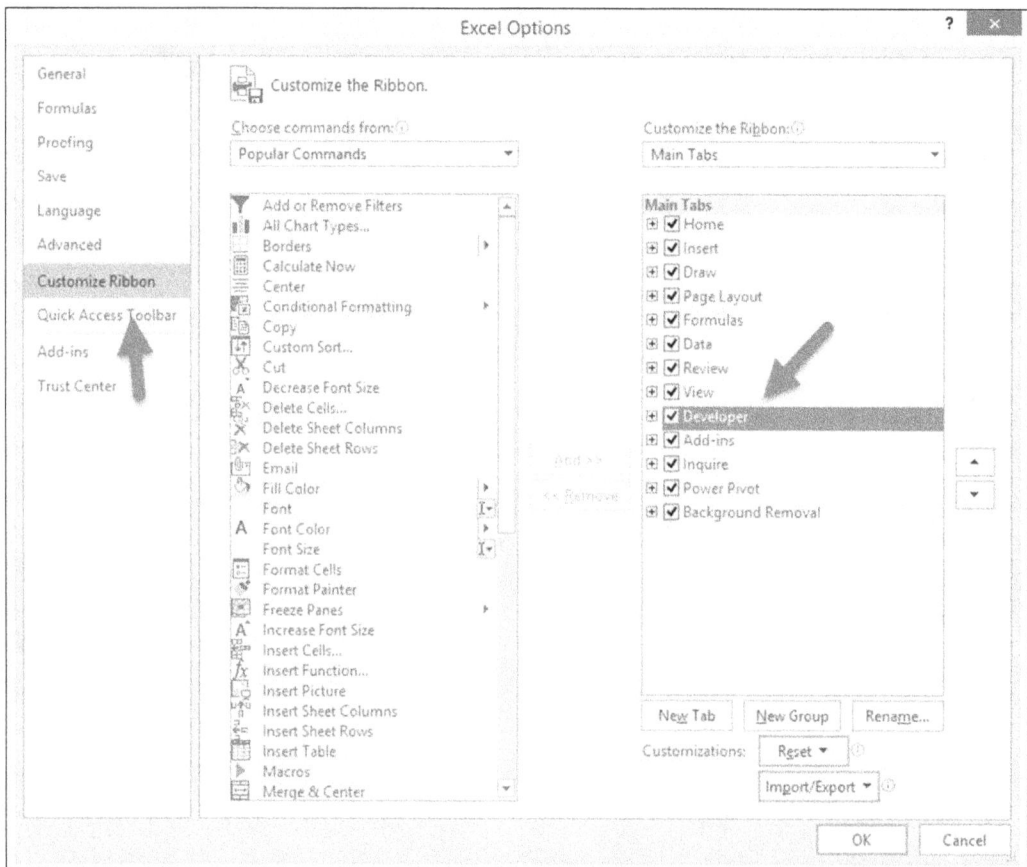

Creating macros

A SmartList Export Solution allows you to run an Excel macro before or after the data arrives to format or manipulate the information so that you only have to do it once. Let's record our Excel macro using these steps:

1. Click on the **Developer** tab and select **Record Macro**. Accept the default name of `Macro1` and click on **OK**:

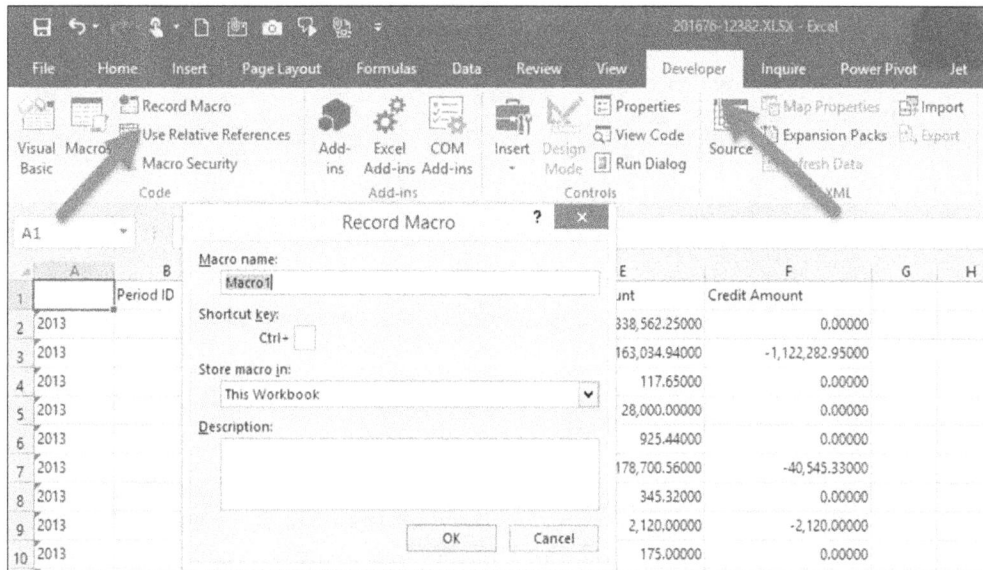

2. In Excel 2016, highlight rows 1-5, right-click, and select **Insert**.
3. Bold the titles in cells A6-F6 by highlighting them and clicking on the **B** icon on the **Home** ribbon.
4. In cell **A1**, enter `Sample Excel Solution`.
5. From the **Developer** tab, select **Stop Recording**.
6. Highlight and delete all the rows.
7. Save the blank file containing just the macro in `C:` drive, with the name as `AccountSummary.xlsm`.

Creating an export solution

Now that we've prepared our Excel 2016 workbook to receive a SmartList, we need to set up and run the SmartList Export Solution using these steps:

1. Access SmartList in the same method used for SmartList exports (where you open SmartList depends on whether you are using the Rich Client or the Web Client of GP).

2. Go to `Financial | Account Summary` in the left pane to generate a SmartList.

3. Click on **Favorites**. Go to **Add | Add Favorite**. The favorite can be named anything. I'm using `Export Solution` for our example:

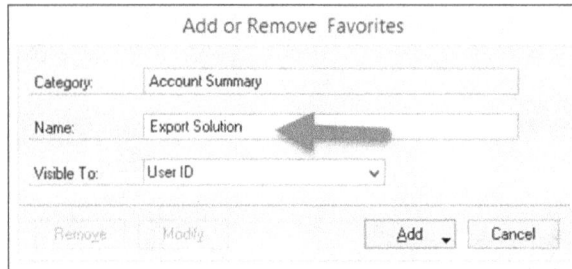

4. Back on the **SmartList** window, go to **SmartList | Export Solutions**. Name the solution `Export Solution`. Set the path to `C:\AccountSummary.xlsm` (or where you saved your Excel file with the macro) and the completion macro to `Macro1`:

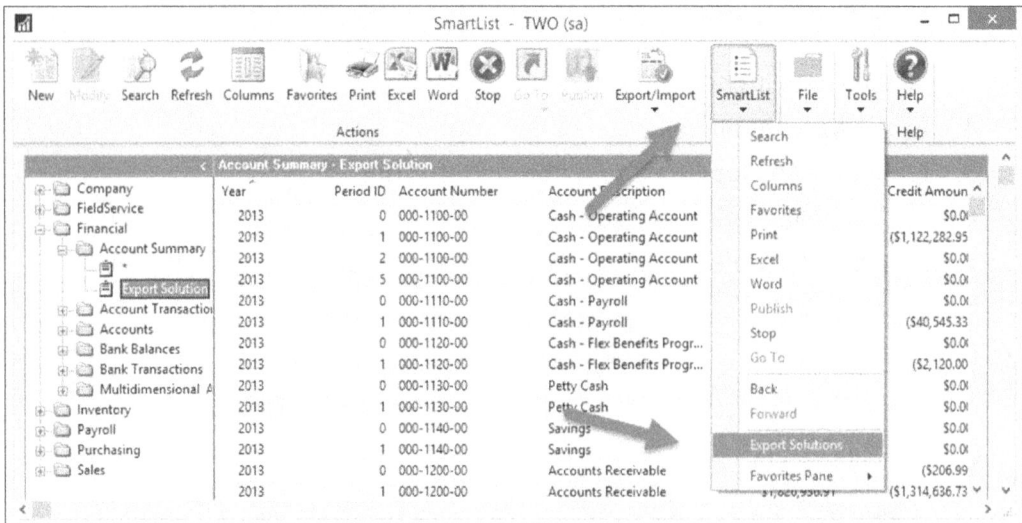

> 💡 There is a length limit of 80 characters for the document name and path. This can be a little on the short side, so it can be difficult to point an export solution to a file deep in a network file tree.

5. Select the box next to the SmartList favorite under `Account Summary` named `Export Solution`:

6. Make sure the **Application** is set to **Excel**. If not, change it:

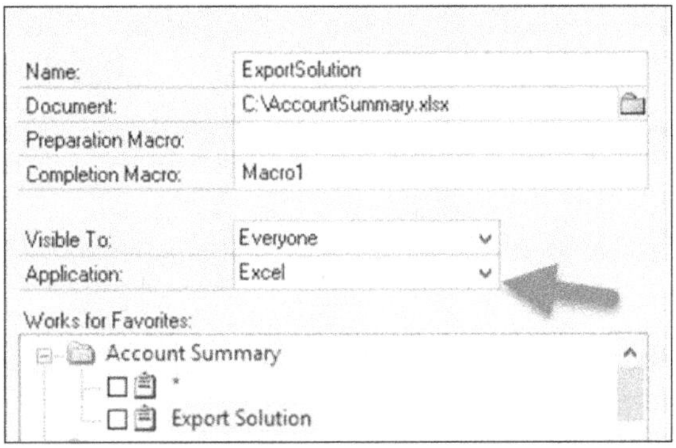

Name:	ExportSolution
Document:	C:\AccountSummary.xlsx
Preparation Macro:	
Completion Macro:	Macro1
Visible To:	Everyone
Application:	Excel

Works for Favorites:
- ☐ Account Summary
  - ☐ *
  - ☐ Export Solution

7. Select **Save** and close the window.

8. Back in the **SmartList** window, select the `Export Solution` favorite under `Account Summary` and click on the **Excel** button.

> 💡 You will have to unselect the `Account Summary` in the **SmartList** window and click back for the new export option to appear.

9. Instead of immediately opening Excel, there are now two options. The **Quick Export** option performs a typical Excel export. We want the second option. Click on the **Export Solution** option. This will open the Excel file named `AccountSummary.xlsm`, export the data, and run the macro named `Macro1`, all with one click:

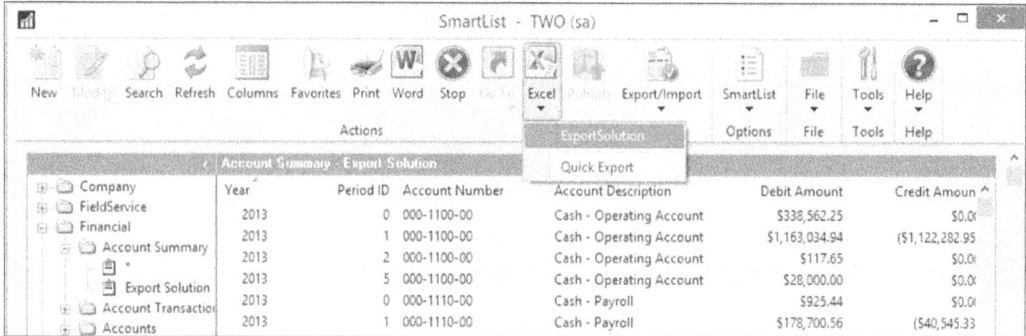

10. Click on the **Export Solution** option and watch the file open and the macro execute:

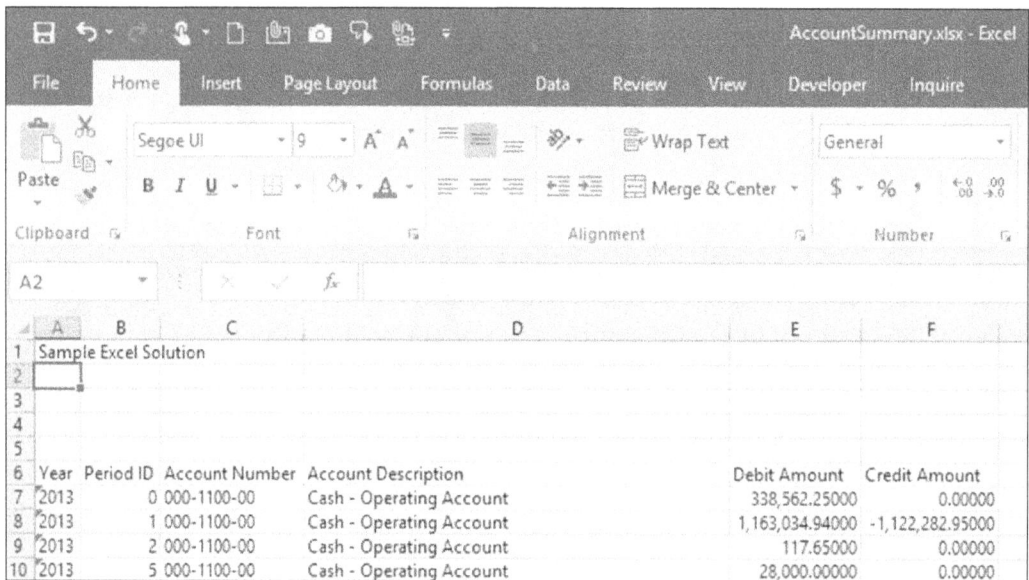

Get and Transform – formerly known as Power Query

Without a doubt, this is a personal favorite method of getting GP data into Excel. "Why?" you ask. The reason is with Get and Transform you can:

- Access your GP (SQL) data

- Combine your GP data with non-GP data

- Edit (or model) your GP data (by this, we mean you can combine fields, extract portions from fields, such as the year from a date, replace null values, and so on)

- Merge or append tables together

And all of this can be done from within Excel without ever logging into a SQL tool such as the SQL Server Studio. You can have developer results while thinking like an Excel user and without being a developer.

> There is a big advantage to learning this tool. It is the same tool that is used in **Microsoft Power BI**. So, learning this one tool in Excel gives you a huge advantage in Power BI.

In Excel 2013 and Excel 2010, this feature can be installed as an add-on called Power Query. Note that this feature only works on specific versions of Excel, so check the system requirements before downloading.

> A table is a file that holds a set of records in the SQL Server. Imagine your chart of accounts being stored in an Excel spreadsheet, which could be a single table for some applications. However, many complex applications (such as Dynamics GP) often break up the information across several tables for efficiency. GP separates the chart of accounts into seven separate tables. Separating the data is good for the application, but confusing to non-developers or database administrators who just want a good Excel report.
>
> To make it easier for users, often these virtual tables are created for the purpose of reporting to combine the data together and making the field names logical. A view is what a virtual table in the SQL Server is called. The chart of accounts information in GP, for example, can be found in an out-of-the-box view called **Accounts**.

Let's extract our list of General Ledger Accounts. Fortunately, Microsoft has already created this as a view in the SQL Database. This view has a lot of fields in it, but let's assume we want to make sure all of the accounts are set up with the correct type (Balance Sheet or Profit and Loss) so that when we close the year in the General Ledger, only the Balance Sheet accounts will roll forward into the new year. Follow these steps:

1. Open Microsoft Excel 2016.

2. Go to **Data** | **New Query** | **From Database** | **From SQL Server Database**:

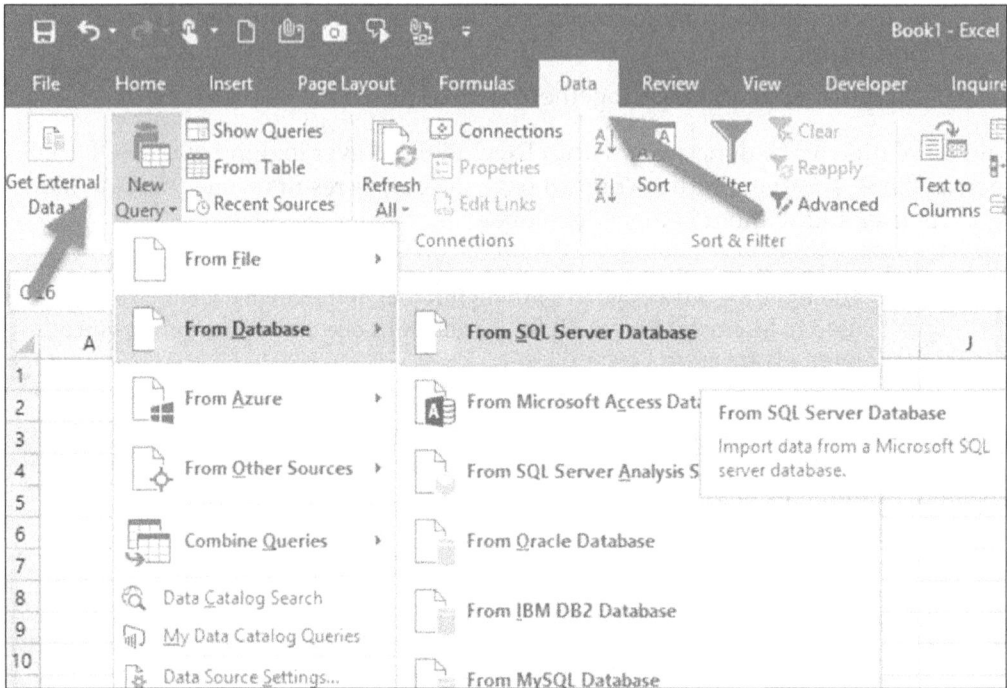

3. In the **SQL Server Database** window that appears, enter the name of your SQL Server instance in the **Server** and **Database (optional)** field. Our GP data is located on the server named `Cherry` and the Database is `TWO`. Click on **OK**:

SQL Server Database

Import data from a SQL Server database.

Server

Cherry

Database (optional)

TWO

▷ SQL statement (optional)

OK   Cancel

> If you do not know the server or database names, consult your IT department or your GP Partner. Usually, the server name is the name of the machine on which the SQL Server is installed. The database name can be found in the upper-right corner on the **Company Setup** window in GP.

4. The **Navigator** window will open, displaying all the tables and views in the SQL Database you selected. Highlight the Accounts view on the left-hand side. You will then get a preview of this view on the right-hand side. Click on **Edit**:

Navigator

Select multiple items

Show All | Show Selected [1]

▲ 🗄 cherry: two [1670]

　🗐 Accounts

　🗐 Account Summary

　🗐 Account Transactions

　🗐 ASIEXP06

　🗐 ASIEXP07

　🗐 ASIEXP08

　🗐 ASIV0001

　🗐 ASIV0002

　🗐 ATP_BOM

Select Related Tables

Accounts

Preview downloaded on Monday, June 27, 2016

Account Number	Account Description	Posting Type	Account C
000-1100-00	Cash - Operating Account	Balance Sheet	Cash
000-1110-00	Cash - Payroll	Balance Sheet	Cash
000-1120-00	Cash - Flex Benefits Program	Balance Sheet	Cash
000-1130-00	Petty Cash	Balance Sheet	Cash
000-1140-00	Savings	Balance Sheet	Short-Term
000-1200-00	Accounts Receivable	Balance Sheet	Accounts F
000-1205-00	Sales Discounts Available	Balance Sheet	Accounts F
000-1210-00	Allowance for Doubtful Accounts	Balance Sheet	Accounts F

Load ▾   Edit   Cancel

5. The **Query Editor** window will open with the `Accounts` data loaded. The first step should always be to rename this query to something that represents something that makes sense to the consumer of this report. We will rename ours to `Chart of Accounts`:

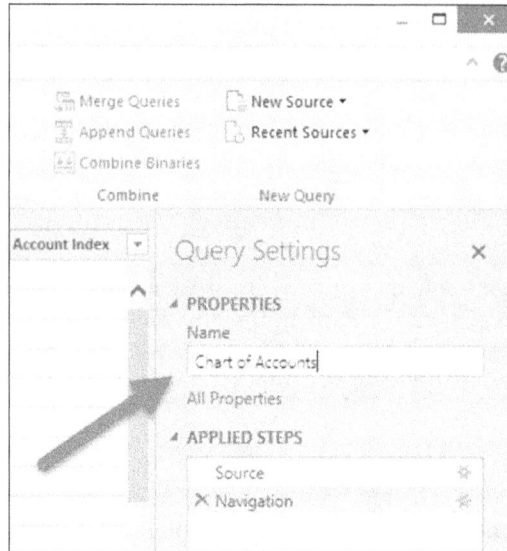

> Note that if you select a table, the query will be named `Query1`, then `Query2`, and so on. If you have multiple queries on a spreadsheet, it can get confusing as to what they represent. This is why renaming them is important and should be our first job.

6. Click on the Table icon and select **Choose Columns**:

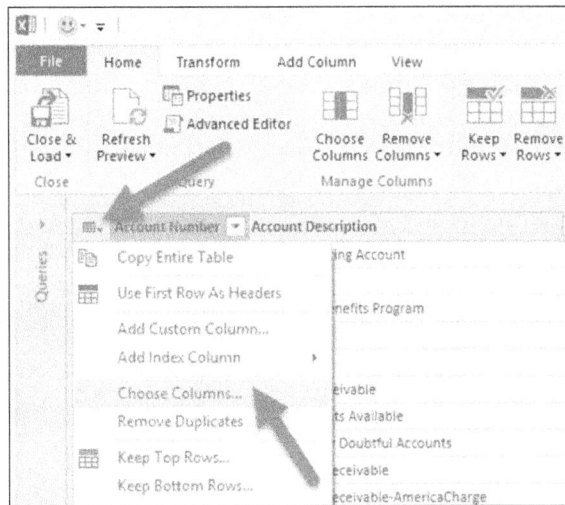

7. The **Choose Columns** window will open. Unmark the first item in the list titled **(Select All Columns)** so that we can manually select the ones we want to keep. Select **Account Number**, **Account Description**, **Posting Type**, **Account Type**, **Active**, and **Created Date**. Click on **OK**. Now, only the columns selected are displayed:

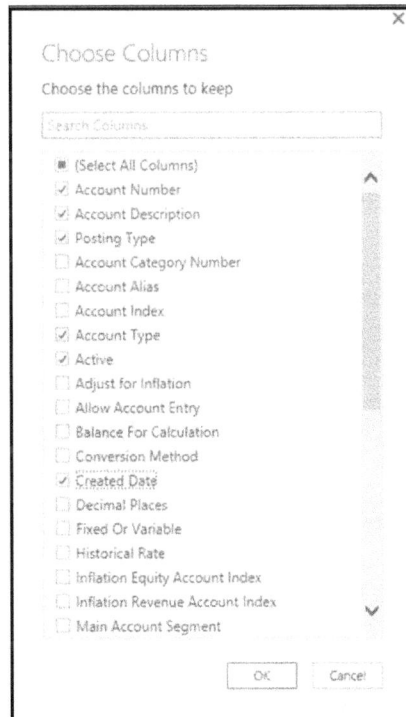

8. The second-most important step is verifying that the column data type is correct. Highlight the **Account Number** column, hold the *Shift* key down, and select the **Active** column so that all columns are highlighted. Right-click on the highlighted area and go to **Change Type | Text**. It might already be **Text**, but this just confirms. You can also highlight the columns one at a time and check the **Data Type in the ribbon.**

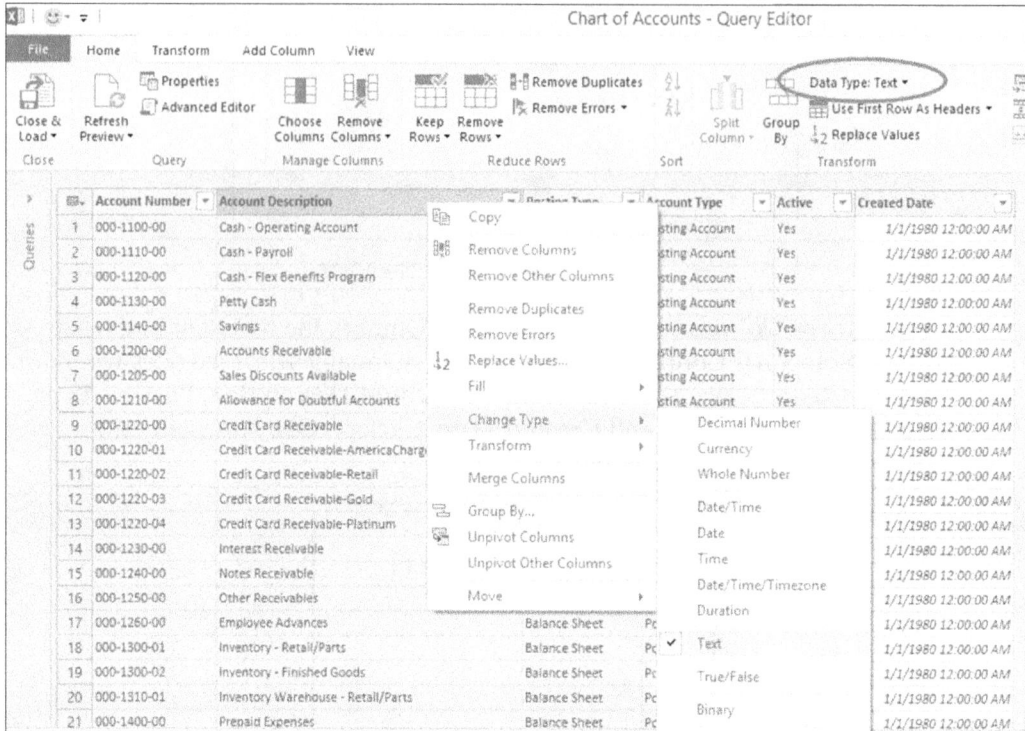

9. Highlight the last column, **Created Date**, right-click and go to **Change Type | Date**. This will change the date format from one that displays the time to one that displays only the date:

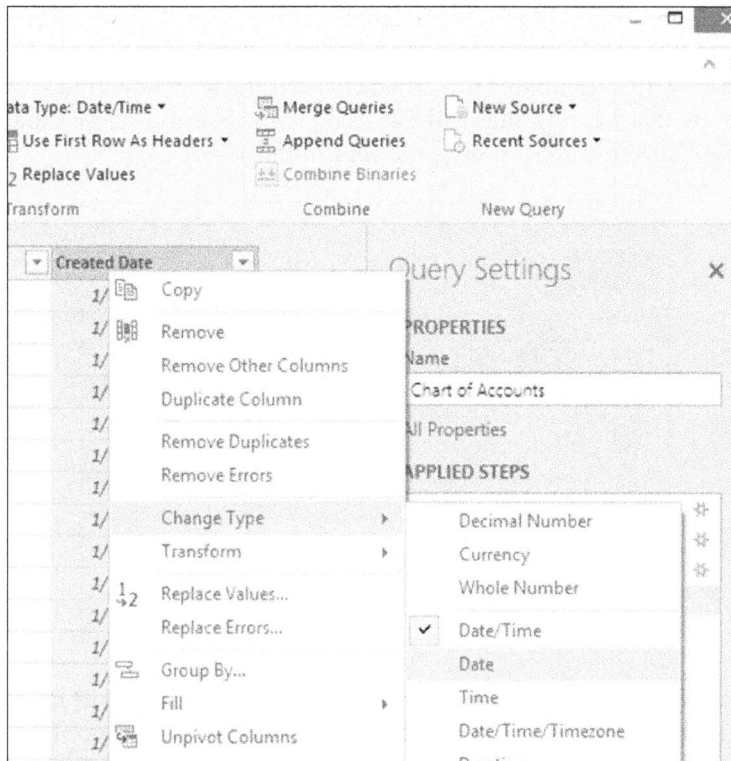

10. You'll notice that as we perform each step, our actions are recorded in the **Applied Steps** area. Get and Transform is actually recording everything we do, so when we use this query again, all of the steps will automatically be performed for us:

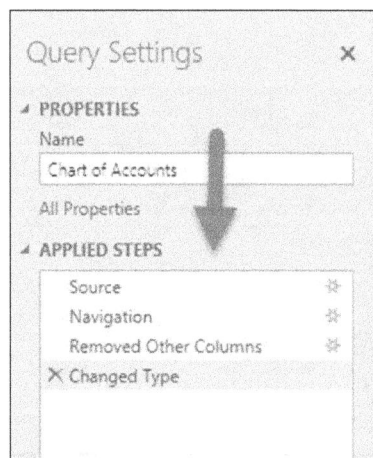

11. Each column has a filter, so you can choose to filter the data if you desire. Click on the words where the down arrow is located (not the icon) for **Close & Load | Close & Load To...** If we click on the icon, the data will flow into a table in Excel. Using the **Close & Load To...** feature, we can load the data into the Excel in-memory data model (**Power Pivot**):

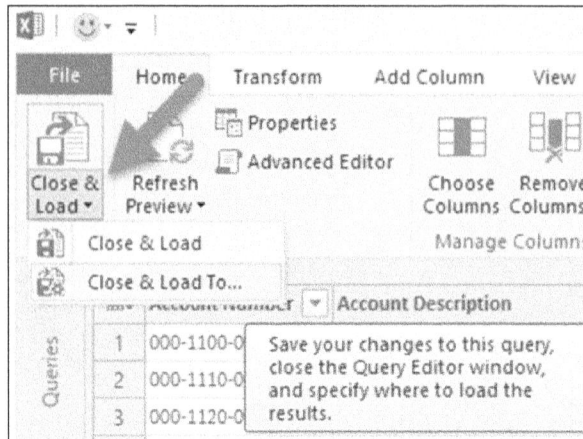

12. The **Load To** window opens. From here, you can either load the data to a table in the worksheet or create the connection only that would allow you to save the Excel file without the data. This allows you to refresh the data without saving a large file (but you must be connected to the SQL Server for this to refresh). You can also choose to add the data to the data model. The data is attached to the Excel file, but not visible to the spreadsheet. This is a great option if you only plan to create a PivotTable. Click on **Load**:

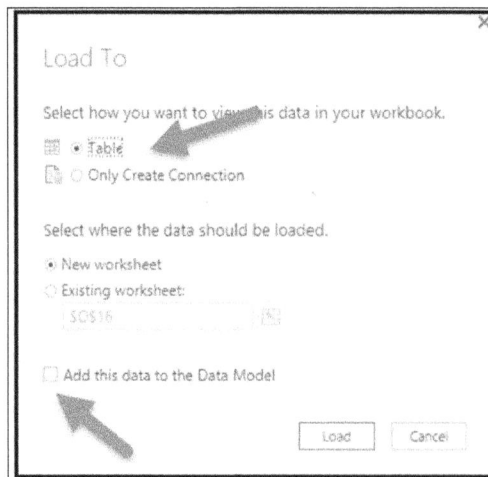

13. The data is now in the Excel spreadsheet as a table.

14. You'll notice there is a **Workbook Queries** pane whose display can be turned on or off using the **Show Queries** option on the **Data** ribbon. Right-clicking on the query provides you with many options, including the ability to **Edit** the query:

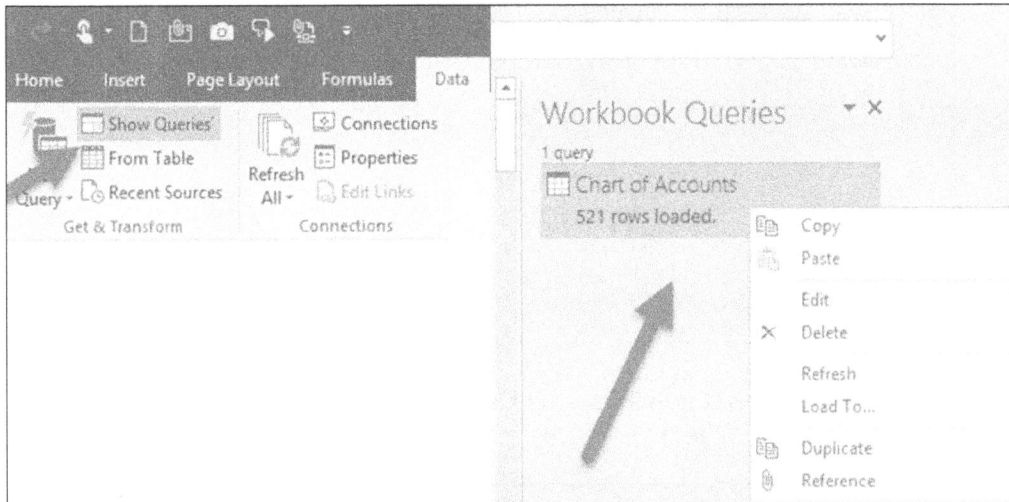

This is only a tiny fraction of what Get and Transform can do. You'll learn more about this great feature in *Chapter 12*, *Sharing and Refreshing Data and Dashboards in Power BI*.

Office Data Connection files

Excel has its own method of importing external data from a variety of sources, including data in the SQL Server. This method can be embedded directly in the workbook or stored in a separate file, the **Office Data Connection** (ODC) file. When this .odc file is created, it can be reused over and over for a quick connection between your GP and Excel that is refreshable.

Creating an .odc file

Let's create an `.odc` file to bring in our vendors using these steps:

1. In Excel 2016, go to **Data | From Other Sources | From SQL Server**:

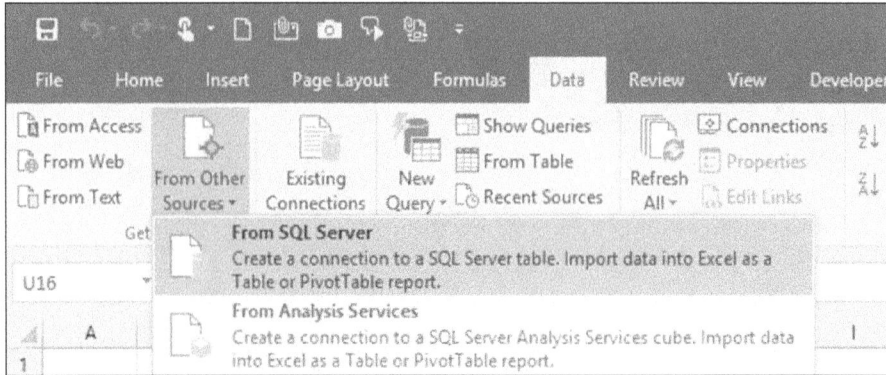

2. The **Data Connection** window will open. Enter the name of your server and your GP log in credentials. Click on **Next**.

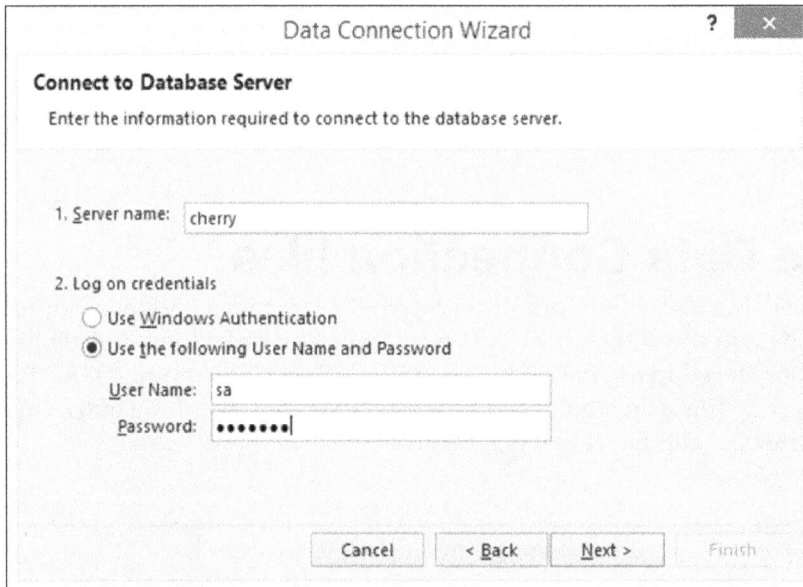

> If you do not know the server or database names, consult your IT department or your GP Partner. Usually, the server name is the name of the machine on which the SQL Server is installed.

3. Select the database you want to report on and then select the view called `Vendors`. Click on **Finish**:

> The database name can be found in the upper-right corner on the **Company Setup** window in GP.
>
> In the Excel **Data Connection Wizard** window, first, SQL Views are displayed in alphabetical order; then, SQL Tables are displayed in alphabetical order.

4. The **Import Data** window will open, providing you with the option of either importing the data into an Excel **Table**, a **PivotTable Report/PivotChart**, or just creating the connection between SQL and Excel. Let's leave the option marked as **Table** and click on **OK**. The data will then import into the spreadsheet:

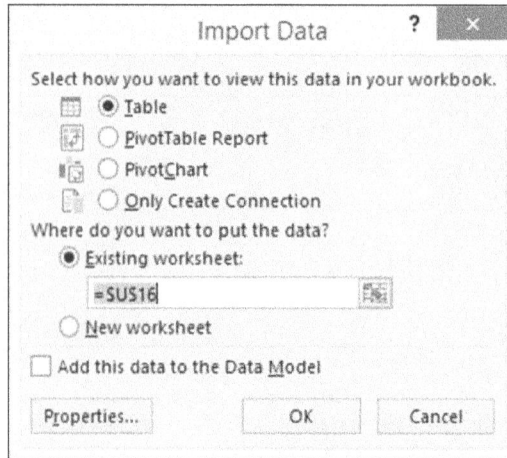

The location of the .odc file

We'll find the location of the .odc file we created earlier, with the spreadsheet still open. Follow these steps:

1. Open the **Connection Properties** window by going to **Data | Connections | Properties...**

2. Click on the **Definition** tab, and the **Connection File** path will be displayed. For me, our file and path is `C:\Users\Belinda Allen\Documents\My Data Sources\cherry TWO Vendors.odc`. As you can see, the actual `.odc` name is a combination of your server, your database, and the table/view you used for the connection:

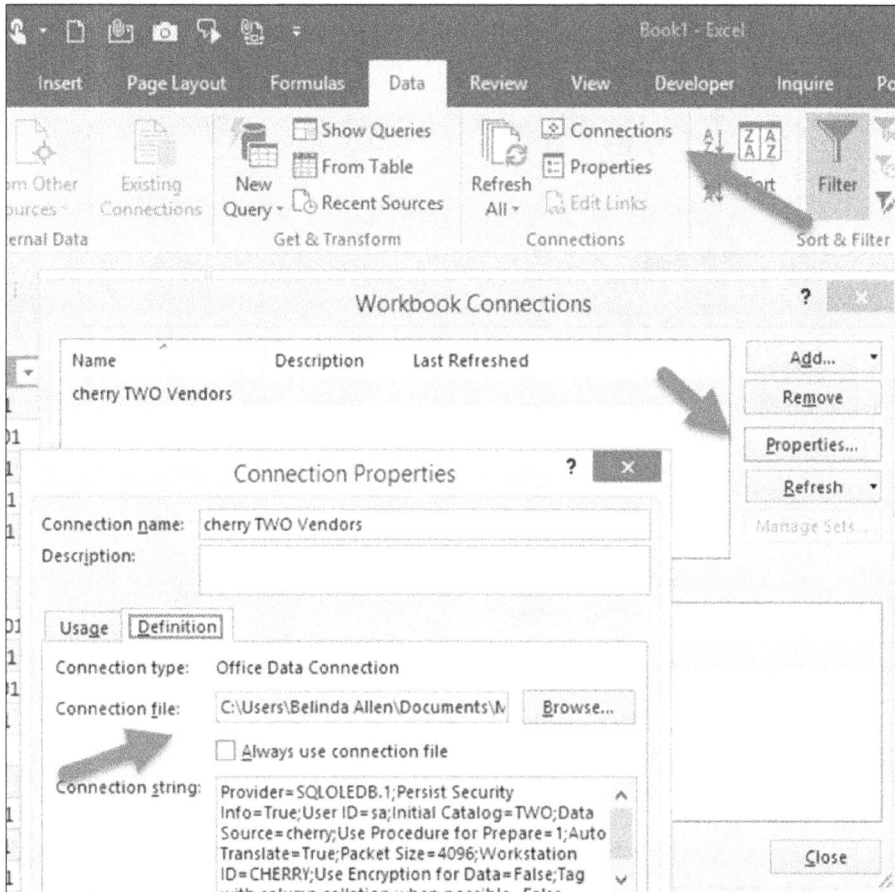

Reusing an .odc fie

One of the great features of using an `.odc` file is that once it is created, it can be used over and over again. Let's reuse the connection file we just created and follow these steps:

1. Open a blank Excel workbook. Go to **Click Data | Existing Connections** and scroll to find the connection you just created. For us, it is **cherry TWO Vendors**. Click on **Open**:

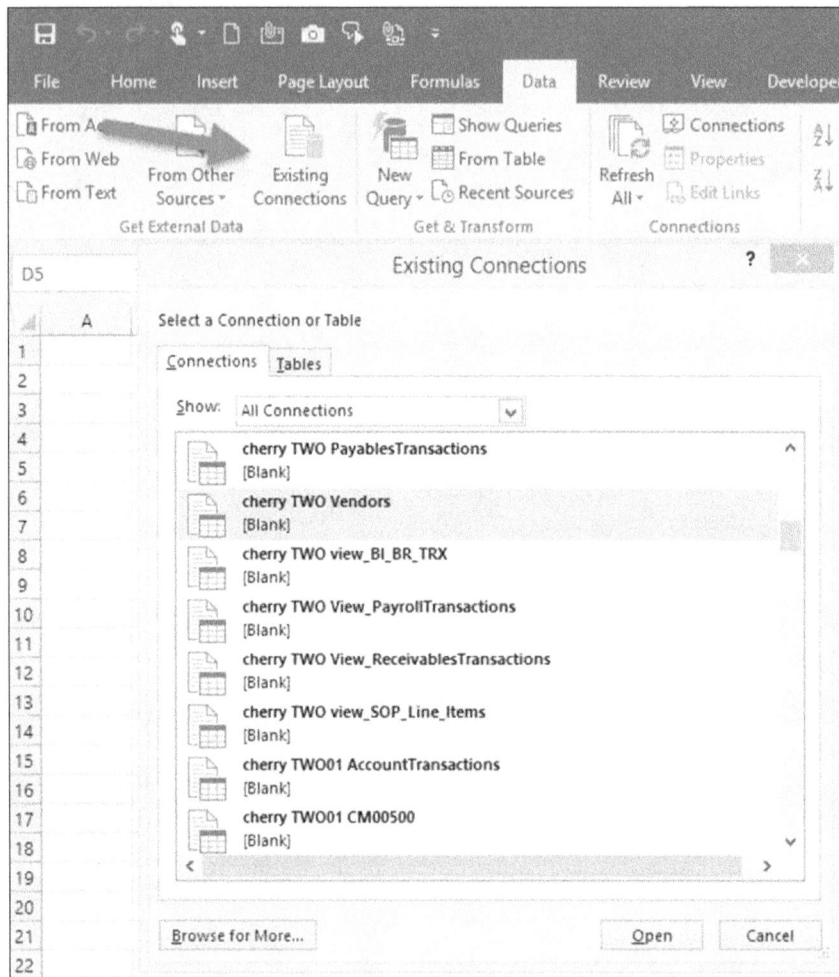

2. The **Import Data** window will open, asking how you want to view your data: **Table**, **PivotTable Report/PivotChart**, or if you just want to create a connection.

> Note that you can also simply double-click on the file in Windows Explorer, which will open Excel and take you directly to the **Import Data** window.

3. You'll then be prompted for your SQL login, which is the same as your GP login.

SQL Server Reporting Services

Microsoft provides prebuilt SSRS reports as part of Dynamics GP 2016. Deploying SSRS reports is included as an option during installation, but they can also be installed later. SSRS provides an easy path to send information to Microsoft Excel 2016.

To demonstrate this, start in Dynamics GP 2016 and follow these steps:

1. Select **Financial** from the navigation pane on the left-hand side.
2. In the list pane which is above the navigation pane, click on **Reporting Services Reports**.
3. In the center pane, scroll down and find **Trial Balance Summary**.
4. Double-click on **Trial Balance Summary** to open the report:

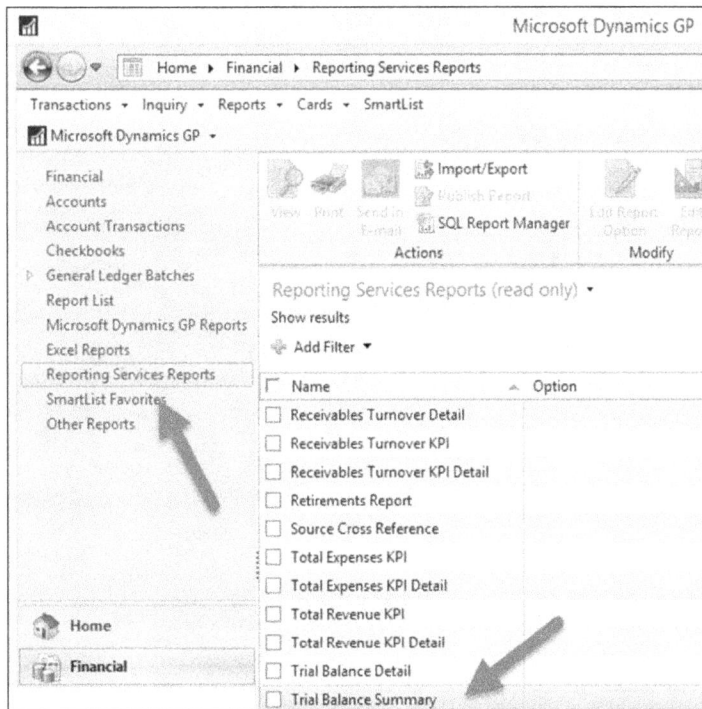

5. Once the report opens in a web browser, change the following criteria:
   - ○ **History Year**: **No**
   - ○ **Year**: **2016**
   - ○ **Starting Account Number**: **000-1100-00**
   - ○ **Ending Account Number**: **999-999-99**
   - ○ **Starting Date**: **12/01/2016**
   - ○ **Ending Date**: **12/31/2016**
   - ○ **Sort By**: **Account**

Show Posting Accounts:	Yes			Show Inactive Accounts:	No	
Show Unit Accounts:	No			Show Zero Balance Accounts:	No	
History Year:	No			Year:	2016	
Account Ranges:	Account			Segment ID:	Division	
Starting Account Number:	000-1100-00			Ending Account Number:	999-9999-99	
Starting Date:	12/1/2016			Ending Date:	12/31/2016	
Sort By:	Account			Subtotal By:	No Subtotal	

6. Click on **View Report** in the upper-right corner to run the **Trial Balance Summary**.

7. Select the disk icon and click on **Excel**:

Show Posting Accounts:	Yes		Show Inactive Accounts:
Show Unit Accounts:	No		Show Zero Balance Accounts:
History Year:	No		Year:
Account Ranges:	Account		Segment ID:
Starting Account Number:	000-1100-00		Ending Account Number:
Starting Date:	12/1/2016		Ending Date:
Sort By:	Account		Subtotal By:

| ◄◄ | ◄ | 1 | of 2 | ► | ►◄ | 100% | | | Find \| Next | | | | |

GL Summary

Fabrik

Genera...

XML file with report data
CSV (comma delimited)
PDF
MHTML (web archive)
Excel
TIFF file
Word

/7/2016   11:25:11 AM

| nactive | Account | Description | | Begining Balance | Debit |

8. If a security bar opens at the bottom asking **Do you want to open or save...**, select **Open**.

9. The **Trial Balance Summary** report now opens in Excel 2016.

Jet Reports Express for Excel

Shortly after the release of Microsoft Dynamics GP 2016, Microsoft announced that the financial report writer, **Management Reporter**, was going into maintenance mode. This meant bug fixes would continue, but there would be no new features added. A large reason for this was Management Reporter's inability to go to the cloud. Entering this situation, Jet Reports to the rescue, offering a special release of the Express product to GP users free of charge.

What is Jet Reports? Jet Reports has an Excel add-on that enables Jet to work directly with your GP data in SQL. So, it's actually Excel that you are using to build reports. You may be wondering why wouldn't we build them in Excel directly. We asked that question. Once we used the product the first time, we had our answers:

- The deliverable report shows no signs of how or where the connection occurred. In the past, we've written a lot of complex Excel reports for customers. More often than not, they have to keep referring to the original copy as they somehow blow away some of the settings. Jet allows the report recipient (viewer) to see only Excel formulas such as SUM, not the connection information. This not only allows for tighter security; it makes the reports easier to consume.

- Changing from one company to the next is just three clicks.

These are just our personal reasons.

There are two elements of this free product: General Ledger (Basic) Financial Report writing and the Jet Table Builder. I'll cover these in more detail in *Chapter 6, Introducing Jet Reports Express*, and *Chapter 7, Building Financial Reports in Jet Express for GP*. Meanwhile, let's take a quick peek at how data flows into Excel from GP via Jet Express.

I also want to point out that Jet Reports will enable you to use your local version of Excel (installed on your computer) with your GP data. Jet Reports will work even if your GP data is in the cloud (hosted by a service data center or hosted in Azure.) The configuration to connect to your data is relatively simple, but outside the scope of this book.

Basic financial data

After Jet Reports is installed and configured, Jet will appear on the Menu bar in your Excel. Once **Jet** is clicked, the Jet ribbon will open. For financial statements, we only need the balance of accounts, so we would use the **GL** function to start building our statements:

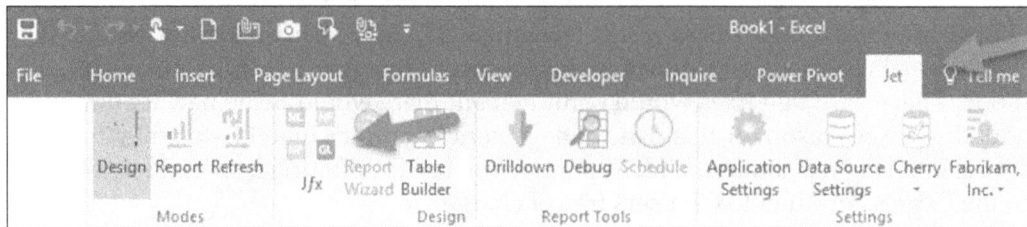

Clicking on the **GL** function will open the **Jet Function Wizard** window. Using the wizard will allow you to simply "fill in the blanks." In the following screenshot, I've selected that we want to see a row for a range of accounts (000-1100-00 through 000-1140-00). There are also fields to add the criteria of a GL **Account** category(s), **Budget**, or to select a specific company (if we want to have a consolidated financial statement.) This will populate Excel with the account numbers:

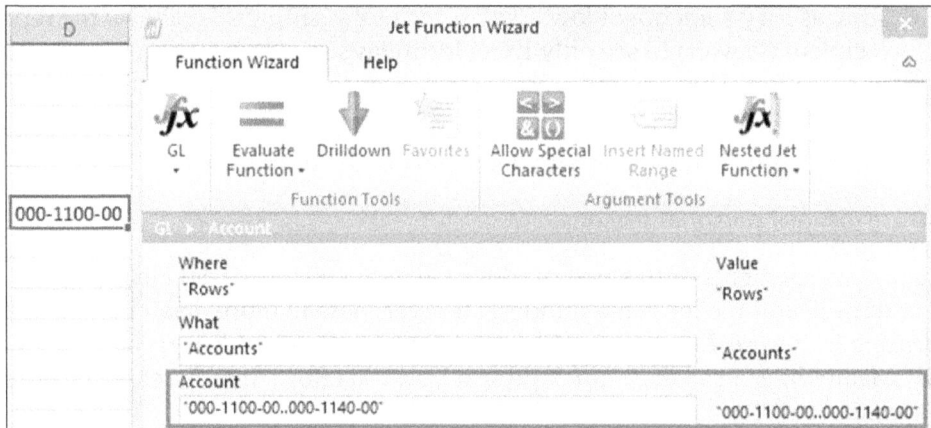

To display the account name, we'll open the **GL** function window again and "fill in the blanks". We add a cell reference next to the number, select **AccountName**, and point to the **Account Number** cell:

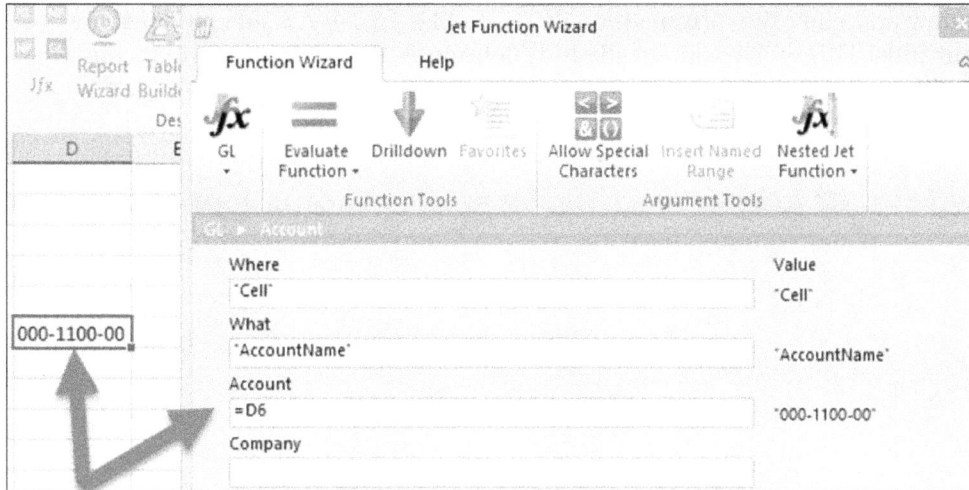

Finally, I'll use the **GL** function to add the account balance. We select cell, **Balance**, and reference the **Account Number** cell like we did earlier. I'll also select the period for which we want to report. I'll select the year 2016 for periods 1 through 12, allowing us to capture the entire year:

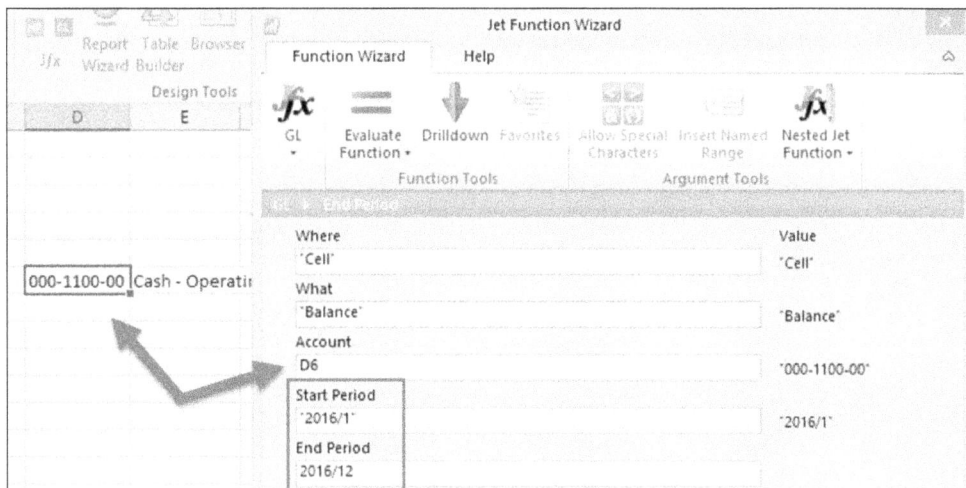

My Excel worksheet now looks like the following screenshot, as we are working (by default) in the **Design** mode. You'll notice that for each Excel cell that we entered data using the GL function wizard, a formula appears in the formula bar. Just as in native Excel, once you become familiar with the formula, you can skip the wizard window and enter the formula directly if you like. In cell A1, Jet entered some commands. This will automatically hide column **A**, so we can use it in formulas if we like:

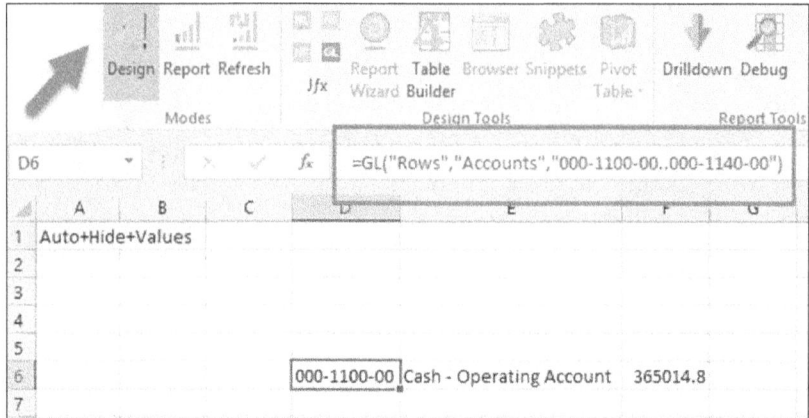

Once we click on the **Report** mode, Jet retrieves all the data requested and displays the accounts, account names, and balances we requested:

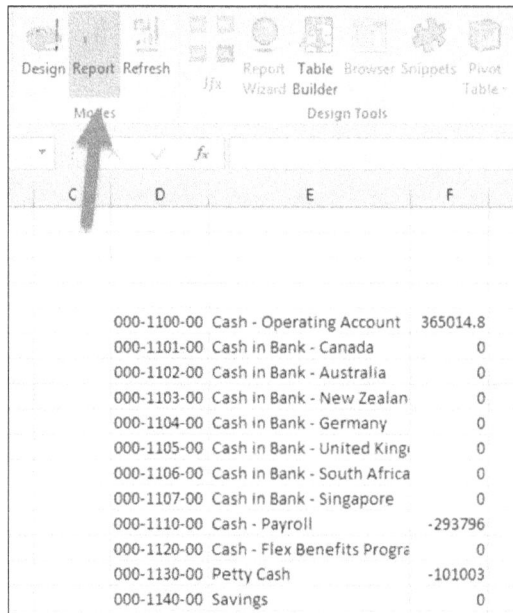

Back in the **Design** mode, I'll quickly perform some normal Excel formatting and add a Sum function:

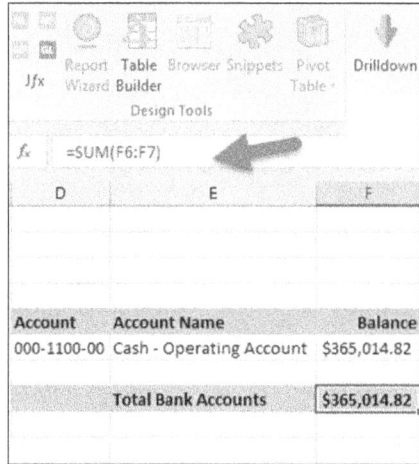

By clicking on the **Report** mode again, our simple report of Cash looks ready for presentation:

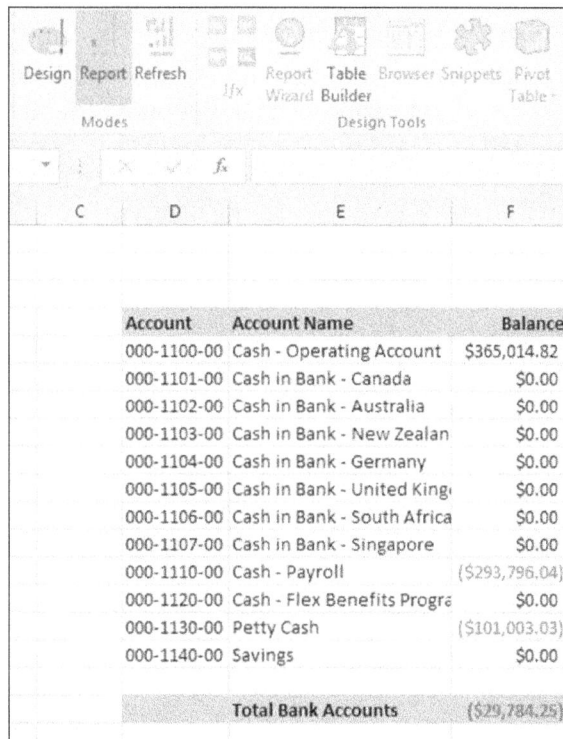

As mentioned earlier, in *Chapter 7, Building Financial Reports in Jet Express for GP*, we'll walk together through building a financial statement.

Table Builder

The Table Builder in Jet Reports retrieves data from GP in a similar wizard-driven fashion, like the GL function earlier. It's easy to use, so I'll just reference you to *Chapter 6, Introducing Jet Reports Express*. We need to give you some reason to keep reading.

SQL Server Management Studio

Microsoft Dynamics GP 2016 runs on SQL Server 2012, SQL Server 2014, and SQL Server 2016. Some companies, in particular those with advanced users, allow read-only access to Microsoft SQL Server to make it easy for users to get just the data they want. Often, this access is provided through the SQL Server Management Studio. Management Studio makes it easy to get data from GP 2016 to Microsoft Excel.

To see how easy this is, follow these steps:

1. Open the SQL Server Management Studio.

2. Connect to the SQL Server instance with Dynamics GP 2016 installed using either **Windows Authentication** or **SQL Server Authentication** with a user ID and password. If you have access to the SQL Server Management Studio, the login method and credentials will be provided by your database administrator. The user's GP login cannot be used.

3. Select **New Query**.

4. In the large, white box on the right-hand side, type `Use TWO` and hit *Enter* to select the sample `TWO` database.

5. Type `Select * from AccountSummary` and click on **Execute** to run the SQL query. The results will appear below the query:

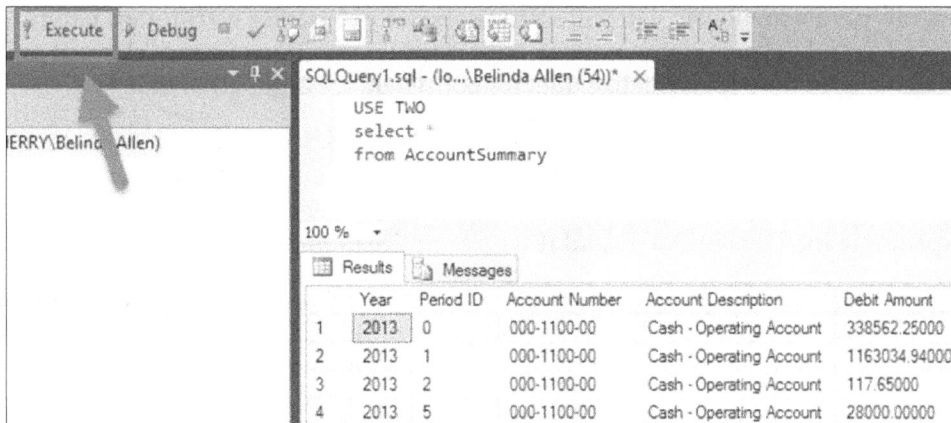

6. Go to **Edit | Select All** from the menu to highlight all of the results.

7. Go to **Edit | Copy with Headers**.

8. Open a blank Excel 2016 sheet. On the **Home** tab, click on the **Paste** icon in the upper-left corner to paste the data to Microsoft Excel.

> There is a setting in the SQL Server that will export headers when copying, even if you forget to pick **Copy with Headers**. The setting can be found by going to **Tools | Options | Query Results | SQL Server | Results To Grid**. To activate it, select **Include column headers when copying or saving the results**.

Analysis Cubes

Microsoft Dynamics GP **Analysis Cubes for Excel (ACE)** is an **Online Analytical Processing (OLAP)** tool from Microsoft, designed for Dynamics GP.

A full implementation of ACE is beyond the scope of this book, but Analysis Cubes are one of the best sources of data for Excel-based dashboards, so we need to spend a few minutes with them.

ACE takes data from Dynamics GP 2016 and places it in a SQL Server based data warehouse for use with the SQL Server Analysis Services. Usually, this is done once a day due to the volume of data that is being pushed through. At its simplest, a data warehouse is a separate place to store information to report off. Often, the data is optimized to improve the reporting process as it moves into the data warehouse. A multidimensional or OLAP cube not only optimizes the structure of the data to improve reporting, it can pre-calculate and aggregate information to make reporting even more powerful.

The term "data warehouse" can scare people. Some companies go through painfully long data warehouse implementations with careful definition of every element and arguments over how to normalize data for consistency. Forget all of that.

The beauty of a powerful ERP system, such as Microsoft Dynamics GP, is that the database design is known, documented, and doesn't change a lot from version to version. This means that a standard data warehouse can be built that works for companies using Dynamics GP, and it won't require months of work to set up.

The Dynamics GP Analysis Cubes product contains well-designed, aggregated tables for most Dynamics GP modules. For people using third-party add-ons, a customized cube with appropriate measures and dimensions would be required.

After you work through this book and build a few dashboards, you'll start to bump into some of the limitations of reporting directly off Dynamics GP data. These can include placing an undue load on the GP server, difficulty in finding and joining tables, and the struggle of calculating measures by hand. You'll also want to build more complex dashboards as you grow. Using Analysis Cubes for Excel is a great next logical step.

As ACE moves data into a data warehouse for reporting, data-heavy dashboards won't put a load on Dynamics GP. Also, because Analysis Cubes prepopulates and calculates information, complex calculations are available for reporting without having to create formulas in Excel. For example, in the next screenshot, you can see that **Budget Variance**, **Current Ratio**, **Debit to Equity**, and **Gross Margin Percentage** are all available in Analysis Cubes to simply drag into a pivot table for use in a dashboard. No calculation needed:

Additionally, users have the option of reporting against the data-warehouse relational database or reporting against the cubes.

From a practical standpoint, using Analysis Cubes is very similar to the process we will walk through in *Chapter 2, The Ultimate GP to Excel Tool – Refreshable Excel Reports*. The techniques used in this book to create a dashboard also work well when building an Analysis Cube based dashboard. Analysis Cubes for Dynamics GP is included in the starter pack in GP 2016, so customers upgrading from previous versions have an even stronger reason to implement it.

> For an in-depth look at some of these reporting solutions, including SSRS and Analysis Cubes, we recommend that you refer to *Microsoft Dynamics GP 2010 Reporting* by Chris Liley and David Duncan from Packt Publishing. Although this book references an older version of Dynamics GP, the content on Analysis Cubes will still be valid and work with the current version, Dynamics GP 2016.

Third-party solutions

All of the solutions we have discussed so far are either included with Microsoft Dynamics GP 2016 or are available as additional software from Microsoft. However, if you want to work with Microsoft Dynamics GP 2016 and Microsoft Excel, there are also a number of third-party solutions available. Selecting a third-party solution can be a challenging proposition.

It seems like every vendor remotely connected to reporting and Excel has put out what they term a **Business Intelligence (BI)** solution for Dynamics GP. Microsoft even referred to **FRx**, the financial reporting forerunner to Management Reporter, as a BI solution. This may be technically true, but when you say BI, the average user thinks of a dashboard, not a financial-reporting package.

The market has finally shaken out into a few categories with a lot of overlap. The options break down into reporting solutions that can produce dashboards. These are generally known as **Corporate Performance Management (CPM)** solutions and are more dashboard-focused solutions that can produce financial reports. For our purposes, I'm labeling these solutions as BI. It's really about where the vendor places the emphasis.

Additionally, the choices break down into those that report directly off data in Dynamics GP, those that use a just a data warehouse, and those that use OLAP cubes for their underlying data sources.

The continuum for costs and sophistication generally breaks down the same way. Solutions that report directly off GP data tend to be the least sophisticated and the cheapest. Solutions using a cube tend to be more expensive and more powerful.

We have an entire section of this book *Section 3, Microsoft Power BI* focusing on Microsoft's own Power BI. This is a simple and inexpensive dashboarding tool. It doesn't cover every company's needs, but it's certainly worth learning for your company's self-service business intelligence needs.

For the purposes of this book, we use the term data warehouse. Some vendors use the term data mart. Generally, a data mart is a specific subset of information in a data warehouse. For example, we might have a data warehouse of operational and financial information, but we segregate just the vendor and AP information into a data mart for use by the purchasing group. Vendors seem to use them interchangeably, with little regard for specific definitions, so for this book, we will use the term data warehouse for both.

The techniques shown in this book work pretty much the same whether you are reporting off a live connection to Dynamics GP, a data warehouse, or a multidimensional cube. Live reporting provides instant gratification. The use of a data warehouse improves the ability to scale reporting without increasing the load on the Dynamics GP server.

Licensing

Accessing Dynamics GP 2016 data from applications such as Excel now only requires a SQL Server **Client Access License** (**CAL**). No additional GP user license is required. Simplicity at its best!

Summary

In this chapter we've looked at a number of ways to get data from Dynamics GP 2016 into Microsoft Excel 2016. Having a lot of options makes it possible to still build an effective dashboard in spite of those restrictions. How data gets extracted from GP totally depends on the rights and needs of the report creator and/or report consumer. We mention this so that you can experiment and find out which options work best for you and your company. Chances are that you'll use more than one option. If you end up needing all of them, let us know. Better yet, write a book for us to read! I've no doubt we'd learn a lot from you.

In the next chapter, we will look at one of the best and easiest options to access Microsoft Dynamics GP 2016 data — (the out of the box) refreshable Excel reports. In that chapter, we will start putting together the data that will eventually go into our dashboard.

2
The Ultimate GP to Excel Tool – Refreshable Excel Reports

The easiest method of getting data out of GP into Excel is with Excel refreshable reports. These were introduced in GP version 10 and provide users with the ability to open an existing report which is connected to GP already. To get the latest data from GP you only need to use the Excel refresh button. What could be better. These work very similarly to SmartList as the data is sorted in the same way and almost all default SmartList objects have a corresponding Excel refreshable report.

Refreshable Excel reports are easy to deploy, easy to update, and easy to work with. That's why they make a great foundation for an Excel 2016 dashboard. In this chapter, you will learn how to:

- Deploy refreshable Excel reports
- Manage security to Excel reports
- Run Excel reports
- Build reports with SmartList Designer

Security

By default, users can view Excel reports and data connections only if they have administrative credentials on the server that is running the SQL Server and if they have access to the network share. Since this isn't a normal setup, users typically need reporting privileges in the SQL Server before they can view the Microsoft Dynamics GP data that is displayed in data connections and Excel reports.

There are three areas of security around Excel reports deployed to a network share or local drive:

- Security to the network share/local folder
- Security at the database level
- Security around Excel

We'll spend a few minutes on each one.

Network share security

Realistically, network share security is normally going to be set by a network administrator. To make a shortcut for administrators, the minimum required security on the shared folder is:

- **Change** option for the share tab
- **Read** option for the security tab

Now, for those of you who want the version that is longer than a (as Mark Polino would say) Latvian wiener dog, follow these steps:

1. In Windows Explorer, right-click on the folder where you deployed the Excel reports and then click on **Sharing and Security...**
2. On the **Sharing** tab, click on **Advanced Sharing...** and select **Share this folder**.
3. Click on **Permissions**.
4. If the user or group already exists in this window, you can skip to the next step. Otherwise, follow these steps:
   - Click on **Add...**
   - In the **Select Users, Computers, or Groups** window, enter the group or users to whom you want to provide access to the shared reports
   - Click on **OK**
5. Select the user or group to apply permission to in the **Group or user names** area.
6. Select the **Allow** checkbox for the **Change** permission and then click on **OK**. The **Change** permission is the minimum required permission.

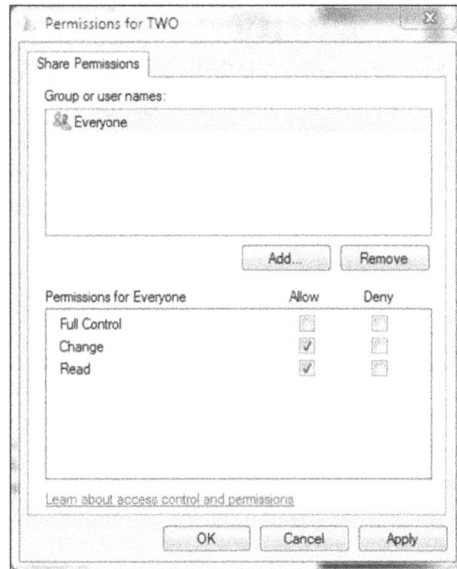

7. Click on the **Security** tab.

8. In the **Groups or user names** area, click on **Add**.

9. If the user or group already exists in this window, you can skip to the next step. Otherwise, follow these steps:

   ° In the **Select Users, Computers, or Groups** window, enter the group or the users to whom you want to provide access to the shared reports

   ° Click on **OK**

10. In the **Groups or user names** area, select each group or user, and then click on the permission that you want the group or the user to have. The minimum required permission is **Read**.

11. Click on **OK**.

> These instructions will vary depending on the version of the Windows server used on the network or the user's version of Windows on a local drive. If you are unsure about setting this up, consult your IT department.

By default, Dynamics GP 2016 deploys reports related to each company and each functional area in their own network folder. This makes it easy to apply different permission levels to sensitive areas such as payroll.

Database-level security

Access to information in the Dynamics GP 2016 database is handled a little differently. A set of fixed security roles is created automatically in the SQL Server when Excel reports are deployed. All of these roles start with `rpt_`. These roles provide access to the underlying tables and views. The process to assign security is to add a user or group to the SQL Server and give them access to the appropriate roles. The users that get added are not Dynamics GP users. They are either SQL Server users (different from the GP login IDs) or active directory users and groups.

> To connect the SQL role with an Excel report to ensure that a user has appropriate access, you really need the spreadsheet from Microsoft that links the two together. You can find it at `https://mbs.microsoft.com/fileexchange/?fileID=e4bb6958-0f07-4451-b72c-f02784e484df.`
>
> This spreadsheet is from version GP 10, but it still works for GP 2016.

In our example, we need access to the `Account Summary Default` Excel sheet. This sheet uses the `Account Summary` view. On the spreadsheet, we see a number of roles that include the appropriate access:

84			rpt_project manager
85	**Financial**		
86	Accounts Defaults	Accounts	rpt_accounting manager
87			rpt_bookkeeper
88			rpt_certified accountant
89			rpt_materials manager
90			rpt_operations manager
91			rpt_order processor
92			rpt_production manager
93			rpt_warehouse manager
94	Account Summary Default	AccountSummary	rpt_accounting manager
95			rpt_bookkeeper
96			rpt_certified accountant
97			rpt_materials manager
98			rpt_operations manager
99			rpt_order processor
100			rpt_production manager
101			rpt_warehouse manager

For our example, we'll give a user access to the **rpt_accounting manager** role. In practice, it's not unusual to add all GP users to a single active directory group and give that group access to all the fixed reporting roles. This is particularly true for companies that don't use payroll and that don't have other sensitive reporting requirements.

To grant database permission using the built-in roles, we have to add the user or group to the SQL Server and then assign the appropriate role(s).

To add a user to SQL Server, follow these steps:

1. Open SQL Server Management Studio and log in using either **Windows Authentication** or **SQL Server Authentication**.

2. Go to **Security | Logins**.

3. Right-click on **Logins** and select **New Login...**

4. Click on **Search**.

5. Enter the domain and user you want to add or enter the group that you want to add to the SQL Server. For my example, I'm entering my domain and user name—Njevity\ballen. This could also be a group of users such as GPUSERS, for example:

6. Click on **Check Names** to validate the entry and click twice on **OK** to finish.

The user has now been added to the SQL Server. Our example used a domain user, but you can also set up a SQL user. In general, a domain user is preferred, because it eliminates the need for the user to manage multiple logins and passwords for reporting. Using a domain login also provides additional control to administrators. If an employee leaves, for example, removing them from the domain removes both their network access and their reporting access in one step.

To grant access to the reporting roles, follow these steps:

1. Go to **Security | Logins**, double-click the user or group that you just created.

2. Select **User Mapping** on the left-hand side.

3. In the upper-center section labeled **Users mapped to this login:**, select the box next to the company that you want to grant report access to. For our example, select **TWO**.

4. In the lower-center section named **Database role membership for: TWO**, select the box next to **rpt_Accounting Manager**:

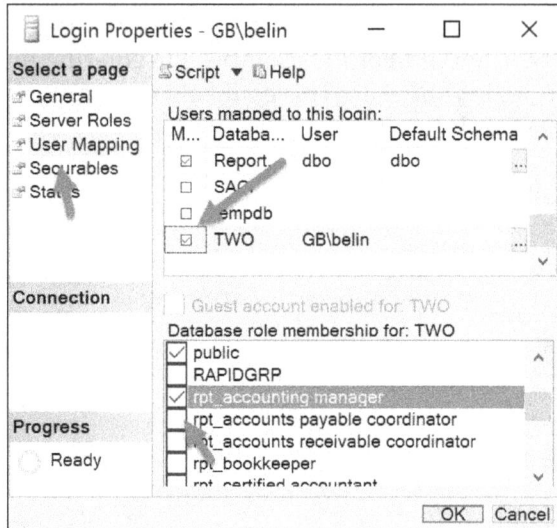

5. Click on **OK** to continue.

The user now has rights to access the TWO AccountSummary default report that we've been working with and any other reports available as part of the **rpt_Accounting Manager** role.

Excel 2016 security

As you connect with database connections in Excel, a security bar may pop up with the message **SECURITY WARNING External Data Connections have been disabled**:

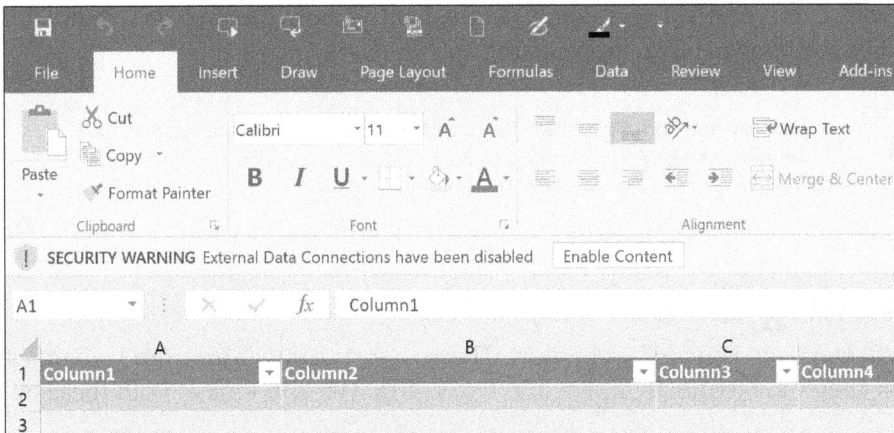

This is an Excel security feature designed to prevent malicious code from running without the user's knowledge. In our case, however, we deployed the reports. We are now running them on our network and controlling access. This is about as secure as it's going to get, and the message is really annoying for users. Let's turn it off.

To disable the Excel security message for these files, follow these steps:

1. Open Microsoft Excel 2016 and go to **File | Options | Trust Center**.

2. Go to **Trusted Center Settings | Trusted Locations**.

3. Click on **Add new location**.

4. Browse to the location where you deployed the Excel reports. In my example, I used C:\GP2016XL. Click on **OK**.

5. Select the box marked **Subfolders of this location are also trusted** and click on **OK**:

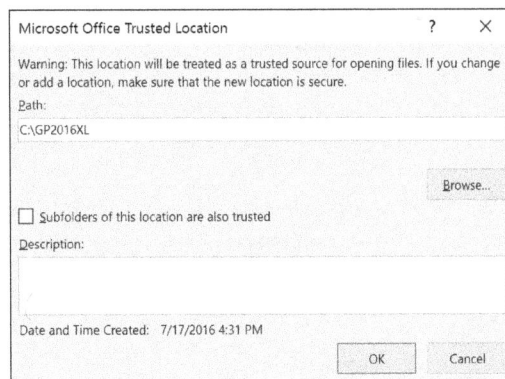

6. Click on **OK** twice to exit.

Now, when you run the Excel reports in the next section, the reports will open in Excel 2016 without the security warning.

> Microsoft offers a great knowledge base article on Excel reports and security at `http://support.microsoft.com/kb/949524` for GP 10, but this portion of security remains the same.

Running Excel reports

Our next step is to run an Excel report. These reports can be run from Dynamics GP 2016, or they can be directly opened in Excel 2016. We will look at both these options.

From Dynamics GP 2016

To run an Excel report from within Dynamics GP, follow these steps:

1. In the navigation pane on the left-hand side, click on **Financial**. The list pane above will change to show financial items.

2. In the list pane, click on **Excel Reports**.

3. In the navigation list in the center, select **TWO AccountSummary Default**. Make sure that you select the **Option** column's options that includes **Reports**:

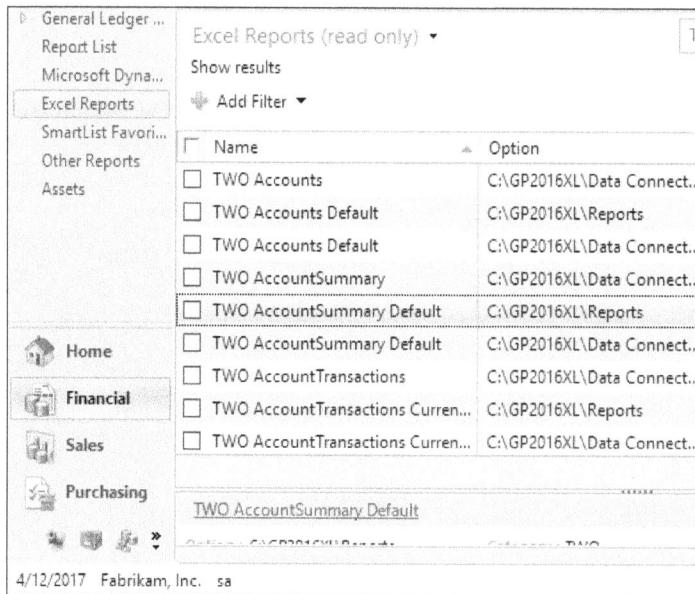

> Options that contain the word **Reports** open Excel reports. Options with **Data Connections** in the string indicate the data connector to build a new report, not an actual report. You can limit the Excel reports list to just **Reports** or **Data Connections** with the **Add Filter** button just above the Excel reports list.

4. Double-click on the **TWO AccountSummary Default** item.

5. We disabled the security warning earlier, but just in case, if Excel 2016 opens with a security warning at the top of the worksheet, click on **Enable Content**.

6. Excel will open with live data from Microsoft Dynamics GP:

	A	B	C	D	E	F
1	Year	Period ID	Account Number	Account Description	Debit Amount	Credit Amount
2	2013	0	000-1100-00	Cash - Operating Account	338562.25	0
3	2013	1	000-1100-00	Cash - Operating Account	1163034.94	-1122282.95
4	2013	2	000-1100-00	Cash - Operating Account	117.65	0
5	2013	5	000-1100-00	Cash - Operating Account	28000	0
6	2013	1	000-1110-00	Cash - Payroll	178700.56	-40545.33
7	2013	0	000-1110-00	Cash - Payroll	925.44	0
8	2013	0	000-1120-00	Cash - Flex Benefits Program	345.32	0
9	2013	1	000-1120-00	Cash - Flex Benefits Program	2120	-2120
10	2013	0	000-1130-00	Petty Cash	175	0

AccountSummary Default

7. As a test, highlight rows seven through 10 (**7-10**) on the left-hand side and press the *Delete* key.

8. Go to **Data | Refresh All** on the ribbon. Excel 2016 will reconnect to Dynamics GP and bring back in the latest data.

> Saving the report with a different name in the same folder as the GP deployed reports will make that report visible in the list of Excel reports in GP.

From Excel 2016

To accomplish this same task (run a GP Excel refreshable report) from Excel 2016, follow these steps:

1. Open Windows Explorer and navigate to the location where you deployed the reports at the beginning of this chapter. In my example, the reports were deployed to `C:\GP2016XL\`.

2. Drill down through the folders to `Reports | TWO | Financial`. This represents the report storage for the sample company's (TWO) financial reports:

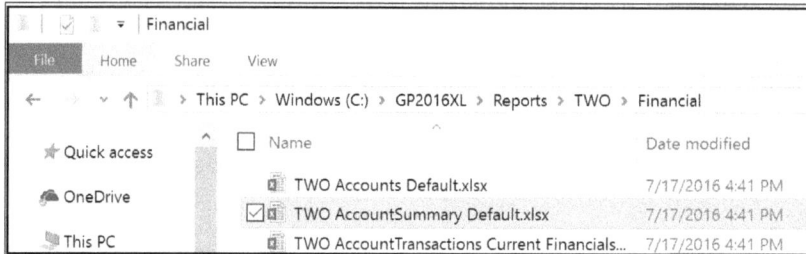

3. Double-click on `TWO AccountSummary Default.xlsx`.

4. Excel 2016 will open with live data from Dynamics GP.

Manual versus auto refresh

Excel reports are refreshable, but that doesn't mean that they have to refresh automatically.

Often accountants ask about saving a static version of the file. They love the idea of refreshing data, but they want it to happen on their terms. Most accountants prefer information that doesn't change once it's been finalized, so this request is perfectly natural. By default, the Dynamics GP 2016 connections are designed to refresh automatically when the file is opened, but you can control this.

To understand how to control the refresh options, follow these steps:

1. Start with the `TWO AccountSummary Default` Excel file that you already have open.

2. In Excel, select the **Data** tab and then go to **Connections | Properties**:

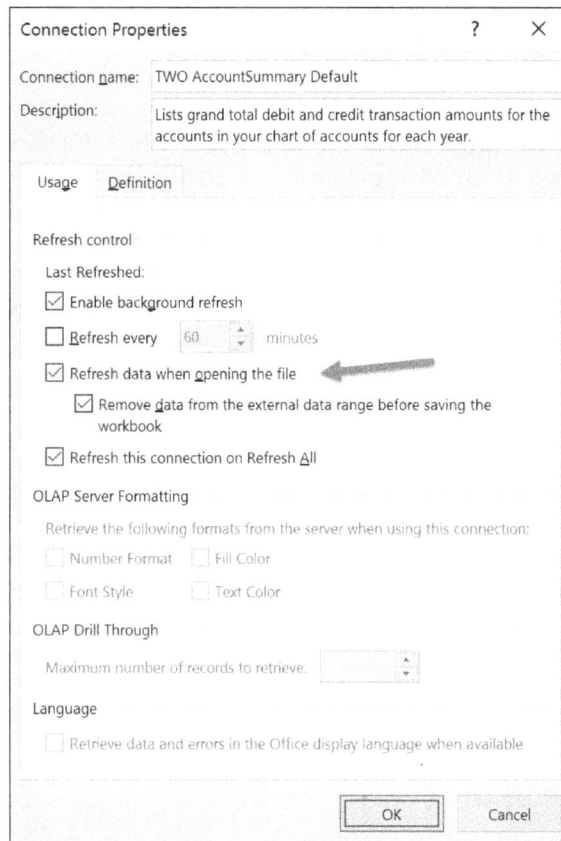

3. Uncheck the **Refresh data when opening the file** box and click on **OK**.

4. Click on **Close** to return to the worksheet in Excel.

5. To validate that this worked, select rows seven through 10 (**7-10**) in the Excel sheet and press *Delete*.

6. Save the Excel sheet to your desktop as `TWO AccountSummary Default Manual Refresh` and close Excel 2016.

7. To reopen the file, double-click on `TWO AccountSummary Default Manual Refresh` on the desktop.

8. Excel will open with data, and rows seven through 10 (**7-10**) will be blank. The sheet did not refresh automatically.

9. To manually refresh the sheet, right-click anywhere in the data area and click **Refresh** or select **Data | Refresh All**.

Excel refreshable reports via SmartList Designer

Since the release of the original version of this book, which focused on Dynamics GP 2013, SmartList has received a few updates. The Designer, which is now part of SmartList, allows for the creation of Excel refreshable reports based on custom SmartList objects that were originated in the Designer. The Designer can easily create both a SmartList object and an Excel refreshable report using a SQL view (which we discussed in *Chapter 1, Getting Data from Dynamics GP 2016 to Excel 2016*.) Let's create a new SmartList object and a new Excel refreshable report now.

Create a new SmartList object

Let's create a new SmartList object that will display the bank accounts and their balances, from the `Bank Reconciliation` module. Microsoft has a view already built to do this very thing, named `CM00500`, which is stored in each company's SQL database. Let's take a look at the following steps to create a new object:

1. Open SmartList as you would to pull up accounts.

2. On the **Actions** part of the SmartList ribbon, select **New**:

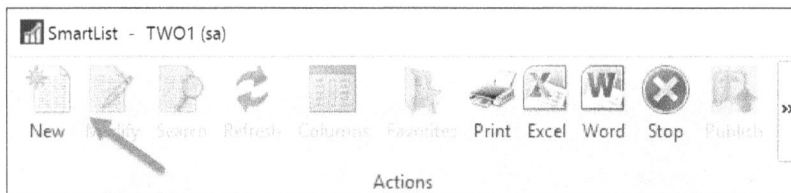

3. In the **List Name**, enter `Bank Balance` and in **Series**, select **Financial** from the drop-down list.

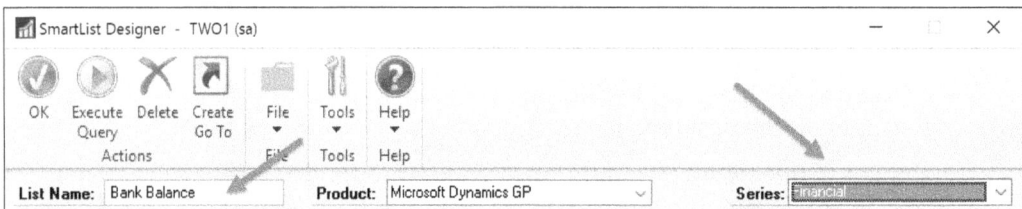

4. On the left **Database View** pane, scroll down and click on the plus (**+**) **Views** | plus (**+**) **Company**. All the views for the database for the company for which you are currently logged in to GP will be displayed.

5. Scroll through the views for **Company**, find CM00500 and click on the plus (+) display the fields (columns) in that view.

6. Select the fields **CHEKBKID, DSCRIPTN, CURNCYID, INACTIVE**, and **CURRBLNC**. The fields will then appear in the **Selected Fields** pane:

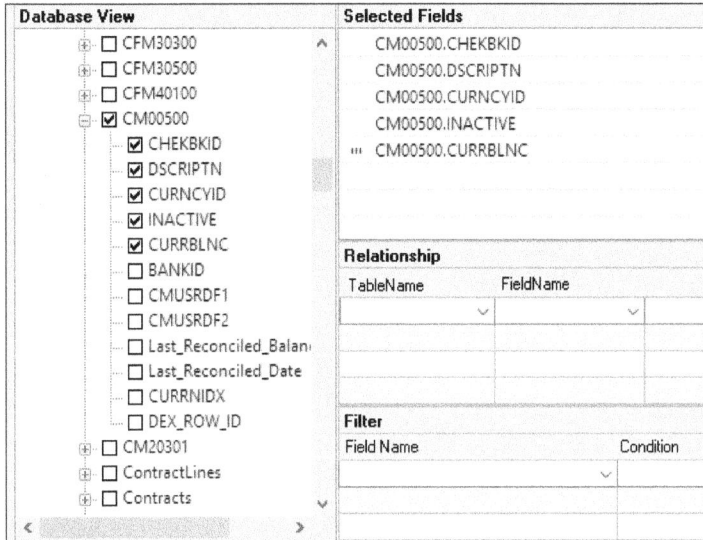

7. Click on **Execute Query** on the ribbon, and you'll see the data displayed in **Result's Preview**:

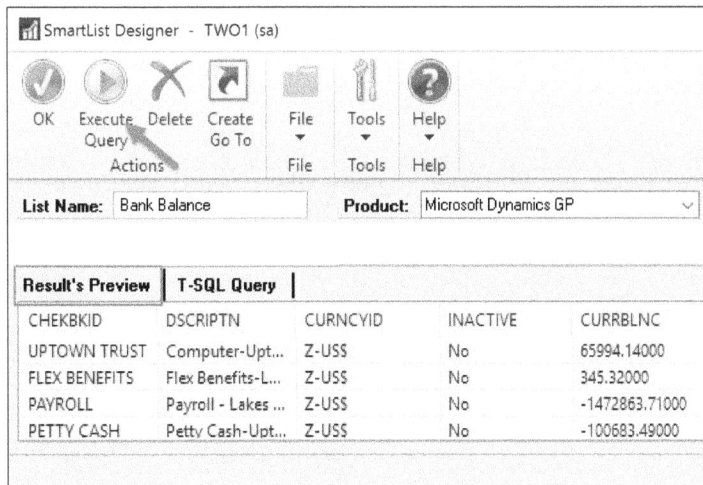

8. If the results look like what you expect, then click on the **OK** button on the ribbon. This will create the new SmartList object.

9. Since we put this new object in the `Financial` Series, you'll now see a new folder called `Bank Balance` that holds our new object:

> You've been given the non-Excel gift of "How to create a new SmartList object in SmartList Designer." And yes, you can use these steps to create other SmartList objects, regardless of whether or not you create an Excel refreshable report from them.

Publish to Excel

Now that we've created our object, let's create the Excel refreshable report using these steps:

1. Open SmartList and highlight the new object we just created.

2. On the SmartList Ribbon, click on **Publish**:

3. You'll receive confirmation that your Excel report was created:

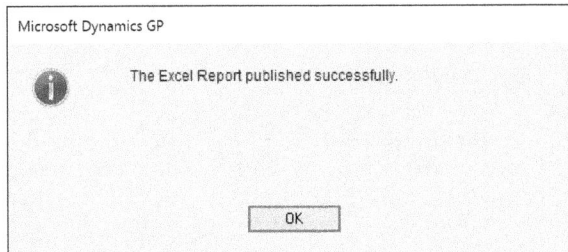

4. Go to the Excel Reports for Financials, that is, go to **Financials | Excel Reports**. Our new report is now in the list and can be used:

5. Double-click on the Excel report version and your bank balances will appear in Excel:

	A	B	C	D	E
1	CHEKBKID	DSCRIPTN	CURNCYID	INACTIVE	CURRBLNC
2	UPTOWN TRUST	Computer-Uptown Trust	Z-US$	No	65994.14
3	FLEX BENEFITS	Flex Benefits-Lakes Bank	Z-US$	No	345.32
4	PAYROLL	Payroll - Lakes Bank	Z-US$	No	-1472863.71
5	PETTY CASH	Petty Cash-Uptown Trust	Z-US$	No	-100683.49
6	FIRST BANK	FIRST BANK	Z-US$	No	0
7					
8					
9					
10					

Sheet1

Summary

We've looked at one of the best methods for getting data for our dashboard. We've deployed, secured, run, and built Excel reports. Now that we've thoroughly explored one of the best ways to get real-time data out of Dynamics GP 2016 and into Microsoft Excel, let's start looking at how to use this information as the foundation for a dashboard.

In the next chapter, we will start to build our dashboard using one of the fundamental building blocks—the pivot tables.

3
Pivot Tables – The Basic Building Blocks

Pivot tables are the basic building blocks of analysis in Excel. The same concept of establishing the pivot table elements, that is, **Rows** (required), **Values** (required), **Columns** (optional), and **Filters** (optional), are used within most of the Microsoft-reporting tools. Very often, I am asked how someone can make a pivot table look like a report and not like a table. With a few clicks of the mouse, your pivot table can become a professional, easy-to-read report.

At their most complex, these tables provide infinite ways to analyze and visualize data. We can't fit an infinite number of ways in this book, so we'll use some common scenarios here.

In this chapter, we will start building our Dynamics GP dashboard by learning about:

- Creating pivot tables from GP 2016 Excel report data
- Creating pivot tables from GP 2016 data connections
- Copying pivot tables
- Creating connected pivot tables from Excel

In the next few of chapters of this book, we will build a dashboard that looks like the one in the following screenshot, and we will use pivot tables as the foundation:

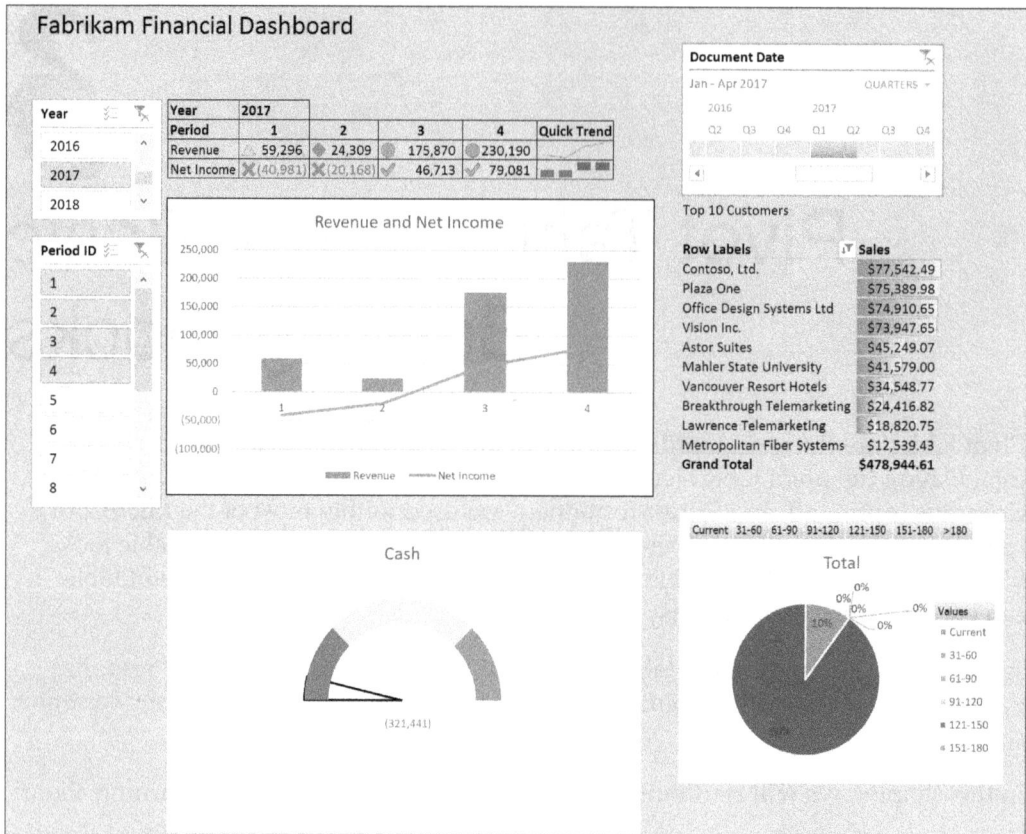

[The term "pivot table" is generic. Microsoft has trademarked the term "PivotTable," so you'll use the items in Excel labeled that way.]

Creating pivot tables from GP 2016 Excel report data

The starting point for pivot tables is simply to use data in Microsoft Excel 2016. I often present a session titled *PivotTables 101*. After almost every presentation, at least one person tells me that they almost didn't attend because they "already knew how to use pivot tables." They then tell me that they are glad they attended as they didn't know about many of the simple Excel features that can turn an ordinary pivot table into an amazing report, chart, or dashboard. Together, we will create and use those features now.

Getting data to Excel

To build our first pivot table, let's start with the TWO AccountSummary Default Excel report that we used in *Chapter 2, The Ultimate GP to Excel Tool – Refreshable Excel Reports*. Then, follow these steps:

1. In Dynamics GP, on the navigation pane on the left-hand side, click on **Financial**. The list pane above will change to show financial items.

2. In the list pane, click on **Excel Reports**.

3. In the navigation list in the center, select TWO AccountSummary Default. Make sure that you select items where the **Option** includes **Reports**.

4. Double-click on the TWO AccountSummary Default item.

5. In *Chapter 2, The Ultimate GP to Excel Tool – Refreshable Excel Reports*, we looked at how to turn off the Excel 2016 security warning at the top of the worksheet. If it still appears, click on **Enable Content** and then circle back to the security section in the previous chapter. I'm assuming that you've got this fixed now, so we won't revisit it.

Building a pivot table with a calculated field

Follow these steps to build the pivot table:

1. Use your cursor to select any cell in the table of data from the Excel report that you just brought into Dynamics GP.

2. Go to **Insert | PivotTable** from the Excel 2016 ribbon.

3. **Select a table or range** should be marked, and the **Table/Range:** should be
   `Table_AccountSummary_Default`:

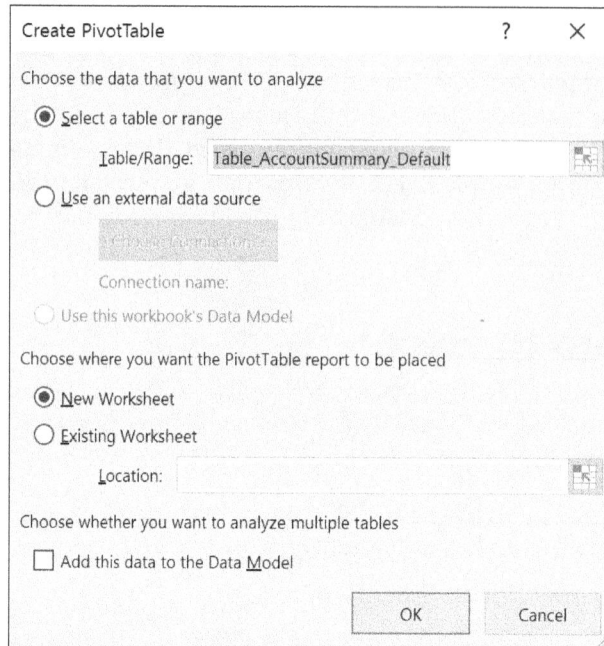

4. Notice that under **Choose where you want the PivotTable report to be placed**, we are putting this pivot table in a **New Worksheet**. Click on **OK**.

5. A new worksheet will open with the canvas for a new pivot table report. In the **PivotTable Fields** box on the right-hand side, use your mouse to drag items into the areas at the bottom. Drag:

   ° **Year** to **Rows**
   ° **Account Number** to **Filters**
   ° **Period ID** to **Columns**

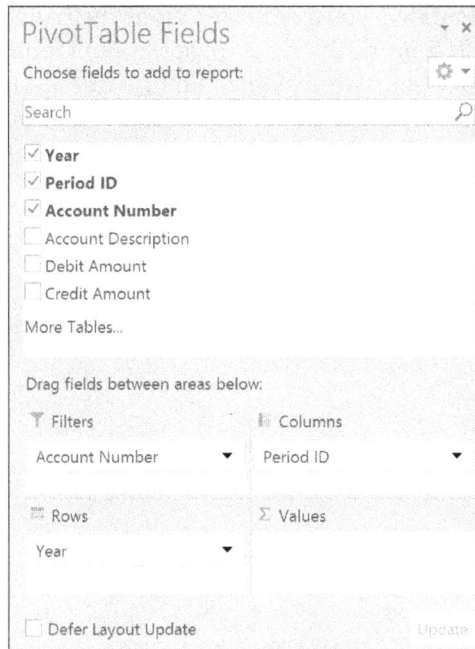

[If you used the (edited) version of the Excel refreshable report that we created in the previous chapter, you'll have a column that displays the net of debits and credits already. You could use that in **Values** and skip this step. But then, you would miss the fun of creating a calculated field.]

6. Click anywhere in the pivot table and a new menu option will appear called **PivotTable Tools**. Go to **PivotTable Tools | Analyze | Fields, Items, & Sets | Calculated Field...** We will create the net balance right in the pivot table:

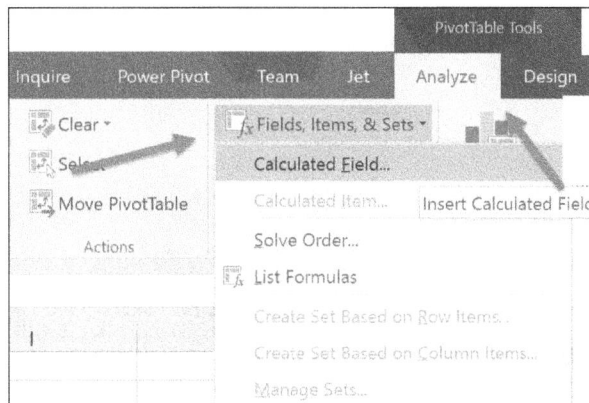

7. In the **Insert Calculated Field** window, enter the name `Net Balance`. In the **Formula** field, remove the zero (0), select the **Debit Amount** field from the **Fields** list, and select **Insert Field**. Enter a minus sign (-) in the formula and then add the **Credit Amount** field. We are creating a formula of *debits - credits*. Click on **OK**. The new calculated field will automatically appear in the **Value** area of the **PivotTable Field** list:

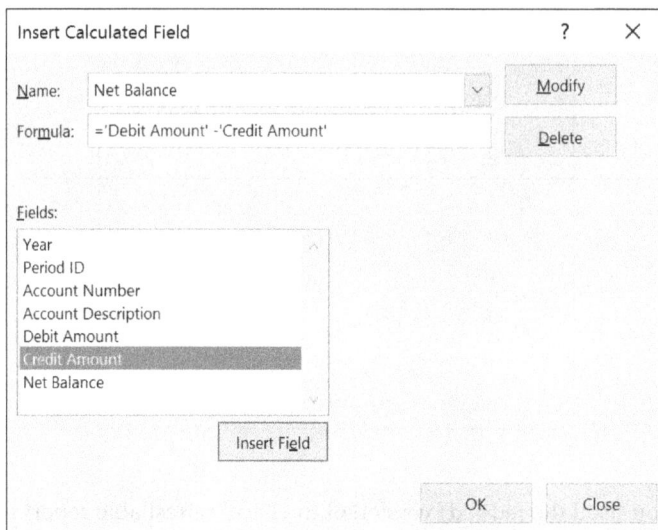

8. This covers all of the accounts. Let's just analyze one account for now. At the top of the pivot table next to **Account Number**, change **(All)** to **000-1100-00**:

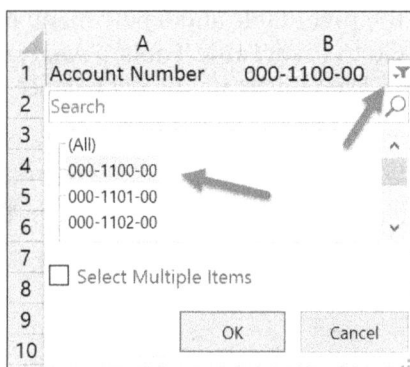

That's it. You've built a pivot table. It's really that easy. Now, we're ready to move into some more building blocks.

Creating pivot tables from GP 2016 data connections

One problem with creating a pivot table from data in Excel 2016 is that we have to bring the data from Dynamics GP 2016 into Microsoft Excel. That's not much of a burden when we're dealing with a few hundred rows, but when you get to transactional data, it's easy to have a couple of hundred thousand rows. This is where pivot table performance starts to bog down. For companies with a lot of accounts, high transaction volume, and a lot of history, it's easy to exceed Excel's maximum row count of 1,048,576 rows. Microsoft Excel 2016 lets us build pivot tables without having to bring the data into Excel.

When we deployed Dynamics GP 2016's Excel reports, we also deployed the data connectors. The connectors let us use data in Dynamics GP to build pivot tables without having to bring detailed data into Excel 2016. Let's use this to start building our dashboard. For much of the rest of the book, you'll want to save the file that we're working with. It will ultimately grow into our dashboard. To build a pivot table from Dynamics GP without having to bring everything into Excel, follow these steps:

1. Open a new worksheet in Excel 2016. Go to **Data | Existing Connections**:

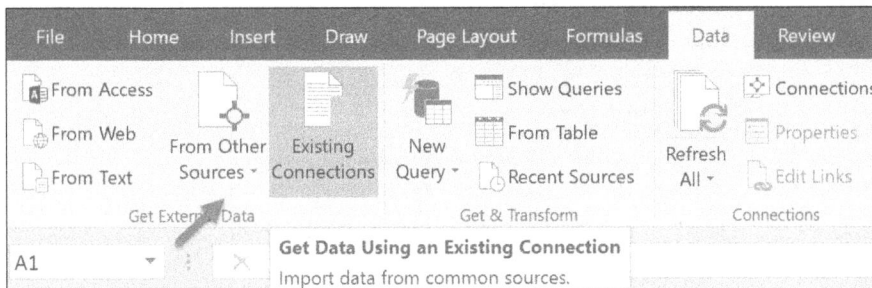

2. In the bottom-left corner of the **Existing Connections** window, click on **Browse for More...**

3. In the **Select Data Source** window, map your way to the location of your deployed GP excel refreshable reports, by going to `Data Connections | <your company ID> | Financial.` Select the `company ID AccountSummary. odc,` in our case `TWO AccountSummary.odc:`

4. Excel 2016 will ask you what to do with the data. Despite also being named `AccountSummary,` this connector is a little different. The `AccountSummary Default` report is actually a limited subset of data from the `AccountSummary` view. The `AccountSummary` connector has everything in the view, so there is a lot more data available:

5. Select **PivotTable Report** and click on **OK**.

> In versions prior to Excel 2016, merely double-clicking on a
> *.odc file would take you right to the **Import Data** window,
> allowing you to create a pivot table or chart without bringing
> the data into a worksheet.
>
> Selecting the **Only Create Connection** option is another cool
> way to create your pivot table and/or chart without storing
> any data in Excel. Each time it opens, it'll refresh with new
> data.

Building a revenue pivot table

Now, we have the canvas for a pivot table again, but this time, it's based on
Dynamics GP data contained in the SQL Server, not on data that we've brought
into Excel. This also makes the Excel files much smaller.

Let's use this data to build a revenue pivot table for our dashboard using these steps:

1. Drag **Account Number** into **Rows**.
2. Drag **Account Category** into **Filters**.
3. Drag **Year** and **Period ID** into **Columns** with **Year** on top.
4. Drag **Period Balance** into **Values**.
5. Click the drop-down box on the **Account Category Number** filter at the top
   of the pivot table next to **(All)**.
6. Select the **Select Multiple Items** box.
7. Uncheck **(All)**.
8. Scroll down and select **Sales** and **Sales Returns and Discounts**:

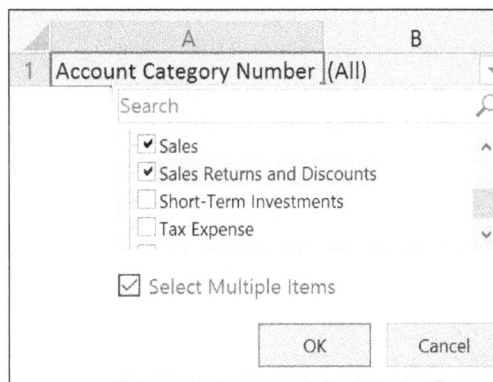

9. Select cell B4. This should contain the year 2013. To filter this to only show 2017, select the drop-down box next to **Column Labels**.

> ![lightbulb icon] Remember that these steps use the lesson data called **Fabrikam**. If you are using your own data, the data will vary, so take that into account.

10. Uncheck **Select All** and select **2017**.

11. Select cell B5. This should now contain period **1**. To filter this to only show the first four months of 2017, select the drop-down box next to **Column Labels**.

12. Uncheck **Select All** and check periods **1** through **4**.

13. Finally, let's clean things up. On the menu bar, go to **PivotTable Tools | Design | Grand Totals | On for Columns Only**:

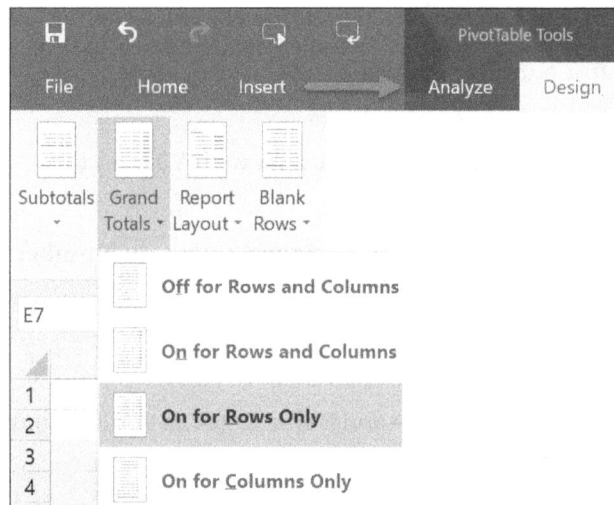

14. Select cells B6 through F6, and right-click and go to **Value Field Settings | Number Format**. Choose the formatting option you desire for the currency values in these columns:

▲	A	B	C	D	E	F
1	Account Category Number (Multiple Items) ⏷					
2						
3	**Sum of Period Balance**	Column Labels ⏷				
4		⊟2017				**2017 Total**
5	**Row Labels** ⏷	**1**	**2**	**3**	**4**	
6	000-4100-00			-539.55	-8,792.14	-9,331.69
7	000-4110-01	-3,799.00		-2,659.30	-579.65	-7,037.95
8	000-4110-02	-55,497.10	-24,308.85	-172,251.95	-220,818.15	-472,876.05
9	000-4140-00			-419.40		-419.40
10	**Grand Total**	**-59,296.10**	**-24,308.85**	**-175,870.20**	**-230,189.94**	**-489,665.09**
11						

> Yes, you could format these cells using the method for any normal worksheet. However, if you want the pivot table to retain these formats, you'll want to use this method.
>
> Formatting can also be achieved by clicking on the down area for **Sum of Period Balance** in the **Values** area of **PivotTable Field** list.

15. Right-click on the tab at the bottom of the worksheet, select **Rename**, and type Revenue.

16. Right-click in the pivot table and select **PivotTable Options**. Name the pivot table Revenue.

17. Save the file as GP 2016 Dashboard.xlsx. Make sure to save it somewhere that you can find it. We will continue working with this file. Saving here is just a precaution.

We've now built the source for the revenue data in our dashboard. This will also become our drill-back to the account numbers to support our revenue total.

Copying pivot tables

We have a pivot table for revenue, but we really need similar information to display net income on our dashboard. Fortunately, we don't have to go through that whole exercise again. Since our net income pivot table is based on the same data as our revenue pivot table, we can copy and paste. To create a net income based pivot table, follow these steps:

1. Click anywhere inside the pivot table on the **Revenue** tab.

2. Select the **Analyze** tab under the **PivotTable Tools** grouping.

3. Go to **Select | Entire PivotTable**.

4. Right-click on the pivot table and select **Copy**.

5. Create a new sheet using the plus (**+**) key at the bottom.

6. In cell A1, click on the **Paste** button on the **Home** ribbon.

Building a net income pivot table

This creates a copy of the sheet on a different tab. Now, we're ready to modify our copied pivot table. Follow these steps:

1. Select the copied pivot table and drag **Account Category** off the **Filters** area and back into the **PivotTable Fields** list.

2. Drag **Posting Type** into the **Filters** area:

▼ Filters			⊞ Columns	
Posting Type	▼		Year	▼
			Period ID	▼
▦ Rows			Σ Values	
Account Number	▼		Sum of Period Balance	▼
☐ Defer Layout Update				Update

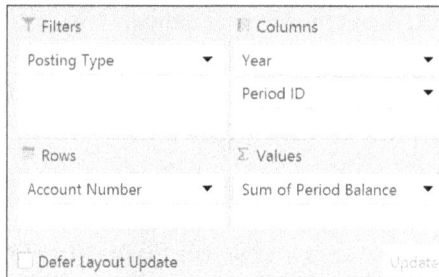

3. Open the drop-down box for the **Posting Type** filter next to **(All)** and select **Profit and Loss**.

4. The periods should show the first four periods. If not, select cell B5 and click the filter button next to **Column Labels**. Uncheck **Select All** and select only periods **1** through **4**.

5. Rename the tab `Net Income`.

6. Right-click in the pivot table and select **PivotTable Options**. Name the pivot table `Net Income`.

7. Save the file:

	A	B	C	D	E	F
1	Posting Type	Profit and Loss 🔽				
2						
3	Sum of Period Balance	Column Labels 🔽				
4		⊟ 2017				2017 Total
5	Row Labels ▾	1	2	3	4	
6	000-4100-00			-539.55	-8,792.14	-9,331.69
7	000-4110-01	-3,799.00		-2,659.30	-579.65	-7,037.95
8	000-4110-02	-55,497.10	-24,308.85	-172,251.95	-220,818.15	-472,876.05
9	000-4140-00			-419.40		-419.40
10	000-4510-01	29,272.62	12,093.06	91,227.81	111,630.94	244,224.43
11	000-4600-00		-1.60	-89.90	-23.94	-115.44
12	000-5100-00	63,045.68	28,147.81	29,141.84	29,019.39	149,354.72
13	100-5150-00	1,431.65	1,430.24	1,432.12	1,431.83	5,725.84
14	100-5170-00	900.00	393.93	408.41	406.60	2,108.94
15	200-5170-00	3,848.23	1,684.56	1,746.19	1,738.60	9,017.58
16	300-5130-00	1,778.92	729.29	5,276.16	6,905.75	14,690.12
17	500-6150-00			15.00		15.00
18	Grand Total	40,981.00	20,168.44	-46,712.57	-79,080.77	-64,643.90
19						
20						

Revenue | Net Income | ⊕

We now have source data for two of the five major elements of our dashboard. We can refresh this data any time from within Excel simply by going to **Data | Refresh All**.

Creating a cash pivot table

We need a couple more pivot tables to round out our dashboard, so let's build them really fast. First, we need cash, and since it's built from our account summary data as well, it makes this easy. For cash, we just want to see total cash. To build the cash pivot table, make another copy of the revenue pivot table with these steps:

1. Click anywhere inside the pivot table on the **Revenue** tab.
2. Select the **Analyze** tab under the **PivotTable Tools** grouping.
3. Go to **Select | Entire PivotTable**.
4. Right-click in the pivot table and select **Copy**.
5. Create a new sheet using the plus (**+**) key at the bottom.
6. In cell A1, click on the **Paste** button on the **Home** ribbon.
7. Rename the worksheet tab to `Cash`.
8. Save the file.

Now, let's modify it to just get the cash total using these steps:

1. In the **PivotTable Field** list area on the right-hand side:
    o   Remove **Year** and **Period ID** from **Columns**
    o   Remove **Accounts** from **Rows**
    o   Move **Account Category Number** to **Rows**
    o   Add **Year** to **Filters**

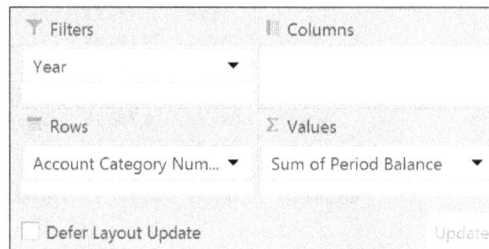

▼ Filters	▥ Columns
Year ▼	

▤ Rows	Σ Values
Account Category Num... ▼	Sum of Period Balance ▼

☐ Defer Layout Update   Update

2. Select the filter symbol next to **Year** and select **(All)**.
3. Select the filter symbol next to **Row Labels** and uncheck everything except **Cash**.
4. Right-click in the pivot table and select **PivotTable Options**. Name the pivot table `Cash`.
5. Save the file:

	A	B
1	Year	(All) ▼
2		
3	**Row Labels** ▼	**Sum of Period Balance**
4	Cash	321,440.94
5	**Grand Total**	**321,440.94**

Nice job. We'll use this information as part of a speedometer graph later on.

> Selecting all years worked in the sample company because of the number of open years in the GP 2016 sample data. In the real world, you would typically only need the open year since it has a beginning balance and subsequent transactions.

Creating connected pivot tables from inside Excel

So far, we've created pivot tables by starting in Dynamics GP 2016 and sending information to Excel. We can also use Excel 2016 to pull data out of Dynamics GP. For our dashboard, we need some sales data and receivables totals. The sales data that we want exists as a Dynamics GP data connection. The receivables data connection doesn't contain quite what we need, so we'll have to adjust it.

Building the sales pivot table

Let's add a sales pivot table first. To create our sales pivot table, follow these steps:

1. In Excel 2016, click plus (**+**) next to the worksheet tabs 2016 to add a new worksheet. Name the worksheet `Top Ten Customers`.

2. Select the **Data** tab and click on **Existing Connections** from the ribbon.

3. Click on **Browse for More...** and navigate to where you installed the GP 2016 data connections for the sample company. Earlier, we deployed it to `C:\GP2016XL\Data Connections\TWO`.

4. Select the `Sales` directory and double-click on `TWO SalesTransactions Posted Invoices.odc`:

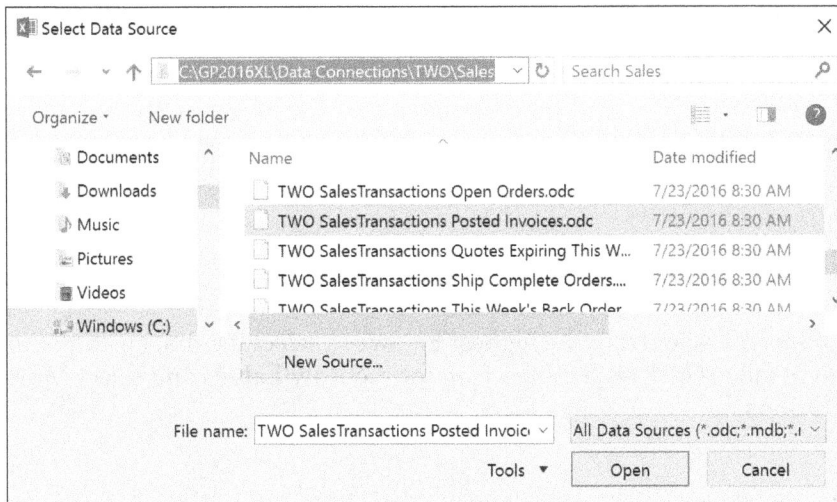

5. The **Import Data** window will open. Select **PivotTable Report** and click on **OK**.

6. Click in the pivot table framework area to bring up the **PivotTable Field** list on the right-hand side.

7. Drag **Customer Name** into **Rows**.

8. Drag **Document Amount** into **Values**.

We don't need all of our customer's sales; that's too much information for a dashboard. Let's limit it to the top 10 customers by sales. To show only the top 10 customers, follow these steps:

1. Click on the first customer name in the sales pivot table.

2. Right-click and go to **Filter | Top 10**.

3. Notice that we're not limited to the top or just to 10 items, but this is good enough for now. So, click on **OK**:

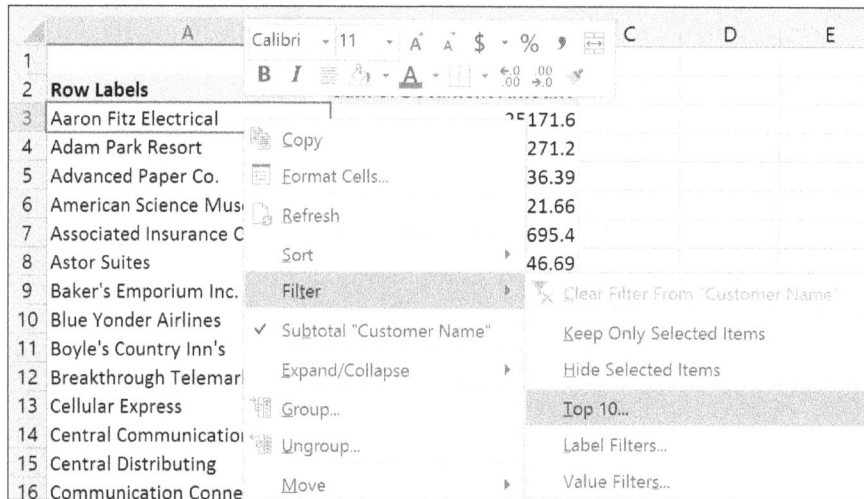

4. To sort the sales from the highest to lowest, select the first customer in the pivot table. Click on the filter icon for the **Row Labels** and select **More Sort Options...**:

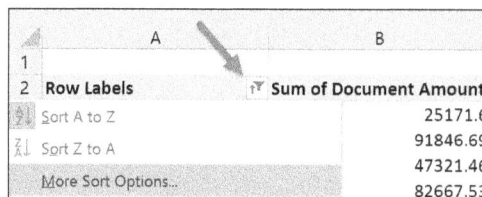

5. In the **Sort (Customer Name)** window, select **Descending (Z to A) by:** and choose **Sum of Document Amount** from the drop-down list:

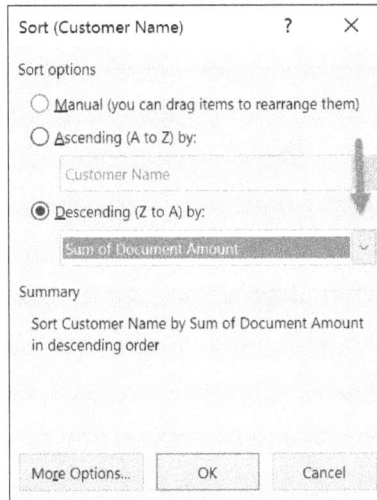

```
Sort (Customer Name)                    ?    ×

Sort options

   ○ Manual (you can drag items to rearrange them)

   ○ Ascending (A to Z) by:

      Customer Name

   ◉ Descending (Z to A) by:

      Sum of Document Amount               ˅

Summary

   Sort Customer Name by Sum of Document Amount
   in descending order


   More Options...        OK          Cancel
```

> Like formatting, if you want to save your sort options for a pivot table, you'll need to perform the sorting in the pivot table itself. Often, formatting and sorting performed from the ribbon will not save.

6. Format the **Sum of Document Amount** column as you did for the previous pivot tables.

7. Right-click in the pivot table and select **PivotTable Options**. Name the pivot table Top 10 Customers.

8. Save the file.

Adding a receivables pivot table

Now, our pivot table has been reduced to just the top 10 customers by sales and ordered appropriately. All that is left for our foundation is adding **receivables aging**. To add receivables, follow these steps:

1. In Excel 2016, click plus (**+**) next to the worksheet tabs to add a new worksheet. Name the worksheet Receivables Aging.

2. Select the **Data** tab and click on **Existing Connections** from the ribbon.

3. Click on **Browse for More…** and navigate to where you installed the GP 2016 data connections for the sample company. Earlier, we installed this in `C:\GP2016XL\Data Connections\TWO`.

4. Select the `Sales` directory and double-click on `TWO Customers Past Due Customers`.

5. The **Import Data** window will open.

6. We need to modify the data coming in, so go to **Properties | Definition**.

This view holds past due customer amounts. We want all customer amounts, not just past due totals, so we have to remove the limitation on this data. Follow these steps:

1. In the **Command text** window, scroll down to the word `where`. Highlight the word `where` with your mouse and select all the rest of the text:

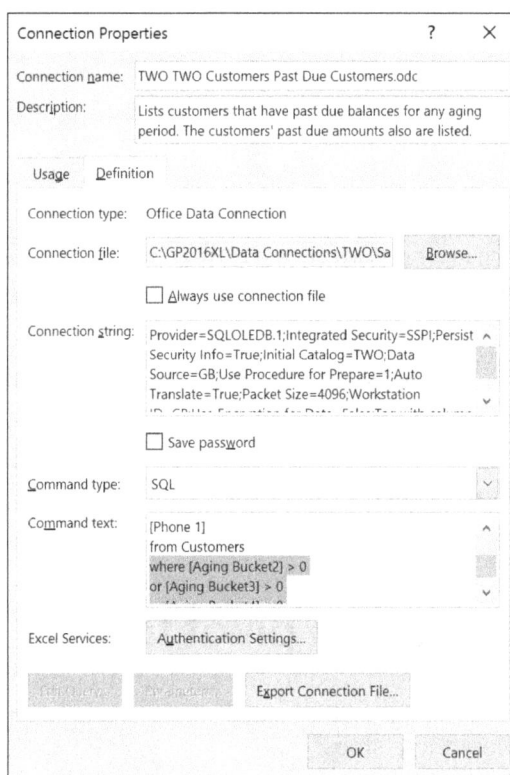

2. Press *Delete* to remove the restrictions. Click on **OK** to confirm the message that this workbook will no longer match the file and click on **OK** to continue.

3. Select **PivotTable Report** and click on **OK**.

4. Click in the pivot table canvas area to bring up **PivotTable Field** list on the right-hand side.

5. Drag each one of the **Aging Buckets** down into **Values**.

6. Drag **Values** from the **Columns** area to **Rows**:

Filters	Columns
Rows	Σ Values
Σ Values ▼	Sum of Aging Bucket1 ▼
	Sum of Aging Bucket2 ▼
	Sum of Aging Bucket3 ▼

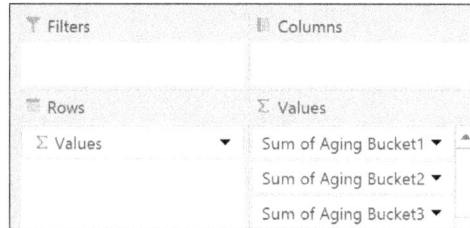

7. Format each **Aging Bucket** on the pivot table to displays a currency or with commas and decimals.

8. Right-click in the pivot table and select **PivotTable Options**. Name the pivot table Receivables Aging.

9. Save the file.

Now, the data foundation of our dashboard is complete.

Summary

So, we've created five different pivot tables, all of which will be used in our dashboard, which we will continue to work on in the next chapter. We created these pivot tables using a few different methods. Since we used data sources that are included as part of your GP, imagine what you could do with your own data sources (custom views).

Pivot tables are super powerful in displaying data. The more variation of rows and columns that you add, the more powerful they become. For example, adding departments in columns with accounts in rows would make for a completely different report than putting months in columns. Experiment with pivot tables and your data, you just might uncover how to make your company more profitable in a way nobody else has thought of yet, making you a Pivot Table Power Hero!

In the next chapter, we will start to build the look and feel of our dashboard with conditional formatting. This is another key element, and it's a big part of making a dashboard look great. We'll perform some custom controls with timelines and slicers. Finally, we'll make all it visually appealing.

4

Making Your Data Visually Appealing and Meaningful with Formatting, Conditional Formatting, and Charts

Now that we have our data elements for a dashboard, we'll start pulling the pieces together and format them. When presenting on dashboards, I often talk about the dashboard in my car. Yes, I know, so does everyone else, but I have a different twist on it. I talk specifically about the gas tank gauge. If it wasn't there, how often would you buy gas, or worse, run out of gas? No doubt, we'd all carry around a canister of spare gas, just in case. With the normal gas gauge of *empty to full*, you can figure out how much gas you have with a little math, provided you know how big your tank is. Trust me, nobody wants me driving while doing math in my head. Would that be a **Driving While Ciphering (DWC)**? Anyway, with the newer visuals of how far I can go with the gas I have in my tank, based on my average driving, I can make informed decisions. That's what a financial dashboard is all about—allowing you to make informed decisions.

> My personal definition of business intelligence is making informed business decisions based on timely and accurate information.

In this chapter, we will start assembling and formatting our dashboard with the help of the following topics:

- Get pivot data
- Excel formatting
- Icon sets
- Sparklines
- Data bars
- Charts
- Slicers and timelines
- Additional formatting

The idea behind conditional formatting is that we want data elements to change visually based on the value of the data. The simplest example is the classic way of presenting positive numbers in black and negative numbers in red. With the conditional formatting options in Excel, we can do so much more. However, first, we have to start building our dashboard.

> The presentation of negative numbers in red is where we get the English phrase "in the red" to describe a company that is losing money.

Recap

As a reminder, we are working to build a dashboard that looks like this:

Fabrikam Financial Dashboard

Year	2017				
Period	1	2	3	4	Quick Trend
Revenue	59,296	24,309	175,870	230,190	
Net Income	(40,981)	(20,168)	46,713	79,081	

Year
2016
2017
2018

Period ID
1
2
3
4
5
6
7
8

Document Date
Jan - Apr 2017   QUARTERS

	2016				2017		
	Q2	Q3	Q4	Q1	Q2	Q3	Q4

Revenue and Net Income

250,000
200,000
150,000
100,000
50,000
0
(50,000)
(100,000)

Revenue —— Net Income

Top 10 Customers

Row Labels	Sales
Contoso, Ltd.	$77,542.49
Plaza One	$75,389.98
Office Design Systems Ltd	$74,910.65
Vision Inc.	$73,947.65
Astor Suites	$45,249.07
Mahler State University	$41,579.00
Vancouver Resort Hotels	$34,548.77
Breakthrough Telemarketing	$24,416.82
Lawrence Telemarketing	$18,820.75
Metropolitan Fiber Systems	$12,539.43
Grand Total	**$478,944.61**

Cash

(321,441)

Current 31-60 61-90 91-120 121-150 151-180 >180

Total

0%
0%
0%
0%
10%
0%

Values
Current
31-60
61-90
91-120
121-150
151-180

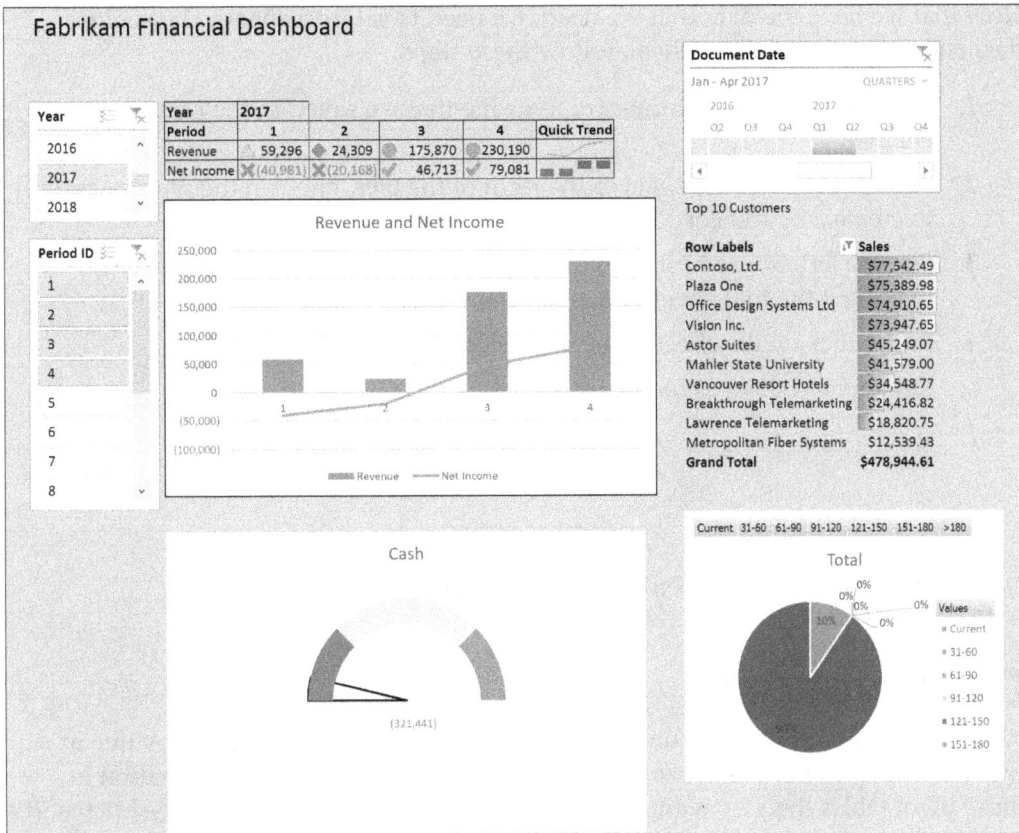

Through the first three chapters, you learned how to get data from Microsoft Dynamics GP 2016 into Excel 2016. Along the way, we built a set of pivot tables to serve as the source data for our dashboard. This chapter is where we start to see the dashboard take shape.

Preparation

The idea behind any financial dashboard is to give users a snapshot of key business metrics. On a car dashboard, more important information is given greater weight, that is, the gauges are bigger, placed in the center, and so on. Periodically important data is highlighted as necessary, for example, when the low fuel light comes on to ensure that you are paying attention to the fuel gauge. It doesn't hurt to think that way for financial dashboards as well. We don't want to clutter up our dashboard with too much information.

Now that we have the data that we need, we need to set up a sheet to hold our dashboard. To create a new sheet, follow these steps:

1. Open the GP 2016 `Dashboard.xlsx` file that we saved in the previous chapter.

2. At the bottom of the sheet to the right of the tabs, click on the plus (**+**) button to create a new sheet.

3. Use the left mouse button to drag the new sheet all the way to the left, making it the first sheet on the left-hand side.

4. Right-click on the sheet name and select **Rename**.

5. Rename the sheet as `Dashboard`.

Now that we have a place to build our dashboard, let's get started.

Get pivot data

We want revenue and net income information on our dashboard, but they live in two different pivot tables in our data. Additionally, there is more information in those pivot tables than we want on our dashboard. The answer to this is—Microsoft's `GetPivotData` formula. Fortunately, you don't really need to spend much time figuring how to use the formula. Let's set up revenue and net income on our dashboard. To do this, follow these steps:

1. In cell D5 of the **Dashboard** sheet, type `Year`.

2. In cell D6, type `Period`.

3. In cell D7, type `Revenue`.

4. In cell D8, type `Net Income`.

Revenue

As a reminder, our revenue pivot table looks like this:

⊿	A	B	C	D	E	F
1	Account Category Number	(Multiple Items) ⊤				
2						
3	**Sum of Period Balance**	**Column Labels** ⊤				
4		⊟ **2017**				**2017 Total**
5	**Row Labels** ▾	1	2	3	4	
6	000-4100-00			-539.55	-8,792.14	-9,331.69
7	000-4110-01	-3,799.00		-2,659.30	-579.65	-7,037.95
8	000-4110-02	-55,497.10	-24,308.85	-172,251.95	-220,818.15	-472,876.05
9	000-4140-00			-419.40		-419.40
10	**Grand Total**	**-59,296.10**	**-24,308.85**	**-175,870.20**	**-230,189.94**	**-489,665.09**

Now that we have our heading information, let's add revenue and expense data using these steps:

1. Select cell E5 on the **Dashboard** sheet.
2. Type the equal sign (=) to start an Excel formula.
3. With your mouse, select the **Revenue** tab.
4. Click on cell B4 on the **Revenue** worksheet. This should be the year value **2017**. Hit *Enter* when done:

Year	2017
Period	
Revenue	
Net Income	

You should now have **2017** sitting in cell E5 next to **Year**. To add periods, follow these steps:

1. Select cell E6 on the **Dashboard** sheet.
2. Type the equal sign (=) to start an Excel formula.
3. With your mouse, select the **Revenue** tab.
4. Click on cell B5 on the **Revenue** worksheet. This should be period **1**. Hit *Enter* when done.

> As these are just filters and not pivot table results, we can copy them.

5. Right-click on cell E6 on the **Dashboard** sheet and select **Copy**.
6. With your mouse, highlight cells F6, G6, and H6.
7. Right-click and select **Paste**.

	A	B	C	D	E	F	G	H
1								
2								
3								
4								
5				Year	2017			
6				Period	1	2	3	4
7				Revenue				
8				Net Income				
9								

Now that we have our year at the top and our periods, let's add some data. Use these steps:

1. On the **Dashboard** worksheet, select cell E7 and type in the equal sign (=).
2. Move to the **Revenue** worksheet, select cell B10 and press *Enter*.

This places the revenue amount for period **1** on the dashboard. If you highlight the amount, you'll see that the formula is a little strange. It looks like this:

```
=GETPIVOTDATA("Period Balance",Revenue!$A$3,"Year","2017","Period
ID",1)
```

This is telling Excel to get the `Period Balance` value from the pivot table that starts in cell A3, where the year is `2017` and `Period ID` is 1. That works great for this cell, but there are two problems with this formula. First, as `2017` and `1` are hardcoded, this formula won't adjust when you copy cells for period 2, period 3, and so on. For the same reason, if the pivot table is changed to a different year or to reflect different periods, our dashboard won't update. We need to improve this formula. Also, since revenue is a credit, the amount appears as a negative, so we need to reverse the sign so that a credit appears as a positive.

To reverse the sign and make the `GetPivotData` formula more flexible, follow these steps:

1. Select the formula in cell E7.

2. Highlight just "2017" in the formula (including the quotes), click on cell E5, press the *F4* key to add anchors (dollar signs), and hit *Enter*. The formula should now look like this:

   ```
   =GETPIVOTDATA("Period
   Balance",Revenue!$A$3,"Year",$E$5,"Period
   ID",1)
   ```

3. Highlight just the number 1 in the formula, click on cell E6 and key in a dollar sign ($) before the number 6 to anchor it. Hit *Enter* when done. The formula should look like this:

   ```
   =GETPIVOTDATA("Period
   Balance",Revenue!$A$3,"Year",$E$5,"Period ID",E$6)
   ```

4. Still editing the formula cell E7, enter minus (-) between = and GETPIVOTDATA to reverse the sign. The final formula should look like this:

   ```
   =-GETPIVOTDATA("Period
   Balance",Revenue!$A$3,"Year",$E$5,"Period ID",E$6)
   ```

5. Now, you can copy the formula to cells F7, G7, and H7:

Year	2017			
Period	1	2	3	4
Revenue	59296.1	24308.85	175870.2	230189.9
Net Income				

Net income

We need to repeat this process to add net income. Our net income pivot table from *Chapter 3, Pivot Tables – The Basic Building Blocks*, looks like this:

	A	B	C	D	E	F
1	Posting Type	Profit and Loss ▾				
2						
3	Sum of Period Balance	Column Labels ▾				
4		2017				2017 Total
5	Row Labels ▾	1	2	3	4	
6	000-4100-00			-539.55	-8,792.14	-9,331.69
7	000-4110-01	-3,799.00		-2,659.30	-579.65	-7,037.95
8	000-4110-02	-55,497.10	-24,308.85	-172,251.95	-220,818.15	-472,876.05
9	000-4140-00			-419.40		-419.40
10	000-4510-01	29,272.62	12,093.06	91,227.81	111,630.94	244,224.43
11	000-4600-00		-1.60	-89.90	-23.94	-115.44
12	000-5100-00	63,045.68	28,147.81	29,141.84	29,019.39	149,354.72
13	100-5150-00	1,431.65	1,430.24	1,432.12	1,431.83	5,725.84
14	100-5170-00	900.00	393.93	408.41	406.60	2,108.94
15	200-5170-00	3,848.23	1,684.56	1,746.19	1,738.60	9,017.58
16	300-5130-00	1,778.92	729.29	5,276.16	6,905.75	14,690.12
17	500-6150-00			15.00		15.00
18	Grand Total	40,981.00	20,168.44	-46,712.57	-79,080.77	-64,643.90

To get net income below revenue, follow these steps:

1. On the **Dashboard** worksheet, select cell E8 and type in the equal sign (=).

2. Move to the **Net Income** worksheet, select cell B18, and press *Enter*. This gives you a default formula:

   ```
   =GETPIVOTDATA("Period Balance",'Net
   Income'!$A$3,"Year","2017","Period ID",1)
   ```

3. Select the formula in cell E8.

4. Highlight just "2017" in the formula, click on cell E5, press the *F4* key to add anchors ($), and hit *Enter*. The formula should now look like this:

   ```
   =GETPIVOTDATA("Period Balance",'Net
   Income'!$A$3,"Year",$E$5,"Period ID",1)
   ```

5. Highlight just the number 1 in the formula, click on cell E6, and key a dollar sign ($) before the number 6 to anchor it. Hit *Enter* when done. The formula should look like this:

```
=GETPIVOTDATA("Period Balance",'Net
Income'!$A$3,"Year",$E$5,"Period ID",E$6)
```

6. Still editing the formula cell E8, enter minus (1) between = and GETPIVOTDATA to reverse the sign. The final formula should look like this:

```
=-GETPIVOTDATA("Period Balance",'Net
Income'!$A$3,"Year",$E$5,"Period ID",E$6)
```

7. Now, you can copy the formula in E8 to cells F8, G8, and H8:

Year	2017			
Period	1	2	3	4
Revenue	59296.1	24308.85	175870.2	230189.9
Net Income	-40981	-20168.4	46712.57	79080.77

Formatting

Now that we have a start to our dashboard, let's improve the look of our revenue and net income table. To do this, follow these steps:

1. On the Dashboard sheet, select cells D5 and E5.

2. Right-click and select **Format Cells**.

3. On the **Font** tab, set **Font Style** to **Bold**.

4. On the **Border** tab, click on the **Outline** and **Inside** buttons.

5. On the **Fill** tab, select a light-gray background for these cells and hit **OK**.

6. Highlight cells D6 through H6.

7. Right-click and select **Format Cells**.

8. On the **Font** tab, set **Font Style** to **Bold**.

9. On the **Alignment** tab, set **Horizontal** to **Center**.

10. On the **Border** tab, click on the **Outline** and **Inside** buttons.

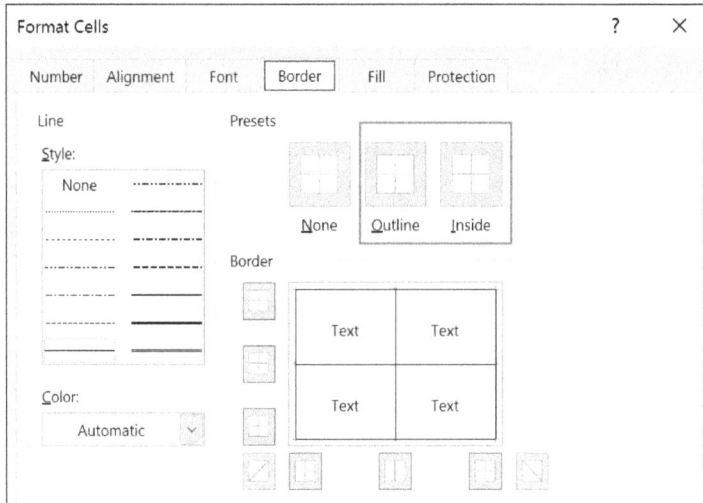

11. On the **Fill** tab, select a light-gray background for these cells and hit **OK**.
12. Highlight cell D6.
13. Right-click and select **Format Cells**.
14. On the **Alignment** tab, set **Horizontal** to **Left (Indent)** and hit **OK**.

Year	2017			
Period	1	2	3	4
Revenue	59296.1	24308.85	175870.2	230189.9
Net Income	-40981	-20168.4	46712.57	79080.77

15. Highlight cells D7 through H8.
16. Right-click and select **Format Cells**.
17. On the **Number** tab, set **Category** to **Number** and **Decimal places** to 0.
18. Select the box next to **Use 1000 separator (,)**.

19. Under **Use Negative Numbers**, select the red numbers with parentheses:

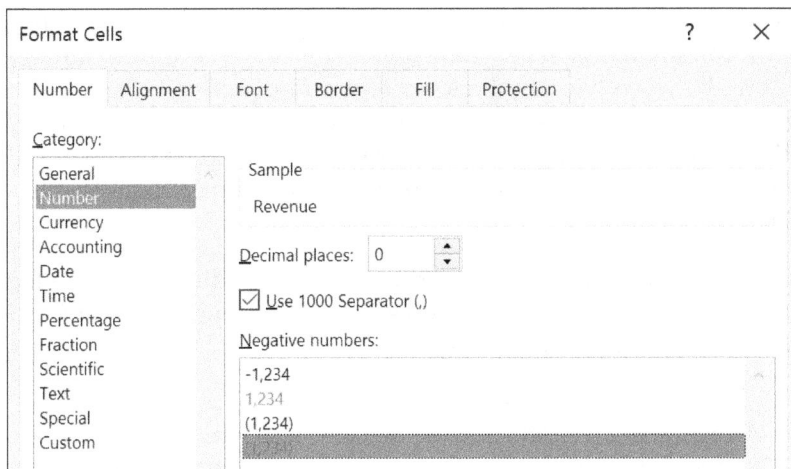

Format Cells	?	×

Number	Alignment	Font	Border	Fill	Protection

Category:

General
Number
Currency
Accounting
Date
Time
Percentage
Fraction
Scientific
Text
Special
Custom

Sample

Revenue

Decimal places: 0

☑ Use 1000 Separator (,)

Negative numbers:

-1,234
1,234
(1,234)

20. On the **Border** tab, click on the **Outline** and **Inside** buttons and hit **OK**.

Year	2017			
Period	1	2	3	4
Revenue	59,296	24,309	175,870	230,190
Net Income	(40,981)	(20,168)	46,713	79,081

We put boxes around the data because at the end, we are going to turn off gridlines in Excel. We want to highlight this data, not have it floating around in space. The lines help set this data off from other elements.

Now that we have the start of our dashboard, let's layer in some conditional formatting, starting with icon sets.

Icon sets

Icon sets are a great way to segregate data with an identifier based on thresholds. For example, if we can say that if at any time revenue is above a certain number, we're doing fine. If it's between two numbers, we're worried, and if it's below a certain number, we're in trouble. Icon sets let you represent data like this graphically. A firm might say that monthly revenue over 1,000,000 is fine, revenue between 750,000 and 1,000,000 is okay, and revenue under 750,000 requires management to intervene to find out what's going on.

The first tier can be represented by a green circle, the middle tier by a yellow triangle, and the last tier by a red diamond. This gives anyone even glancing at the dashboard a good idea of what needs their attention.

An option in Excel 2016 is to use the same icon but a different color to represent the different tiers, for example, a circle in red, yellow, or green. This isn't a great idea for two reasons. First, some people have trouble distinguishing colors. Second, the dashboard may get printed out for someone to take with them. If it's printed in black and white, the power of color is lost. I recommend that you use both symbols and color when using indicators.

You can also build icon sets based on any number of other criteria, including percent, a formula, or percentile rank.

For our dashboard, we'll use a straightforward example:

Status	Revenue	Net Income
Acceptable (green)	>60,000	>40,000
Concerned (yellow)	>25,000 and <60,000	>0 and <40,000
Requires attention (red)	<25,000	<0

To set up our icon sets, follow these steps:

1. Select cells E7 through H7.
2. On the **Home** ribbon, go to **Conditional Formatting | Icon Sets**.

3. Under **Shapes**, select the second option, which displays a green circle, a yellow triangle, and a red diamond:

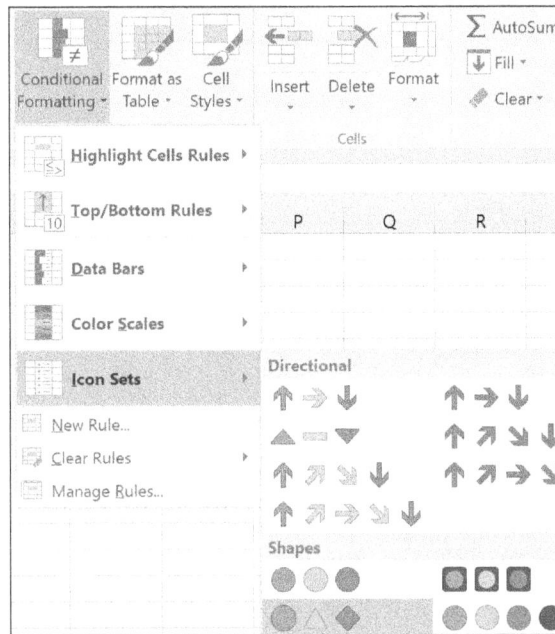

4. Back on the ribbon, go to **Conditional Formatting | Manage Rules...**
5. Click on the **Edit Rules** button:

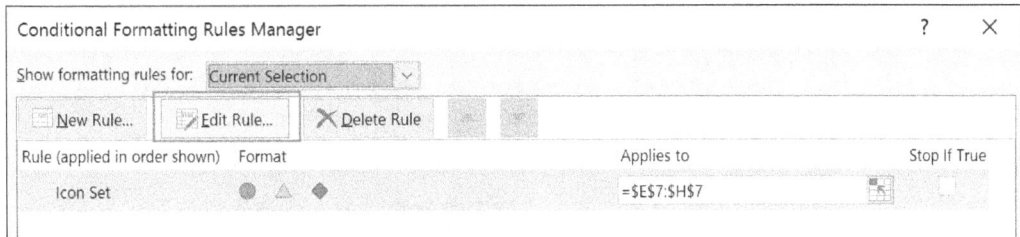

6. To the right of the green circle icon, change **Type** to **Number**.
7. Set **Value** equal to 60000.
8. To the right of the yellow triangle, change **Type** to **Number**.

9. Set **Value** equal to 25000, click on **OK**, and click on **OK** again to close both windows:

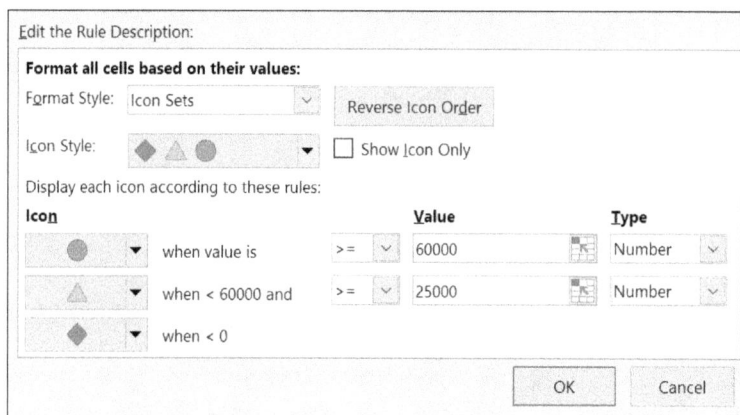

Now, you should have icons next to the revenue amounts:

Year	2017			
Period	1	2	3	4
Revenue	⚠ 59,296	◆ 24,309	● 175,870	● 230,190
Net Income	(40,981)	(20,168)	46,713	79,081

Let's do the same thing for net income using these steps:

1. Select cells E8 through H8.
2. On the **Home** ribbon, go to **Conditional Formatting | Icon Sets**.
3. Under **Indicators**, select the option on the right-hand side, which displays a green check mark, a yellow exclamation mark, and a red X:

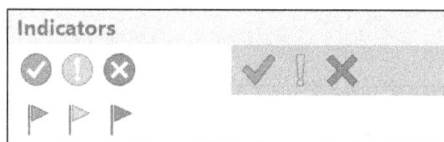

4. Back on the ribbon, go to **Conditional Formatting | Manage Rules**.
5. Click on the **Edit Rules** button.
6. To the right of the green circle icon, change **Type** to **Number**.
7. Set **Value** equal to 40000.

8. To the right of the yellow triangle, change **Type** to **Number**.

9. Set **Value** equal to 0, click on **OK**, and click on **OK** again to close both windows:

Now, you should have revenue and net income with status indicators based on icon sets:

Year	2017			
Period	1	2	3	4
Revenue	⚠ 59,296	◆ 24,309	⦿175,870	⦿230,190
Net Income	✗(40,981)	✗(20,168)	✔ 46,713	✔ 79,081

Normally, I wouldn't recommend mixing symbols like we do in this example. Mixing symbols is confusing to users. It's better to pick an icon set and stick with it, but I'm willing to break a rule or two to show off some cool options, and I think that this is a good time to break some rules.

Our initial formatting of negative numbers as red provided the bare minimum for conditional formatting. By adding them in icon sets, we were able to give context to the numbers. Even though a number is positive, it doesn't mean that the number is acceptable. Icon sets are one tool that can be used to provide that additional information. Let's move on to the very cool feature of data bars.

Though there are arrows in the icon sets, the arrows don't necessarily represent a trend. They could be used, for example, to show amounts over or under a goal. You can use a formula and arrows to show the latest direction of change. An example is when newspapers put an up or down arrow next to a sports team based on their last performance. This typically includes something like "W3" and an up arrow to show three wins in a row and a positive indicator.

Sparklines

By utilizing icons in the previous section, we can easily see if each period had an acceptable increase or if we need to be alarmed. What if we want to look for a trend? Are we steadily increasing? Decreasing? It is for these questions that Sparklines can provide value. Imagine a tiny little chart next to our set of numbers. When the focus is the numbers themselves, adding these tiny little charts (aka Sparklines) can give enough visual information to know where you need to focus your attention. Let's add them now.

Preparing for Sparklines

We'll add some Sparklines to our revenue and net income data. First, let's set up the formatting.

1. Open the GP 2016 `Dashboard.xlsx` file that we've been working with.
2. Click on the **Dashboard** tab to open the worksheet.
3. Select cell I7. This should be the cell next to the header for period 4.
4. Type `Quick Trend` in the cell I7 and widen the cell to ensure that it fits.
5. Select cell H7.
6. Select the **Home** tab and click on the paintbrush icon to copy the formatting:

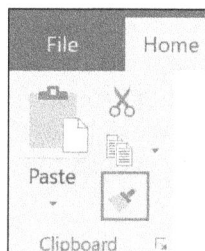

7. Click on cell I7 to apply the formatting:

Year	2017				
Period	1	2	3	4	Quick Trend
Revenue	△ 59,296	◆ 24,309	●175,870	●230,190	
Net Income	✗(40,981)	✗(20,168)	✔ 46,713	✔ 79,081	

Adding Sparklines

Now that we're set up, let's build a Sparkline using these steps:

1. Highlight cells E7 through H7. These are the amounts on the **Revenue** line.
2. Click on **Insert** to open the insert ribbon.
3. In the **Sparklines** section, click on **Line**.
4. The **Create Sparklines** box will open. The **Data Range** box will be prepopulated with the highlighted cells.
5. Select the **Location** box and click on the lookup button next to it.
6. Pick cell I7 and hit *Enter*:

Create Sparklines	?	✕
Choose the data that you want		
Data Range: E7:H7		
Choose where you want the sparklines to be placed		
Location Range: $I$7		
	OK	Cancel

7. Click on **OK** to create the Sparkline:

Year	2017				
Period	1	2	3	4	Quick Trend
Revenue	△ 59,296	◆ 24,309	●175,870	●230,190	
Net Income	✗(40,981)	✗(20,168)	✔ 46,713	✔ 79,081	

Adding a Sparkline to cell I7 creates a small line graph in that cell. It's a great way to get a quick read on how the data has changed. Let's add another Sparkline to the **Net Income** line. This time, we'll add a Win/Loss chart to show negatives.

To add a Sparkline to the **Net Income** row as shown in the screenshot, follow these steps:

1. Highlight cells E8 through H8.
2. Click on **Insert** to open the insert ribbon.
3. In the **Sparklines** section, click on **Win / Loss**.
4. The **Create Sparklines** box will open. The **Data Range** box will be pre-populated with the highlighted cells.
5. Select the **Location** box and click on the lookup button next to it.
6. Select cell I8 and hit *Enter*.
7. Click on **OK** to create the Sparkline.
8. Select the Sparkline in cell I8.
9. The tab for the **Sparkline Tools Design** ribbon lights up. At this point, you can opt to change the color scheme if you are so inclined (perhaps to match your logo):

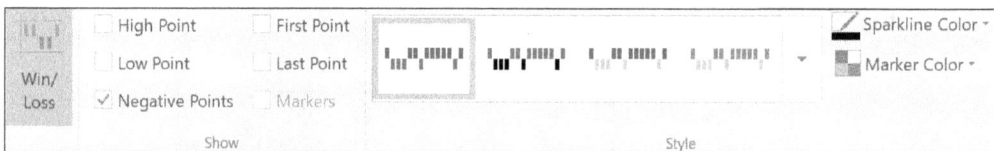

10. Right-click and select **Format Cells**.
11. Pick the **Border** tab.
12. Click on the **Outline** and **Inside** boxes to put lines around the Sparkline cells.
13. Click on **OK** to finish.
14. Save the file:

Year	2017				
Period	1	2	3	4	Quick Trend
Revenue	⚠ 59,296	◆ 24,309	⬤ 175,870	⬤ 230,190	
Net Income	✗ (40,981)	✗ (20,168)	✓ 46,713	✓ 79,081	

The **Sparkline Tools Design** tab lights up when you select a Sparkline. It contains additional tools to improve the usability of Sparklines. Here is an example.

Go to **Sparkline Tools Design | Edit Data | Hidden and Empty Cells**. This will allow you to control blank data points. You can show a gap in your Sparkline, default that point to zero, or simply connect lines by skipping the gap.

With the options in the **Show** section, you can mark data points such as the high and low points, first and last points, and negative numbers.

Sparkline idiosyncrasies

Sparklines are an interesting combination of charts and cells. This combination creates some idiosyncrasies when working with them. As we wrap up Sparklines, we'll look at a few.

Deleting Sparklines

Since Sparklines reside in a cell, you might think that you can simply hit the *Delete* button and remove a Sparkline, but you can't. To remove a Sparkline, select the Sparkline, right-click, and go to **Sparklines | Clear Selected Sparklines**.

Changing Sparkline data

Sparklines are attached to a selection of cells in a row. In our case, we don't have them directly connected to a pivot table. Our revenue and income boxes are intentionally not dynamic, so putting a Sparkline to the right works. If we connect a Sparkline to a pivot table row, changes to the pivot table can cause it to grow beyond the location of the Sparkline. The pivot table overlaps the Sparkline, and the Sparkline appears behind the overlapping data. Usually, this isn't ideal. If you're connecting a Sparkline directly to a pivot table, consider adding it to the left or farther out to the right.

Since Sparklines are based on a range, adding data to a cell outside the range will not be picked up by a Sparkline. For example, if Sparkline data runs from cells E7 to H7, adding data in D7 will not change the Sparkline. Adding a cell in the middle of the range will update a Sparkline. Named ranges can be used when creating a Sparkline to help overcome this limitation.

Like any other cell, Sparklines can be cut, copied, and pasted to a different cell. The cells they are in can be formatted with backgrounds and borders.

Data bars

Data bars are most often used to show how data points relate to each other, for example, earlier we created a pivot table with our top 10 customers. It would be nice to know how much larger the top customer is when compared to the number 10 customer. Data bars make this a very easy visualization to create without taking up additional space.

Let's add our top 10 customers to our dashboard and create data bars to enhance the information. Since everything we need is in our pivot table, we don't have to use GetPivotTable formulas. We can just copy our pivot table on to the dashboard.

To get our top 10 customers on the dashboard, follow these steps:

1. On the **Dashboard** worksheet, select cell K10.

2. In cell K10, type Top 10 Customers. We'll use this later.

3. Select the **Top 10 Customers** tab.

4. Select cells A2 through B14 (or the entire pivot table). This should be the entire Top 10 Customers pivot table.

5. Right-click and select **Copy**.

6. Select the **Dashboard** worksheet.

7. Select cell K12, right-click, and select the leftmost paste icon. Hovering over this icon shows **Paste (p)** in the tip.

Top 10 Customers	
Row Labels ↓▼	**Sum of Document Amount**
Plaza One	$159,211.89
Mahler State University	$94,697.45
Vancouver Resort Hotels	$93,235.36
Lawrence Telemarketing	$93,105.17
Astor Suites	$91,846.69
Contoso, Ltd.	$82,667.53
Office Design Systems Ltd	$74,910.65
Vision Inc.	$73,947.65
Breakthrough Telemarketing	$47,321.46
Aaron Fitz Electrical	$25,171.60
Grand Total	**$836,115.45**

8. This will drop a copy of the Top 10 Customers pivot table on the dashboard. Now, we need to clean it up and add data bars.

9. Use the handles at the top of cell K to widen the cell so that the data fits.

10. Select cell L12, Sum of Document Amount, and right-click.

11. Click on **Value Field Settings**.

12. Change the **Custom Name** field from Sum of Document Amount to Sales and click on **OK**:

Value Field Settings	?	✕
Source Name: Document Amount		
Custom Name: Sales		

13. If the number format did not copy (and it should have), perform the following steps:

    1. Highlight cells L13 through L23.

    2. Right-click and select **Format Cells**.

    3. On the **Number** tab, set **Category** to **Number** and **Decimal places** to **0**.

    4. Select the box next to **Use 1000 separator (,)**.

    5. Under **Use Negative Numbers**, select the red numbers with parentheses.

14. Adjust the width of column **L** as necessary to ensure that all of the numbers are shown properly:

Top 10 Customers

Row Labels	Sales
Plaza One	$159,211.89
Mahler State University	$94,697.45
Vancouver Resort Hotels	$93,235.36
Lawrence Telemarketing	$93,105.17
Astor Suites	$91,846.69
Contoso, Ltd.	$82,667.53
Office Design Systems Ltd	$74,910.65
Vision Inc.	$73,947.65
Breakthrough Telemarketing	$47,321.46
Aaron Fitz Electrical	$25,171.60
Grand Total	**$836,115.45**

Now let's add data bars using these steps:

1. Select cells L13 through L22. This is the sales column for `Top 10 Customers` table without any headers or totals.
2. On the **Home** ribbon, go to **Conditional Formatting | Data Bars**.
3. Under **Gradient Fill**, select the blue data bar.
4. Save the file:

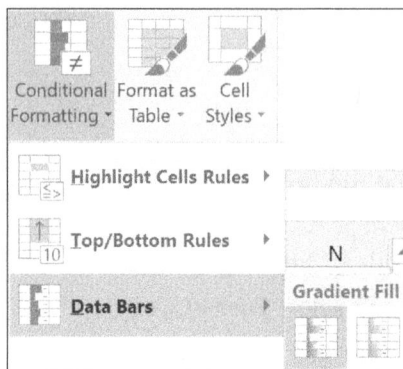

Blue data bars will appear inside the cells with sales numbers. Each bar represents how a customer's sales compare to the other top 10 customers:

Top 10 Customers	
Row Labels ⬇▼	**Sales**
Plaza One	$159,211.89
Mahler State University	$94,697.45
Vancouver Resort Hotels	$93,235.36
Lawrence Telemarketing	$93,105.17
Astor Suites	$91,846.69
Contoso, Ltd.	$82,667.53
Office Design Systems Ltd	$74,910.65
Vision Inc.	$73,947.65
Breakthrough Telemarketing	$47,321.46
Aaron Fitz Electrical	$25,171.60
Grand Total	**$836,115.45**

The sample company data visually shows that **Plaza One** has significantly higher sales than all of the others. The next seven are relatively close, with a dramatic drop off for the ninth and tenth highest customers.

Visualizations like this can put a relationship into perspective. Clearly, the top eight customers should get the most attention. The difference between number eight and number two is pretty small. Just as clearly, **Plaza One** needs special attention because of their size. This data isn't yet limited by date. We'll tackle that when we get to slicers, so you'll get to see this information change before we are done.

> Data bars show the relationship against the other items in the data set, not against the total. For example, **Mahler State University** value is roughly 60 percent of **Plaza One** value and the bar is about 60 percent as long. There is a great, in-depth discussion of how data bars work at http://blogs.office.com/b/microsoft-excel/archive/2009/08/07/data-bar-improvements-in-excel-2010.aspx.

Bar chart with trend line

For our dashboard, we will add a bar chart showing revenue over time to enhance our revenue table. Then, we'll layer over a line to show net income as a complement to revenue. With this technique, we can show income, even when it's technically a loss, against revenue.

Let's start building our bar chart. To build a revenue chart, follow these steps:

1. Open the GP 2016 `Dashboard.xlsx` file that we've been working with.
2. Select the **Dashboard** worksheet.
3. Highlight cells D7 through H8. They should contain the revenue and net income information from the table.
4. Select the **Insert** tab from the ribbon.
5. Select the icon for **Combo Charts** from the ribbon:

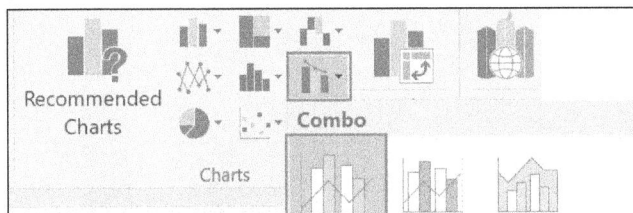

6. The bar chart will automatically appear. Use your mouse to drag the new chart directly under the revenue table:

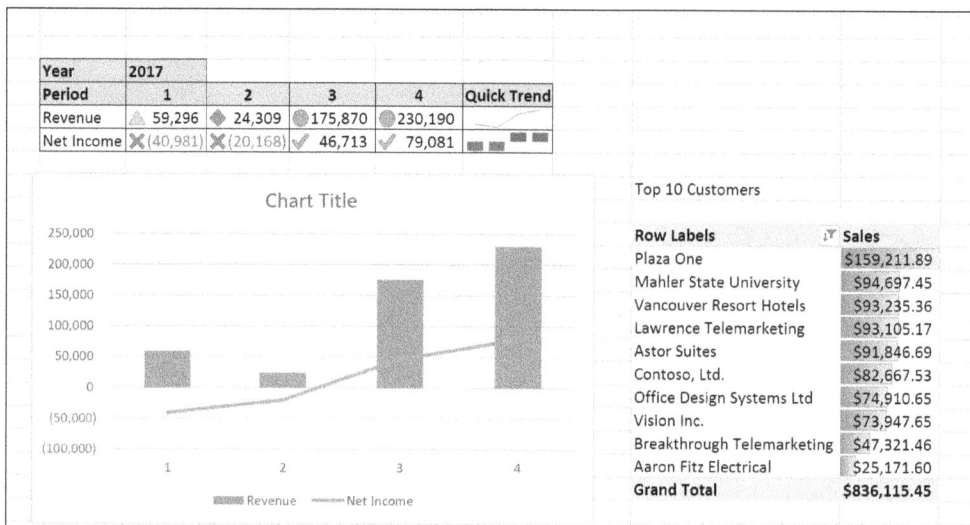

Year	2017				
Period	1	2	3	4	Quick Trend
Revenue	59,296	24,309	175,870	230,190	
Net Income	(40,981)	(20,168)	46,713	79,081	

Chart Title

Top 10 Customers

Row Labels	Sales
Plaza One	$159,211.89
Mahler State University	$94,697.45
Vancouver Resort Hotels	$93,235.36
Lawrence Telemarketing	$93,105.17
Astor Suites	$91,846.69
Contoso, Ltd.	$82,667.53
Office Design Systems Ltd	$74,910.65
Vision Inc.	$73,947.65
Breakthrough Telemarketing	$47,321.46
Aaron Fitz Electrical	$25,171.60
Grand Total	**$836,115.45**

7. Click anywhere on the chart (select), and the handle bars will appear around the chart. This will open a new menu option called **Chart Tools**:

Chart Tools

Design   Format

8. If your **Revenue** shows up as the bars and your **Net Income** shows as the line, your fine:

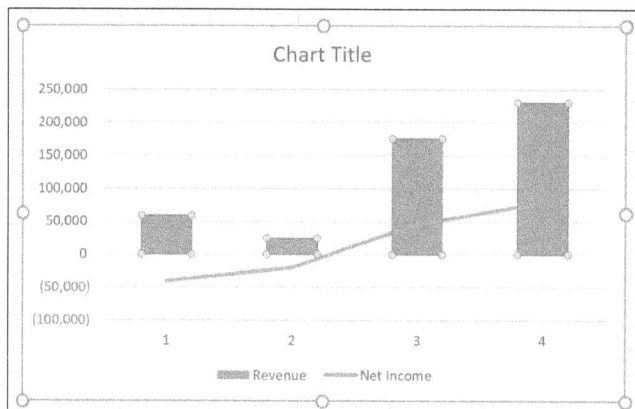

Chart Title

9. If it is reversed, click on **Switch Row/Column** by going to **Chart Tools | Design**:

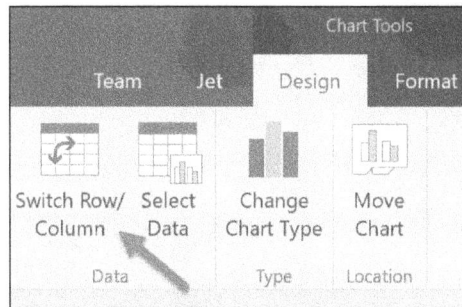

Now let's complete this chart with a little bit of formatting cleanup using these steps:

1. Double-click on **Chart Title** and change the name to **Revenue and Net Income**:

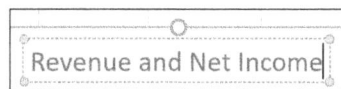

2. With the chart still selected, add **Shape Outline** by going to **Chart Tools | Format**. This will put a box around our chart:

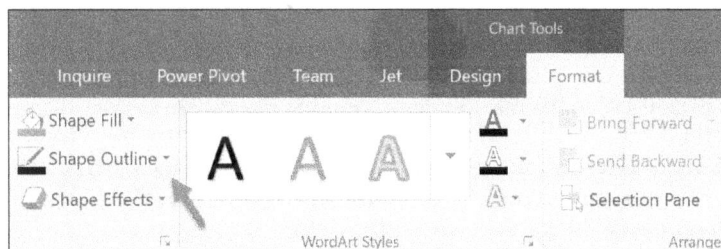

Our dashboard is becoming a working, informative tool. Soon, it'll be a work of art that can change the way we think about our business. I'm already excited!

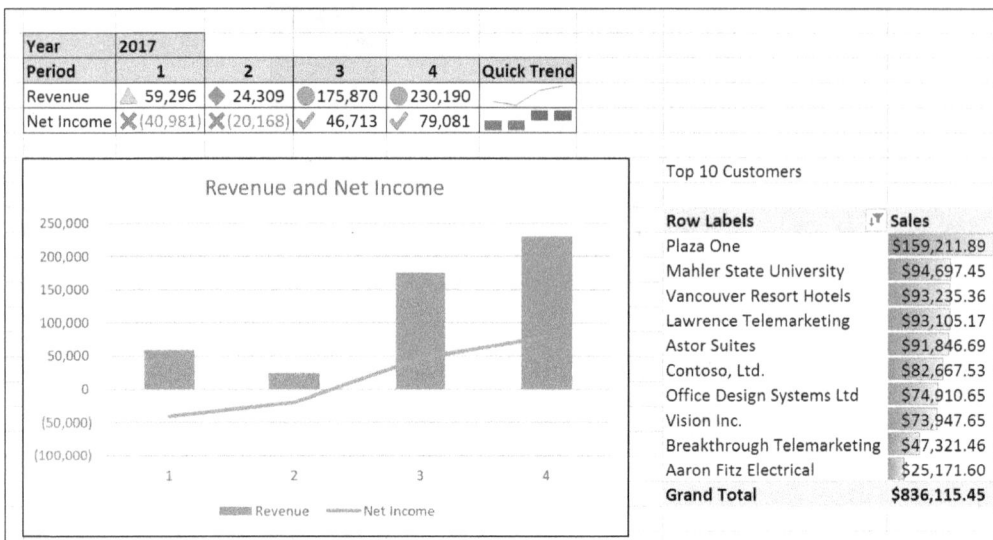

Year	2017				
Period	1	2	3	4	Quick Trend
Revenue	△ 59,296	◆ 24,309	◐ 175,870	◑ 230,190	
Net Income	✖ (40,981)	✖ (20,168)	✔ 46,713	✔ 79,081	

Revenue and Net Income

Top 10 Customers

Row Labels	Sales
Plaza One	$159,211.89
Mahler State University	$94,697.45
Vancouver Resort Hotels	$93,235.36
Lawrence Telemarketing	$93,105.17
Astor Suites	$91,846.69
Contoso, Ltd.	$82,667.53
Office Design Systems Ltd	$74,910.65
Vision Inc.	$73,947.65
Breakthrough Telemarketing	$47,321.46
Aaron Fitz Electrical	$25,171.60
Grand Total	**$836,115.45**

You'll notice that this combo chart displays negative net income without cluttering up revenue. Now, we've got our combo chart for revenue and net income. Next up, let's look at receivables.

Pie chart

Pie charts are useful for showing percentages and portions. They are great for segmenting data. In our dashboard, we want to show the breakdown of receivables to understand what buckets our receivables fall into. In other words, we need to understand what percentage of our receivables is new and what percentages are aged at various lengths.

A pie chart is not a one size fits all for visualizations. Be careful when deciding to use a pie chart that you need to show various sums or counts and how they pertain to the grand total. Pie charts work for receivables, but not to show your cash balance. Be thoughtful!

> Never use 3D charts, especially for pie charts. Depending on the angle or the rotation, your numbers will look skewed. Unless, of course, you want them skewed and you do not want anyone to see what your numbers really look like.

To build our receivables aging pie chart, use these steps:

1. Select the **Receivables Aging** worksheet.
2. Click on any cell in the pivot table to select the pivot table.
3. On the ribbon, select the icon for **Pie Charts** and select the first 2D pie chart:

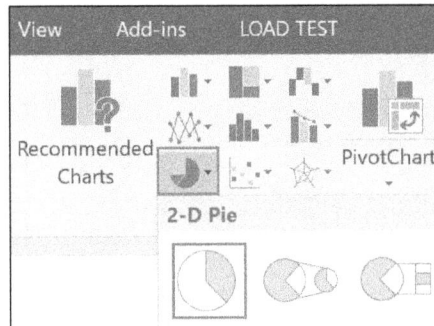

4. Click on the blue pie to select it.
5. Right-click on the pie and go to **Add Data Labels | Add Data Labels**:

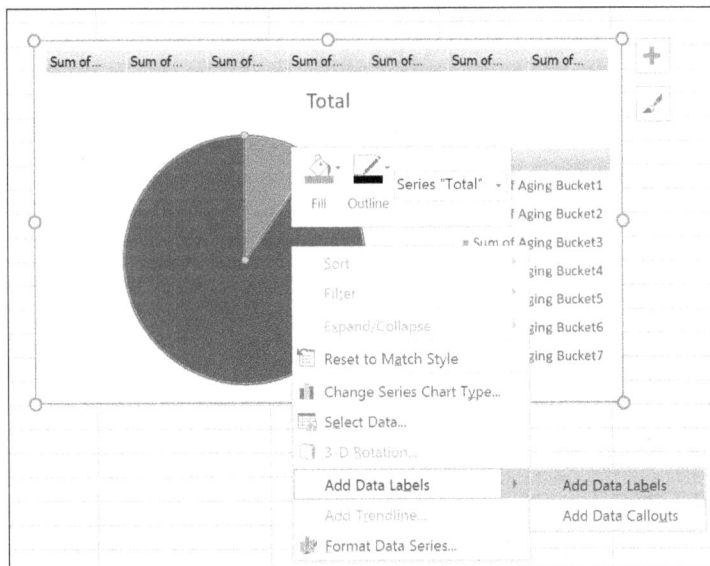

6. Click on one of the data labels.
7. Right-click and select **Format Data Labels**.

8. In the **Format Data Labels** section to the far right of your Excel window, select **Percentage** and deselect **Value**. Leave the **Show Leader Lines** box selected:

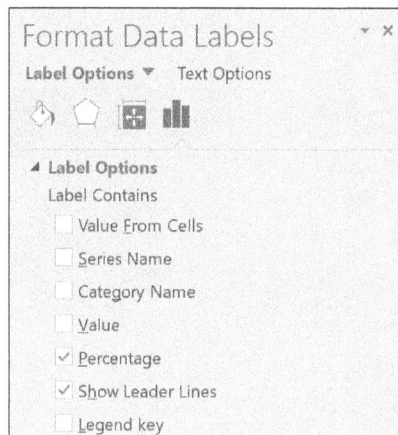

Format Data Labels ▾ ✕

Label Options ▾   Text Options

✎ ⬠ ▦ ılı

▴ **Label Options**

Label Contains

☐ Value From Cells

☐ Series Name

☐ Category Name

☐ Value

☑ Percentage

☑ Show Leader Lines

☐ Legend key

9. In the pivot table, change the value of cell A2 to **Current**.

10. Repeat this process with all the items in column **A** to match this table:

Value
Current
31-60
61-90
91-120
121-150
151-180
>180

The values will change in the chart as well.

11. Select the chart, right-click, and select **Cut**.

12. Select the **Dashboard** worksheet.

13. Select a cell in column **K** under the `Top 10 Customers` table on the **Dashboard** worksheet.

14. Right-click and select `Paste`.

15. Click on the pie chart.

16. Grab the sizing handle on the right-hand side and shrink the chart to fit in columns **K** and **L**:

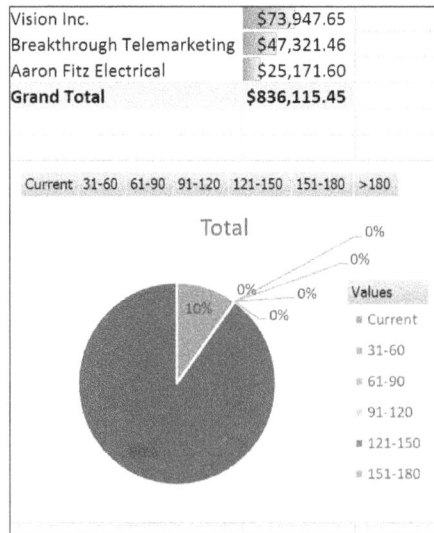

Vision Inc.	$73,947.65
Breakthrough Telemarketing	$47,321.46
Aaron Fitz Electrical	$25,171.60
Grand Total	**$836,115.45**

Current 31-60 61-90 91-120 121-150 151-180 >180

Total

0%
0%
0%   0%   Values
10%   0%   ▪ Current
                ▪ 31-60
                ▪ 61-90
                ▪ 91-120
                ▪ 121-150
                ▪ 151-180

Now, we've got a breakout of the receivables aging. This is sample data, but in a real business, this looks bad. Ninety percent of our receivables are over 180 days. That's a scary scenario.

> If your company's aging looks like this, yikes! Typically, companies don't have most of their receivables in the longest timeframe. I decided to leave it like this, even though the sample data isn't terribly realistic. I think you are smart enough to understand what this might look like in the real world. If your company looks like this, I applaud you for sharpening your Excel skills as you hunt for a new job.]

Speedometer chart

A speedometer chart is a classic dashboard presentation tool, but it's not a chart available in Microsoft Excel. This tool exists in Microsoft Power BI (we'll discuss this in the next chapters), so I am expecting it to appear in Excel at some point. Since it doesn't exist, we will build one.

Speedometer charts are just what you would expect. Like a car speedometer, a speedometer chart has a dial and a needle with the needle moving from left to right, depending on the value. They are extremely useful for showing levels. In our case, we will build one that shows the level of cash. We'll add some red, yellow, and green indicators to help users understand whether the level of cash is acceptable. Our finished speedometer chart should look like this:

As a speedometer chart doesn't exist as a type in Excel 2016, we will build it with an optical illusion. Our speedometer chart uses half of a pie chart to make the needle and half of a doughnut chart to make the dial. Pies, doughnuts, and so on. Doesn't Microsoft know it's trendy to stay away from carbs?

The green/yellow/red limit

Excel 2016 provides another conditional formatting option that is a kind of mix between icon sets and data bars. It's called **Color Scales**. Color Scales behave more like icon sets but are closer in appearance to data bars. We will do some setup along the Color Scales line to support a speedometer chart. A speedometer chart is surprisingly hard to create in Excel, so we will do the pre-work here. This setup sets the green/yellow/red limits for that chart.

1. Select the **Cash** worksheet.
2. In cell D6, type `Cash`.
3. In cell E5, type `Actual`.
4. In cell F5, type `Meter Use Only`:

5. In cell E6, type the equal sign (=) and the negative sign (-), and select cell B4. This is the cash amount from the pivot table. You should see a formula that looks like this:

```
=-GETPIVOTDATA("Period Balance",$A$3,"Account Category
Number","Cash")
```

6. In cell D9, type `Meter Level`.

7. In cell E9, type `Difference`.

8. In cells D10 through D12, type `Red`, `Yellow`, and `Green`, respectively.

9. In cell E10, type `1000000`.

10. In cell E11, type `3000000`.

11. In cell E12, type `4000000`. These are the red, yellow, and green values.

12. In cell F10, type `=E10`.

13. In cell F11, type `=E11-E10`:

	Actual	Meter Use Only
Cash	(321,441)	8,321,441
Meter Level	**Difference**	
Red	1,000,000	1,000,000
Yellow	3,000,000	2,000,000
Green	4,000,000	1,000,000
		4,000,000

We will use column E later to set the green, yellow, and red levels for the user. Column F will set the difference between those levels to ultimately control the meter. A speedometer chart in Excel is effectively an optical illusion, and the **Meter Use Only** field is used to make the illusion work.

Building a doughnut

Since this isn't a standard chart, it takes a little more work. The first step is to build a speedometer chart with these steps:

1. Continue with the GP 2016 `Dashboard.xlsx` file that we've been using.

2. Select the **Cash** worksheet.

3. Highlight cells F10 through F13. These should be under the header **Difference**.

4. Click on **Insert** to open the insert ribbon.

5. Select the pie chart dropdown in the **Charts** section.

6. Select the **Doughnut** chart.

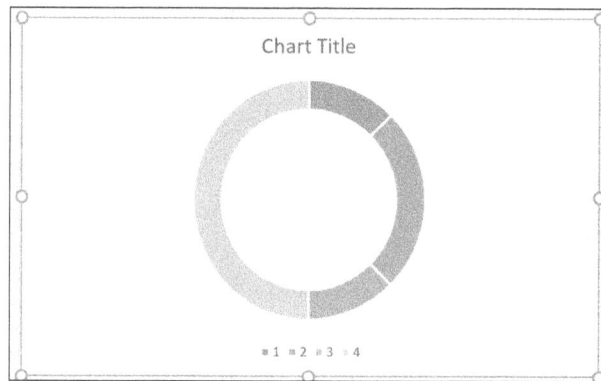

7. Click on the largest slice of the doughnut twice to select it.

8. Right-click on the largest slice and select **Format Data Point**.

9. The **Format Data Point** sidebar opens on the right-hand side. Choose the icon that looks like a graph. Change the value of **Angle of First Slice** to 270 and hit *Enter*. This rotates the doughnut to put the total slice at the bottom:

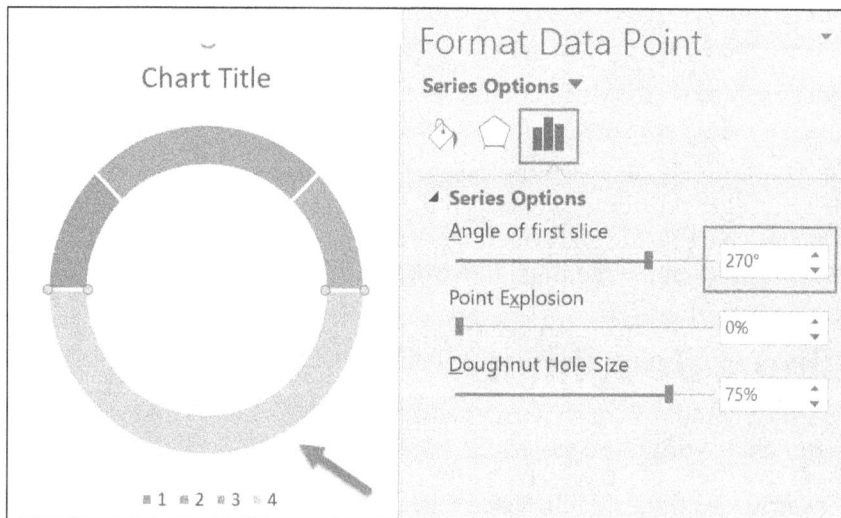

Cutting the doughnut in half

This is how cutting the doughnut in half is done:

1. With the largest segment still selected, select the paint bucket icon in the **Format Data Options** sidebar.
2. Select the **No Fill** box to make the segment disappear.
3. Select the legend at the bottom of the chart and hit the *Delete* key.

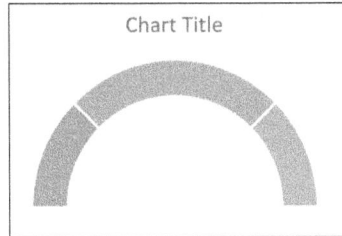

Chart Title

4. Click to select the leftmost visible segment.
5. Right-click and select **Format Data Point**.
6. On the **Format Data Point** sidebar, click on the paint bucket icon.
7. Change the color to red.
8. Repeat this process with the middle slice and change the color to yellow.
9. Finally, do this one more time with the rightmost slice and change the color to green:

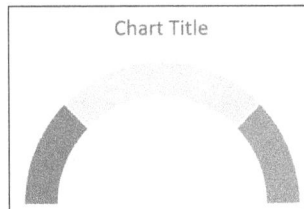

Chart Title

Building a needle

Now, we have the outside dial of our speedometer chart. Up next, we'll build the needle with a pie chart. To do this, follow these steps:

1. Right-click inside the doughnut chart.

2. Click on **Select Data...**

3. Click on **Add** to add a second data series:

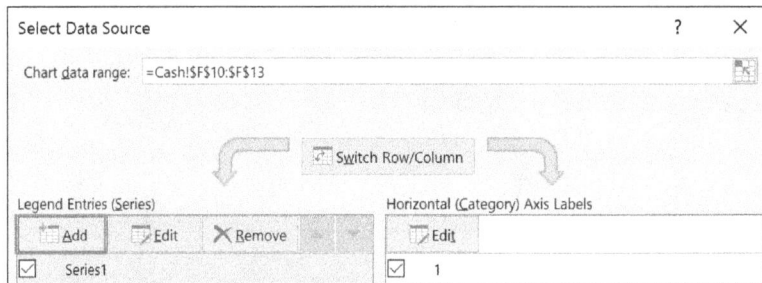

4. Under **Series name**, type Cash.

5. Select the **Series value** box and use your mouse to select cells E6 and F6 and click on **OK** twice. These are the values under the **Actual** and **Meter Use Only** headings.

6. Click on the largest section of the outer ring to select it.

7. Right-click on the largest section of the outer ring and select **Format Data Point**.

8. Click on the paint bucket icon and set **Fill** to **No fill** and **Border** to **No line**:

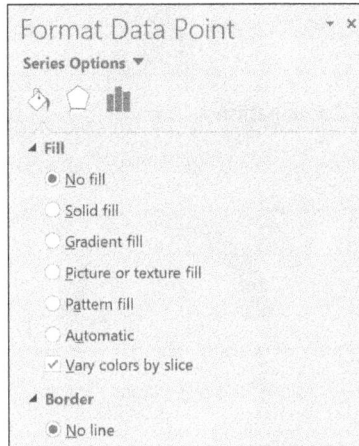

9. Click on the remaining visible outer ring section to select it:

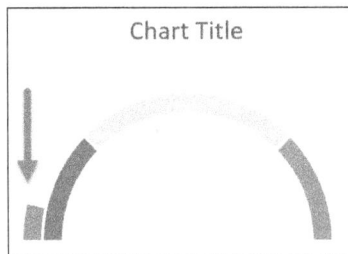

10. Right-click and select **Change Series Chart Type**.

11. At the bottom, change the dropdown for the **Cash** series from **Doughnut** to **Pie** and click on **OK**:

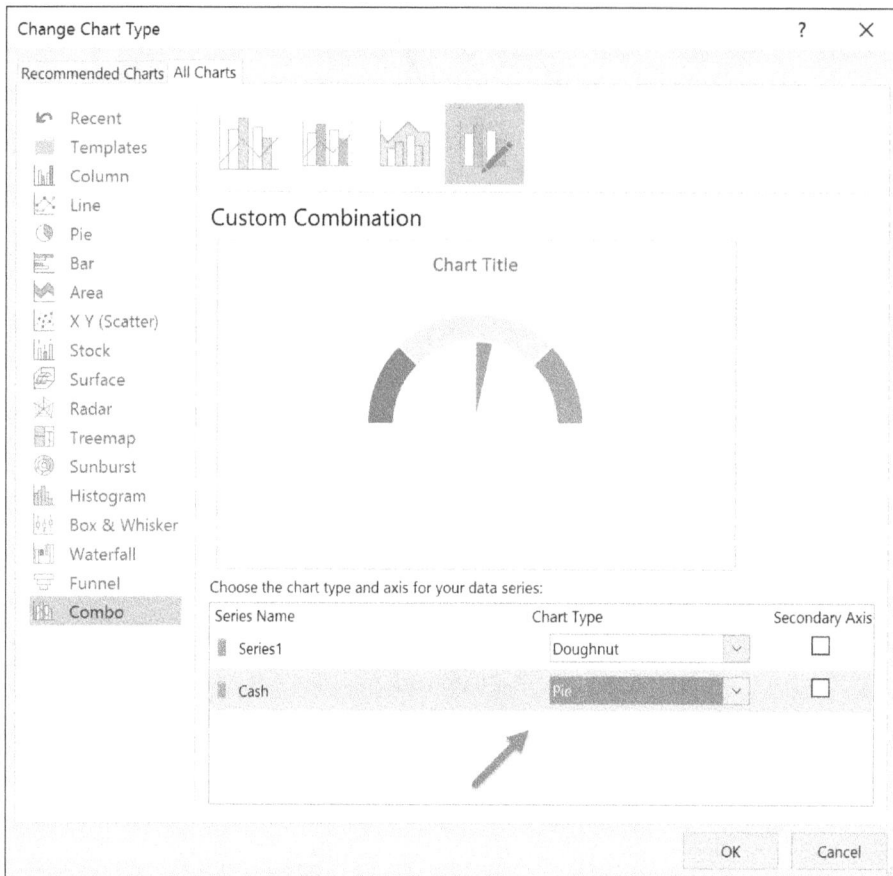

12. Click on the filled-in section in the center of the chart to select it.

13. Right-click on the filled-in section in the center of the chart and select **Format Data Point**.

14. Select the icon that resembles a graph and set the **Angle of first slice** to **270**.

15. Click on the paint bucket icon and set **Fill** to **No fill**.

16. Set **Border** to **Solid line**.

17. Set the **Color** of the border to black:

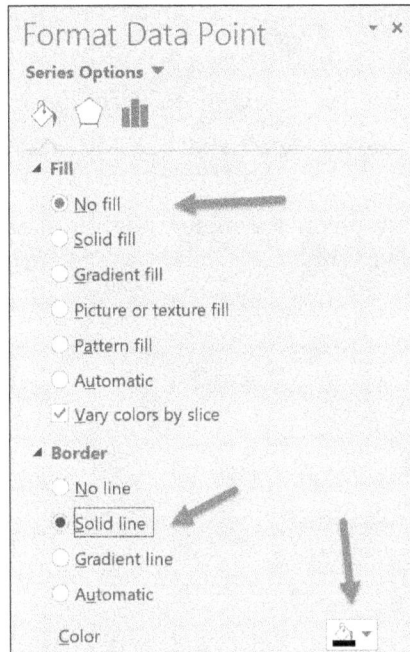

By now, you should see the framework of our speedometer chart taking shape. We have red, yellow, and green indicators with a needle showing our position on the scale:

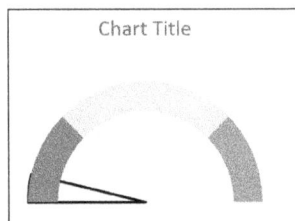

Finishing it off with Sprinkles

We need to finish formatting our chart and move it onto our dashboard. To finish things up, follow these steps:

1. Click on the center needle. You want to select the section in the upper left.

2. Right-click and go to **Add Data Label | Add Data Label** to display the value of the cash amount.

3. Drag this value down below the meter. Highlight and delete the upper value, which was **Meter Use Only**:

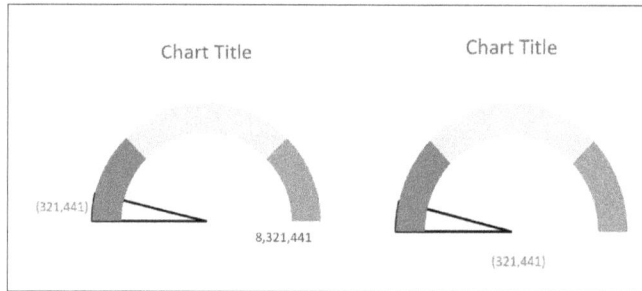

4. Double-click on **Chart Title** and change it to **Cash**.

5. Right-click in the white space of the chart to select the whole chart.

6. Click on **Cut**.

7. Select the **Dashboard** worksheet.

8. Select cell D27.

9. Right-click and select **Paste** to paste the chart onto the dashboard:

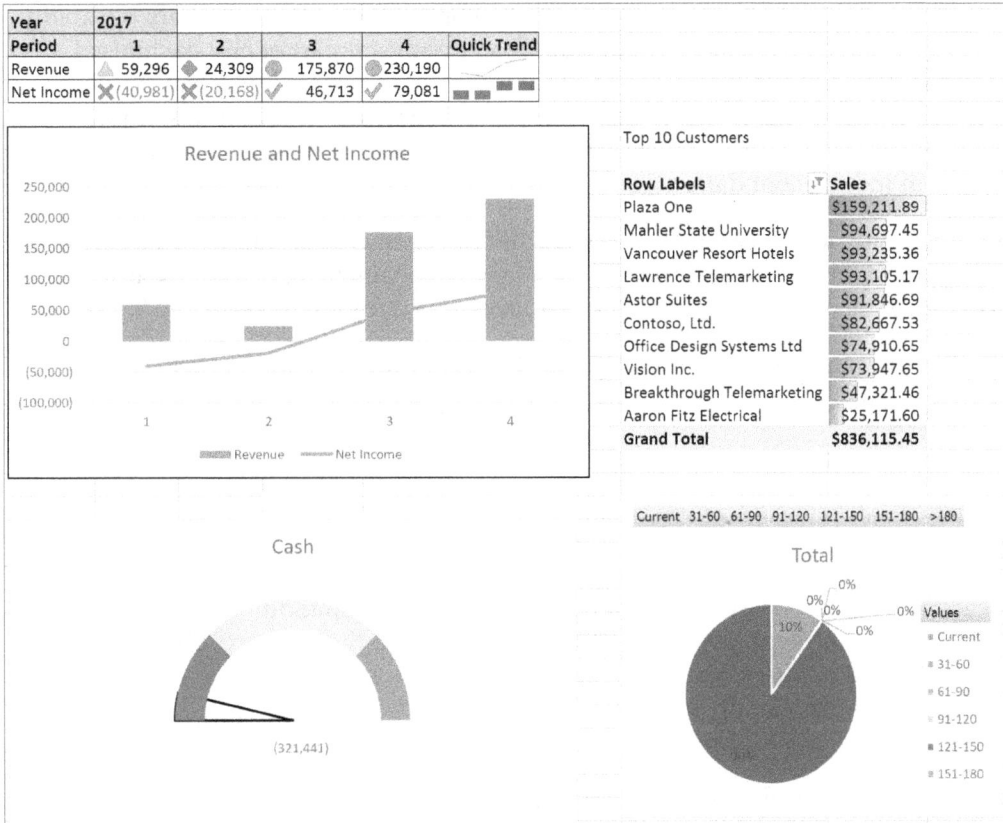

Year	2017				
Period	**1**	**2**	**3**	**4**	**Quick Trend**
Revenue	⚠ 59,296	◆ 24,309	◉ 175,870	◉ 230,190	
Net Income	✗ (40,981)	✗ (20,168)	✓ 46,713	✓ 79,081	▪▪ ▪▪

Revenue and Net Income

250,000			
200,000			
150,000			
100,000			
50,000			
0			
(50,000)			
(100,000)			
1	2	3	4

▪▪▪ Revenue   ━━ Net Income

Top 10 Customers

Row Labels ↓▽	Sales
Plaza One	$159,211.89
Mahler State University	$94,697.45
Vancouver Resort Hotels	$93,235.36
Lawrence Telemarketing	$93,105.17
Astor Suites	$91,846.69
Contoso, Ltd.	$82,667.53
Office Design Systems Ltd	$74,910.65
Vision Inc.	$73,947.65
Breakthrough Telemarketing	$47,321.46
Aaron Fitz Electrical	$25,171.60
Grand Total	**$836,115.45**

Current 31-60 61-90 91-120 121-150 151-180 >180

Cash

(321,441)

Total

0%
0%
0%
0%
10%	0%
0%

Values
- ▪ Current
- ▪ 31-60
- ▪ 61-90
- ▪ 91-120
- ▪ 121-150
- ▪ 151-180

That is how you build a speedometer chart in Excel 2016. It's a lot of steps, but once you understand how it's built, the process is straightforward.

> OK, so maybe Mark Polino's section name *Finish it off with sprinkles* took the doughnut metaphor too far. I am not a sprinkles girl, so I would have said "Frosting on the doughnut," which would have been just the right metaphor. Hey, it's Mark's work getting updated, so...
>
> This speedometer chart is loosely based on the technique described at `http://www.brainbell.com/tutorials/ms-office/excel/Create_A_Speedometer_Chart.htm`
>
> (short link: `http://bit.ly/13LssJN`). You can find additional information there.

Slicers and timelines

A dashboard without interactivity is simply a pretty report. Giving users the ability to review scenarios and explore the data is an important part of any dashboard. However, you also want to provide enough control over user interaction to ensure that the results are meaningful. For example, if a user selects a year, it's important that all of the related pivot tables update to that year; otherwise, a user might be looking at inconsistent data.

Slicers provide a way to give the user additional control over the information being delivered. Excel 2013 added a new type of slicer, the timeline. A timeline is a date-based slicer designed to make it easy for users to work with dates.

Let's add these elements to our dashboard to help provide that interactivity:

- Slicers
- Timelines

Slicers

Slicers provide interactivity to pivot tables. The simplest definition is that they are replacements for pivot table filters, but that doesn't do them justice. Slicers don't have to be tied to filters, and a slicer can be applied without creating a filter. The key is that slicers are generally easier to use than filters for end users. Some examples of this include:

- When multiple filters are applied at the same level (such as the Year and Period column filters on our `Revenue` pivot table), it can be confusing to the user to select the right level to change the filter.

- Slicers follow the familiar pattern of using the *Shift* key to select all items in a range and the *Ctrl* key to select non-sequential items.

- Slicers can be shared across multiple pivot tables, so one change by the user can affect data in several tables. Filters don't work this way.

- Slicers provide greater formatting options, making it easier to build a good-looking dashboard. They can also be formatted with an Excel theme to match the color of the rest of a workbook.

- Selecting multiple items in a filter prevents you from seeing what is being filtered. Slicers will highlight the filters themselves, thus displaying what is being filtered.

Creating slicers

Slicers are easy to build, so let's add some slicers to our dashboard to see how powerful they can be. To do this, follow these steps:

1. Select the **Revenue** worksheet in the `Dashboard.xlsx` workbook of GP 2016 that we've been working with.

2. Click on any cell in the pivot table to select the entire pivot table.

3. Select the **Insert** ribbon and then click on **Slicer**:

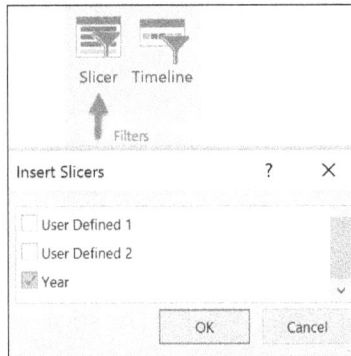

4. Select the box next to **Year** to create a slicer based on years.

5. Select the slicer and hit *Ctrl + X* to cut the slicer so that we can move it to the dashboard.

6. Move to the **Dashboard** worksheet and select cell B5.

7. Hit *Ctrl + V* to paste the slicer.

8. Use the handles on the side of the slicer to resize the **Year** slicer to fit roughly into cells B5 through C10. The slicer should show three years and a vertical scroll bar:

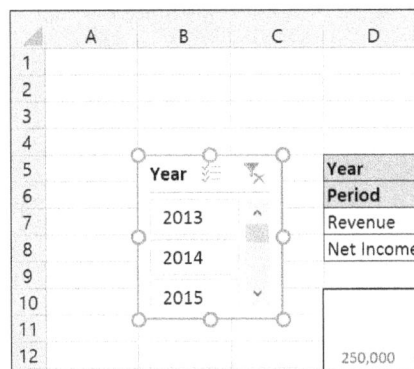

9. Use the vertical scroll bar to scroll down until the years **2016**, **2017**, and **2018** are being shown in the slicer.

10. Ensure that the year **2017** is selected in the slicer.

Notice that the year **2018** is grayed out. This is an indicator that there is no data for **2018** that matches either our slicers or filters. There may be **2018** data, but there isn't any for **2018** for period **1** to **4** and the filtered accounts that we are using. Remember that we've already pre-filtered our pivot table, and the slicer is acting on that pivot table.

Now that we've sliced on years, let's go ahead and slice on periods as well. To add a period slicer, follow these steps:

1. Select the **Revenue** worksheet in the `Dashboard.xlsx` workbook of GP 2016 that we've been working with.

2. Click on any cell in the pivot table to select the entire pivot table.

3. Select the **Insert** ribbon and then click on **Slicer**.

4. Select the box next to **Period ID** to create a slicer based on periods.

5. Select the slicer and hit *Ctrl + X* to cut the slicer so that we can move it to the dashboard.

6. Move to the **Dashboard** worksheet and select cell B12.

7. Hit *Ctrl + V* to paste the slicer.

8. Use the handles on the side of the slicer to resize the **Period** slicer to fit roughly into cells B12 through C24.

9. Hold down the *Ctrl* button and select periods **1** through **4** in the **Period** slicer.

> In the **Period ID** slicer, select just period **1** and watch the graph move. Repeat this with period **2**. Notice the animation of the bars as the graph changes. This movement was added in Excel 2013. Animating charts used to be really hard to do, but Excel 2013 (and higher versions) makes it easy.

Let's dig a little deeper into our slicers for just a minute:

In the **Period ID** slicer, hold down *Ctrl* and select period **1**, **2**, **3**, and **8**.

Notice that in our table, **Net Income** shows a #REF error. This is because our slicer is really only connected to our **Revenue** pivot table. As the GETPIVOTDATA formulas look at the table headers, the net income graph moves around, but it's really not being driven by the slicer.

Connecting slicers

Slicers can be connected to a single set of data, or they can be shared. If we want revenue and net income reporting to move together, and we usually do, we can connect a single slicer to both sets of data. This is much more convenient to the user than having to change the settings on slicers for each dataset. If we were only using filters, the user would have to change the filters for revenue and net income. To connect our slicers to net income as well as revenue, follow these steps:

1. Right-click on the **Year** slicer and select **Report Connections**.

2. Select the box next to **Net Income** and click on **OK**:

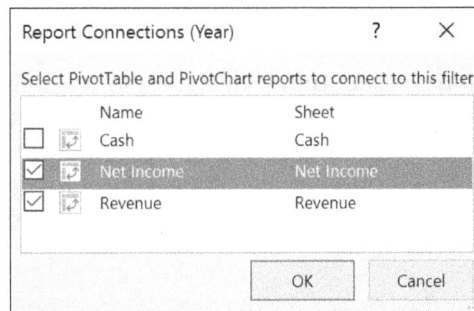

3. Back on the **Dashboard** tab, right-click on the **Period ID** slicer and select **Report Connections**.

4. Select the box next to **Net Income** and click on **OK**:

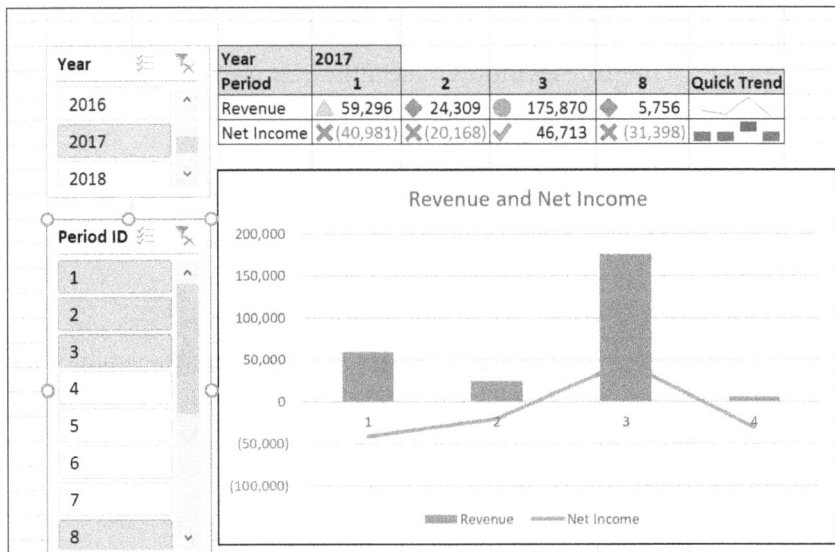

Once you connect the **Period ID** slicer, the net income error we just created in period **8** disappears, and the graph rebuilds with the appropriate information.

5. On the **Period ID** slicer, hold the *Shift* button and select periods **1** and **4** to select the range.

6. We normally want to see revenue and income for the same periods. It doesn't make much sense to evaluate revenue from January against net income from August. Connecting these two pivot tables with a single slicer not only makes things easier for the user, it helps keep them out of trouble too.

Timeline

A timeline is a special kind of slicer that is designed to work with a range of dates, and it's perfect for working with our Top 10 Customers pivot table. Our Top 10 Customers pivot table is based around sales over a period of time, so if we want to see the top 10 customers based on sales over the last month, quarter, or year, it's easy to adjust the timeline slicer to show that information. The conditional formatting that we've put in place will follow along as well.

Let's add a timeline to our dashboard for the Top 10 Customers pivot table using these steps:

1. Select the **Dashboard** tab.

2. Click on cell K13 to select the Top 10 Customers pivot table on the dashboard.

3. Go to **Insert | Timeline** to start creating the timeline slicer.

4. On the **Insert Timelines** window, select the box next to **Document Date**:

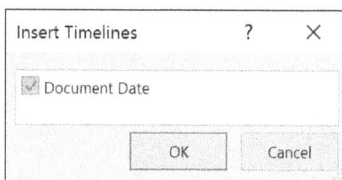

> Notice that only **Document Date** is available. Timelines only work with dates, so the only fields that are visible in the **Insert Timelines** window are date fields in the pivot table.

5. Click on **OK** to finish creating the timeline slicer.

6. Now that we have our timeline slicer, we need to position it on the page.

7. Drag the timeline so that the upper-left corner rests in cell K2.

8. Use the handles to resize the timeline to fit in cells K2 through L9:

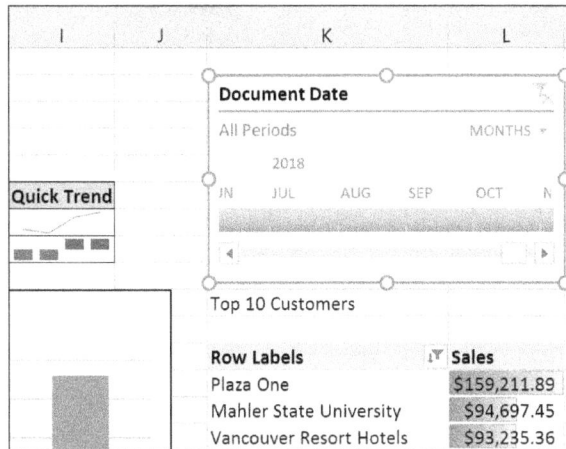

Now, we have our timeline to control our `Top 10 Customers` pivot table. Let's see how this works using these steps:

1. On the timeline, click **JAN** under **2017**. The top 10 customers will be updated to reflect only sales for January:

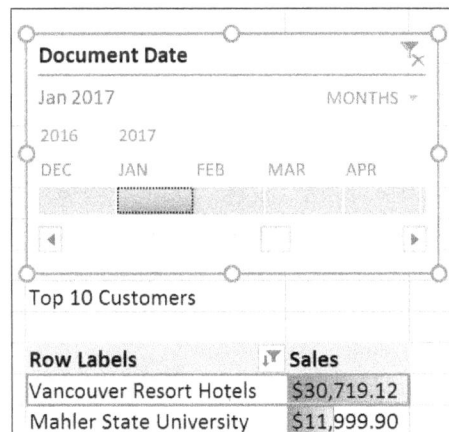

Notice that **Vancouver Resort Hotels** is the top-selling customer.

2. Hover over the timeline until handles appear to the right of January. Drag the timeline to include January through April of 2017. The timeline updates to reflect sales for the four-month period:

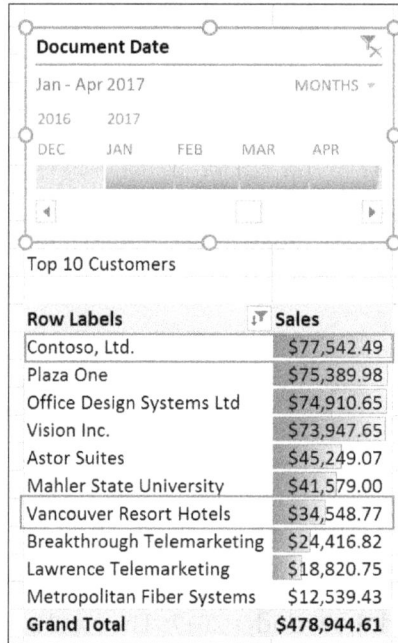

Top 10 Customers	
Row Labels	**Sales**
Contoso, Ltd.	$77,542.49
Plaza One	$75,389.98
Office Design Systems Ltd	$74,910.65
Vision Inc.	$73,947.65
Astor Suites	$45,249.07
Mahler State University	$41,579.00
Vancouver Resort Hotels	$34,548.77
Breakthrough Telemarketing	$24,416.82
Lawrence Telemarketing	$18,820.75
Metropolitan Fiber Systems	$12,539.43
Grand Total	**$478,944.61**

With this change, notice that **Contoso, Ltd.** moves to the top of the list. **Vancouver Resorts** moves to the number seven slot. Apparently, Vancouver spent a lot in January and then tapered off. With the change, our list is re-sorted to move the customer with higher sales to the top, and our conditional formatting in the form of data bars is maintained.

The timeline has a horizontal scroll bar at the bottom to move back and forth through the available date range. Above the horizontal line is an indicator to show where you are on the timeline in relation to the selected dates:

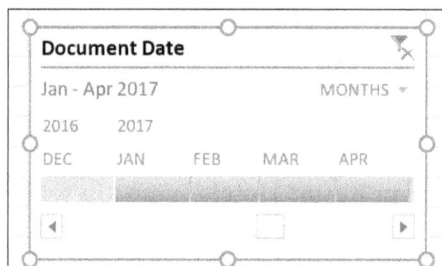

Notice that our slicer field, **Document Date**, doesn't appear at all in the pivot table. The field used in the slicer timeline doesn't have to show in the timeline to still be used to limit the date.

There is a key element to timelines that I don't want you to miss. We did not do anything with the date information to separate it out into months. Excel 2016 did that all by itself. We picked **Document Date** that includes month, day, and year elements, and the timeline defaulted to months. Excel calls this the time level.

What's nice about time level is that we're not limited to whatever Excel 2016 chooses. In our example, next to the word **Months**, is a drop-down box. The drop-down selection contains **YEARS**, **QUARTERS**, **MONTHS**, and **DAYS**. As this is important, let's take a quick look at how this works before we move on.

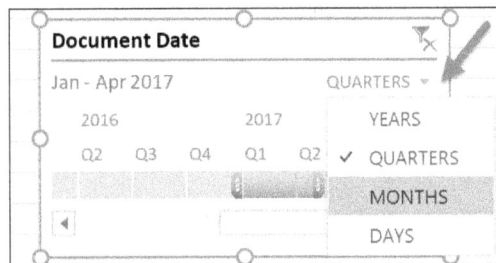

Let's continue with our timeline:

1. In the **Document Date** timeline, select the dropdown next to the word **Months** and pick **Quarters**. The display will change to reflect **Q1** through **Q4** for each year.

2. Now, change **Quarters** to **Days**. The timeline will update to allow you to pick individual days.

3. Finally, set **Days** back to **Months**, since that is most appropriate for our dashboard.

There are more features to show for slicers and timelines. We'll cover some of these features in the next chapter.

Some more formatting

Let's wrap up this dashboard with just a few final formatting touches. We'll add a title and adjust the background using these steps:

1. Click in cell B2 and enter Fabrikam Financial Dashboard.

2. Click on the **Home** tab and change the font size to **20**:

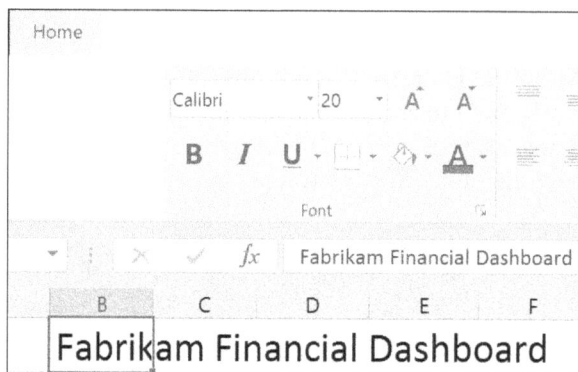

3. Click on the **View** Tab and unmark **Gridlines**. This will create a blank white background:

Finally, let's fill in the background with a color.

1. Right-click on the gray header cell between **A** and **1** (it resembles a triangle) to select the entire sheet and pull up the floating formatting menu:

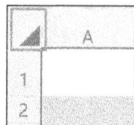

2. Select the **Fill** icon dropdown (it looks like an arrow to the right of the paint bucket) and select your background color. Click anywhere in a cell to close the floating formatting menu:

If you want to add a logo, you can go to **Insert | Pictures**. There are a lot of other things we can do to make this dashboard better, from both a functional and formatting point of view. The goal here is to provide you with an introduction. Here is our final dashboard:

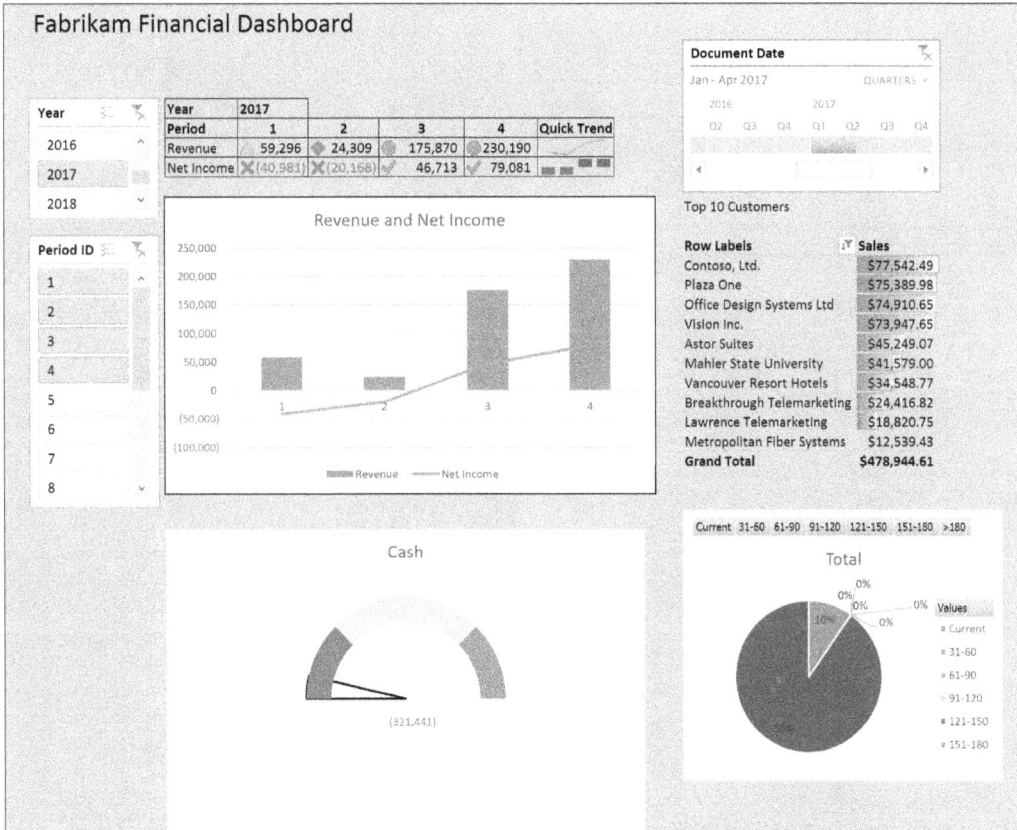

Summary

Together, we've built comparisons between revenue and net income, we've identified our top 10 customers, and we've created reviews of our cash and receivables aging. Is this the perfect dashboard for you and your company? Probably not. And it shouldn't be. Creating reports and dashboards with the tools we are providing in this and future chapters will allow you to create exactly what you need, including those things that make you and your company unique.

In the next chapter, we'll review more Excel 2016 features that can make your reports go from good to great!

5
Drilling Back to the Source Data and Other Cool Stuff

Our dashboard is looking great and is already providing real value. Now, let's polish it and add some additional functionality.

Once you deploy a dashboard, it's obvious that people would want more information. A great way to manage this is to build a couple of dashboards. Usually, this looks like a primary dashboard with secondary dashboards that break out more information about sales, cash, or departments. We've done this at a very simple level with our **Revenue** tab and **Net Income** tabs. Another great way to deal with the need for detail and to take your dashboard beyond what everyone else is doing is to allow users to drill down into specific transactions or accounts in Microsoft Dynamics GP 2016.

In this chapter, we will look at the following topics:

- Slicer and timeline options
- Hyperlinks and drill downs
- Other cool Excel stuff
- Refreshing data
- Final cleanup
- Sharing

Recap

Throughout this book, we've been building a dashboard that looks like the following screenshot:

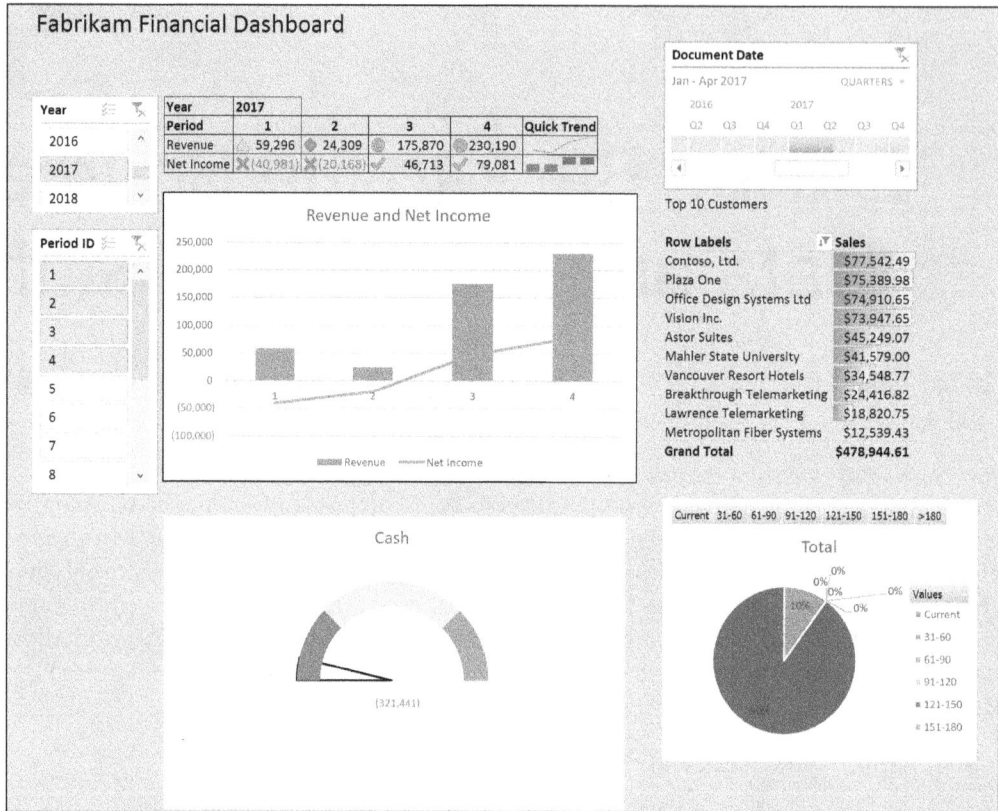

We're done with the hard parts, and now, we will connect the pieces and clean things up.

Slicers and timelines options

We've already seen how slicers and timelines provide interactivity to pivot tables. Let's spend a little more time on slicers and timelines. We can change them visually, which enables them to fit into tight spaces and/or become more visually efficient and appealing.

Slicer orientation

The two slicers that we've created so far are vertical slicers, that is, the selections are oriented up and down. Depending on how a dashboard is laid out, it may make sense to reduce the height and increase the width of the slicer visual/tile. If you are going to increase the width, you may want to increase the number of columns in the slicer. The default number of columns is one. In effect, we'll create a horizontal slicer. To create a horizontal slicer, follow these steps:

1. Open the GP 2016 `Dashboard.xlsx` file that we've been working with and save it as GP 2016 `DashboardTest.xlsx`. This will allow you to learn about some additional options and tools before we add them to our finished product.

2. Select the **Year** slicer on the **Dashboard** worksheet.

3. Go to **Slicer Tools | Options** to open the slicer options ribbon:

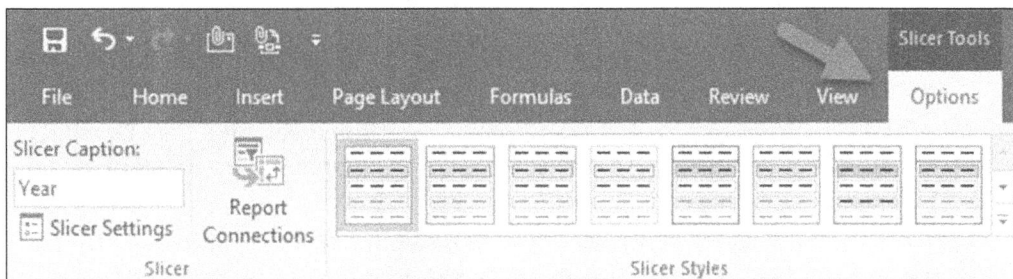

4. Set **Columns** to **4** (or **6**). With the **Year** visual selected (handle bars or circles will appear around it), you can resize the slicer and move it to a place that makes sense to you:

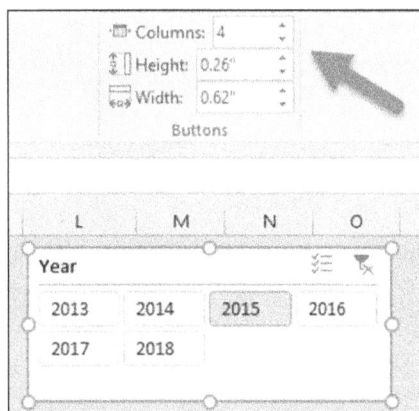

Navigate to **Slicer Tools | Options**, you'll see the **Buttons** area. Here, you can edit the actual height and width of the buttons. To the right of the **Buttons** area is a **Size** area with an expansion icon. This will enable you to get super detailed in the sizing and positioning of the slicer.

Although the timeline does not have the equivalent of columns, it has the sizing options available, which you can access by going to **Timeline Tools | Options**.

Slicers and timelines color and alignment

If multiple slicers or multiple timelines appear on the report or dashboard, you may want to display them in the same area, creating the need for uniformity to make the report(s) more visually appealing. This can be achieved using the same colors and arranging them neatly. To add color and arrange them, follow these steps:

1. Open the GP 2016 `DashboardTest.xlsx` file that we created in the previous section.

2. Move your **Year** and **Period ID** slicers to the same area of the dashboard so that they are on top of each other. No need to be precise. We will let Excel line them up for us.

3. Click on the **Year** slicer, press and hold down the *Ctrl* key, and select the **Period ID** slicer. The handles should be around both slicers as both have been selected.

4. Go to **Slicer Tools | Options** and then to **Arrange | Align | Align Left**. This will line both slicers on the left-hand side:

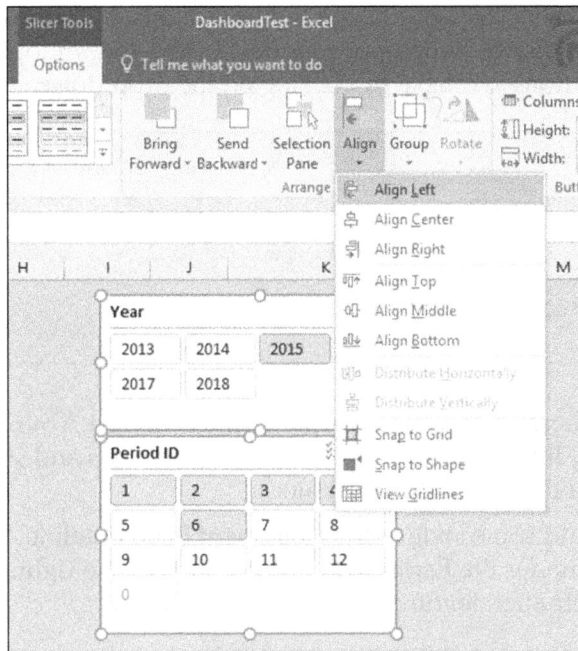

5. With both slicers still selected, go to **Slicer Tools | Options | Buttons**. In the **Buttons** area, enter 3.5" in the **Width** field, or whatever amount works for your slicers:

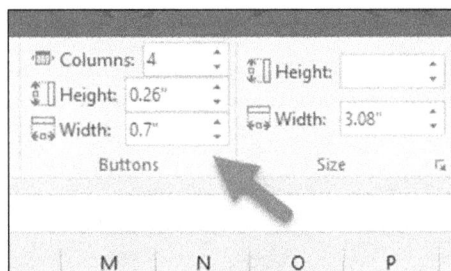

6. With both slicers still selected, go to **Slicer Tools | Options | Slicer Styles** and select a color that matches your dashboard and/or logo. Note that there are more options available by clicking on the drop-down list:

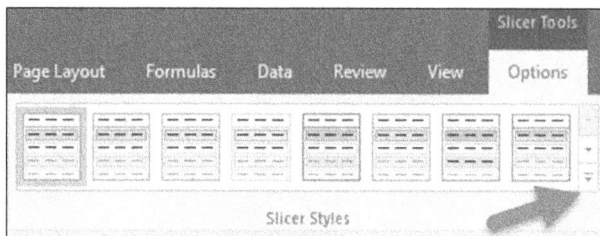

7. Click anywhere on the Excel spreadsheet to unselect. Your slicers are now the same width, lined up on both the right and left sides and styled, giving your dashboard a better overall appearance.

8. Now, let's add some style to the **Document Date** timeline. Select the timeline and drag it under the **Period ID** slicer, slightly to the right. This will allow us to use the left-align feature again:

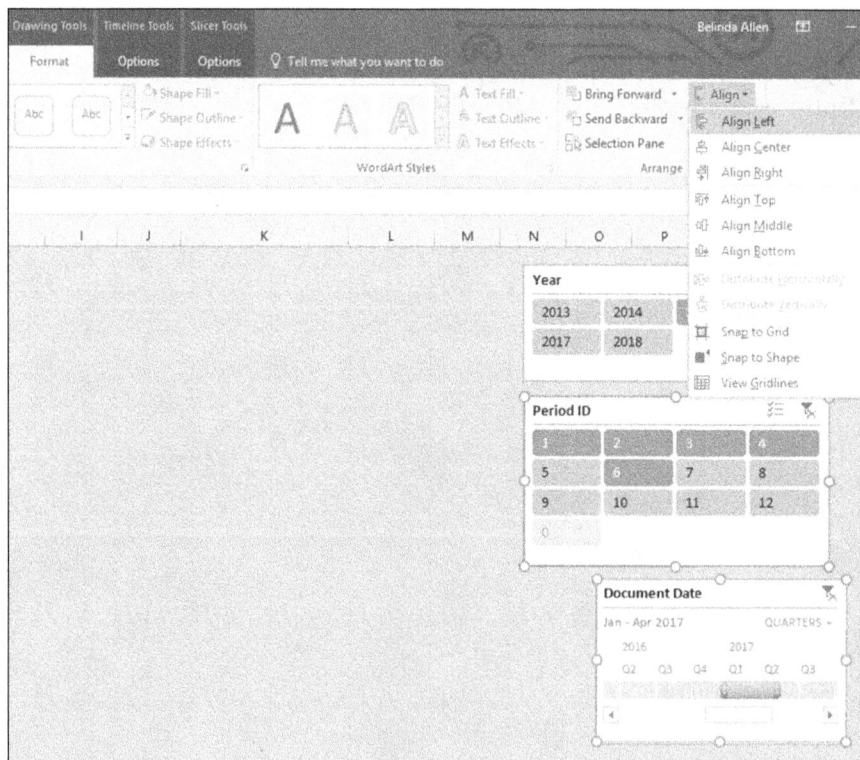

9. With the timeline still selected, press and hold down the *Ctrl* key and select the **Period ID** slicer. Go to **Drawing Tools | Format | Arrange | Align | Align Left**. This will align the timeline on the left-hand side to the two slicers. The width can be edited as well, if you want them to line up on both sides.

10. Click anywhere to remove the multi selection. Then, click to reselect (only) the **Document Date** timeline.

11. The timeline caption can be changed from `Document Date` to `Transaction Date` by going to **Timeline Tools | Options | Timeline | Timeline Captions:**. Slicers can be changed by going to **Slicer Tools | Option:**

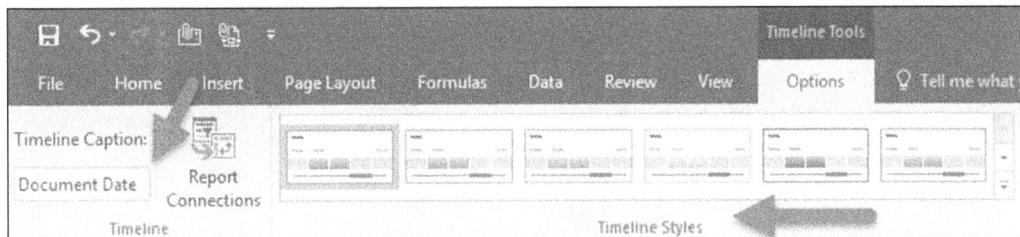

12. In the **Timeline Tools | Options | Timeline Styles** field are other color and style themes for the timeline. Select the one that best fits your background and/or log.

When selecting styles for the slicers and timelines, be mindful and consistent in the colors. Many colors can be distracting to the dashboard consumers. Too many colors can look like a circus, which, of course, would be a good thing if your business is indeed a circus; but bad if your business is a law firm for example.

Slicer additional options

By default, when a slicer is added, all options appear. This may sound like what you want, but sometimes, it just adds clutter to the dashboard. Here's an example of where this clutter would occur. In our example, we have two slicers, namely, **Years** and **Period ID**. If I select the year **2017** on my year slicer, I only want to see periods that have data in the **Period ID** slicer. If I only have 2017 data for periods 1-4, I do not want to see the options of periods 5-12 in my slicer. We can hide items with no data by following these steps:

1. Open the GP 2016 `DashboardTest.xlsx` file that we created earlier.

2. Select (only) the **Period ID** slicer then go to **Slicer Tools** | **Options** | **Slicer** | **Slicer Settings**:

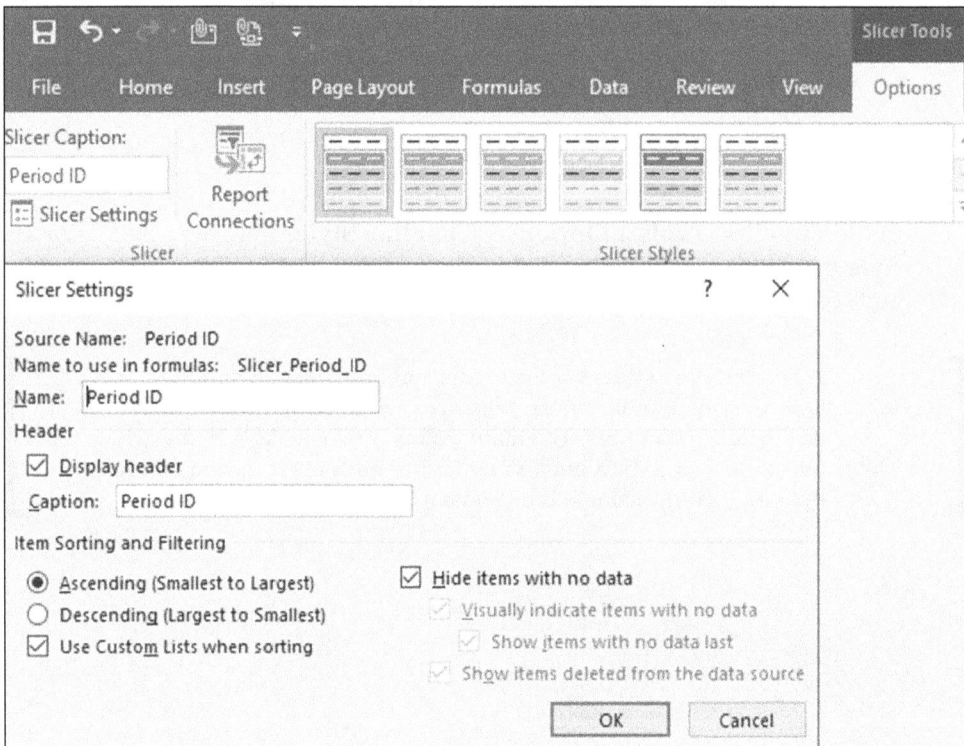

3. In the **Slicer Settings** window, select the **Hide items with no data** field. Click on **OK**.

Now, our slicers and timelines look great and are easier to use.

In Excel 2016, the multiselect feature was added for slicers. In prior versions of Excel, you had to hold the *Ctrl* key down to multiselect slicer data. In Excel 2016, you only need to click on the **Multi-Select** icon in the top-right corner of each slicer. Then, just click (select or unselect) on the data you want to include:

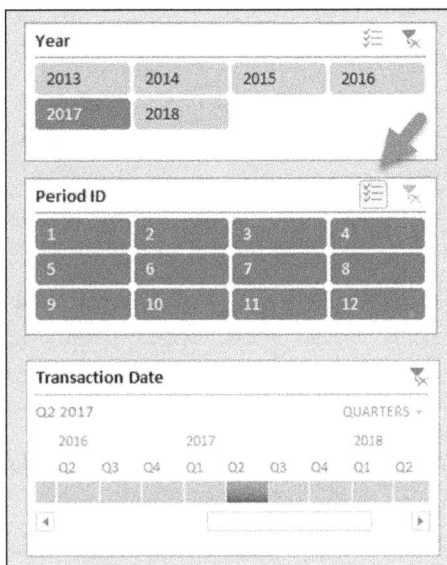

Learning about hyperlinks

Hyperlinks are a feature of Excel 2016 that have been in the product for a while. Links can be built via the interface or with a formula. They provide a great way to link sheets together, open website pages, and even drill into a GP window (for users of on-premise GP, not the web client).

In previous chapters, we added additional information to our **Revenue** and **Net Income** tabs. We'll start by linking these tabs to our dashboard. To build our hyperlinks, follow these steps:

1. Open the `Dashboard.xlsx` file of GP 2016 that we've been working with.
2. On the **Dashboard** tab, select cell D7. This should be the **Revenue** label.
3. Go to **Insert | Links | Hyperlink** on the Excel ribbon.
4. In the **Link to:** section, on the left-hand side, select **Place in This Document**.

5. In the center section, under **Or select a place in this document:**, pick **Revenue**, as shown in the following screenshot:

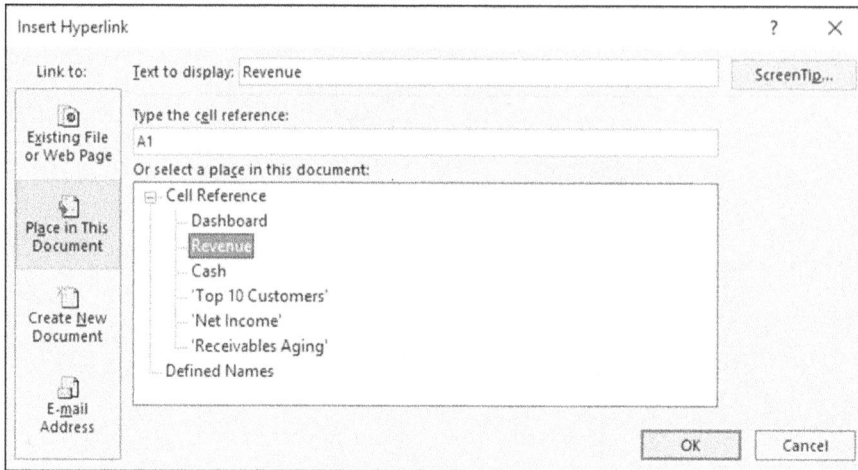

6. Click on **OK**. The **Revenue** label will turn blue and be underlined indicating a hyperlink, as shown in the following screenshot:

Year	2017				
Period	1	2	3	4	Quick Trend
Revenue	59,296	24,309	175,870	230,190	
Net Incom	#####	#####	46,713	79,081	

7. Click on the new **Revenue** link to drill down to the **Revenue** tab. By simply clicking on the word **Revenue** with the hyperlink, the worksheet for **Revenue** opens.

We need to do the same thing for the **Net Income** line. To link to additional net income information, follow these steps:

1. Click on the **Dashboard** tab.
2. On the **Dashboard** tab, select cell D8. This should be the **Net Income** label.
3. Go to **Insert | Hyperlink** on the Excel ribbon.
4. In the **Link to:** section, on the left-hand side, select **Place in This Document**.
5. In the center section under **Or select a place in this Document**, pick 'Net Income' and click on **OK**.
6. Save the file.

Hyperlinks don't have to link back to another Excel sheet. They can also link to more information on the web or to a location in SharePoint, for example. Finally, we can link them back to a transaction in Dynamics GP 2016. That's up next.

Using drill downs in GP 2016

At its simplest, a drill down is a hyperlink that links back into Dynamics GP. When the user clicks on the hyperlink, the focus changes to Microsoft Dynamics GP 2016, and the linked window opens in GP with the appropriate data. In the real world, a dashboard might display cash balances for each bank account or checkbook in GP terms. The operating checkbook would have a hyperlink attached on the dashboard. Clicking on the link would cause the checkbook register inquiry window to open in Dynamics GP and display information from the operating checkbook.

Drill down background

With regard to Dynamics GP, Microsoft uses the terms "drill down" and "drill back" interchangeably. For our purposes, they are the same thing.

A drill down link can work for inquiries and transactions throughout GP. Since there is little to no documentation on these drill downs, you would think that they would be hard to use, except that Microsoft gave us a huge shortcut. The **Office Data Connector** (**ODC**) files that we've been using for our dashboard contain drill down links. Each ODC file has one or more columns that link back into Dynamics GP.

Next, we will review how they work and add some to the dashboard.

Before we get rolling, there are a few things that you need to know:

- The user must have Dynamics GP 2016 open and be logged in to the company they are drilling into for the drill down to work. The hyperlink will not open Dynamics GP 2016 for you. This arrangement also makes licensing and security straightforward since it's controlled by the GP 2016 interface.
- The user must have permission in Dynamics GP 2016 to open the window that they are trying to drill back into. For example, if a user doesn't have access to payroll inquiry via GP, we certainly don't want them to be able to drill down into that data via Excel.
- At the release of Microsoft Dynamics GP 2016, drilling down from Excel to GP via the new web client was not available. It may be made available later via a service pack. Fingers crossed!

Now that we have all the background out of the way, let's drill down!

Using drill downs

Drill downs are the simplest to explain when we bring the data into Microsoft Excel 2016, so we'll go down that route with a common example. To build your first drill down, follow these steps:

1. Open the sample company in Microsoft Dynamics GP 2016.
2. Select **Financial** in the navigation list on the left-hand side.
3. In the pane above, select **Excel Reports**.
4. Double-click the selection marked `TWO AccountTransactions`. The type should be **Data Connections**:

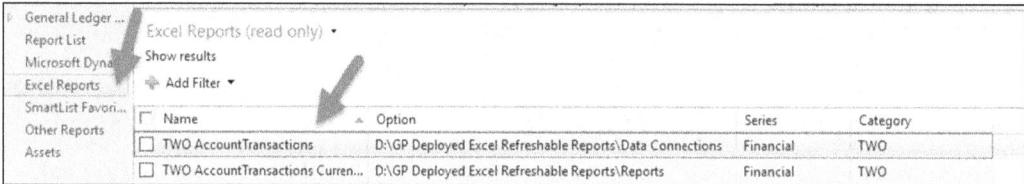

	Name		Option	Series	Category
General Ledger ...		Excel Reports (read only) ▾			
Report List		Show results			
Microsoft Dyna		⊕ Add Filter ▾			
Excel Reports	☐	Name ▲	Option	Series	Category
SmartList Favori...	☐	TWO AccountTransactions	D:\GP Deployed Excel Refreshable Reports\Data Connections	Financial	TWO
Other Reports	☐	TWO AccountTransactions Curren...	D:\GP Deployed Excel Refreshable Reports\Reports	Financial	TWO
Assets					

5. If you receive **Microsoft Excel Security Notice**, select **Enable**.
6. On the **Import Data** window, select **Table** and click on **OK**.
7. Scroll all the way to the right-hand side of the resulting Excel file. You should see two columns labeled **Account Index for Drillback** and **Journal Entry for Drillback**. These are the two default drill down URLs for journal entry transactions. They are explained here:

    ◦   **Account Index for Drillback**: This entry will open the **Account Maintenance** window for this account. That's not terribly helpful in most cases since it just lists the account setup.

    ◦   **Account Index for Journal**: This entry will open the **Journal Entry Inquiry** window for posted transactions and the **Transaction Entry** window for unposted entries. Both these windows then allow drill back into additional detail.

DP
Account Index For Drillback
dgpp://DGPB/?Db=&Srv=BUSYBEE&Cmp=TWO&Prod=0&Act=OPEN&Func=OpenAcctIndx&ACTINDX=1
dgpp://DGPB/?Db=&Srv=BUSYBEE&Cmp=TWO&Prod=0&Act=OPEN&Func=OpenAcctIndx&ACTINDX=1
dgpp://DGPB/?Db=&Srv=BUSYBEE&Cmp=TWO&Prod=0&Act=OPEN&Func=OpenAcctIndx&ACTINDX=447

We have the link details, but it's not yet a link in Dynamics GP. To build a formula-based link in Excel 2016, follow these steps:

1. In the Excel sheet, insert a column between columns **A** and **B** to create a blank column **B**.

2. In cell B1, type JE Link.

3. In cell B2, type =HYPERLINK(DR2,A2). Cell DR2 should be the first cell under **Journal Entry for Drillback**. Here, we're building a hyperlink using a formula instead of the interface. Unlike the interface-based link we used for revenue, a formula-based link is dynamic, making it easy to build a link per line.

4. Column **B** now contains the journal entry number with a link:

	A	B	C	D
1	Journal Entry	JE Link	Series	TRX Date
2	1543	1543	Financial	5/8/2017 0:00
3	1546	1546	Purchasing	2/15/2017 0:00
4	1545	1545	Purchasing	2/15/2017 0:00

B3 =HYPERLINK(DR3, A3)

Normally, when creating formulas in tables, I reference column data name rather than the column worksheet reference. For example, I would use =HYPERLINK([@[Journal Entry For Drillback]],[@[Journal Entry]]) rather than =HYPERLINK(DS2, A2). In the steps earlier, it was just easier walking you through it with the column worksheet reference. In many ways, an Excel table is like a "mini database," so using the column data names is more in line with using a database.

5. Scroll down to journal entry **27** and click on the link in column **B**. Click on any row for journal entry **27**.

6. Click on **Yes** when the security notice appears:

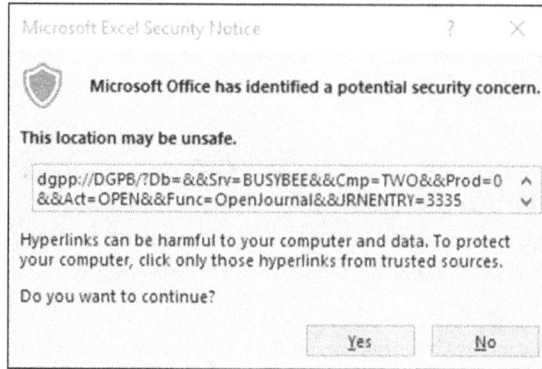

> There is a way to disable this box using a registry entry, but there are variations based on your version of Windows and Office. You can find out more at http://www.msoutlook.info/question/245. Make sure to back up the registry before making changes. Better yet, get your IT team or your Microsoft partner to do this for you.

7. The **Journal Entry Inquiry** window will open for journal entry on row **27**. A user can then click on **Source Document** to continue drilling back into the source of this journal entry.

The reason why we selected journal entry **27** to drill back into is because this is a posted journal entry. If we had selected an unposted journal entry, the **Transaction Entry** window would have opened. In the Dynamics GP interface, you can't use an inquiry window to inquire on an unposted journal entry.

Drill down link structure

Since we have so much flexibility with drill downs, it's worth understanding what the structure of a drill down looks like.

Here is my drill down link for journal entry **27**:

```
dgpp://DGPB/?Db=&Srv=BUSYBEE&Cmp=TWO&Prod=0&Act=OPEN&Func=OpenJournal
Inq&JRNENTRY=27&RCTRXSEQ=1&YEAR1=2014&TRXDATE=01/01/2014
```

That thing is huge! The good news is that it breaks down pretty easily. All the elements are connected by the ampersand (&) symbol. The description of other elements is given in the following table:

Drill down elements	Description
dgpp://DGPB/?	This is the drill back URL that indicates that the program to work with is Dynamics GP.
Db=	This is the database instance. You won't see a database instance if your GP installation uses the base SQL server instance. The base instance is more common and is how you see it here.
Srv=BUSYBEE	This is the server name. In our example here, the server name is BUSYBEE.
Cmp=TWO	Cmp represents the database name for the company to drill back to. Our example uses TWO, the sample company.
Prod=0	This is the product. Product 0 equates to Dynamics GP. Other product numbers might refer to Fixed Assets, Project Accounting, or an ISV solution. Product numbers are listed in the Dynamics.set file.
Act=OPEN	This is the action where we are going to open a window.
Func=OpenJournalInq	Func represents the function. The function we are performing is opening the **Journal Inquiry** window.
JRNENTRY=27	This is the first parameter; we want to return journal entry 27.
RCTRXSEQ=1	Recurring transaction sequence is the second parameter, and it is set to 1. Since recurring transactions can have the same journal entry, this specifies which instance of a recurring transaction to use.
TRXDATE=01/01/2014	The final parameter is the transaction date, January 1, 2014.

Drill down links for inventory, sales, or other transactions will be similar. In our case, the links are already built for us, and the link elements are static.

Other cool Excel stuff

Let's take a look at all the other exciting stuff that Excel has in store for us!

Adding a logo

In almost every case, you'll want to add a company logo to a dashboard. Logos help dress up even a plain dashboard. Often, they end up in the left-hand corner, so you may need to move your titles around. They don't have to end up there though.

For our example, I wanted something available to every Excel user, so we'll use a star symbol available in Excel 2016 as our company logo. Perform these steps to add a logo:

1. Open the `Dashboard.xlsx` file of GP 2016 that we've been working with.

2. Select the **Dashboard** tab.

3. On the ribbon, go to **Insert | Illustrations | Pictures Online**.

4. In the **Bing Image Search** box, type `Star` and press *Enter*:

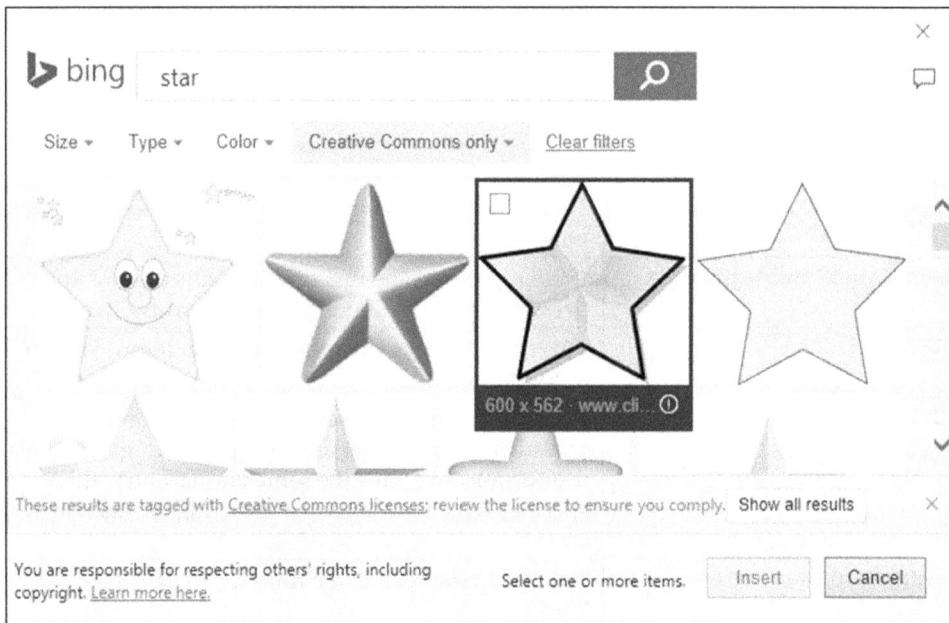

5. Select the star you wish to use and click on **Insert**.

6. Drag the star to your desired location. I chose to insert it directly under column **I**.

7. Use the handles to resize the star to fit in the unused space:

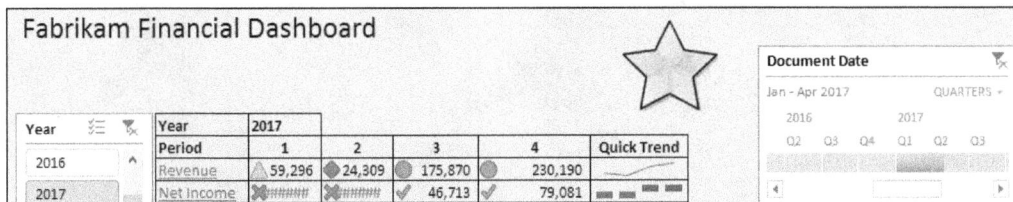

Fabrikam Financial Dashboard													

Year			Year	2017					Document Date				
			Period	1	2	3	4	Quick Trend	Jan - Apr 2017			QUARTERS	
2016			Revenue	59,296	24,309	175,870	230,190		2016			2017	
2017			Net Income	######	######	46,713	79,081		Q2 Q3 Q4			Q1 Q2 Q3	

For your company logo, your process will be slightly different. I needed a graphic that everyone has access to. Rather than selecting **Online Pictures** from the **Insert** ribbon, you'll likely select **Pictures**. Windows Explorer will open, allowing you to locate your logo and click on **Insert**.

Good design

In our example dashboard, we have limited graphics that are available to us. I wanted to use pictures that are available to the widest number of users. However, I also don't want you to be limited to what everyone else does. If you use Google or Bing to look up images of Excel-based dashboards, they all quickly start to look alike. We will look at a different example to help provide some inspiration.

Author Tyler Chessman has written a book on the U.S. national debt. The book is appropriately titled *Understanding the United States Debt*. What's really cool for us is that Chessman has taken the U.S. national debt and broken it down in Excel using all the elements that we've used for our dashboard. It is, without a doubt, a very cool Excel dashboard and one of Mark Polino's (the original author of this book) favorites.

The debt data is loaded via PowerPivot, and the Excel sheet is available for download at `http://understandingtheusdebt.com/data.aspx`. This fantastic dashboard looks like the following screenshot:

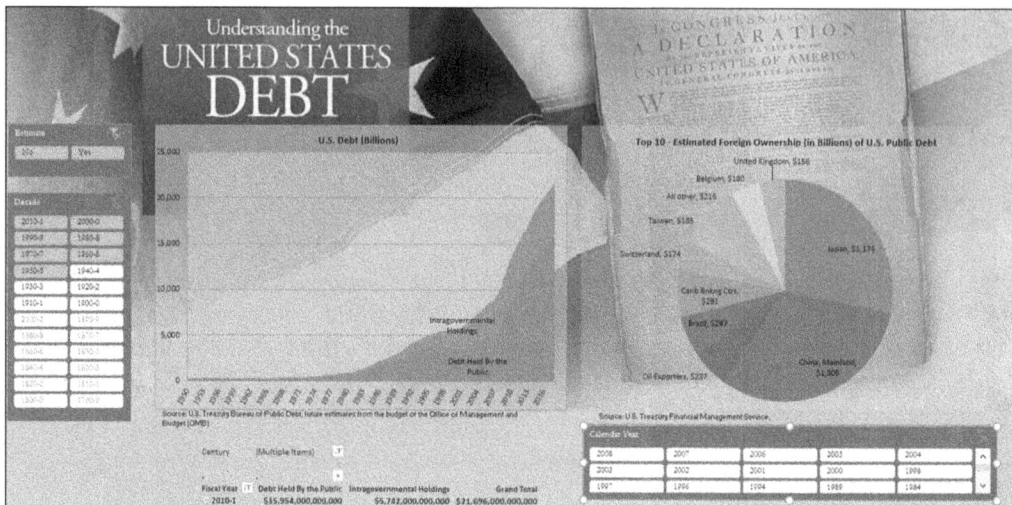

This is a great example of using reporting and dashboards to think outside the box. Use visual reporting for anything you need to monitor. Remember: "*You cannot improve what you do not measure.*"

Refreshing the data

One problem with hiding the ribbon is that it makes it hard for the user to refresh the data. Certainly the **Refresh data when opening the file** or the **Refresh every 60 (you define the number of) minutes** settings in the data sources can help with that, but there are plenty of good reasons for a user to want to be able to refresh data on demand. Pressing *Alt + F5* on the keyboard will also refresh all, so that is an option when the ribbon is hidden.

You can put a note in the sheet to remind folks how to complete an on-demand refresh with the button or with *Alt + F5*. We've tried to minimize the effort on the part of the user, but we are asking users to interpret and make decisions based on the data in this dashboard. Learning to click on the **Refresh All** or a simple keystroke combination button should be within their skill set.

Sharing

We've now built this great dashboard. We can refresh it and see the latest numbers at will. Rarely are we the only users of our dashboard. We've built this dashboard to support the organization, and we've built it in a way that is easy to use and understand. Now we have to figure out how to make it available to more users. There are a number of options available. We will explore the various options, but some of them can be quite complex, so we won't go into them in detail. In the real world, if you've got a great dashboard and it makes the controller and/or the CFO happy, you'll get the resources to get it deployed.

Some common options for sharing an Excel-based dashboard include:

- E-mail
- Network sharing
- Hosting via OneDrive
- Downloading via OneDrive
- Downloading via SharePoint
- Hosting via SharePoint Office 365 services
- Microsoft Power BI

We will briefly look at each of these.

The quick option – e-mail

E-mail is still the most common way to share an Excel-based dashboard, certainly at the start. One of the benefits of our dashboard is that if the users we e-mail it to are on the network and have appropriate security, we don't have to send it to them repeatedly. The users can simply save the dashboard and refresh it. However, if you make structural changes to the dashboard, you will need to resend it. This can result in users having different versions of the dashboard. Usually, that's not a good thing.

Whether or not users can update a dashboard delivered via e-mail depends on a couple of factors. If the connection is embedded in the spreadsheet and the user has access to the source via the network, VPN, or some other method, they should be able to update it. If the connection is embedded in an ODC file, the ODC file may need to travel with the spreadsheet as well.

Network sharing

Typically, the next step is to place the dashboard in a shared network location. This ensures that all users are using the same versions. Any new versions would overwrite the old ones, keeping everyone up to date.

Hosting via OneDrive

OneDrive is one of Microsoft's cloud options for file storage and access. Documents stored on OneDrive can be opened via Excel on the Web. Before you get all excited that this is the answer you've been looking for, you also need to understand that there are a lot of limitations. Some of them are as follows:

- There is a maximum file size when opening an Excel file. Microsoft continues to increase the size, but it's still relatively easy to hit the limit.
- Many dashboard elements won't work on the web version of Excel.
- Users won't be able to refresh data from Dynamics GP using OneDrive.

These limitations are pretty severe, but there are scenarios where it makes sense to publish a static version of a dashboard for remote locations and host the file on OneDrive.

Downloading via OneDrive

OneDrive can also be used to download an Excel file, much like a network location. File sizes typically aren't an issue, but again, without a connection back to Dynamics GP, these files can't be refreshed. However, we've looked at a number of techniques for building dashboards. Some of them included embedding data in the file. While this isn't preferred, it could be used to give remote users a regularly updated dashboard to work with, especially if the analysis only requires periodic data, such as monthly financial information.

Downloading via SharePoint

A step that many companies take after they try the downloading from the network option is to move the file into SharePoint and let users download from there. SharePoint provides options such as version control and even more extensive security. This is really just a tiny step up from downloading from the network. Users still download the file and run it locally, and users still need appropriate access to update the dashboard.

Hosting via SharePoint Office 365 services

Now, we start to approach the answer that most folks are looking for: Office 365 SharePoint technology that allows users to make Excel workbooks available via SharePoint. End users don't need to have Microsoft Excel on their machines. The information is actually displayed using Excel Services, not using Microsoft Excel 2016. Files can be uploaded, secured, displayed, refreshed, and shared via Excel Services on SharePoint. Microsoft's Office 365 cloud offering contains similar functionality to make Excel data available to users online and refreshable by the user.

Microsoft Power BI

The final sharing option is the new business intelligence service, Microsoft Power BI. We'll go much more into detail on this from *Chapter 9, Getting Data in Power BI,* to *Chapter 12, Sharing and Refreshing Data and Dashboards in Power BI.* For now, it would suffice to say that this data can be shared as an Excel report in Power BI and become available to users to consume. Refreshing can be tricky, but we'll cover that later in the Power BI portion of this book.

Summary

That's it, we've built a pretty nice dashboard. It connects to Dynamics GP 2016; it's refreshable and portable. You can do the same thing for your company. The core is just the basic building blocks of pivot tables, conditional formatting, and charts. But wait, we're not done! I've already mentioned that we have a whole section dedicated to Microsoft Power BI, but up next is the new product by Jet Reports, Jet Express for GP. This product will enable you the ability to build financial statements and create tables of financial and non-financial data in GP within Excel. Go ahead, turn the page!

6
Introducing Jet Reports Express

As we mentioned in *Chapter 1, Getting Data from Dynamics GP 2016 to Excel 2016*, shortly after the release of GP 2016, Microsoft announced that **Management Reporter** was moving to maintenance only mode. This announcement was made in conjunction with the announcement that Jet Reports was releasing a version of **Jet Express for Excel** that works with GP, in collaboration with Microsoft. This offering will fill in the gap that was being left by Management Reporter. Jet Express for Excel has different feature sets than Management Reporter. For starters, it is an Excel add-on, which is why we included a few chapters in this book on this very cool product. Also, did we mention it is free to GP users? Well it is, so why not use it?

In this chapter, you will learn more about Jet Express for Excel and create our first report. We'll achieve these goals by covering the following topics:

- Jet Reports overview
- Jet **Table Builder**
- Other Jet Reports offerings for GP

Recap

Before we begin with Jet Reports, let's review what we've done so far. We've connected to GP data for use in Excel in a variety of ways, using several of these methods to create an Excel dashboard. Now that we are moving into Jet Reports, we'll begin using a combination of Jet Express for GP and native Excel functions to create a general ledger trial balance. Once you obtain these skills, you can tap into pretty much any GP data (that you have the rights to) and create an Excel table and, therefore, some power Excel reports.

Here is a sample of the report we will build in this chapter. This sample is currently only reviewing the accounts for the cost of goods sold for a fiscal period:

General Ledger Trial Balance

Months			
Jan	Feb	Mar	Apr
May	Jun	Jul	Aug
Sep	Oct	Nov	Dec
<1/1/2017	>12/2/2017		

Account Number	Account Description	Date	Journal Entry	Reference	Debit	Credit	Sum of Net
000-1110-00	Cash - Payroll				$0.00	$20,632.78	($20,632.78)
000-2150-00	Taxable Benefits Payable				$0.00	$1,428.95	($1,428.95)
000-2161-00	IL State Withholding Payable				$0.00	$710.81	($710.81)
000-2170-00	Federal Withholding Payable				$0.00	$6,165.81	($6,165.81)
000-2200-00	Payroll Deductions Payable				$0.00	$1,914.68	($1,914.68)
000-5100-00	Salaries and Wages				$27,402.56	$0.00	$27,402.56
100-5150-00	Employee Benefits - Administration				$1,428.95	$0.00	$1,428.95
100-5170-00	Payroll Taxes - Administration				$383.16	$0.00	$383.16
200-5170-00	Payroll Taxes - Accounting				$1,638.36	$0.00	$1,638.36
Grand Total					$30,853.03	$30,853.03	$0.00

What is Jet and why should I use it?

Jet Express for Excel is not so much of a report writer, but rather a special tool box for Excel. This toolbox can enable you to not only access your GP data, but also extract exactly what you want from GP. This means you can use native Excel tools to create financial and operational statements. A great example of getting exactly the data you want would be the net change of a general ledger account for a certain period. You can set it so that the period is hard coded in the formula or you can have an Excel field for the period that you reference. This means you do not have to change every formula if the period changes. You can also set your reports to not show accounts if the balance is zero. Yes, you can do these things in Excel, but it is much easier with the Excel add-on from Jet. Using Jet makes it easier to create the report, and certainly makes it easier for the person consuming the report.

As mentioned earlier, Jet Express for Excel can be used to create both financial statements and operating statements. Let's review how we are defining these terms for the purpose of this book. Financial statements include (but are not limited to) balance sheets, profit and loss statements, and cash flow statements. Operating statements would typically be either supporting report for financial statements or simply some sort of business intelligence reports. Operating statements include (but are not limited to) general ledger trial balances, accounts payable trial balances, inventory item sales reports, customers on hold reports, fixed assets property ledger, and so on.

For those of you using GP that is installed on servers in your network, the setup is super easy. If your GP data is hosted or on a cloud server such as Microsoft Azure, unlike Management Reporter, you can use your locally installed version of Excel to access your data in the cloud. We'll not go into the installation or setup in this book. We'll simply focus on getting you started with Jet.

I would like to add one additional point for using Jet Express for Excel. Most customers I've worked with typically export their reports to Excel for distribution. They typically do this because Excel is usually installed on everyone's machine and almost everyone knows how to at least navigate around in Excel. Why not just start in Excel?

You can easily create these tables using data from GP.

Prebuilt reports

Jet Reports tries to give you some instant success with their product by providing around 20 sample reports from which you can just pull up a report and use. This is a tool that's so valuable, even if you choose to create your financial statements elsewhere, you can still use this free version of Jet to assist in the creation of Excel reports. Some of these reports require additional installation of custom Jet Views, which we will cover later in this chapter.

Let's spend a little time on one of these pre-built reports, the **Item Sales over time** report. When you open the report for the first time, you will need to enable it for editing. Since this report was not created on your computer, Windows needs you to verify that it is safe. You can do this by simply clicking on **Enable Editing**:

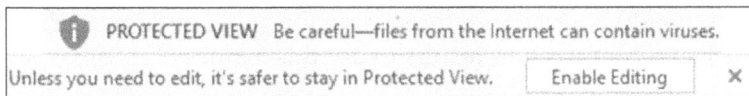

Let's start by reviewing the different worksheets (tabs) on this report:

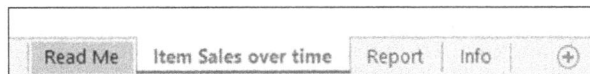

When you open the report for the first time, you'll start with the second tab, the **Item Sales over time**. This is the actual report, and it contains a graph of the sales, in dollars, of items over all the years in GP. In this image, I've collapsed (summarized) all the years, except **2017**. As a result, the graph shows the years as sums, except **2017** (which shows as months). You'll also notice that the pivot table of the data is to the right of the graph (chart). This pivot table makes it easier to review the actual numbers. This worksheet is made up of pure Excel formulas, functions, and tools:

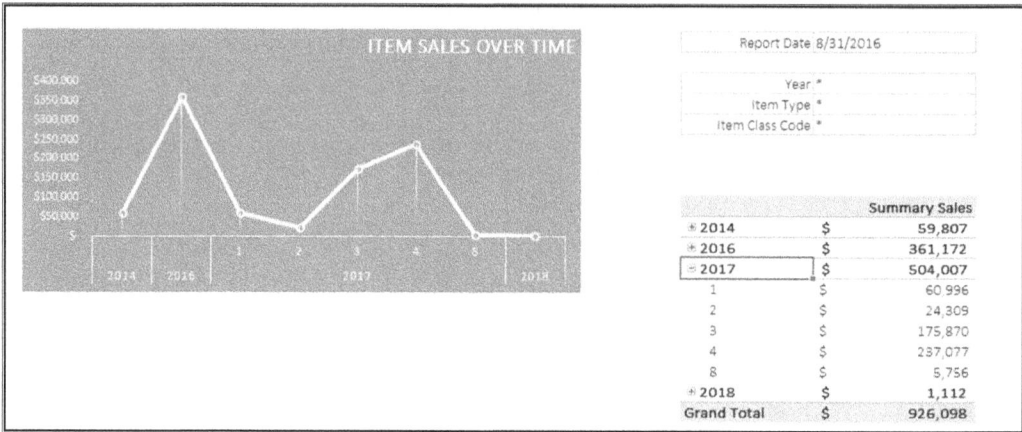

In the top-right corner, below the **Report Date** (which is a formula to display today's date), are the parameters, or options, used to run this report. When the report data is refreshed against the GP data, the following window appears, allowing you to enter specific data to filter (reduce) the results received. For this report, I could enter a single **Item Class Code** and the report will display the sales amounts for items in that class. As you build your own reports using the Table Builder, you may find it necessary to achieve your desired results to use this feature:

The next (or third) tab is the **Report** worksheet. This is the worksheet that holds the table of data retrieved from GP via Jet. Not only does the table of GP data appear, but the filters and parameters being used for this table are also displayed. This helps the report consumer understand exactly what data is being extracted from GP:

Tables and Fields	Filters	
InventorySalesSummaryPeriod_History		
Location Code	<>''	
Summary Type	Calendar	
Year	*	
Items		
Item Type	*	
Item Class Code	*	
Selling U of M	*	

Item Description	Item Number
Green Phone	100XLG
Green Phone	100XLG
Green Phone	100XLG

The last tab, or worksheet, is the **Info** tab. The geek in me loves this tab. This shows me from which tables and/or views the data is being pulled and how it links together:

> This report pulls information from the **InventorySalesSummaryPeriod_History** view which contains records of item sales by item number, period and year.
>
> It also returns Item information from the **Item** table

InventorySalesSummaryPeriod_History		Item
Item Number	←---- Link ----→	Item Number
Item Description		Item Type
Location Code		Item Class Code
Summary Costs		Selling U of M
Summary Prd/Mth		
Summary QTYS		
Summary Sales		
Summary Type		
Year		

> 💡 Although this is a good *best practice* when building your own reports, it is not necessary to include this level of detail.

Last and certainly not least is the **Read Me** tab. This contains general information about the report. This includes links for support, training, and report services.

Jet Views and Friendly Names

When working in (any version of) GP, we are accustomed to seeing data logically organized using natural language. Do not be afraid of the example that follows; it is only intended to show you how important **Jet Views** and **Friendly Names** are to us all. Here is one example. If we look at our chart of accounts in the general ledger (using the **Account Maintenance** window), we see a required field for each account number is **Posting Type**. There are two options, and we select the option that pertains to this account, either **Balance Sheet** or **Profit and Loss**. We also see the required **Category** field, which is a drop-down list with items such as **Cash**, **Accounts Receivable**, **Inventory**, and so on. In the database, this data is stored in a table named GL00100. The **Posting Type** is stored in a field named PSTINGTYP. When **Balance Sheet** is selected, the PSTINGTYP field stores a 0, and when **Profit and Loss** is selected, the PSTINGTYP field stores a 1. When building a report and, even more importantly, when consuming a report, you should not need to know what GL00100 or PSTINGTYP means, or even what a 0 or a 1 means, because it can change with every field. The **Category** (ACCATNUM) field is even more cryptic. Depending on the **Category** you choose, a numeric value of 1-48 can be stored. To get the exact name of the **Category**, because you can change it in GP or even add to the 48 existing categories, you have to link GL00100 to another table. OK, I'm done talking geek!

Tables	Filters - GL00100		
GL00100	Show Results:		User Defined:
Add Table Remove	Where PSTNGTYP ▾ Equals ▾		☐
Fields - GL00100	Add Filter		
Search		0	
ACCATNUM		1	
ACCTENTR			
ACCTTYPE			

Versus

Tables	Filters - Jet GL Account		
Jet GL Account	Show Results:		User Defined:
Add Table Remove	Where Posting Type ▾ Equals ▾		☐
Fields - Jet GL Account	Add Filter		
Search		Balance Sheet	
☐ Active		Profit and Loss	
☐ Category Description			
☐ Category Number			

To make the report-writing experience easier for you (and the report consumer), Jet has created some custom views and edited the field names, making them friendlier. This means, in the example earlier, Jet created a view called `Jet GL Account`. This view can be used to access the GL account number, the posting type, the category, and so on. Here's why this is a big deal:

- Getting data from something called `Jet GL Account` type makes more sense than `GL00100`

- The `Category` table is already properly linked so that I get the right category

- The **Posting Type** field is populated with either **Balance Sheet** or **Profit and Loss,** as opposed to 0 or 1

- The **Category** field actually displays the names for the category, even if you change the category names in GP, rather than a number

This is just one example of how Jet Views and Friendly Names are important, not just in Jet for report writing, but in any tool. Jet makes it easy for us, though, by adding the views and giving the fields friendly names. You'll know it is a view created by Jet because they start each view name with the word `Jet`.

> To install Jet Custom Views and Friendly Names, the **GP Update Utility** option must be run. This utility installs when you install Jet and is found through your Windows program manager (or **All apps**).

What is Table Builder?

Before we start with the Jet Table Builder, let's review the definition of an Excel table. A table in Excel is similar to a mini database in Excel. Each row contains one and only one record, and all rows and columns are related to each other and work as one. Using a range of data in a single group (or grid), the data is easier to manage and use in other Excel features such as **PivotTables**. Jet Express for Excel provides us with the ability to create table directly from our GP data.

> GP usually stores open, work, and history data in different tables. This is another great reason to use views. A view can be created to access all these tables so that you can have all corresponding data on the same report without having to link the tables together yourself. If you create an incorrect link, your data will not be correct.

Create a general ledger trial balance

Now, let's do what we came to do here: write a report in Excel. In the next chapter, we'll build some financials statements.

[💡 At this point, you should have installed Jet Express for GP and installed the Jet Views and Friendly Names.]

So, let's use the Table Builder to create a general ledger trial balance to accompany the financial statements. Follow these steps:

1. Open a blank workbook in Excel 2016.

2. Go to **Jet** | **Design Tools** | **Table Builder**. A new workbook will open in Excel, along with the **Table Builder** window. The reason a new workbook opens is to make sure you are starting with a clean slate. The Table Builder will use specific cells in the spreadsheet, and if you have anything in those cells, it would be overwritten:

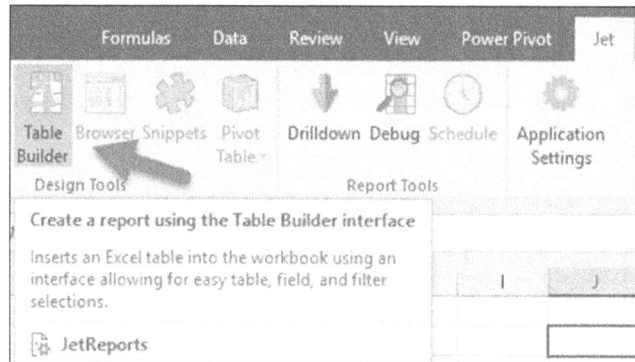

3. In the **Table Builder** window, select **Add Table**. Make sure the option at the bottom is set to **Views** (which is where you can opt to see tables as well.) Double-click on **AccountTransactions** from the drop-down list to open this view in the **Tables** pane:

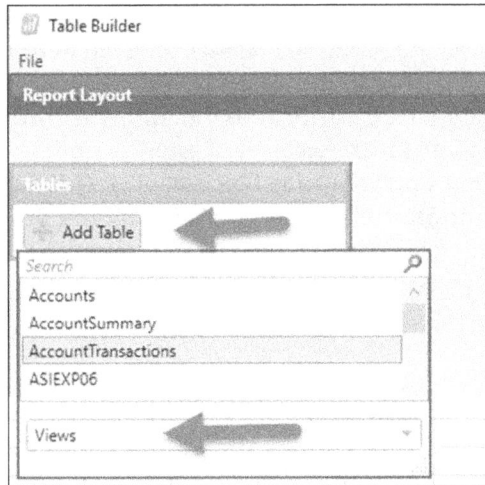

4. All the fields in this view will display. Click on the corresponding checkbox to select the following fields: **Account Number, Account Description from Account Master, Account Category Number, Credit Amount, Debit Amount, Description, Originating Master Name, Journal Entry, Reference, Source Document**, and **TRX Date**:

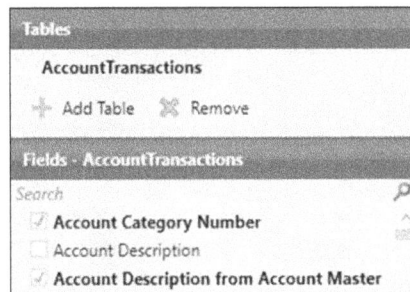

The **Table Builder** window can be enlarged or set to full screen to make working in it easier.

5. The selected fields will appear in the **Report Layout** pane in the order that they were selected. Grab the header for each field to drag and drop (left-click and hold, drag to the position you want the field, and let go of the mouse button) so that they appear in the following order: **Account Number, Account Description from Account Master, Account Category Number, TRX Date, Journal Entry, Source Document, Debit Amount, Credit Amount, Description, Reference,** and **Originating Master Name**. If this data is only going to appear in a pivot table, you can forego this step:

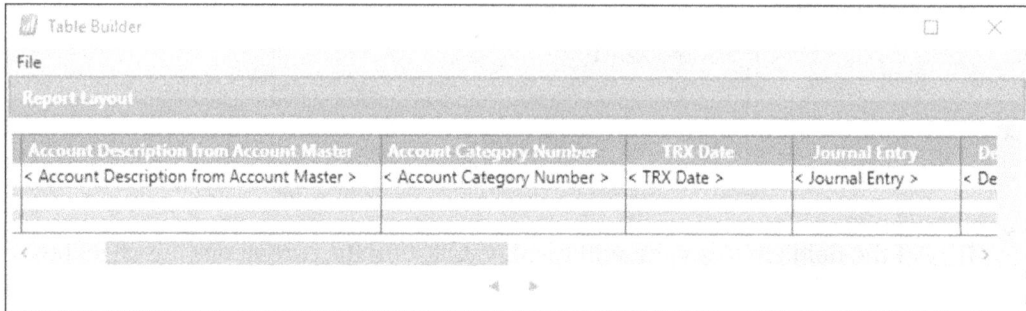

6. Let's change the name of a few of the fields. Double-click on the header and just type in the new name. Change **Account Description from Account Master** to Account Description. Change **Account Category Number** to Category. Change **TRX Date** to Date. Change **Originating Master Name** to Master Name:

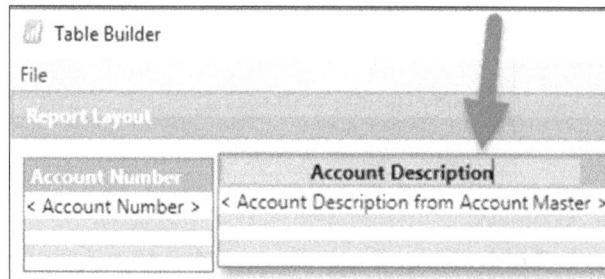

7. Let's exclude voided transactions. Click on the **AccountTransactions** view name in the **Tables** pane, and a new pane will appear on the right-hand side, named **Filters – AccountTransactions**. Click on **+ Add Filter**. Select the field to **Voided**, set the function to **Equals**, and enter **No**:

Tables	Filters - AccountTransactions	
AccountTransactions ←	Show Results:	User Defined:
✛ Add Table ✖ Remove	✖ Where Voided ▼ Equals ▼ No ▼	☐
Fields - AccountTransactions	✛ Add Filter	
Search 🔍		

> It's a good habit to automatically exclude all voided transactions anytime you use transaction data in GP. In the case of GL data, unposted transactions can be voided. Voided transactions will appear with posted data as part of your audit trail.

8. Now, let's create a parameter for the open fiscal year. On the **Filters – AccountTransactions** pane, click on **+ Add Filter**. Set the field to **Open Year** and enter **2017**. Click to select the **User Defined:** box on the right-hand side. This will enable users to enter any open year to be used when refreshing the report:

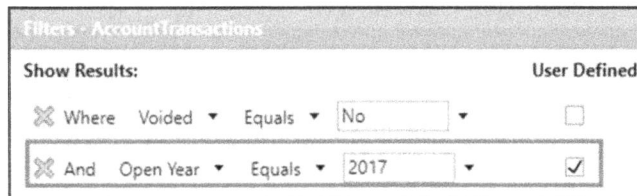

Filters - AccountTransactions	
Show Results:	User Defined:
✖ Where Voided ▼ Equals ▼ No ▼	☐
✖ And Open Year ▼ Equals ▼ 2017 ▼	☑

> We could have used the **TRX Date** field instead of the year. To make a date range, just enter two dots (. .) between the dates. For example, I could have entered 1/1/2017..12/31/2017 for the year 2017. I opted to use the years so that beginning balances would be included in the correct fiscal year.

9. In the event you want to print this report using historical data, add a filter for the **History Year** field as well. However, rather than selecting a year, select the blank spot above the year, rather than leaving the field blank:

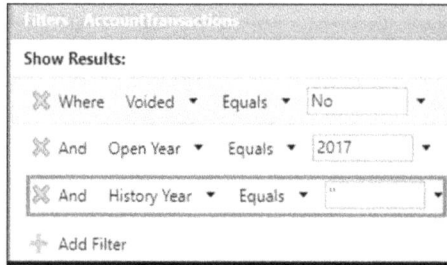

> In GP, a transaction can only exist in either an open year or a history year. When using the report for an open year, we'll use the blank in history year. When using the report for a history year, we'll use the blank in open year.
>
> You might also add some of your account segments in filters, enabling you, for example, to print a trial balance for just a particular department.

10. Click on **OK**. You'll then be prompted with the option to save your work as a Table Builder template. Click on **Yes**.

> It's always a good idea to save this setup as a template. It's a small XML file that will be saved on your PC. This will save you time if you want to alter this table or create a new table using this one as a starting point.

11. The report will now be displayed in Excel in the **Design** mode:

	A	B	C	D	E	F
1	Auto+Hide+Values	Title+Fit		Value	Lookup+Hide	
2						
3			Tables and Fields	Filters		
4			AccountTransactions			
5	Hide		Voided	No		
6	Option		Open Year	2017		
7	Option		History Year	''		
8						
9	Hide			Headers:	Account Number	Account Description
10	Hide			Fields:	Account Number	Account Description from Account Master
11				Table		

12. Go to **Jet | Modes | Refresh** to display the **Report Options** window. You can edit these fields to display the data you desire. If you enter a year in **Open Year** field, enter an asterisk (*) in the **History Year**. If you enter a year in the **History Year** field, enter an asterisk (*) in **Open Year**. Click on **Run** to populate the table with data:

13. The report will now display in Excel. We do not see the void filter because we did not mark the user-defined checkbox when creating filters. Save the file with the name `GLTrialBalance.xlsx`:

To finish the trial balance report, we'll move to pure, native Excel. The data we just brought in from Jet is now stored as an Excel Table.

1. Click anywhere inside the table. In the Excel menu, go to **Insert | Tables | PivotTable**. The **Create PivotTable** window will open. Click on **OK**.

2. A new worksheet will open in this workbook, with the pivot table canvas appearing. I'm renaming this tab `Trial Balance` to make it easier for the user to know which tab to open:

3. In the **PivotTable Field** list on the right-hand side, drag **Account Number,
Account Description, Date, Journal Entry,** and **Reference** (in that order) to
the **Rows** pane. In Excel 2016, the **Date** fields will split up hierarchically into,
potentially, **Years, Quarters, Months,** and **Days**:

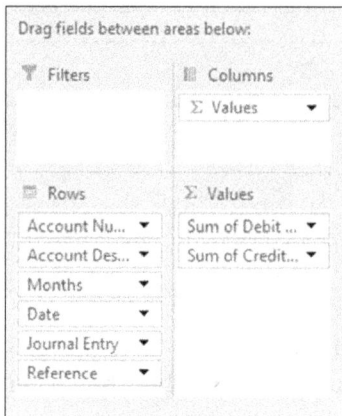

4. In the **PivotTable Field** list on the right-hand side, drag **Debit Amount** and
Credit Amount (in that order) to the **Values** pane.

5. Go to **PivotTable Tools | Design**. Go to **Report Layout | Show in Tabular
Form**. The pivot report now places all row fields in a separate Excel column,
making the report easier to read:

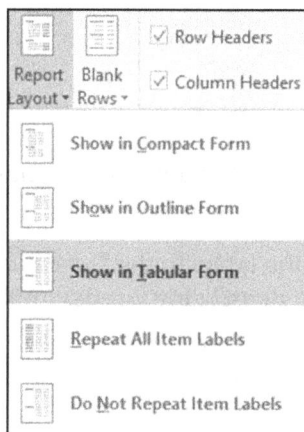

6. Go to **PivotTable Tools** | **Design**. Go to **Subtotals** | **Do Not Show Subtotals**. This will remove all the rows that are subtotals. Using the Excel feature of collapsing will give the effect of **Subtotals**, without them cluttering the detailed (expanded) version:

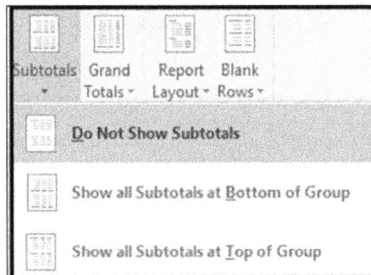

7. Go to **PivotTable Tools** | **Analyze**. Go to **Calculations** | **Fields, Items & Sets** | **Calculated Field**. The **Insert Calculated Field** window will open:

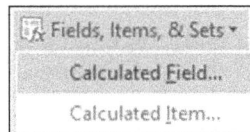

8. Change the **Name** to Net. In the **Formula** field, remove 0 but leave =.

9. In the **Fields:** box, double-click on **Debit Amount**. This will place the **Debit Amount** field in the **Formula** box. Enter minus (-) after **Debit Amount**. Double-click on **Credit Amount** in the **Fields:** box. The formula should now read: = 'Debit Amount' - 'Credit Amount'. Click on **OK**:

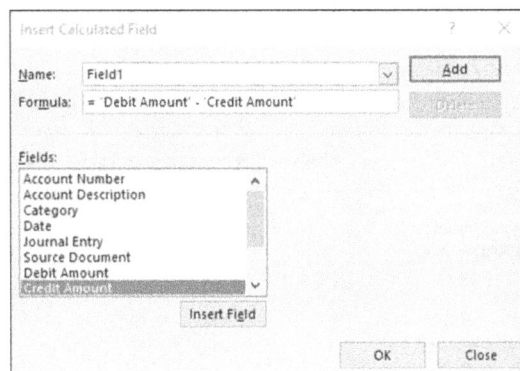

10. Let's format the currency fields in the columns. For all three fields in the **Values** pane in the **PivotTable Fields** list, click on the drop-down arrow and select **Value Field Settings...**:

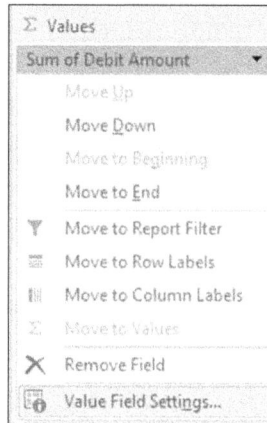

11. The **Value Fields Settings** window will open. Click on **Number Format** in the bottom-left corner and choose **Currency**. Click on **OK** on each window to complete formatting.

You can use some of Excel's simple techniques discussed in the previous chapters to clean this report up a bit. I moved the **Month** field (created by adding the date to the rows) out of the **Rows** pane and created a slicer for them instead:

General Ledger Trial Balance

Months			
Jan	Feb	Mar	Apr
May	Jun	Jul	Aug
Sep	Oct	Nov	Dec
<1/1/2017	>12/2/2017		

Account Number	Account Description	Date	Journal Entry	Reference	Debit	Credit	Sum of Net
000-1110-00	Cash - Payroll				$0.00	$20,632.78	($20,632.78)
000-2150-00	Taxable Benefits Payable				$0.00	$1,428.95	($1,428.95)
000-2161-00	IL State Withholding Payable				$0.00	$710.81	($710.81)
000-2170-00	Federal Withholding Payable				$0.00	$6,165.81	($6,165.81)
000-2200-00	Payroll Deductions Payable				$0.00	$1,914.68	($1,914.68)
000-5100-00	Salaries and Wages				$27,402.56	$0.00	$27,402.56
100-5150-00	Employee Benefits - Administration				$1,428.95	$0.00	$1,428.95
100-5170-00	Payroll Taxes - Administration				$383.16	$0.00	$383.16
200-5170-00	Payroll Taxes - Accounting				$1,638.36	$0.00	$1,638.36
Grand Total					$30,853.03	$30,853.03	$0.00

The goal of this report was to connect to GP and show you how normal Excel tools and formatting can make a master report writer. This report happened to access general ledger transactions, but it could have been inventory items, customers, invoices, bank accounts, or whatever data is stored in your GP database. The possibilities are limited to only what you store in GP and what you need to manage your business better.

Other Jet offerings

Jet Express for GP is not the only tool available for Microsoft Dynamics GP. There are two other tools in the Jet Reports toolbox: **Jet Professional** (formerly Jet Essentials) and **Jet Enterprise**. Depending on your needs, you may find that you need to upgrade to one of these advanced versions. Both these versions offer more advanced report-creation options and mobile/web reporting options. Jet Enterprise takes it another step further with business dashboards, KPIs, and security.

The cost-free Jet Express for GP is the bare bones of each of these offerings, but they have many more features, more than I've just mentioned. This being said, Jet Express is a great place to start. If you need more, you can leverage everything you've learned and built in Jet Express, which means a shorter time to the return on your investment.

Summary

Now that we've built an Excel table, providing us with the detailed information in the GL for a year and/or fiscal period, let's build some financial statements. In the next chapter, we will build a basic balance sheet and a basic profit and loss statement. As with the Table Builder in this chapter, once you know the financial statement (GL function) basics, you can utilize your Excel knowledge to create some serious kick-ass statements.

7
Building Financial Reports in Jet Express for GP

We all know that financial statements are a necessity of running and managing any business or organization where money flows in and/or out. It's required for tax purposes, yes, but looking at your business through pure numbers can help you analyze how your business is changing. Monitoring statements can help you stop a problem before it runs you out of business, it can help you find an opportunity that will allow your business to grow, or it can show you that your business is staying flat or not changing at all, which can be bad or good.

In this chapter, we will build the following core financial statements:

- Balance sheet
- Profit and loss statement

Recap

In the previous chapter, we reviewed why Jet Express for GP is now free and available for all GP users. We also used the Jet Table Builder to create an Excel table to generate the effect of a general ledger trial balance. While the Table Builder is a great tool, it does not provide users with an easy method of getting the data from a table into a format that looks like the traditional balance sheet, or profit and loss statement. The Jet Express for GP GL function makes creating financial statements a snap. The GL function only reads data from the general ledger transactions, so we'll use the GL function to create reports for this chapter.

> Create reports in the order of this chapter. Start with the balance sheet, then the profit and loss and, finally, the additional elements. To maximize your learning experience, we will use different approaches for each topic beginning with the easiest approach.

Building a balance sheet

The first statement we'll build is a simple balance sheet. The balance sheet is critical because it shows us what the business owns, what it owes, and what it is worth. Our final result should look similar to the following screenshot:

Fabrikam, Inc.

Balance Sheet - Compared to Last Year

Year to Date as of:

| Year: | 2017 |
| Period: | 4 |

Assets		This Year	Last Year	Variance
000-1100-00	Cash - Operating Account	$ 163,080.49	$ 359,735.32	$ (196,654.83)
000-1110-00	Cash - Payroll	$ (108,548.93)	$ (97,266.20)	$ (11,282.73)
000-1130-00	Petty Cash	$ -	$ (101,003.03)	$ 101,003.03
000-1200-00	Accounts Receivable	$ 217,591.35	$ 4,444.58	$ 213,146.77
000-1300-01	Inventory - Retail/Parts	$ (52,538.52)	$ (36,562.89)	$ (15,975.63)
000-1300-02	Inventory - Finished Goods	$ 1,942.50	$ (1,102.90)	$ 3,045.40
000-1312-00	Inventory Offset	$ (77,550.00)	$ (284.60)	$ (77,265.40)
000-1360-01	WIP - Material	$ (620.00)	$ -	$ (620.00)
	Total Assets	**$ 143,356.89**	**$ 127,960.28**	**$ 15,396.61**

Liabilities		This Year	Last Year	Variance
000-2100-00	Accounts Payable	$ 429.43	$ 50.25	$ 379.18
000-2111-00	Accrued Purchases	$ 1,103.84	$ 142.30	$ 961.54
000-2120-00	Commissions Payable	$ 14,690.12	$ 10,836.51	$ 3,853.61
000-2150-00	Taxable Benefits Payable	$ 5,725.84	$ 5,754.44	$ (28.60)
000-2161-00	IL State Withholding Payable	$ 4,596.18	$ 3,932.36	$ 663.82
000-2170-00	Federal Withholding Payable	$ 39,476.70	$ 34,222.42	$ 5,254.28
000-2200-00	Payroll Deductions Payable	$ 7,859.43	$ 8,431.08	$ (571.65)
000-2300-00	IL State Sales Tax Payable	$ 18,490.41	$ 5,106.06	$ 13,384.35
000-2310-00	Chicago City Sales Tax Payable	$ 3,081.85	$ 851.06	$ 2,230.79
000-2320-00	GST Collected-Canada	$ 9,514.45	$ 2,680.20	$ 6,834.25
000-2340-00	GST Collected -New Zealand	$ 54.98	$ -	$ 54.98
000-2740-00	Advances from Customers	$ (27,500.00)	$ -	$ (27,500.00)
000-4730-00	Purchase Price Variance - Unrealized	$ 1,189.76	$ 1,496.43	$ (306.67)
	YTD Profit (Loss)	$ 64,643.90	$ 54,457.17	$ 10,186.73
	Total Liabilities	**$ 143,356.89**	**$ 127,960.28**	**$ 15,396.61**

> This is a final reminder that we will use the simplest elements first and adopt some alternate, although still simple, methods to make the reports easier to use and consume as we progress through this chapter.

Let's begin building our balance sheet with some general report information using basic Excel:

1. Open a blank Excel workbook and save it as FinancialStatements.xlsx.

2. In cell D3, enter Fabrikam, Inc. which is the name of our sample company.

3. In cell D4, enter Balance Sheet - Compared to Last Year. This is the name of the report. We will compare our current year to the previous year for a user defined fiscal period.

4. Highlight cells D3 and D4, increase the font size to **16**, and make the text bold. Report headers are usually bigger and bolder than the data in the statement itself.

5. In cell D5, enter Year to Date as of:. This portion of the report header will explain which period the report displays.

6. In cell D6, enter Year:, and in cell D7, enter Period:. We will manually enter the reporting fiscal year and fiscal period as defined in Dynamics GP **Fiscal Periods Setup**.

7. In cell E6, enter 2017, and in cell E7, enter 4. This is the first fiscal period/ year for which we will report.

8. Highlight cells D5, D6, D7, E6, and E7, increase the font size to **12**, and make the text bold. We want this portion of the header to be only slightly bigger than the report body as shown in the following screenshot:

9. In cell D10, enter Assets. This row will define both the report section for Assets and act as our column headers for this section.

10. In cell F10, enter This Year, in cell G10, enter Last Year, and in cell H 10, enter Variance.

11. Highlight Cells D10, E10, F10, G10, and H10. Feel free to format these column/section headers anyway you like. I will use the predefined formats in Excel by going to **Home | Styles | Cell Styles | Accent 5** (under **Themed Cell Styles**.) While I have the cells highlighted, I will also make the font bold, which makes fonts in white easier to read.

12. Precautionary save.

Now, that we have begun the layout of our balance sheet using Excel, let's start adding some Jet functionality. You'll notice that we began adding information several rows down and several columns from the left. Jet uses, at a minimum, the first row and the first column for functions and formatting. I like to highlight the rows and columns Jet uses, so when I am in the **Design** mode, I can easily see what is visible and what is not visible when the finished report (**Report** mode) is displayed.

1. Highlight columns **A** and **B** and highlight (**Home | Font | Fill Color**). Highlight row **1** and highlight (**Home | Font | Fill Color**). As I mentioned earlier, I like to highlight the columns that will be used for Jet functions and hidden so when I am building the design of the report, I know where I can hide cells and where I can make cells visible.

2. Verify Excel is pointing to the sample company data, **Fabrikam, Inc. (Jet | Settings**). In case you are wondering, this is how you will change the company data that is being displayed in the report:

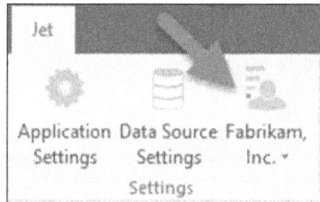

3. Click on cell D11 and select the **GL** function (**Jet | Design Tools | Jfx | GL**). The **Jet Function Wizard** window will open.

4. The first field in the **Jet Function Wizard** window is **Where**. Click on the **Where** field and select **Rows**. We will create a series of rows based on some element we'll define in this wizard.

5. The next field is the **What** field. Click on **What** and select **Accounts**. We will create a row for every account that is an asset, tying **Where** and **What** in this wizard together.

6. Now, we will define the accounts to be displayed. We can open the field for **Account** and highlight the accounts one at a time, or in a range, using the *Shift* key. Instead, let's make this report using the categories defined in Dynamics GP (**Financial | Setup | Category**). Any changes you make to the categories in GP will be reflected here as we are reading data from the database itself.

7. Click on the **Category** field. Select **1-Cash**, scroll down and hold the *Shift* key down, then select **12-Other Assets**. This will select the entire range of assets. Click **Insert** and then click outside the dropdown list:

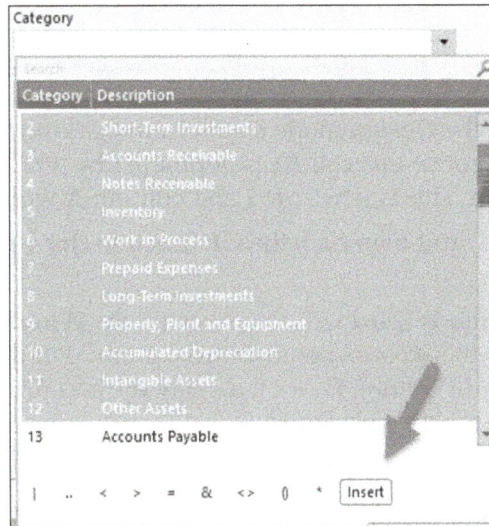

You'll notice that the two ends of the range are separated by two dots (..). Anytime you need to enter a range in Jet, this is how you will separate the beginning and ending of a range.

8. Click **OK** to close the **Jet Function Wizard** window. You'll see the first (and only the first) account that meets the criteria we specified in cell D11.

9. Let's check to make sure our function is working by running the report. Click on **Refresh** (**Jet | Modes | Refresh**). The **Jet Express** window will open, showing the progress while connecting to the GP data and populating the Excel workbook. You should now see a list of accounts in column **D**. Row **1** and column **A** should be hidden, but you should see the highlighted column **B**:

7	Period:	4
8		
9		
10	Assets	
11	000-1100-00	
12	000-1101-00	
13	000-1102-00	

10. Let's go back to the **Design** mode to continue working (**Jet | Modes | Design**). You'll notice that cell A1 is populated by Jet. The word **Hide** exists in the expression. This is why row **1** and column **A** were hidden.

11. Click on cell E11, and then click the **GL** function (**Jet | Design Toll | Jfx | GL**).

12. In the **Jet Function Wizard** window, click on the **Where** field and select **Cell**. We will display the account name in this column. For every row that has an account number in column **D**, we'll display the account name in the cell next to the account number (column **E**).

13. In the **What** field, select **AccountName**.

14. In the **Account** field, click once to place your cursor in the field, then click on cell D11. D11 is where we placed the GL function that displays the account number. Now this GL function is set to display the name of the account for the account number in the column to the left. You will now see the first account number display.

15. Click **OK**.

16. Before we run the report again, let's set the report to automatically resize the columns. In row **1**, place the word Fit in columns **D, E, F, G,** and **H**:

D	E	F	G	H	
Fit	Fit	Fit	Fit	Fit	
Fabrikam, Inc.					
Balance Sheet - Compared to Last Year					
Year to Date as of:					
Year:	2017				
Period:	4				
Assets		This Year	Last Year	Variance	
000-1100-1 Cash - Operating Account					

17. Let's check to make sure our function is working by running the report. Click on **Refresh** (**Jet** | **Modes** | **Refresh**). Now, you should see the columns resize with detail of the account numbers and names. Let's go back to the **Design** mode to continue working (**Jet** | **Modes** | **Design**).

18. Precautionary save.

We've now extracted the account numbers and names, and we will need to put the balance information on the report. For the most part, adding account balances is the same as adding the account numbers; however, there is one major difference. We need to limit the amounts to the reporting period, so we'll need to reference a starting period and an ending period.

> When referencing the starting period and ending period, we can use a full date format YYYY/M/D or M/D/YYYY (D/M/YYYY based on regional settings). The formatting option that is the fastest is YYYY/PPP (a 4 digit year, a slash (/), and a 1-3 digit period number.) We'll be using this fastest method throughout the chapter.

You may opt to leave either the starting period or ending period blank, but if you do, you may not receive the desired data. The following is a chart that will explain what your results will be based on, your decision to populate or leave blank the starting period and ending period fields:

	End Date	No End Date
Start Date	Net change in period range	Net change from start date to current date
No Start Date	Balance on end date	Current balance

> While using GP, keep in mind if you include multiple years; balance sheet accounts may appear doubled because the totals will include the **Balance Brought Forward** (**BBF**). Due to this BBF, I encourage you to always use a starting and ending date. Also note that this BBF is period 0, so when using balance sheet accounts, always start with period 0.

Let's add the amount columns now:

1. As we will compare this year to the previous year, we will need to define the previous year. Click on cell A5 and enter `Last Year`. When I use some of the hidden space for formulas and functions, I like to have a label that explains why I am using it. This is the label for our formula to define the previous year.

2. Click on cell A6 and enter the formula, `=E6-1`. This will subtract a year from our reporting year. As we entered `2017` as our reporting year in cell E6, we will see `2016` displayed in cell A6 as a result of our formula.

3. Click on cell F11 and select the **GL** function (**Jet | Design Tools | Jfx | GL**).

4. In the **Jet Function Wizard** window, click on the **Where** field and select **Cell**.

5. In the **What** field, select **Balance**.

6. In the **Account** field, click once to place your cursor in the field and then click on cell D11. D11 is where we placed the GL function that displays the account number.

7. Click on the **Start Period** field. We'll want our starting period to be period `0` for the year 2017. We can hardcode it as `"2017/0"`, but who wants to edit this and every amount function every time we change our reporting period? Let's use a formula instead. Click on cell E6, and it will populate in the **Start Period** field. We'll need to make this reference to cell E6 absolute, otherwise row **12** will use E7, row **13** will use row E8, and so on. We want every row to use cell E6. We can either press the *F4* key or edit the field so the dollar sign (**$**) is before the **E** and the **6**. The dollar sign before the **E** means always column E. The dollar sign before the **6** means always row **6**.

8. Next, enter `&` to concatenate (add together text like a sentence) the cell reference to `"/0"`. The double quotes indicate that the slash and the zero are to be treated like text. Tab off the field, and it should look like the following: `$E$6&"/0"`. If you like, you can add spaces before and after `&` to make it easier to read. To the right of the field, you can see the **Value** as **"2017/0"**. It's a good habit to make sure this displays as you intend while you are editing the function.

9. Click on the **End Period** field and repeat the preceding step, but leave off the period `0`. Your formula should like `$E$6 & "/"`. You can copy, paste, and edit if you like (I did). At the end of the formula, add another `&` and then select field E7, which is where we entered the reporting period. Make the E7 cell absolute as well. Your finished formula should look like `$E$6 & "/" & $E$7`.

You'll notice some additional fields that we can populate using the **Jet Function Wizard** window when **Cell** is selected. We can opt to **Include Unposted** transactions in the general ledger by selecting **True**; if you select **False** or leave it blank, Jet assumes that you do not want unposted transactions included.

There is a **Company** field. You can create a multi-company statement, putting each company in a separate column, by selecting the company you want in this column and repeating column setup for other companies.

The **Data Source** field does not apply to the free Jet Express for GP.

10. Click **OK**.

11. Copy the formula we did for This Year in F11 to cell G11, which is for Last Year. We'll just edit the GL Function.

12. Click on cell G11 and select the **GL** function (**Jet | Design Tools | Jfx | GL**).

13. The **Jet Function Wizard** window will open and have the fields completed based on the This Year column. We will only need to edit the **Start Period** and **End Period** fields. Rather than reference cell E6, we want to reference cell A6, which is where we created the formula to define Last Year. I manually edited the formulas, just by changing the E to an A. Starting to see the benefits of building reports in Excel now, right?

14. Click **OK**.

15. Click on Cell H11. Add a formula =F11-G11 to find the variance between this year and last year.

16. Highlight columns **F, G**, and **H** and format as **Currency**. After highlighting, I right clicked and selected **$**.

17. Let's check to make sure our function is working by running the report. Click on **Refresh** (**Jet** | **Modes** | **Refresh**). Now, we will see numbers for this year, last year, and the variance between the two. Let's go back to the **Design** mode to continue working (**Jet** | **Modes** | **Design**).

18. Precautionary save.

Now that we have the details of the asset accounts displaying, let's add a total. There are also a lot of accounts that have zero balances for both this year and last year; we do not need to see those, so let's add a formula to hide those rows.

1. Click on cell E13 and enter Total Assets. This is the row where we will place the totals. I'm sure you are wondering why we are leaving a blank row. We will use the Excel SUM function to sum up all the asset accounts. If we did not leave a blank row, the formula would read SUM from cell F11 to F11. If that were the formula, when we run (**Refresh**) the report, the total line would not include any row but 11. By adding a blank row, we are saying add all account balances up to and including the blank row.

2. Click on cell F13. Add the SUM formula, including rows **11** and **12** (**Home** | **Editing** | **AutoSum**). The formula will look as follows:

   =SUM(F11:F12).

3. Copy the formula in cell F13 to cell G13.

4. Copy the formula in cell H11 to cell H13. For variances, I find better consistency (due to rounding) when using the variance formula for the totals, rather than totally the rows.

5. Highlight cells E13, F13, G13, and H13. Feel free to format these totals anyway you like. I will use the predefined formats in Excel by navigating to **Home** | **Styles** | **Cell Styles** | **20% - Accent 5** (under **Themed Cell Styles**). While I have the cells highlighted, I will also make the font bold, which makes it easier to read.

6. Precautionary save.

7. Click on cell B1 and enter `Hide+?`; it will allow us to use this column to decide which rows we should hide and which we should not. This function will also hide column **B**.

In my experience, this feature only works in column **B**.

8. Click on cell B11, and we'll enter a formula that evaluates the cells for this year and last year to see if they both are zero. On the Excel menu, go to **Formulas**. From the **Function Library** group, select **Logical** and then **IF**. The **Function Arguments** window will open.

9. Click on the **Logical_Test** field to put your cursor there and then select cell F11. We'll start by checking the current year balance. Back in the **Logical_Test** field, enter `=0` after the cell reference. Your formula should look like `F11=0`. You'll also notice that to the right, you'll see the word **FALSE** indicating that cell F11 has a balance, and it is not zero.

10. Click on the **Value_if_true** field and enter the word `Hide`.

11. Click on the **Value_if_false** field and enter the word `Show`:

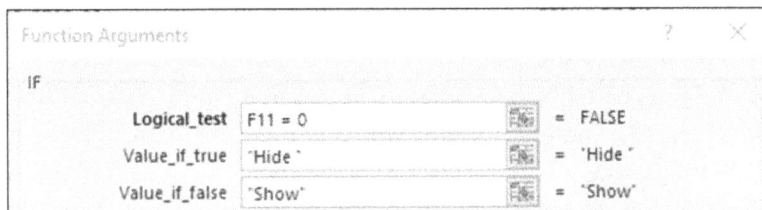

Function Arguments		?	×
IF			
Logical_test	F11 = 0	=	FALSE
Value_if_true	"Hide "	=	"Hide "
Value_if_false	"Show"	=	"Show"

12. Click **OK**. We have now evaluated the current year amount; now, we need to evaluate the previous year's amount.

13. With your cursor still on cell B11, you should see the formula you just created using the **Function Arguments** window. Copy the entire formula (`=IF(F11 = 0,"Hide ","Show")`) to your clipboard (*CTRL + C*).

14. With your cursor still on cell B11, click on the function icon to the left of the address bar to reopen the **Function Arguments** window:

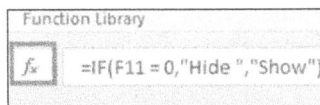

Function Library
f_x =IF(F11 = 0,"Hide ","Show")

15. In the **Function Arguments** window, paste the formula you just created in the **Value_if_true** field. We are nesting one formula inside the other. Delete the equal (=) sign at the beginning of the formula you just pasted in.

16. Change the **Logical_test** field to G11=0. The formula is now performing the following:

17. Is last year zero? If not, show the row.

18. Is last year zero? If yes:

    ° Is this year zero? If not, show the row.

    ° Is this year zero? If yes, hide the row:

Function Arguments		?	✕
IF			
Logical_test	G11 = 0	=	TRUE
Value_if_true	IF(F11 = 0,"Hide ","Show")	=	"Show"
Value_if_false	"Show"	=	"Show"

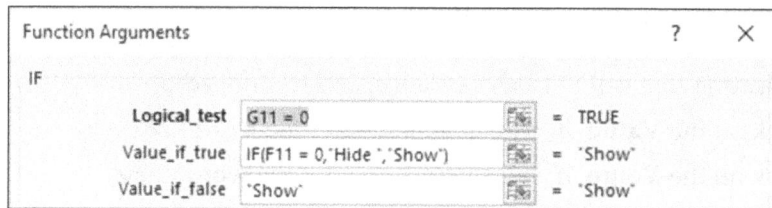

19. Click **OK**. The formula now looks like the following: =IF(G11 = 0,IF(F11 = 0,"Hide ","Show"),"Show").

20. Click on cell B12 and enter **Hide**. This will hide the blank row we created to assist in totals.

21. Let's check to make sure our function is working by running the report. Click on **Refresh (Jet | Modes | Refresh)**. Now, all zero amount rows are hidden and all the highlighted rows and columns are hidden. We also have a formatted total row. Let's go back to the **Design** mode to continue working **(Jet | Modes | Design)**.

22. Precautionary save.

Now, we are ready to add our liabilities and equities. Due to the nature of Excel's copy and paste, we can make fairly quick work of this.

1. Highlight rows **10** through **13**, right click and choose to **Copy**.

2. Click on row **15** and choose **Paste**. We have now duplicated the Assets section.

3. Click on cell D15 and change the word Assets to Liabilities and Equity.

4. Click on cell E18 and change the word `Total Assets` to `Total Liabilities and Equity`.

5. Click on cell D16 and select the **GL** function (**Jet | Design Tools | Jfx | GL**).

6. Erase `"1..12"` on the **Category** field. Click on the **Category** dropdown list and select **13-Accounts Payable** through **30-Preferred Dividends**, just like we did for the `Assets` earlier. Click on **Insert** and click elsewhere to close the dropdown list. The field now has the value `"13..30"`.

7. Click **OK**.

Excel reads the numbers in GP as debit balances are positive and credit balances are negatives. Whenever you have an account like liabilities and equities, they should have a credit balance; the sign needs to be reversed.

---

8. Click on cell F16. In the address bar, the GL function appears. Put a minus sign (-) between the equals (=) and the `GL`. It should now look like the following: `=-GL("Cell","Balance",D16,$E$6 & "/0",$E$6 & "/" & $E$7)`.

9. Click on cell G16. In the address bar, the GL function appears. Put a minus sign (-) between the equals (=) and `GL`. It should now look like the following: `=-GL("Cell","Balance",E16,$A$6&"/0",$A$6&"/"&$E$7)`.

10. Now, we will need to add a line for the net profit and loss amount. Insert a blank row between rows **18** and **19**.

11. Click on cell E19 and enter `Year to Date Profit (Loss)`.

12. Copy cell F16 to F19.

13. Copy cell G16 to G19.

14. Copy cell H16 to H19.

15. Click on cell F19 and select the **GL** function (**Jet | Design Tools | Jfx | GL**).

16. Remove the value (`D17`) from the **Account** field so it is blank. We do not want to reference a single account, but all profit and loss accounts.

17. In the **Category** field, add `31..47` (don't forget, it is two dots or periods to make the range). The profit and loss accounts begin with category `31` and run through `47`. You can either enter the range or select it from the dropdown list:

> Unit accounts use category `48`. If you've added any categories, they will begin with `49` and continue from there; so, be careful when selecting categories for your live company.

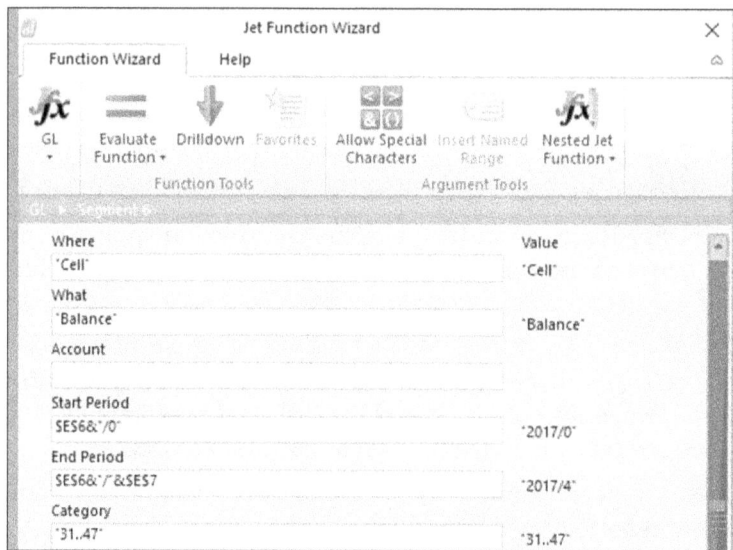

	Jet Function Wizard	×
Function Wizard	Help	⌃

fx GL ▾   Evaluate Function ▾   Drilldown   Favorites   Allow Special Characters   Insert Named Range   *fx* Nested Jet Function ▾

Function Tools   Argument Tools

GL ▸ Segment 6

Where	Value
`Cell`	`Cell`
What	
`Balance`	`Balance`
Account	
Start Period	
`SES6&`/0``	`2017/0`
End Period	
`SES6&`/`&SES7`	`2017/4`
Category	
`31..47`	`31..47`

18. Click on cell G19 and repeat the previous step for the `Last Year` column.

19. Edit cells F20 and G20 so the sum includes the new row **19**. The new formulas should look as follows:`=SUM(F17:F19)` and `=SUM(G17:G19)`

20. Let's check to make sure our function is working by running the report. Click on **Refresh (Jet | Modes | Refresh)**.

21. Precautionary save.

In theory, the balance sheet is complete. However, I like to add the three following additional elements:

1. Right click on the **Sheet1** tab and rename it to `Balance Sheet`.

2. When creating a report that has an internal balancing (for example, *Assets = Liabilities and Equity*), I like to add a row that stands out if the report doesn't balance. Let's do this now.

3. Let's go back to the **Design** mode to continue working (**Jet | Modes | Design**).

4. Click on cell E24 and enter Out of Balance. Format the font to be large and bright red.

5. Click on cell F24 and create a formula that takes assets and subtracts liabilities and equities, for example, =F13-F20.

6. Copy cell F24 to G24.

7. Copy cell B17 to B24. Now, if you have an imbalance, you'll see a bright red "**Out of Balance**" at the bottom.

8. Finally, we'll remove the gridlines. In Excel, click on the **View** tab, then unmark **Gridlines** (**View | Show | Gridlines**).

9. Let's check to make sure our changes are working by running the report. Click on **Refresh** (**Jet | Modes | Refresh**).

10. Click on **Save**; our balance sheet is complete. Along the way, you learned a lot about the Jet GL function:

Fabrikam, Inc.

Balance Sheet - Compared to Last Year

Year to Date as of:

Year:		2017
Period:		4

Assets		This Year	Last Year	Variance
000-1100-00	Cash - Operating Account	$ 163,080.49	$ 359,735.32	$ (196,654.83)
000-1110-00	Cash - Payroll	$ (108,548.93)	$ (97,266.20)	$ (11,282.73)
000-1130-00	Petty Cash	$ -	$ (101,003.03)	$ 101,003.03
000-1200-00	Accounts Receivable	$ 217,591.35	$ 4,444.58	$ 213,146.77
000-1300-01	Inventory - Retail/Parts	$ (52,538.52)	$ (36,562.89)	$ (15,975.63)
000-1300-02	Inventory - Finished Goods	$ 1,942.50	$ (1,102.90)	$ 3,045.40
000-1312-00	Inventory Offset	$ (77,550.00)	$ (284.60)	$ (77,265.40)
000-1360-01	WIP - Material	$ (620.00)	$ -	$ (620.00)
	Total Assets	**$ 143,356.89**	**$ 127,960.28**	**$ 15,396.61**

Liabilities		This Year	Last Year	Variance
000-2100-00	Accounts Payable	$ 429.43	$ 50.25	$ 379.18
000-2111-00	Accrued Purchases	$ 1,103.84	$ 142.30	$ 961.54
000-2120-00	Commissions Payable	$ 14,690.12	$ 10,836.51	$ 3,853.61
000-2150-00	Taxable Benefits Payable	$ 5,725.84	$ 5,754.44	$ (28.60)
000-2161-00	IL State Withholding Payable	$ 4,596.18	$ 3,932.36	$ 663.82
000-2170-00	Federal Withholding Payable	$ 39,476.70	$ 34,222.42	$ 5,254.28
000-2200-00	Payroll Deductions Payable	$ 7,859.43	$ 8,431.08	$ (571.65)
000-2300-00	IL State Sales Tax Payable	$ 18,490.41	$ 5,106.06	$ 13,384.35
000-2310-00	Chicago City Sales Tax Payable	$ 3,081.85	$ 851.06	$ 2,230.79
000-2320-00	GST Collected-Canada	$ 9,514.45	$ 2,680.20	$ 6,834.25
000-2340-00	GST Collected -New Zealand	$ 54.98	$ -	$ 54.98
000-2740-00	Advances from Customers	$ (27,500.00)	$ -	$ (27,500.00)
000-4730-00	Purchase Price Variance - Unrealized	$ 1,189.76	$ 1,496.43	$ (306.67)
	YTD Profit (Loss)	$ 64,643.90	$ 54,457.17	$ 10,186.73
	Total Liabilities	**$ 143,356.89**	**$ 127,960.28**	**$ 15,396.61**

Building a profit and loss statement

The simple balance sheet we created has a line for net profit and loss, so now we need a statement that breaks out how this number was determined. As we build a simple profit and loss statement, we'll build on what you've learned building the balance sheet. We'll take a different approach to selecting accounts and period ranges:

Profit and Loss
Period Ending: April 30 2017

B. I. BELINDA

Sales		This Year	Budget	Variance
000-4100-00	Sales	$ 12,159.46	$ -	$ 12,159.46
000-4110-01	US Sales - Retail/Parts	$ 7,037.95	$ -	$ 7,037.95
000-4110-02	US Sales - Finished Goods	$472,876.05	$ -	$472,876.05
000-4140-00	US Sales - Repair Charges	$ 419.40	$ -	$ 419.40
	Total Sales	$492,492.86	$ -	$492,492.86

Cost of Goods Sold		This Year	Budget	Variance
000-4510-01	Cost of Goods Sold - Retail/Parts	$244,524.43	$ -	$244,524.43
000-4600-00	Purchases Discounts Taken	$ (115.44)	$ -	$ (115.44)
000-4730-00	Purchase Price Variance - Unrealized	$ (1,189.76)	$ -	$ (1,189.76)
	Total Cost of Goods Sold	$243,219.23	$ -	$243,219.23
	Gross Profit	$249,273.63	$ -	$249,273.63

Expenses		This Year	Budget	Variance
000-5100-00	Salaries and Wages	$149,354.72	$ -	$149,354.72
100-5150-00	Employee Benefits - Administration	$ 5,725.84	$ -	$ 5,725.84
100-5170-00	Payroll Taxes - Administration	$ 2,108.94	$ -	$ 2,108.94
200-5170-00	Payroll Taxes - Accounting	$ 9,017.58	$ -	$ 9,017.58
300-5130-00	Commissions - Sales	$ 14,774.94	$ -	$ 14,774.94
500-6150-00	Supplies-Allocated - Consulting/Training	$ 15.00	$ -	$ 15.00
	Total Expenses	$180,997.02	$ -	$180,997.02

Other Income & (Expenses)		This Year	Budget	Variance
000-7402-00	Rounding Difference - Australia	$ 0.01	$ -	$ 0.01
	Other Income & (Expenses)	$ 0.01	$ -	$ 0.01
	Net Profit	$ 68,276.62	$ -	$ 68,276.62

Do not make yourself crazy, like I did when I was building these reports the first time. When comparing my balance sheet to my profit and loss statement, I was off. After a while, I noticed there was a **Profit and Loss** account that had a **Balance Sheet** category. As my balance sheet was based on categories, and my profit and loss statement was built on accounts, the account was on both reports. Learn from my frustration.

Let's begin building a statement that should look like the above screenshot when we are finished:

1. Open the Excel report we used for the balance sheet, which is `FinancialStatements.xlsx`.

2. Create a new tab and rename it as `Profit and Loss`.

3. Click on cell D4 and enter `Profit and Loss`.

4. Click on cell A3 and enter `Reporting Date`.

5. Click on cell A4 and enter `4/30/2017`. This is where we will put the reporting date that we want to use for this report.

6. Click on cell D5. We will enter a header line that references the report date. When we created the balance sheet, the reporting year and month appeared disconnected from their labels. By creating a field that strings together text and a date, we can make a single field that displays the label and the date.

7. From the Excel menu, select **Formulas** and then **CONCAT** from the **Text** formulas (**Formulas | Function Library | Text | CONCAT**). The **Functions Arguments** window will open.

8. On the **Text1** field, enter `For the Period Ending:` (make sure there are two spaces after the semicolon). Press the *Tab* key.

9. On the **Text2** field, enter `TEXT(A4, "MMMM dd YYYY")`. This is a formula that converts the date entered in cell A4 (the reporting date) to text so that we can see the month, the day, and the year. Press the *Tab* key:

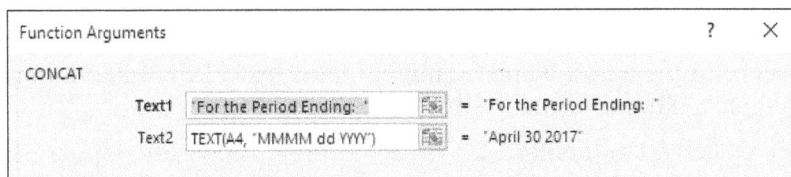

Function Arguments		?	✕
CONCAT			
Text1	`For the Period Ending: `	=	"For the Period Ending: "
Text2	`TEXT(A4, "MMMM dd YYYY")`	=	"April 30 2017"

10. Click **OK**.

11. Select cells D4 through H4, right click, and choose **Format Cells**.

12. Click on the **Alignment** tab in the **Format Cells** window.

13. Change **Horizontal Text Alignment** to **Center Across Selection**:

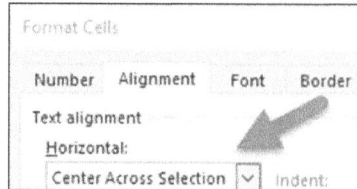

14. Click **OK**.

15. Select cells D5 through H5, right click, and choose **Format Cells**.

16. Click on the **Alignment** tab in the **Format Cells** window.

17. Change **Horizontal Text Alignment** to **Center Across Selection**.

18. Click **OK**.

19. Select cells D4 and D5, increase the font to **16**, and make the font bold. These two fields are the header for our report.

20. Click on cell A5 and enter `Year`.

21. Click on cell A6 and enter the following formula to display the reporting year: `=YEAR($A$4)`

22. Click on cell A7 and enter `Period`.

23. Click on cell A8 and enter the following formula to display the reporting period:

    `=Month($A$4)`

24. Select columns **A** and **B** and highlight them. Select Row **1** and highlight it. Navigate to **Home | Font | Fill Color**.

25. Click on cell A1 and enter `Auto+Hide+Values`. As we are populating information in column **A** before we start using Jet, Jet will insert a column once we use a function, creating a new column **A**, and this will prevent a new column from being inserted.

26. Click on cell B1 and enter `Hide+?`:

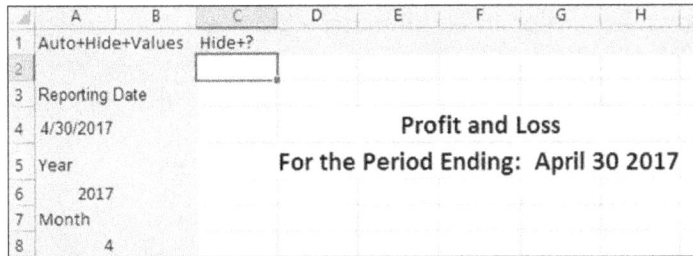

	A	B	C	D	E	F	G	H
1	Auto+Hide+Values	Hide+?						
2								
3	Reporting Date							
4	4/30/2017					Profit and Loss		
5	Year				For the Period Ending: April 30 2017			
6	2017							
7	Month							
8	4							

27. Precautionary save.

We are now ready to begin making sections and populating these sections with data from GP.

1. Click on cell D9 and enter `Sales`.

2. Click on cell F9 and enter `This Year`.

3. Click on cell G9 and enter `Budget`.

4. Click on cell H9 and enter `Variance`.

5. Select cells D9 through H9 and format. I use Excel **Cell Styles**. This is the same process we used for the balance sheet. Navigate to **Home | Styles | Cell Styles | Accent 5**.

6. Rather than using account categories, we'll build this financial statement using ranges of the main account segment, which is segment 2 in the sample company. Click on cell A10 and enter `4000..4500`. This represents the entire range of sales accounts.

7. Click on cell D10 and select the **GL** function (**Jet | Design Tools | Jfx | GL**).

8. In the **Jet Function Wizard** window, select **Rows** for the **Where** field and **Accounts** for the **What** field, just as we did for the balance sheet. Leave the **Account** field blank.

9. We want to make sure we exclude Unit Accounts from this range. The easiest method to do this is to select all the categories in the **Category** field drop-down list except **48-NonFinancialAccounts** or you can enter `1..47` in the **Category** field.

10. Click on the **Segment 2** field, the point to cell A10 that references the sales accounts. Be sure to make it absolute: `$A$10`:

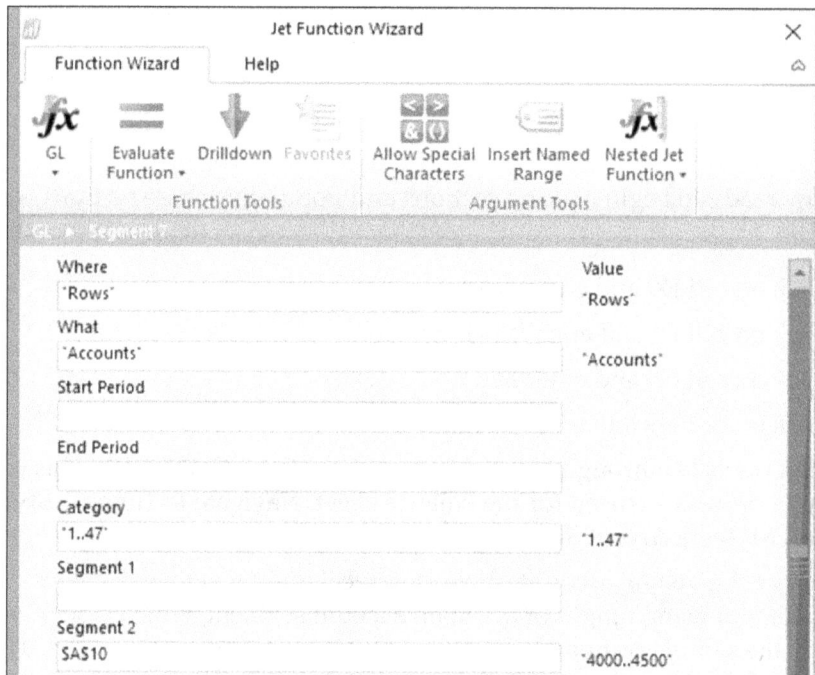

11. Click **OK**.

12. Click on cell E10 and select the **GL** function (**Jet | Design Tools | Jfx | GL**).

13. In the **Jet Function Wizard** window, select **Cell** in the **Where** field, **AccountName** in the **What** field, and reference cell D10 in the **Account** field. As the full account displays in column **D**, we'll reference the full account name and not the range of **Segment 2** account numbers:

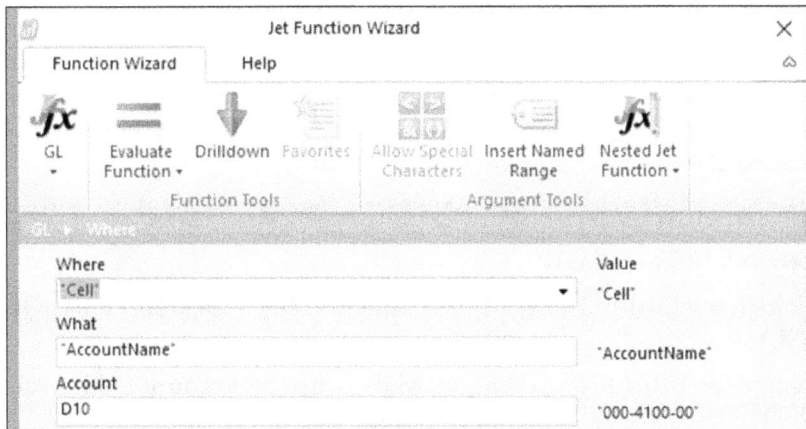

14. Click **OK**.

15. Click on cell F10 and select the **GL** function (**Jet | Design Tools | Jfx | GL**).

16. In the **Jet Function Wizard** window select **Cell** in the **Where** field, **Balance** in the **What** field, and reference cell D10 in the **Account** field. As the full account displays in column **D**, we'll reference the full account name and not the range of **Segment 2** account numbers.

17. We'll populate the start and end periods as we did for the balance sheet referencing the year in cell A6 and the month in cell A8. **Start Period** will be $A$6&"/0" and the **End Period** will be $A$6&"/"&$A$8:

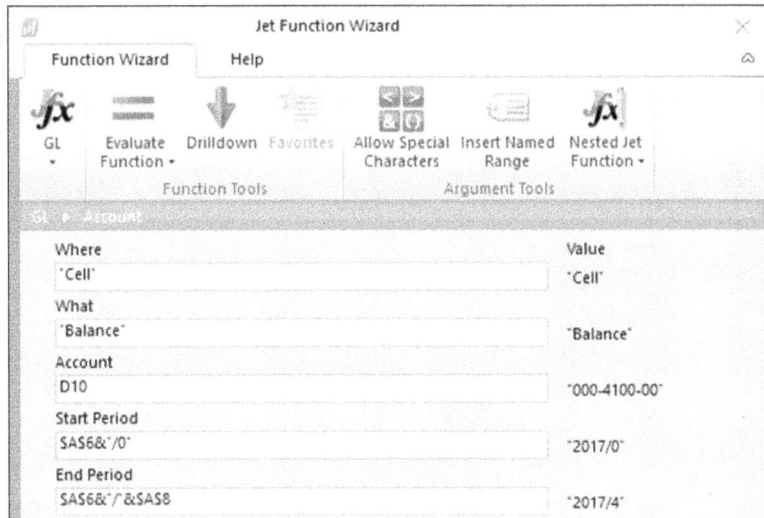

18. Click **OK**.

19. Click on cell F10 and enter a minus (-) between the equals (=) and the GL function to reverse the sign. Remember sales accounts should have a credit balance, and we do not want the credit balance showing as a negative. The formula should look as follows:

```
=-GL("Cell","Balance",D10,$A$6&"/0",$A$6&"/"&$A$8)
```

20. Copy cell F10 to cell G10.

21. Click on cell G10 and select the **GL** function (**Jet | Design Tools | Jfx | GL**).

22. Change the **What** field to **Budget**. Make sure the **Account** field is referencing cell D10, copying the field might change this cell to E10.

> You may want to make the column absolute by putting the dollar ($) in front of the column when referencing, for example, cell D10 will become $D10. This will always look at column **D**, but the row will vary.

23. In the **Budget** field, select **Budget 4**. The budgets you see in the drop-down list are the budgets that are entered in GP:

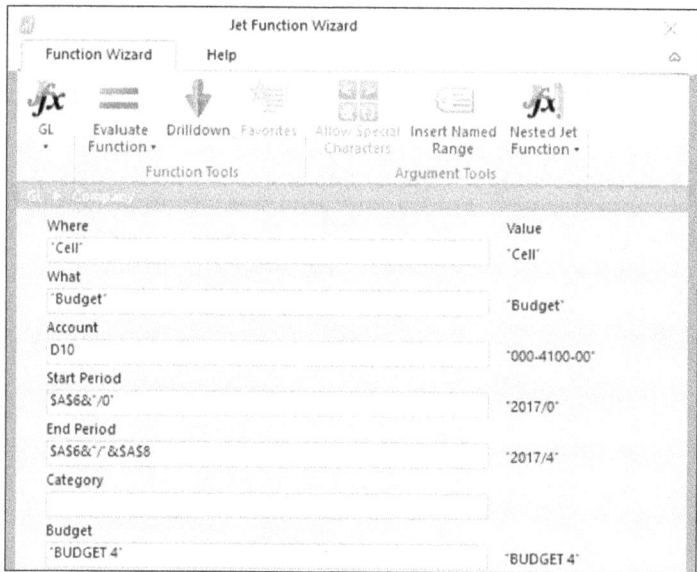

24. Click **OK**.

25. Click on cell G10 and enter a minus (-) between the equals (=) and the GL function to reverse the sign. Remember sales accounts should have a credit balance, and we do not want the credit balance showing as a negative. The formula should look as follows:

```
=-GL("Cell","Budget",D10,$A$6&"/0",$A$6&"/"&$A$8,,,,,,,,,,,,"BUDG
ET 4")
```

26. Click on cell H10 and enter the formula to take the actual minus budget, `=F10-G10`.

27. Click on cell E12 and enter **Total Sales**.

28. Click on cell F12 and enter a sum formula `=SUM(F10:F11)`, adding cells F10 through F11.

29. Copy cell F12 to G12.

30. Copy cell H10 to H12

31. Format cells E12 through H12; I use **20% - Accent5**.

32. Let's check to make sure our function is working by running the report. Click on **Refresh (Jet | Modes | Refresh)**.

33. Precautionary save.

While looking at the report, I see we need to hide the zero columns and resize the columns.

1. Let's go back to the **Design** mode to continue working (**Jet | Modes | Design**).

2. Enter the word `Fit` in cells D1 through H1; it will auto-resize the columns. As we centered the headers, the resizing will occur for the data in the column, not the data, in cells D4 and D5.

3. Let's enter the column to evaluate the values in the **This Year** column and the budget column. If both of these are zero, the row will hide. The formula I used is as follows:

```
=IF(G10 = 0,IF(F10 = 0,"Hide","Show"),"Show")
```

> To avoid repeating text as much as possible, I am just showing the formula in some cases, if and only if, we covered the same topic while building the balance sheet.

4. Click on cell **B11** and enter `Hide` to avoid showing the blank row.

5. Highlight columns **F**, **G**, and **H** and format to **Currency** or **Number**.

6. Let's check to make sure our formatting is working by running the report. Click on **Refresh (Jet | Modes | Refresh)**.

7. Precautionary save.

Let's add the next section of our report—the `Cost of Goods Sold` section.

1. Highlight rows **9** through **12** and choose to copy. Paste on row **14**. The entire sales section is duplicated.

2. Click on cell **D14** and change the section title to `Cost of Goods Sold`.

3. Click on cell **E17** and change the total line to `Total Cost of Goods Sold`.

4. Click on cell **D15** and select the **GL** function (**Jet | Design Tools | Jfx | GL**).

5. In the **Segment 2** field, change the value to look at the absolute value of cell A15: `$A$15`.

6. Click on cell **A15** and change the range to `4501..4999`. Now this report includes all posting accounts where the second segment begins with a `4`.

7. Click on cell **F15** and remove the minus sign between the equal and the GL function. Cost of goods sold should have a debit balance, so we want to ensure that the debit numbers are shown as positive. As we copied it from sales, the minus sign made debits that are shown as negative.

8. Click on cell **H15** and change the formula (`=G15-F15`) to budget minus actual.

> When comparing actual numbers to historical or budget numbers, the variance can change depending on whether you are looking at revenue or expenses. This is called **favorable versus unfavorable**. For example, if your actual sales is less than budget, your variance should be negative because you haven't met budget yet. On the other hand, if your expenses are more than your budget, this should also be negative because you spent more than your budget. In Excel, it's just a matter of changing the formula.

9. Click on **H17** and change the formula (`=G17-F17`) for the total line as well. If you copy, you may need to reformat that cell.

10. Click on cell **E19** and enter `Gross Profit (Loss)`.

11. Click on cell **F19** and enter a formula to take sales from this year and subtract cost of goods sold. `=F12-F17`.

12. Copy cell F19 to G19.

13. Click on cell H19 and enter a formula (`=F19-G19`) for the variance, actual minus budget (if we have more gross profit than budget, that's a positive!).

14. Format cells E19 through H19; I use **40% - Accent5**.

15. Let's check to make sure our formatting and formulas are working by running the report. Click on **Refresh (Jet | Modes | Refresh)**.

16. Precautionary save.

Let's add the final section to display the Expenses.

1. Let's go back to the **Design** mode to continue working **(Jet | Modes | Design)**.

> Quick note on the different report modes: Design is where you edit and create reports, Refresh will go to GP and get the latest data, load the data in the cache (memory) and display the report. Report is the mode where the data displays. If you are building a report, you can go from **Design** to **Refresh** and the report will load using the data in the cache so it'll run faster. Just an FYI...

2. Highlight rows **14** through **19** and choose to copy.

3. Paste the rows to row **20**. This will duplicate the **Cost of Goods Sold** section.

4. Click on cell D21 and change the header to `Expenses`.

5. Click on cell E24 and change the total to `Total Expenses`.

6. Click on cell A22 and change to `5000..9999`. Now every account whose main account segment is greater or equal to 4,000 will display on this report.

7. Click on cell D22 and select the **GL** function **(Jet | Design Tools | Jfx | GL)**.

8. In the **Segment 2** field, change the value to look at the absolute value of cell A22. `$A$22`.

9. Click on cell E26 and change the value to `Net Profit (Loss)`.

10. Let's check to make sure our formatting and formulas are working by running the report. Click on **Refresh (Jet | Modes | Refresh)**.

11. Save.

Just as I added the out of balance line to the balance sheet, I'd like to do the same thing to the profit and loss statement when they are in the same workbook.

1. Let's go back to the **Design** mode to continue working (**Jet | Modes | Design**).

2. Click on cell E29 and enter `Out of Balance`.

3. Click on cell F29 and enter a formula that looks at the current year net profit from the profit and loss statement and subtracts the **year to date (YTD)** net profit from the balance sheet. For me, the formula is `=F26-'Balance Sheet'!F19`. If the result is zero, the profit and loss is in balance with the balance sheet. If not, I will need to figure out what is wrong.

4. Format cells E29 and F29 something terrible to look at so it really stands out if you are out of balance:

		Profit and Loss			
		For the Period Ending: April 30 2017			
Sales		**This Year**		**Budget**	**Variance**
000-4100-00	Sales	$	12,159.46	$ 12,767.44	$ (607.98)
	Total Sales	$	12,159.46	$ 12,767.44	$ (607.98)
Cost of Goods Sold		**This Year**		**Budget**	**Variance**
000-4510-01	Cost of Goods Sold - Retail/Parts	$	244,524.43	$256,750.65	$ 12,226.22
	Total Cost of Goods Sold	$	244,524.43	$256,750.65	$ 12,226.22
	Gross Profit (Loss)	$	(232,364.97)	##########	$ 11,618.24
Expenses		**This Year**		**Budget**	**Variance**
000-5100-00	Salaries and Wages	$	149,354.72	$156,822.45	$ 7,467.73
	Total Expenses	$	149,354.72	$156,822.45	$ 7,467.73
	Net Profit (Loss)	$	(381,719.69)	##########	$ 19,085.97
	Out of Balance	$ (449,996.31)			

5. Copy the formula to hide if zero from cell B23 to B29.

6. Remove the gridlines. Navigate to **View | Show | Gridlines**.

7. Add a logo. Go to Navigate to **Insert | Illustrations | Pictures**.

8. Let's check to make sure our formatting and formulas are working by running the report. Click on **Refresh (Jet | Modes | Refresh)**.

9. Save:

B. I. BELINDA

Profit and Loss
For the Period Ending: April 30 2017

Sales		This Year	Budget	Variance
000-4100-00	Sales	$ 12,159.46	$ 12,767.44	$ (607.98)
000-4110-01	US Sales - Retail/Parts	$ 7,037.95	$ 7,389.85	$ (351.90)
000-4110-02	US Sales - Finished Goods	$472,876.05	$496,519.86	$(23,643.81)
000-4140-00	US Sales - Repair Charges	$ 419.40	$ 440.37	$ (20.97)
	Total Sales	$492,492.86	$517,117.52	$(24,624.66)

Cost of Goods Sold		This Year	Budget	Variance
000-4510-01	Cost of Goods Sold - Retail/Parts	$ 244,524.43	$256,750.65	$ 12,226.22
000-4600-00	Purchases Discounts Taken	$ (115.44)	$ (109.66)	$ 5.78
000-4730-00	Purchase Price Variance - Unrealized	$ (1,189.76)	$ (1,130.27)	$ 59.49
	Total Cost of Goods Sold	$243,219.23	$255,510.72	$ 12,291.49
	Gross Profit (Loss)	**$249,273.63**	**$261,606.80**	**$(12,333.17)**

Expenses		This Year	Budget	Variance
000-5100-00	Salaries and Wages	$149,354.72	$156,822.45	$ 7,467.73
000-7402-00	Rounding Difference - Australia	$ (0.01)	$ (0.01)	$ -
100-5150-00	Employee Benefits - Administration	$ 5,725.84	$ 6,012.13	$ 286.29
100-5170-00	Payroll Taxes - Administration	$ 2,108.94	$ 2,214.39	$ 105.45
200-5170-00	Payroll Taxes - Accounting	$ 9,017.58	$ 9,468.46	$ 450.88
300-5130-00	Commissions - Sales	$ 14,774.94	$ 15,513.69	$ 738.75
500-6150-00	Supplies-Allocated - Consulting/Training	$ 15.00	$ 15.75	$ 0.75
	Total Expenses	$180,997.01	$190,046.86	$ 9,049.85
	Net Profit (Loss)	**$ 68,276.62**	**$ 71,559.94**	**$ (3,283.32)**

Now that we created a balance sheet and a profit and loss statement, the foundation exists to start creating custom reports that are more complex, by sampling using Excel formatting and the narrowing of data by accounts, account segments, and/or categories.

Summary

You can see why I love Jet Express for GP. It is so easy to use and so powerful. When I get to leverage knowledge I already have, such as Excel, learning a new tool becomes a piece of cake.

What's in the next chapter? We will take a look at Microsoft's dashboarding tool, Power BI. It is an incredible tool that enables you to look at your GP data in new and exciting ways. The best part is that it is so easy and fun, and there is a free version.

8
Introducing Microsoft Power BI

So far we've built Dashboards in Excel, and we've built Financial Statements (and tables) using Jet Express for GP. Now, we will review one of the coolest new Microsoft products since slicedbread. No kidding. A couple of years ago, Microsoft introduced a cool new product, a dashboarding tool called **Power BI**. This tool can be used on your computer (desktop), in the cloud (service), and even on your iPad or phone (mobile).

We will review some of the basics about the product itself. Understanding these fundamentals can help in planning where and how you should and could implement. In this chapter, we'll cover the following topics:

- Power BI Desktop versus Service versus Mobile
- Power BI Professional (paid) versus Power BI (free)
- Typical workflow of Power BI
- Update speed

Recap

So far, we've discussed using standard Excel features and Jet Express for Excel features. Using Excel itself can provide some amazing dashboards, and this book is about Excel and dashboards. This last section, however, is taking a bit of a detour. As we cover Microsoft Power BI, we'll use Excel in some areas. However, Microsoft Power BI is not an Excel tool or add-on. In fact, it usually works without the use of Excel at all. However, as we are discussing dashboards, and this is a book about Microsoft GP data, it only seems appropriate to include Power BI. I think you'll love what you see, so let's get started.

Power BI Desktop versus Service versus Mobile

There are three major methods to consume data using Power BI: the Desktop, Service, and Mobile. Let's talk about each one in detail and what is special about each tool.

Power BI Desktop

The first tool we'll discuss is the **Power BI Desktop**. This is a tool that you can download right to your PC or notebook; it is free to download and use. It kind of works like Excel. You create a `*.pbix` file that connects to your data and displays a report. The report can, and usually does, consist of multiple tabs with a separate report on each tab. Once you create your connection and report(s), you can upload the data in the file directly to Power BI in the web. Some companies only need/want to work in the Desktop version. The `*.pbix` file contains the imported data, so the file can be shared with others who can use the report, even refreshing the data if the new report recipient has access to the original datasource.

The Power BI Desktop tool provides you with the ability to connect to your data, edit/mold/transform your data, store your data in the `*.pbix` in-memory-data model, and consume your data in the form of reports you create. The reports created in the Desktop tool are a compilation of charts, graphs, and tables. These report elements are called **visuals** or **visualizations**:

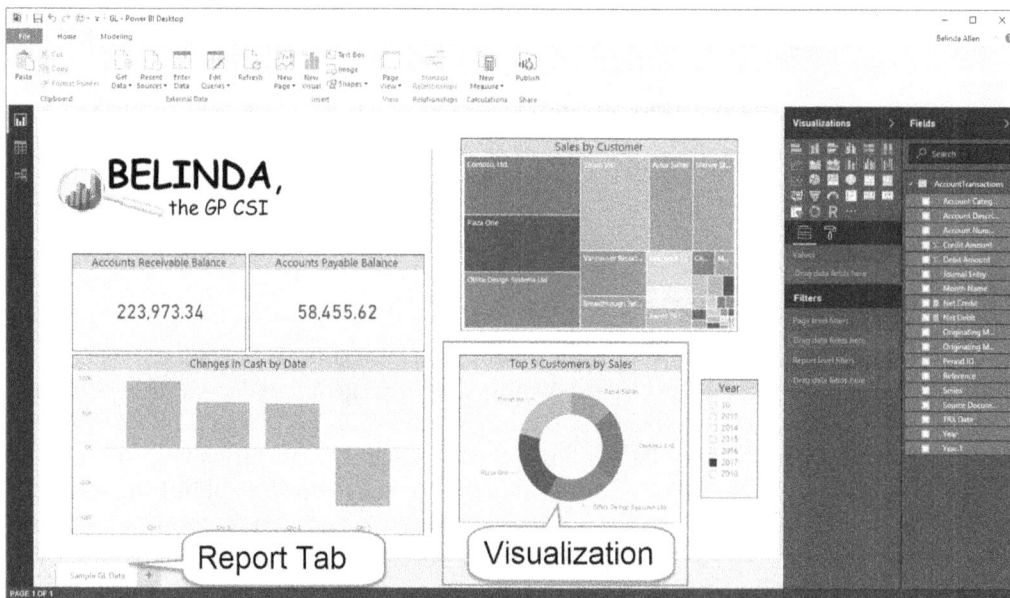

The preceding screenshot shows a lot in a very small image. For now, just note that there are tabs at the bottom of each file, just like worksheet tabs in Excel. Separate and unique reports are created on these tabs. Also note that each graph, chart, card, image, and more, are the visualizations that we will be building, entering, or importing in later chapters. These visuals are what we can place on dashboards later.

The Power BI Desktop tool can be downloaded at `https://powerbi.microsoft.com/en-us/desktop/`.

Power BI Desktop files can be uploaded to the web when you are ready/wanting to consume the visuals via the Internet or mobile device. The process of uploading is very simple. We'll review the steps to upload after we've built some content.

Probably, the biggest advantage to using the Power BI Desktop is to build content/visuals for use on the service and/or mobile devices. It's also a great tool if you have an e-mail address that will not allow you to sign up for the Power BI services.

Power BI services require an e-mail address with a unique domain. This means no Yahoo, MSN, Hotmail, Gmail, AOL, and so on. It must be an e-mail associated with a unique domain, and it must be an e-mail address where you can verify the validity of that e-mail. The first person to sign up for the Power BI services will be required to verify the domain by clicking on a link on an e-mail received by that e-mail address.

Power BI Service

The next tool that we'll discuss is the **Power BI Service**. In this case, service is referring to web services. Basically, this means that the Power BI webpage is organized in such a way that it can use standardized integration tools. It's these integration tools that enable the webpage to get the latest data to display. So, in short, when you see the Power BI Service, the `www.PowerBI.com` website is what they are referring to.

Everyone accesses their data from the same website (www.PowerBI.com). After you sign up, when you go to this page, you'll click on the **Sign In** option at the top right-hand corner to access your data:

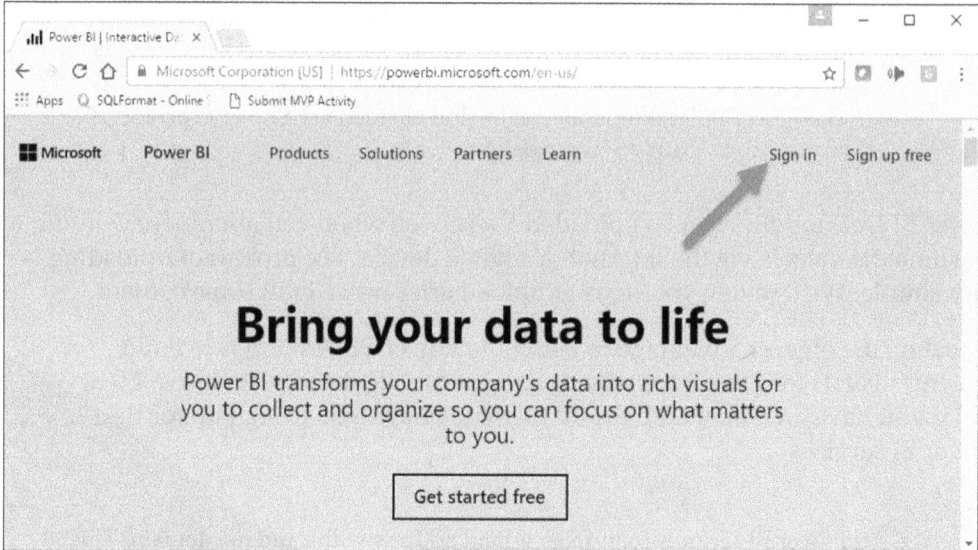

It is on this site that you will also create your Power BI account. Once you log in, (one of) your dashboard(s) will be displayed:

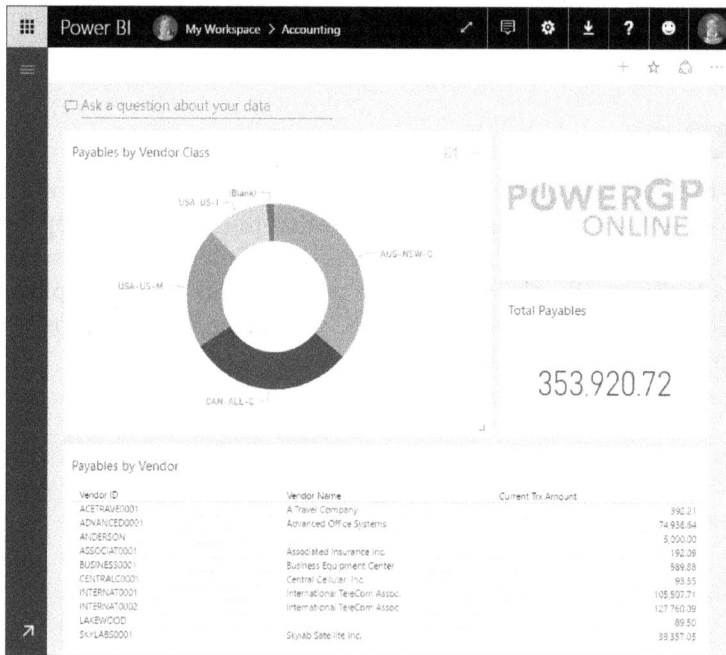

Click on the hamburger icon in the top-left corner to open the navigation pane:

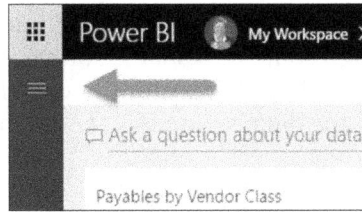

It is from this navigation pane that we can access our dashboards, reports, and datasets:

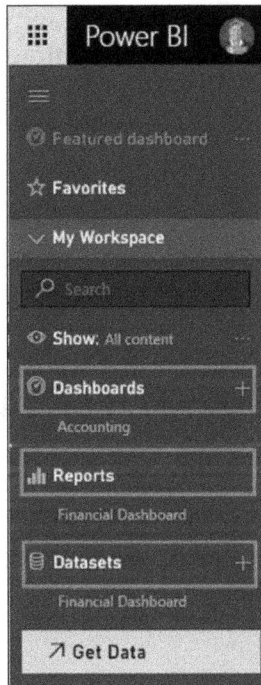

Unlike the Power BI Desktop, the Power BI Service can contain as much data as you like. Where the Power BI Desktop is like a single Excel file, containing one or more sources of data (datasets) and, usually, a single topic of area of interest; the Power BI Service can (and usually does) contain as many topics as your business dictates. The only limitation on the volume of data is that it can hold it solely based on whether you have the free or paid version, but we'll talk about that later.

In the normal workflow for Power BI, users create the initial content in the Power BI Desktop, and then publish it to Service. Once it is published, the connections to the data and the reports built in the desktop are uploaded into the service (web page). If the data is connected through some refreshable source, such as OData, API, web page, and so on, then the service has the capabilities of refreshing the data directly. The ability to directly refresh the data is why `www.PowerBI.com` is a web service and not just a web page.

Power BI Mobile

Power BI Mobile is a free app that you can download and use from the iOS, Android, and Windows app stores. The Power BI Mobile is even available on the Apple watch. Imagine checking the bank balance for your business by looking at your wrist! Once you download, you can log into your Power BI account and see everything that is on the Power BI Service. Power BI Mobile is only used for consumption of data, not for creating and editing reports/dashboards:

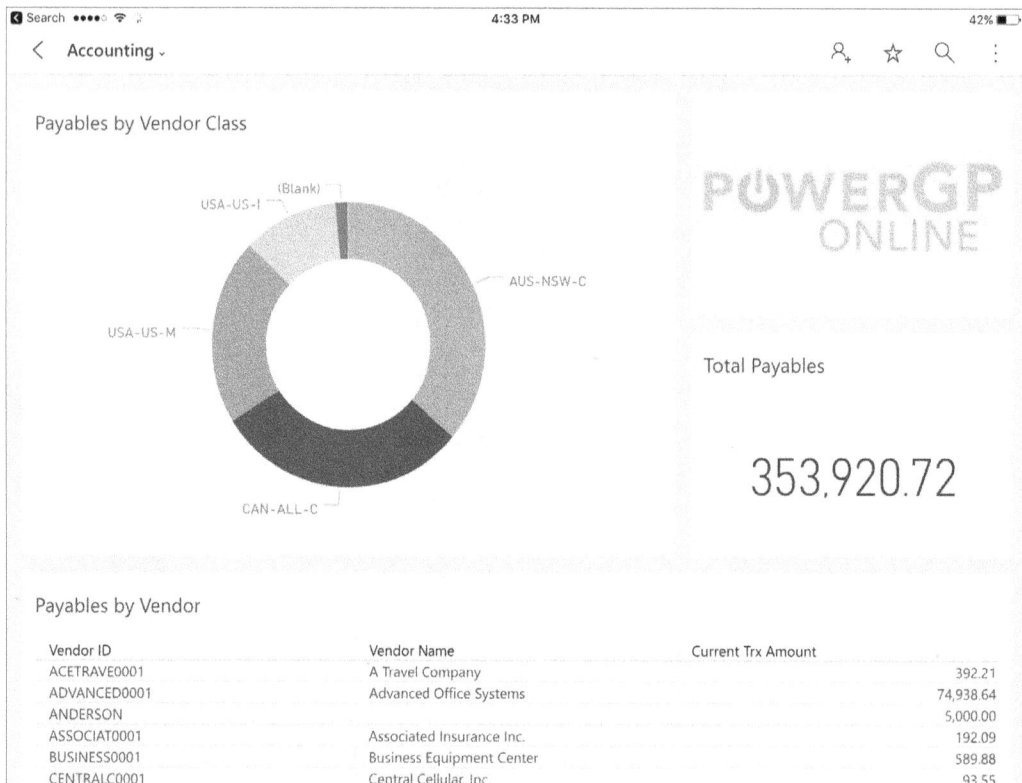

My favorite feature of Power BI Mobile using my iPhone or iPad is annotating and sharing a snapshot of a visual (tile.) In the following screenshot, I, using my iPhone, selected a single visual, circled parts of the legend, wrote a note (although it's hard to tell in a black and white image, I changed the color to red), and added some thumbs up and down. Once I annotate, I can click on the share icon at the top-right corner and e-mail this to whomever I choose:

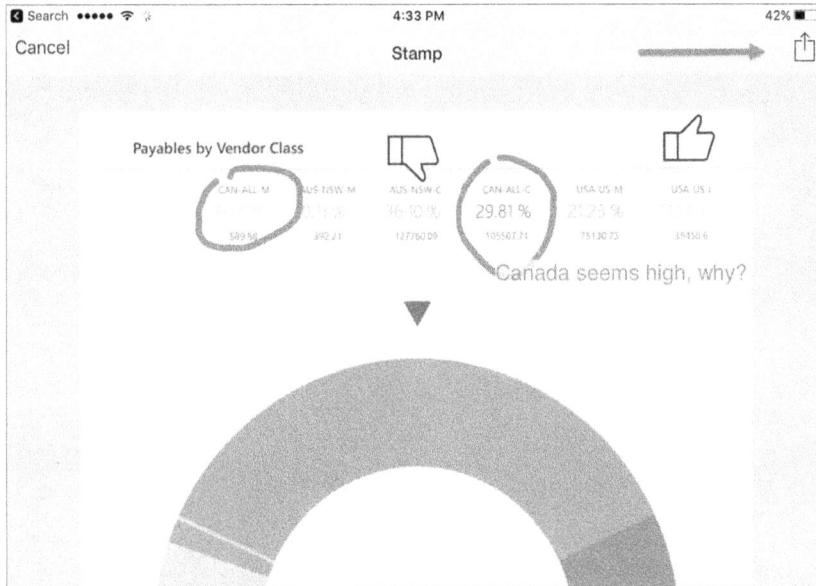

Dashboards can be *favorited* on the Power BI Service and within the Power BI Mobile. In the Power BI Mobile, a **Favorites** page is available.

Another cool feature of the mobile product is filters for locations. If a visual is created with geographical data, a push pin will appear on the visual at the top-right corner. Clicking on the push pin will give you the ability to filter by city, state/province, or country/region. This feature truly helps when you are consuming data on a smaller window/screen.

Other ways to view Power BI

Power BI visuals can also be *embedded* in another application. What does this mean? The best example I can give you is to show you a new feature in GP 2016. Look at the following screenshot of my GP Desktop:

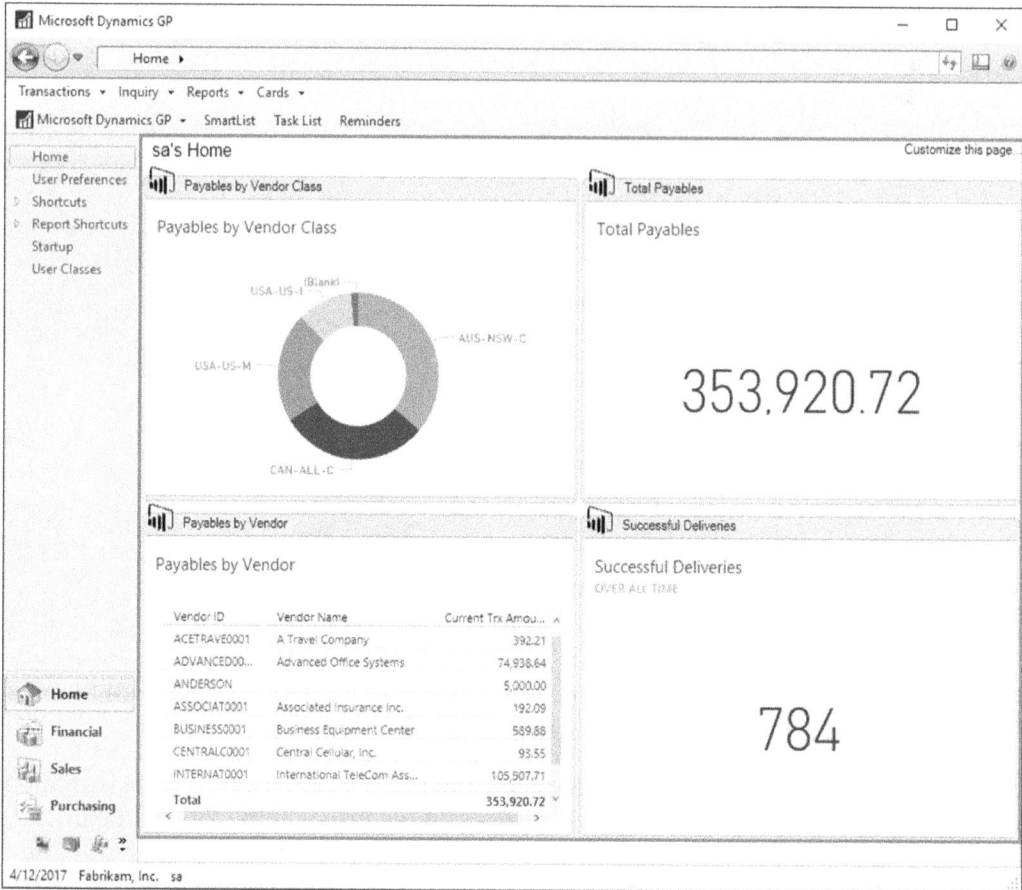

Everything in the red box in the preceding screenshot comes from my Power BI Service (web page). These four visuals are part of my Power BI that I can see on the web page and my mobile device. I've incorporated just these four visuals onto the desktop of my GP, making my GP home page a dashboard. The bottom-right visual (**Successful Deliveries—784**) did come from my Power BI, but it originated in an e-mail service I use called **MailChimp**. The other three visuals come from GP data. Placing these visuals in my GP application is called embedding.

Embedding visuals to an application like GP takes some development, but it is important to know that it can be done.

Visuals can be embedded on a web page much more easily. To share a visual to a web page, you must be a Power BI user, but the people who consume the visual on the web page do not need to be a Power BI user. This is an excellent method to present data on a website, both private and public.

Power BI Professional (paid) versus Power BI (free)

As amazing as Microsoft Power BI is, the price is even better. There are two versions: Power BI and Power BI Pro. Power BI is free! Power BI Pro is $9.99 USD/month. All this power, no pun intended, and it is that inexpensive. The icing on the cake is that if you need a paid user license (Power BI Pro), it does not mean that everyone in your company needs a paid user license. Within your company, you can mix the license options, as they are a user by user case.

> We will only focus on the major feature differences between the two versions, not all the features.

Let's review the major differences between the two options:

The first big difference is the amount of data that can reside in the Power BI Service, and therefore, Power BI Mobile. The free version can only contain 1 GB of data per user, while the paid version can contain 10 GB per user. The dashboards are based off visuals that are on the Power BI reports, and the Power BI reports are built off data in the report memory. So, all the data that the report is based on will make up part of the 1 GB or 10 GB amount.

Auto refreshability is another area with differences between the paid and the free versions. If data is scheduled to refresh automatically within Power BI, the free version can only refresh once a day while the paid version can refresh hourly. Some data can be streaming, which means it updates every time the data changes. The free version can only stream 10,000 rows an hour, while the paid version can stream 1 million rows an hour.

For companies who want their Power BI to refresh against data that is located on premises using a schedule (opposed to manually refreshing), Power BI has a tool that can be used to do this. The tool is called a **Data Connectivity Gateway**. This Gateway is only available with the paid version. If you are using the free version, you'll need to manually refresh the data.

With the paid version, users who also use Office 365 can utilize groups that are built-in Office 365. This is a wonderful feature. You can choose to share information with a group and not have to worry about selecting specific individuals. With the paid version, comes the ability to share reports with Active Directory (local network) groups, even without Office 365.

Templates, data connections, and reports can be organized into what Power BI calls Content Packs. Content Packs allow users to start with connections and reports that are already built. These content packs only work with the paid version.

The last item that I'll mention, which comes only with the paid version, is row-level security. If you build a report/dashboard that contains sales information with row-level security setup for sales people, each salesperson will only see data related to them. For example, if I'm over **New York (NY)**, **Connecticut (CT)**, and **New Jersey (NJ)**; then I would only see data pertaining to those states. If, for the period I was reviewing, those states had no sales, I would see nothing.

> For detailed information, visit `https://powerbi.microsoft.com/en-us/pricing/`.

Typical workflow of Power BI

There is no one right way to work in Power BI. It's a very individualized product and process:

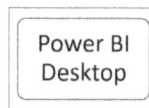

```
Power BI
Desktop
```

That being said, let's review the typical workflow in Power BI:

1. A user can begin by creating a connection to data using the Power BI Desktop and pulling the data into the in-memory data model.
2. The data is then modeled, that is, edited, transformed, and so on.
3. Reports are built in the Power BI Desktop.

> I like to see multiple report pages built, with each page covering a particular area. By this, I mean that if you are displaying sales information, you may have a page for products sold, customer sales, salesperson information, and so on. My reasoning is that once the visuals are in the service on a dashboard, clicking on the visual will open the report on which the visual resides. If I click on a Salesperson visual, I will probably want more information based on Sales people. Organizing your reports will achieve this kind of organization.

4. The data connection, data, and reports are then published to the Power BI Service:

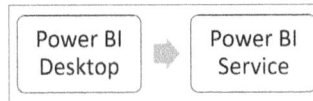

Power BI Desktop	➡	Power BI Service

5. The user then connects to the Power BI Service. They will *pin* select visuals to a dashboard. Once the dashboards are created in full, the data is ready to consume. At this point, the user may even choose to share dashboards with other users:

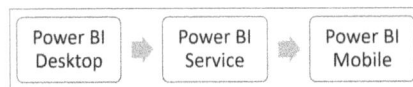

Power BI Desktop	➡	Power BI Service	➡	Power BI Mobile

6. The data can now be viewed on mobile devices via the Power BI Mobile.

Again, this is just the typical workflow. You may opt to skip the Power BI Desktop altogether and just build everything in the Power BI Service. Personally, I use both of these methods.

Update speed

This is an extremely important section. The rate at which this application is being enhanced is mind-blowing. There is a new version of the Power BI Desktop every month, and a new version of the Power BI Service every week. It is because the product is being enhanced and developed so quickly, we'll only cover the basics in this book.

When the Power BI Desktop has a new version, you'll receive a notification in the bottom-right corner of your PC when you log in. This notification will prompt you to download and install the latest version. You do not need to uninstall first, but you will need to close the application prior to performing the installation.

As the Power BI Service is actually on a web page, you do not need to do anything. Just use as normal and the enhancements will be there.

> I strongly encourage referring to the blog to see what new features are added. Even with this fast rate of updating, the features that get added each time are super awesome. The blog can be found at `https://powerbi.microsoft.com/en-us/blog/`

Summary

In this chapter we've covered some pretty important elements that should be considered as you create a Power BI methodology. We've discussed the different methods of accessing visuals: Power BI Desktop, Web Service and Mobile. We've also reviewed the Professional version versus the free version; and the speed at which versions are being released. Finally, we discussed the typical workflow of creating reports and dashboards.

We've covered the foundation for Power BI so we are ready to move forward. In the next chapter, we will begin using Power BI and bringing in data from GP and other sources. Now, the fun begins!

Getting Data in Power BI

9

The most important element of Microsoft Power BI is data itself, so getting the data into Power BI is essential. In this chapter, we'll spend some time discussing different methods of getting data from GP into Power BI. Although we'll be focusing on getting data from GP, the same principles can be used for any kind of data. It should also be noted that we will not be covering every method of getting data into Power BI.

In this chapter, we will connect to data in GP through the following listed methods. We'll also throw in a few notes about some data connection options that can be used for non-GP data just to spice things up and also because you are likely to have data in multiple sources that you want to include in your dashboards:

- Getting data from files
- Connecting to data in Dynamics GP directly
- Content packs
- Getting data from folders

Recap

In *Chapter 8, Introducing Microsoft Power BI*, we discussed Desktop Application versus Mobile Application versus Service (website). Previously, we mentioned the typical workflow was Desktop to Service to Mobile. We'll be following the typical workflow and use the Power BI Desktop for this chapter.

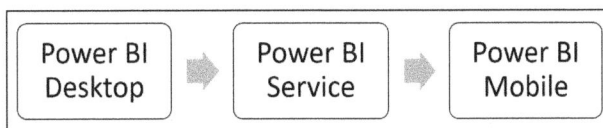

```
Power BI          Power BI          Power BI
Desktop    ▶▶    Service    ▶▶    Mobile
```

Getting data from files

Getting data from a file, such as Excel, CSV, XML, or text, is the most straightforward method of getting data into Power BI. We'll start here with an Excel file. Download and install the Power BI Desktop from www.PowerBI.com before you begin.

> Your Power BI Desktop may look a little different than mine, based on when you downloaded it, although the foundation will remain the same. A new version is released every month.

Using Excel reports in Power BI

Our goal here is to solely connect the data in an Excel file to the Power BI Desktop and import the data into the in-memory data model for Power BI. This will allow the data to reside in Power BI for use with its many visuals:

1. Open Microsoft Dynamics GP SmartList and export the default SmartList Customers Balance * to Excel and **Save**:

Customers - Customer Balance*		
Customer Number	Customer Name	Customer Balance
AARONFIT0001	Aaron Fitz Electrical	$24,394.17
ADAMPARK0001	Adam Park Resort	$20,800.09
ADVANCED0001	Advanced Paper Co.	$327.08
ADVANCED0002	Advanced Tech Sat...	$4,702.20
ALTONMAN0001	Alton Manufacturi...	$75,375.00
AMERICAN0001	American Science ...	$25,838.97
AMERICAN0002	American Electrical...	$7,800.13
ASSOCIAT0001	Associated Insuran...	$1,093.04
ASTORSUI0001	Astor Suites	$1,127.47
ATMORERE0001	Atmore Retirement...	$13,746.14
BAKERSEM0001	Baker's Emporium ...	$9,428.74
BERRYMED0001	Berry Medical Center	$50,796.79
BLUEYOND0001	Blue Yonder Airlines	$36,646.45
BOB		$0.00

Tree: Company, FieldService, Financial, Fixed Assets, Human Resources, Inventory, Payroll, Purchasing, Sales > Customer Addresses, Customer Items, Customers > *, Average Days to Pay*, Customer Balance*, Customer Contact List*

2. Open Microsoft Power BI. Upon opening it, you may receive a **Getting Started** window. This window contains links to the last few dashboards you've built, such as **POWER BI BLOG, FORUMS, TUTORIALS**, and **WHAT's NEW**. You can also begin a new dashboard with **Get Data** and/ or **Sign In** to Power BI online. If this window pops up, close it by clicking on **X** in the top-right corner. Although this window is super handy, let's do everything via the application so you know how to navigate without having to open this window each time.

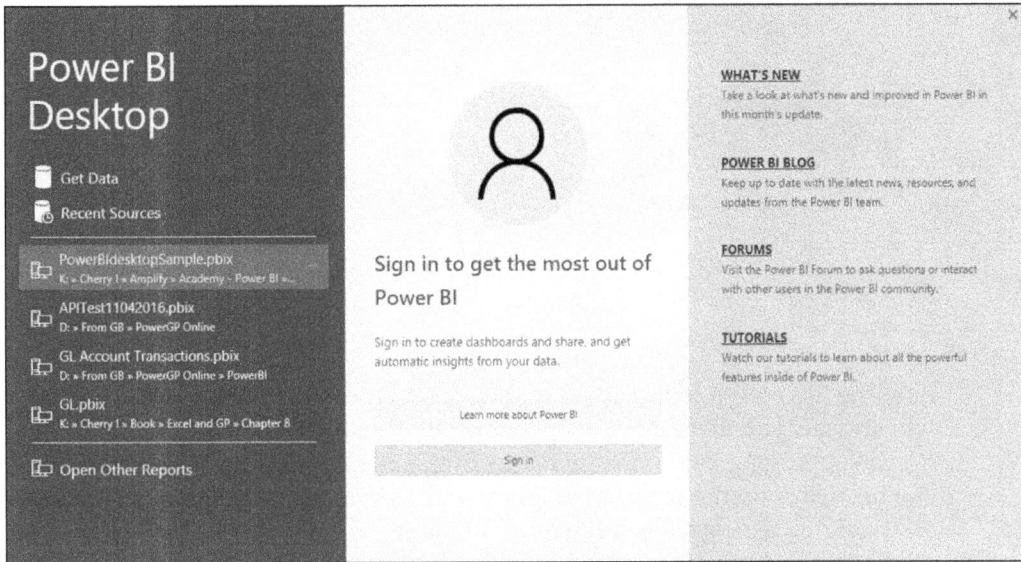

3. On the Power BI ribbon, in the **External Data** section of the **Home** tab, select **Get Data** (the icon, not the words with the arrow), as shown in the following screenshot:

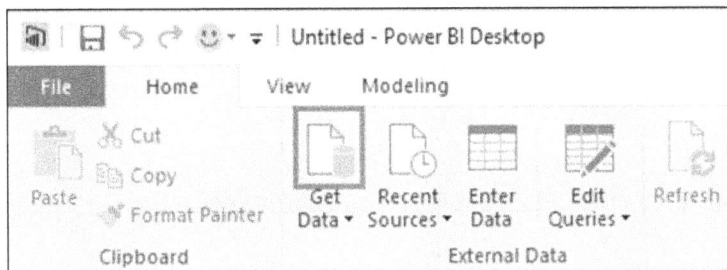

4. In the **Get Data** window, select **File** on the left and **Excel** on the right, then click on **Connect**, as you can see in this screenshot:

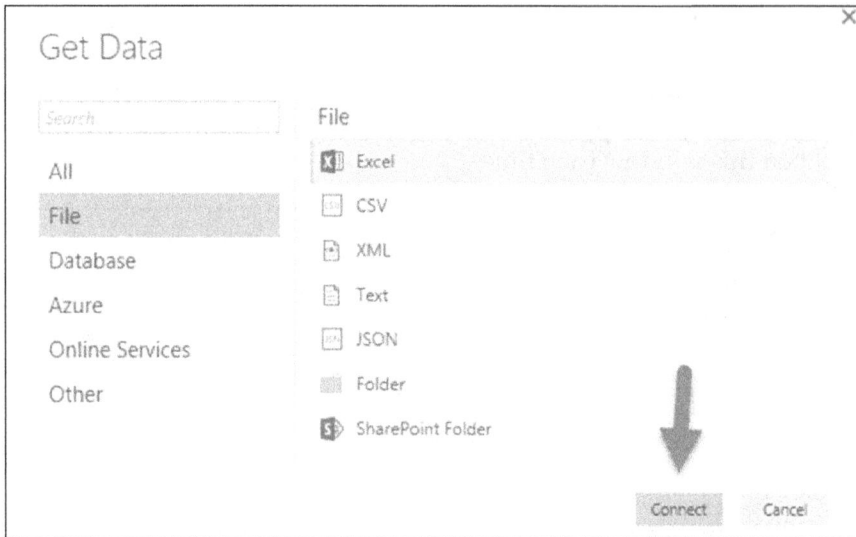

5. Find the file you saved in step 1 and click on **Open**. The **Navigator** window will appear. The filename will appear on the left with each tab and table in the file appearing below the filename. In this file, there is no table and only one tab. Click on the tab to highlight it and a preview of the data will appear on the right. The preview allows you to make sure we are getting the data we desire.

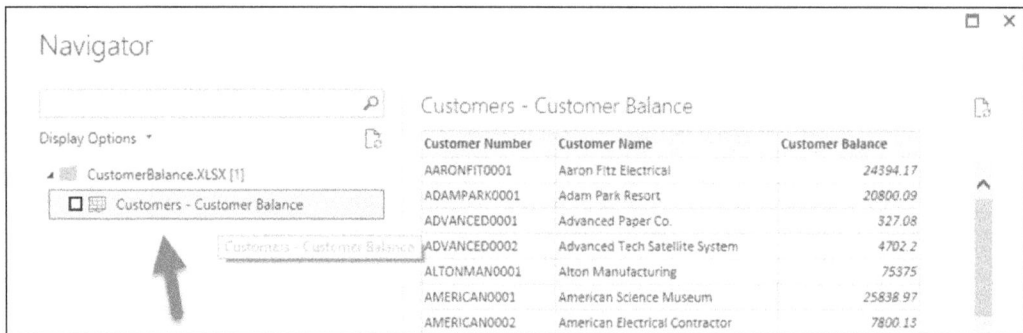

6. Click on the tab checkbox and select **Load**, as shown in the following screenshot:

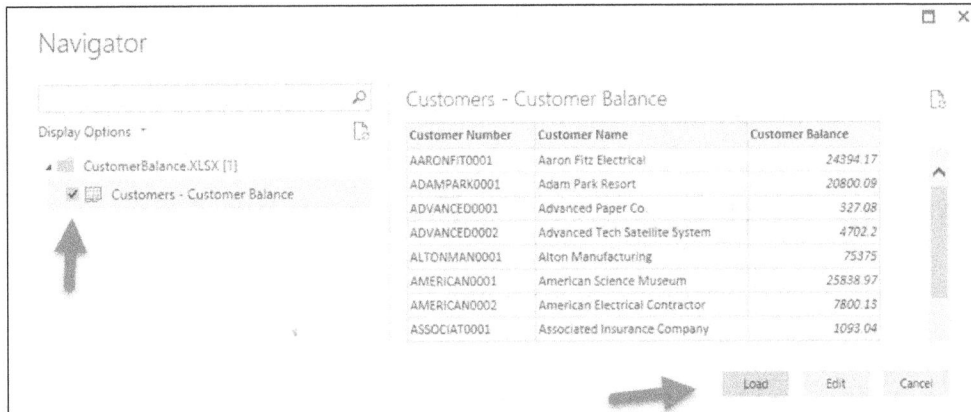

7. The data from the spreadsheet is now in the data model for Power BI. You'll see the data listed with the name of the file and each field in the file listed below the filename in the **Fields** pane, as you can see in the following screenshot:

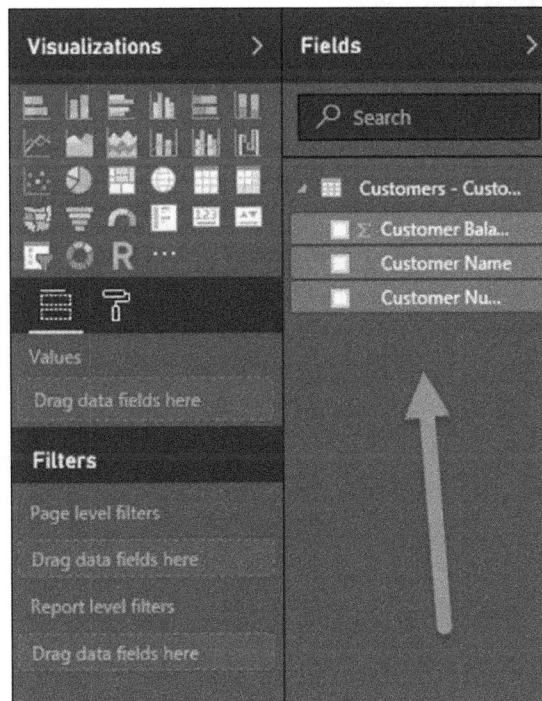

> The data was imported into Power BI just as it was in the Excel file. In the next chapter, we'll work on cleaning/enhancing the data so it provides more value in the visuals.

8. Save your Power BI Desktop files (`*.pbix`) as `CustomerInfo.pbix`. If someone asks you if you "Got Data?", you can now say YES!

Connecting to data in Dynamics GP

Now that we have made a simple Excel data connection, let's focus on getting data from Dynamics GP. The first step in connecting to data is knowing where the data resides. In the case of Dynamics GP, that would be a Microsoft SQL Server Database. No worries, you do not have to go into SQL, be an SQL God, or even know SQL. We'll provide you with tips to help you get to the data you want and make sure the data requires as little cleanup as possible. We'll discuss cleaning, which is also known as transforming, cleansing, editing, modeling, and so on, in a later chapter. There are three ways to get data from SQL into Power BI; we'll review those options in the following sections.

Direct SQL Connect

Let's begin with directly connecting to the SQL database. Power BI makes this super easy:

1. Open Microsoft Power BI. Upon opening, if you receive a **Getting Started** window, close it. We'll connect to the data from within the Power BI application.

2. On the Power BI ribbon, in the **External Data** section of the **Home** tab, select **Get Data** (the icon, not the words with the arrow), as shown in the following screenshot:

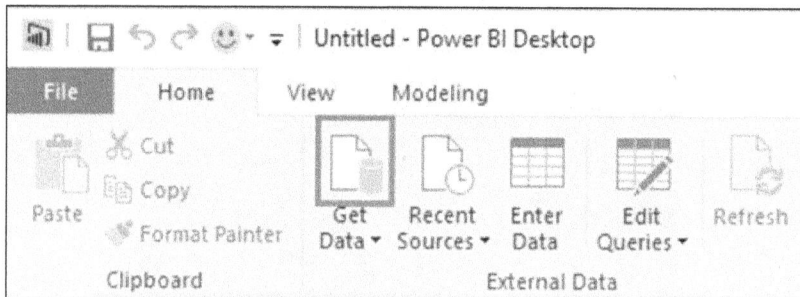

3. In the **Get Data** window, select **Database** on the left and **SQL Server Database** on the right, then click on **Connect**, as you can see in the following screenshot:

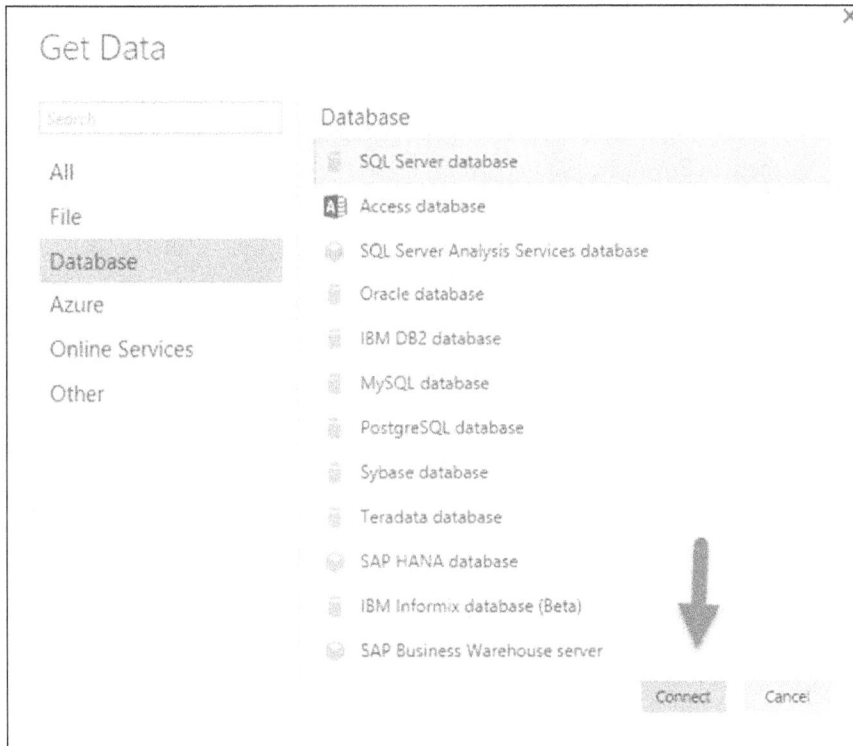

> Even if your data resides in **Azure**, you'll choose the **Database** option, not the **Azure** option. SQL Server in Azure is different than the SQL Server that GP uses.

4. The **SQL Server database** window will open. Populate the **Server** field with your SQL Server name. Populate the **Database** field with your database name. Make sure the **Import** option is selected and click on **OK**.

We discussed how to get these two names in the Excel section of this book. If you do not know the server or database name, contact your IT department to obtain them.

Although the **Database** field is optional, you'll save yourself a lot of scrolling by entering the name here. Each data connection (or Query) is to a specific set of data. That being said, you can have two data connections that contain, for example, a list of General Ledger Transactions, each coming from a different database. You can combine them in Power BI, but each data connection will be for only one database for one specific set of data:

By choosing **Import**, we are pulling the data into the Power BI file. If we chose **DirectQuery**, the data would not be in the Power BI file. With **DirectQuery**, every time we open the Power Bi file, the data would refresh from the SQL data. Sometimes, this is a good thing. If you intend to use the **Publish** button to push the data to the Power BI Service (website), then I would not suggest it. If you tried to access the data when you are not connected to your server, you would receive an error, unless you have a gateway installed. We'll talk about gateways and other methods of refreshing data in a later chapter.

5. The **Navigator** window will open, displaying all the tables and views, which we discussed in the Excel portion of this book, for the database we selected on the previous window.

> Unless you are extremely familiar with the data schema, which most people are not, stick to using views. Views make the data easier to read and use better field names as a general rule. If you cannot find a view that suits your needs, contact your partner to build some views for you. One well-built view can save hours and hours of trying to connect tables and clean them up on your own.
>
> As a rule, views will be named with words rather than a combination of letters and numbers; this makes it easier to distinguish a view from a table.

6. In the **Navigator** window, we'll select a view that contains vendor information. Type in the word Vendor in the blank lookup field. Only tables, views, and stored procedures that contain Vendor in the name will display. You can also just scroll down to find the field you want. Select **Vendors** and verify on the right that this is the data (list of vendors) that we want:

7. Click on **Load**.

8. Navigate to **File | Save As** and save it as VendorInfo.pbix. We'll add more data to it in the next section, and we'll use this file in the next chapter when we begin creating visuals.

Just a reminder: in a couple of chapters, we'll be covering how to edit the data, even adding some custom fields. In the meantime, let's add a few more data connections or Queries using SQL Server; I'll be referring to them as **Queries** from here on out to stay consistent with Microsoft Power BI terminology.

SQL statement

Living in the era of social media, we often see great pieces of information on blogs, forums, and even this book (right???) Suppose you come across an SQL view that can provide you with the data organized just the way you want but you do not have access to the SQL Server itself. What do you do? The Microsoft Power BI team has thought of this scenario and has built a solution for you. We can create a Query (data connection) that contains the view, rather than accessing a view in the SQL Server. Let's walk through the steps for creating this type of Query:

1. Open the Power BI file we created in the last step: VendorInfo.pbix.

2. On the Power BI ribbon, in the **External Data** section of the **Home** tab, select **Get Data** (the icon, not the words with the arrow).

3. In the **Get Data** window, select **Database** on the left and **SQL Server Database** on the right, then click on **Connect**.

4. The **SQL Server database** window will open. Populate the **Server** field with your SQL Server name. Populate the **Database** field with your database name. Make sure the **Import** option is selected. Click on the expansion for **Advanced options**. This will open some additional fields:

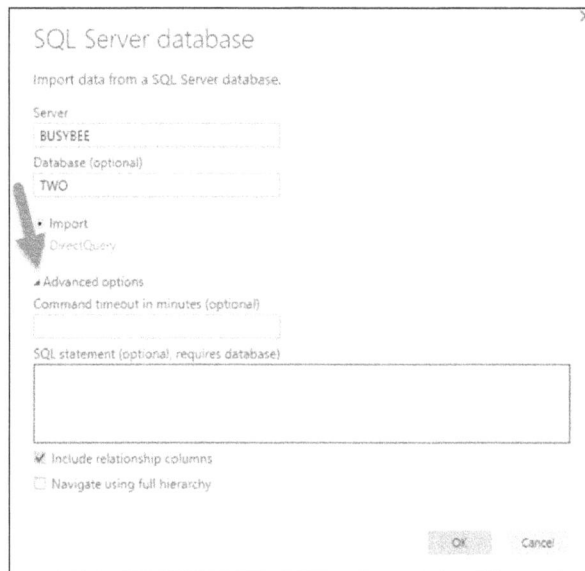

One of the fields that opens up when we expand **Advanced options** is the SQL statement. We will paste (or enter) a **Transact-SQL (TSQL)** statement here. A TSQL statement is just a SQL command that could be used to create a view.

5. I've created an TSQL statement that displays all GP Payables Transactions with a status of Open. This statement shows credit memos, returns, and payments as negative amounts. The statement is listed as follows:

```
SELECT PT.VCHRNMBR AS [Voucher Number],
       PT.VENDORID AS [Vendor ID],
       VM.VENDNAME AS [Vendor Name],
       CASE PT.DOCTYPE
           WHEN 1 THEN 'Invoice'
           WHEN 2 THEN 'Finance Charge'
           WHEN 3 THEN 'Misc Charge'
           WHEN 4 THEN 'Return'
           WHEN 5 THEN 'Credit'
           WHEN 6 THEN 'Payment'
           WHEN 7 THEN 'Schedule'
           ELSE 'Other'
       END AS [Document Type],
       PT.DOCNUMBR AS [Document Number],
       PT.TRXDSCRN AS Description,
       PT.DOCDATE AS [Document Date],
       PT.DUEDATE AS [Due Date],
       CASE PT.DOCTYPE
           WHEN 1 THEN PT.DOCAMNT
           WHEN 2 THEN PT.DOCAMNT
           WHEN 3 THEN PT.DOCAMNT
           WHEN 4 THEN (- 1 * PT.DOCAMNT)
           WHEN 5 THEN (- 1 * PT.DOCAMNT)
           WHEN 6 THEN (- 1 * PT.DOCAMNT)
           WHEN 7 THEN PT.DOCAMNT
           ELSE PT.DOCAMNT
       END AS [Document Amount],
       CASE PT.DOCTYPE
           WHEN 1 THEN PT.CURTRXAM
           WHEN 2 THEN PT.CURTRXAM
           WHEN 3 THEN PT.CURTRXAM
           WHEN 4 THEN (- 1 * PT.CURTRXAM)
           WHEN 5 THEN (- 1 * PT.CURTRXAM)
           WHEN 6 THEN (- 1 * PT.CURTRXAM)
           WHEN 7 THEN PT.DOCAMNT
```

```
            ELSE PT.CURTRXAM
        END AS [Amount Unapplied],
        PT.PORDNMBR AS [PO Number],
        CASE PT.HOLD
            WHEN 0 THEN 'Yes'
            WHEN 1 THEN 'No'
            ELSE 'Unknown'
        END AS HOLD
    FROM dbo.PM00200 AS VM
    INNER JOIN dbo.PM20000 AS PT ON VM.VENDORID = PT.VENDORID
    WHERE (PT.VOIDED = 0)
```

6. Copy the statement and paste in the **SQL statement** field of the **SQL Server database** window, then click on **OK**:

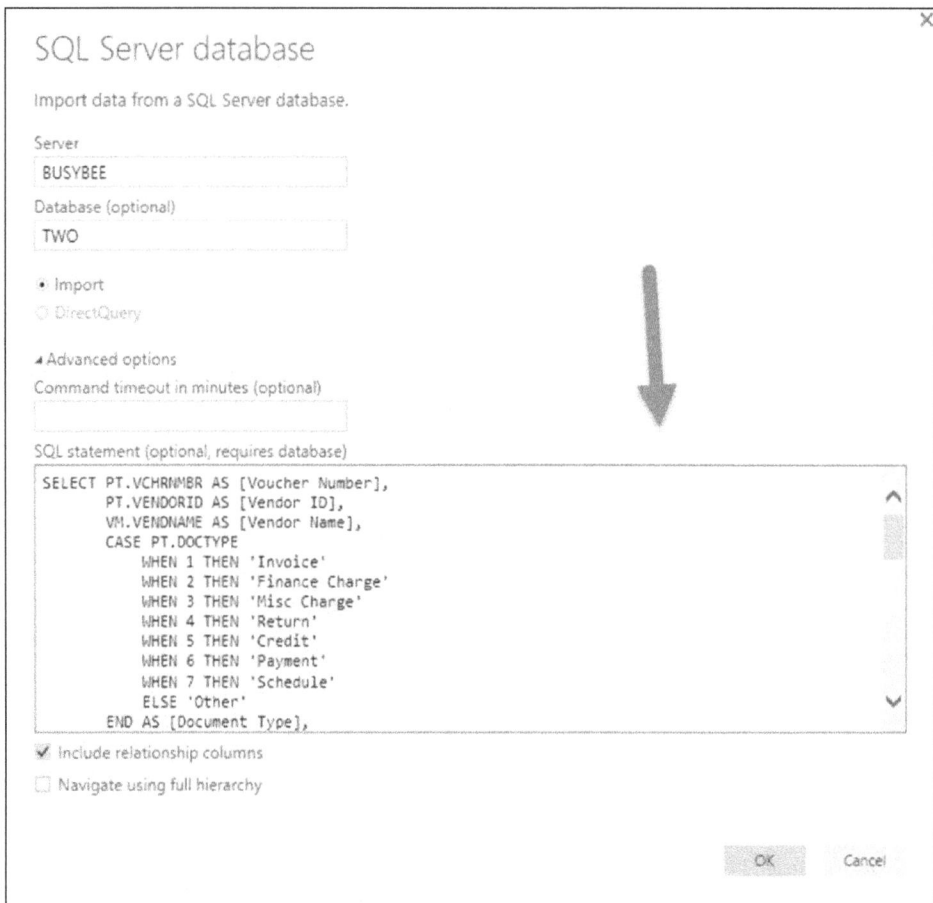

7. A preview window will appear; click on **Load**:

You have now successfully added data from your SQL server using a TSQL statement.

> When using TSQL statements, you must have privileges to the tables being referenced. The same principles we discussed in *Chapter 2, The Ultimate GP to Excel Tool – Refreshable Excel Reports*, on security apply here as well. Refer to that chapter on handling security to your SQL data.

OData

With the release of GP 2016, a new GP feature, called **Open Data Protocol (OData)**, was added. It is a service that allows for the accessing of data via the web (or network if internal). For the non-developer, you only need to know it allows you a method of getting to your data from anywhere, over the Internet.

At the time this book was being written, there are still some issues being worked out with the GP OData, but it will get there. As a result, let's connect to another OData source--they all pretty much work the same way. In our example, we'll use some real New York City data. New York has quite a few open databases available and, in this example, we'll review the database of *.nyc Domain Registrations by Zip Code*. It's a small database, but it'll give you some experience in creating a Query using OData. The first part of these steps is obtaining the OData Endpoint. Once we have the Endpoint, the steps will be the same as using the GP OData.

> An OData Endpoint is a specific source of data. It can be a table or view, such as customers, vendors, payable transactions, and so on. It can also be a single record, such as one customer, or a single field, such as total accounts receivable for all customers. For the use of GP, an OData Endpoint will be either an SQL view or an SQL table.

So let's connect to some OData data!

1. Open any Internet browser and connect to `https://data.cityofnewyork.`
   `us/Business/-nyc-Domain-Registrations-by-Zip-Code/ymvu-4x4s`.
   This will open the NYC OpenData page for the specific dataset for which we
   want to connect.

2. At the top of the page, there is a menu that allows you to either view the data
   or download/share the data. On this menu, click on the ellipsis (three dots).
   Select **Access Data via OData**, as you can see in the following screenshot:

3. A new window will appear that displays the OData Endpoint (URL link to
   the specific data table). Click on **Copy** to put the link in your clipboard; the
   field will change to green and read **Copied** when your clipboard is updated.
   Then, click on **Done**, as shown in the following screenshot:

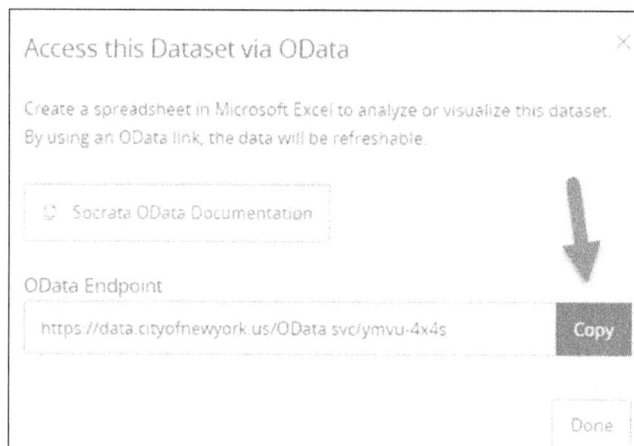

4. Open the Power BI file we created in the last step: `VendorInfo.pbix`.

5. On the Power BI ribbon, in the **External Data** section of the **Home** tab, select **Get Data** (the icon, not the words with the arrow).

6. In the **Get Data** window, select **Other** on the left and **OData Feed** on the right, then click on **Connect**.

7. The **OData Feed** window will open. Paste the URL from your clipboard into the **URL** field. Click on **OK**, as you can see in this screenshot:

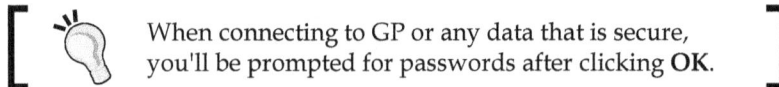

OData Feed

• Basic   ○ Advanced

Enter the URL for an OData feed.

URL

https://data.cityofnewyork.us/OData.svc/ymvu-4x4s

OK   Cancel

> When connecting to GP or any data that is secure, you'll be prompted for passwords after clicking **OK**.

8. A preview window will appear; click on **Load**, as shown in this screenshot:

https://data.cityofnewyork.us/OData.svc/ymvu-4x4s

__id	zip_code	borough	total
23	10055	Manhattan	1
28	10311	Staten Island	1
42	10176	Manhattan	21
53	11256	Brooklyn	3

Load   Edit   Cancel

You have now successfully created a Query via OData. One of the best parts about using OData is that the link is refreshable, even if you are not in your office.

Content packs

As you begin building dashboards, what if you want to share them with other members of your team? What if you want to take these dashboards and put them in a library for easy access? Have you wondered if some of your software providers are providing you libraries of dashboards you can use? Microsoft has thought of these questions already and has provided you with a feature called **content packs**.

Now, I suppose you are wondering why I am discussing a library of dashboards in a chapter about getting data. The explanation is not only simple but cool. These content packs not only provide you with sample or template dashboards, but they also provide you with connection information already built-in; you will only need to supply the login, if required. So you get data on a content pack and log in, and voila, you are up and running!

There are two kinds of content packs: **Online Services** and **Organizational**. Let's review each of these now.

Online Services

Online Services content packs are prebuilt reports and dashboards that are created by software (application) companies, which (usually) offer the product as an online service. This means you typically do not install their application on your machine, but rather access it through a web browser.

> When using Online Services from Power BI Desktop, often, only the connection is created. When using Online Services from within Power BI Service (web), more often than not, sample reports and dashboards are also created.

As there is probably no one application that everyone who is reading this book subscribes to, we'll walk you through locating these content packs together; and, at that point, we'll show you some screenshots connecting to one such service (Facebook). This will provide you with a good idea of how Online Services content packs work using the Power BI Desktop:

1. Open the Power BI file we created in the last step: `VendorInfo.pbix`.
2. On the Power BI ribbon, in the **External Data** section of the **Home** tab, select **Get Data** (the icon, not the words with the arrow).

3. In the **Get Data** window, select **Online Services** on the left. On the right, you will see all the available Online Services content packs, as shown in the following screenshot:

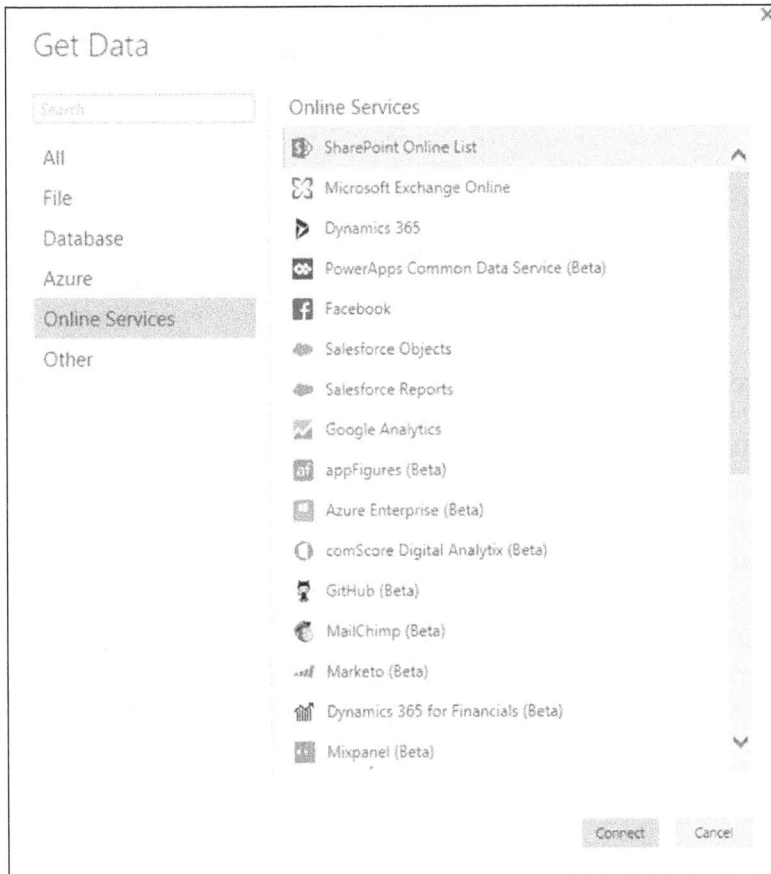

It's also important to note that not all Online Services content packs will exist in both Power BI Services (web page) and the Power BI Desktop. Online Services content pack providers have the option to decide where they want their content packs to be made available.

You may also get a **Connecting to a third-party service** window. This will provide you with some information about the connection. You can learn more or click on **Continue**.

Microsoft has a screening process for Online Services content pack providers. This is to ensure quality and benefits for consumers.

Next, we'll show you how we connect to **Facebook** content packs. This will give you a better idea of what to expect when you begin using Online Services content packs yourself.

The following steps are not necessarily for you to follow along, as we'll be using our own login for Facebook. If you have a Facebook account, please feel free to give it a try:

1. In the **Get Data** window, we will select **Facebook** from the **Online Services** option. We'll then click on **Connect**.

> Microsoft tests new Online Services by putting them in beta mode. If your option is in beta, you'll receive a **Preview connector** window. If you receive this, click on **Continue**.

2. A **Facebook** window will open. This allows for unique login information to be entered. All Online Services will require your unique login information to be entered to connect to your data.

3. The **Navigator** window will open. On the left, you can select one (or more) connections. This will be individual Power BI Reports and dashboards, if you are performing this step from the Power BI Service. The data will preview on the right.

4. A **Facebook** window will open that asks what data we want to get. We leave **Object ID** listed as **me**. We'll be prompted next for our Facebook login. We will leave the **me** object for personal information as opposed to a particular page. We'll access our likes for music pages, as you can see in the following screenshot:

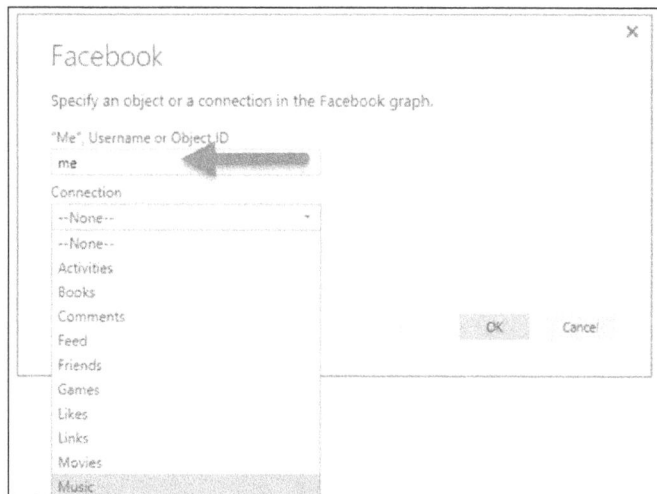

> A good use of Facebook BI is likes for your business or product page.

5. The **Access Facebook** window appears. As we have not logged on to Facebook yet, we'll get a not authorized error. Click on the **Sign in** button and log in as you normally would. Upon successful login, you'll return to the **Access Facebook** window. Click on **Connect**, as shown in the following screenshot:

6. The data preview window will appear. Apparently, music is not something we click the **Like** button on very much, which is shown in the following screenshot:

https://graph.facebook.com/v2.2/me/music

name	category	id	object_link	created_time
Allen Herman	Musician/Band	104797862930320	Record	2014-05-14T11:21:44+0000
JennieGirl Music	Record Label	185141738210910	Record	2014-05-14T11:21:30+0000
Jennie Walker	Musician/Band	183139575401	Record	2009-04-17T21:53:23+0000
Harry Connick Jr	Musician/Band	41043175538	Record	2009-07-25T00:02:42+0000

The following is a screenshot of a report created by the Online Service for MailChimp. In the case of MailChimp, we not only connected to our data, we received prebuilt reports as well. We can use the reports right out of the box or edit them for our particular needs. To get this dashboard, we only need to connect to MailChimp's Online Service and log in.

Note that the actual dashboard shows much more than the following screenshot:.

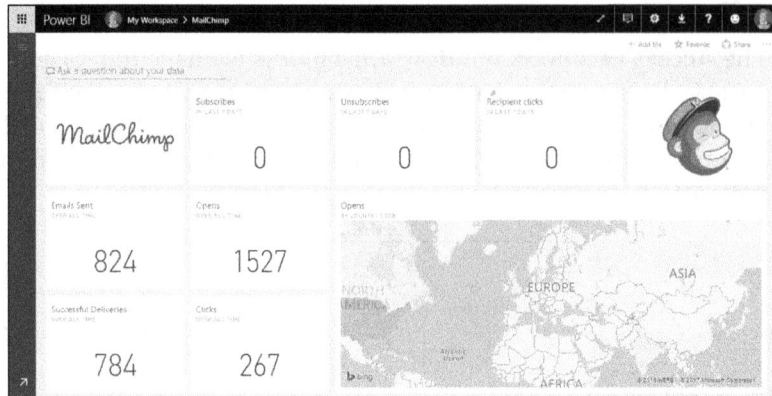

Organizational

When you are ready to share your reports with your co-workers, creating library dashboards and reports with the connection information setup is the easiest and more organized approach.

To create content packs, you must have Power BI Pro, the paid version. For your co-workers to access the content pack library, they must also have a Power BI Pro license. If you and/or your co-workers do not have the paid version of Power BI, you'll need to create a .pbix file using the Power BI Desktop and share it as you would an Excel or Word file.

You can share individual content packs with a single person, all co-workers, a group you create in Power BI, and even a group you create in Office 365 (if your organization is an Office 365 subscriber).

When a Power BI Desktop report is published to the Power BI Service, we are prompted with the option of publishing to just our Power BI account, or to either a Power BI group or an Office 365 group, as you can see in the following screenshot:

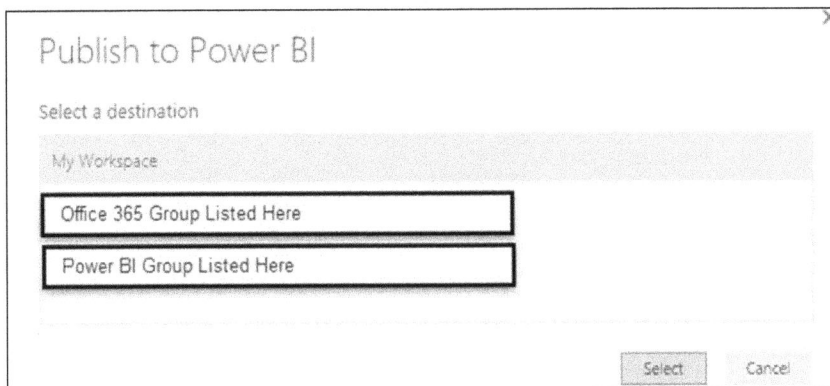

Getting data from folders

In this final source of getting data, we'll review folders. Sometimes, you'll get information from sources in individual files, but you need to report on all the data as one file. Maybe it's sales information being polled monthly from a point of sale system. You could create a separate Query for each month, but at the end of one year, you would have 12 separate Queries. What if you have 10 stores? At the end of the year, you would have 120 separate Queries. Not only is that more Queries for a single source than you would want to have, you wouldn't want to have to create a new Query each month. If the data is in the same format and in the same file type, you can just get the data from the folder, rather than individual files.

We will not be walking through getting data from a folder in this chapter. We'll cover it when we review editing/modeling data. It is the **Query Editor** tool that makes data usable as one complete data source. Use the **Get Data** window to connect to the folder, as you can see in the following screenshot:

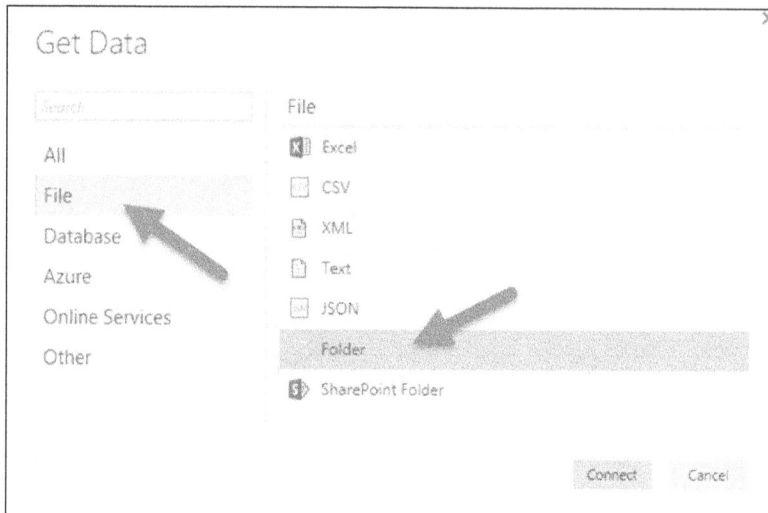

Summary

We've covered a variety of methods of getting into Power BI Desktop for reporting. We've connected to SQL data, data from websites, and from Excel files. We've even discussed using content packs and multiple files in a folder. Now that the data is loaded, we can build reports.

Reports in Power BI are a collection of charts, graphs, tables, and so on. Each item on the report is called a visual. In the next chapter, we'll begin building visuals. (By the way, I'm so excited. Building Power BI visuals is as much fun as popcorn at the movies!)

10
Creating Power BI Visuals

So here is the exciting part where we *see* (we're laughing because it's a pun off visuals) data starting to appear on the screen. As data artists, we've gathered our paints and supplies (data), the (Power BI) blank canvas lays before us, and we're about to paint realistic views of our data. Too far with the imagery? Sorry, it's the most fun part, and we got a little carried away.

In this chapter, we will cover the basics on visuals. There are more visuals and improvements to visuals being constantly added. As a result, understanding some of the basics is essential. Specifically, we will cover the following topics:

- Filters
- Formatting
- Standard visuals
- Development options
- R overview

Recap

Now that we understand the typical workflow (the Power BI Desktop, published to Power BI Service, shared with others and consumed in Power BI Mobile), we know where to begin in creating visuals. We've extracted/imported data into the Power BI Desktop using the **Get Data** feature. We're finally ready to begin populating the canvas and see the rewards of our hard work.

Using Filters

Without the ability to filter, you can still see some pretty important information in a Power BI report. We could look at our payables aged trial balance and see everything that we owe. However, what if I want to narrow down the report and see only the cost of goods sold to vendors or just 1,099 vendors? What if I was looking at a receivables aged trial balance, and I wanted to see only customers for a particular salesman? After all, if we're looking at financial numbers from the general ledger, wouldn't we all want to see just a particular period or year? Enter: filters. Filters can be set in the **Visualizations** pane of the Power BI Desktop.

We can filter for:

- The entire report/file, perhaps eliminating all voided transactions.

- The entire page; maybe we have a page on the report that has only unpaid invoices and another page that has all active vendors.

- A single visual. This would allow a single page on the report to contain a visual for unpaid transactions and a visual for active vendors.

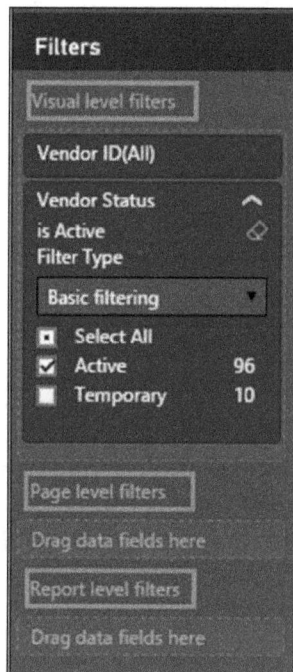

We will cover filtering as we work on creating each individual visual later in the chapter.

Formatting as a tool

Do not postpone or ignore formatting options. It's not just about making the report pretty; it's about adding more value to the visual. Sure, you can make it more visually appealing with formatting; however, with formatting, you can also add some static information that provides more value on the report. A great example of this is the gauge, which we'll create in this chapter. When you first create the visual, the amount will always be set at 50%, which doesn't provide much value. With formatting, you can set a maximum target amount and a minimum which makes the visual more valuable, as you can see in the following screenshot:

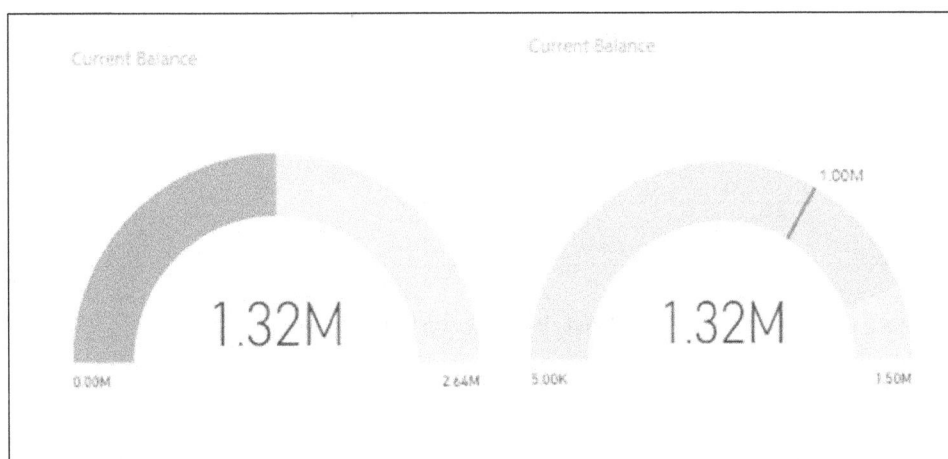

The preceding image shows the out-of-the-box gauge on the left and the same gauge formatted on the right. If all your gauges looked like the one on the left, you might as well just list the amount, which is a card visual, rather than using a gauge.

We will cover formatting (and filtering from earlier) as we create visuals, which is next.

Understanding standard visuals

Let's begin creating visualizations. We'll only cover a few visuals, providing you with the foundation to create some amazing reports and dashboards.

Getting quick information with cards

The first visual we'll create is a card; specifically, a single number card. It's probably the least exciting, but it certainly has its place in business intelligence. We'll create a visualization that displays the total balance of our **Accounts Payable (AP)**. In our example, if there is only one number, putting in a chart or graph will not offer any additional information and, in fact, might make it harder to read quickly. Look at the following image. I've displayed the total AP balance using three different chart visuals: **Column**, **Pie**, and **Line**. None of these visuals are easy to read or make sense of. Using these would be having a chart for the sake of having a chart, not for providing valuable insight:

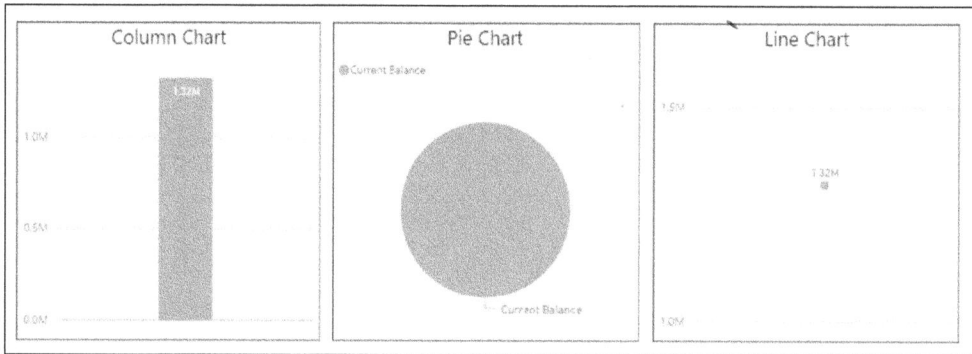

Let's create our first visual, the **Card**, by following these steps:

1. Open the Power BI file we created in *Chapter 9, Getting Data in Power BI*, `VendorInfo.pbix`.

2. Make sure you are viewing the **Report** on the canvas. This will be the chart icon in the black bar on the left side of the window. Nothing will appear in the canvas yet. However, that is about to change!

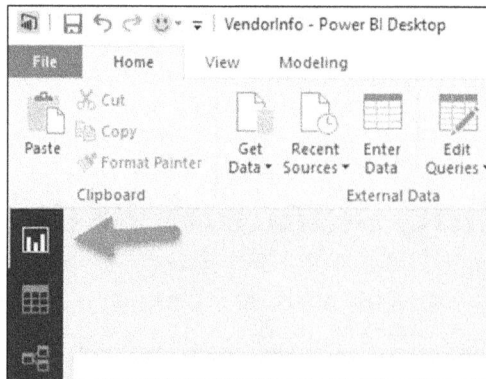

3. In the **Visualizations** pane, select the **Card** icon. The **Card** icon is the one that has **123** visible. A blank visual will now appear on the canvas.

> As you hover over each icon, the name or type of the visualization will appear.

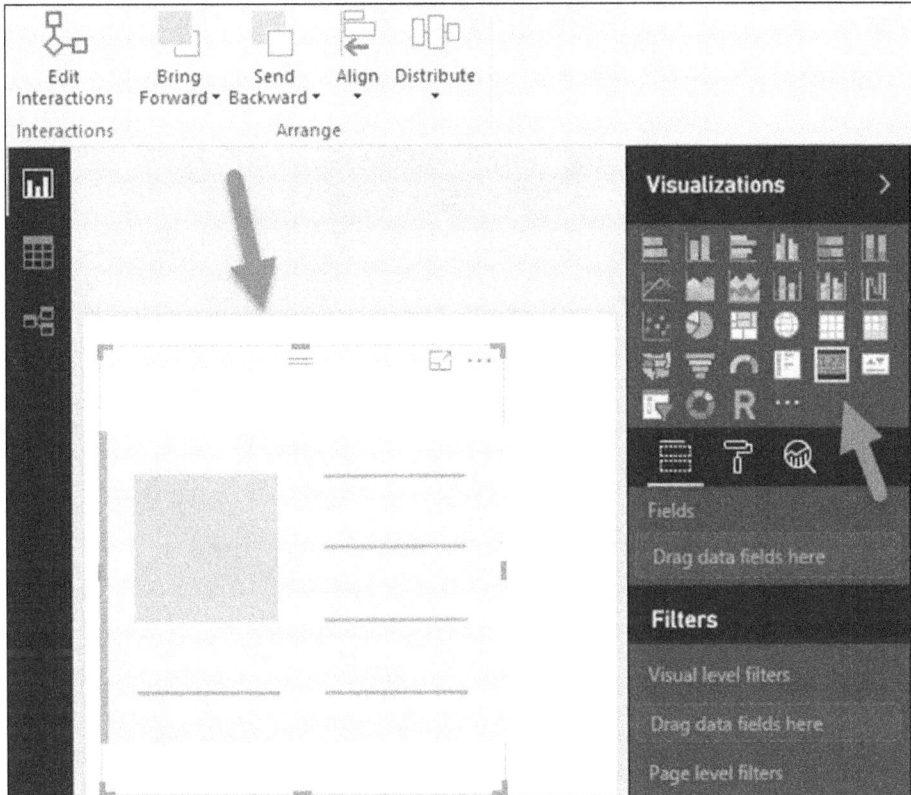

4. Make sure the new visual is selected. You'll see what I refer to as handlebars around the visual in this screenshot:

You'll also notice that the **Visualizations** pane includes a **Fields** area and **Filters** now has **Visual level filters**. This will enable us to use this pane to customize this specific visual.

5. In the **Fields** pane, expand the query named **Vendors** by clicking on the arrow. Scroll down and click on **Current Balance**, as shown here:

6. The total AP balance will appear in the visual as follows:

In theory, this visual is complete. It definitely can be used just as it is; however, some formatting can make it much more valuable. Let's add some formatting now:

1. Make sure that the new visual is selected. You'll see what I refer to as handlebars around the visual.

2. In the **Visualizations** pane, click on the formatting option (paint/roller brush). You'll notice the visual type is highlighted for reference, as depicted in the following screenshot:

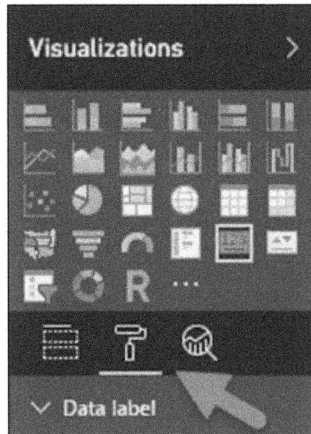

3. Expand the **Data label** option and change the **Display...** option from **Auto** to **None**. This will stop the value on the visual from rounding, as you can see in this screenshot:

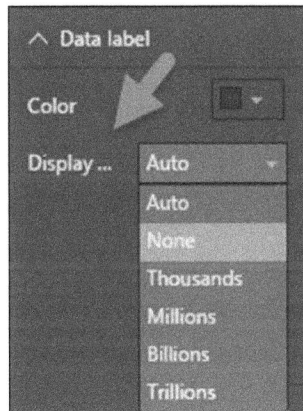

4. Expand the **Title** option and slide the bar to **On**, enter `Accounts Payable` in the **Title Text**, change **Font color** to black, change **Alignment** to center in the middle, and change **Text** to **14** (you can slide the bar to increase text). This will give an easy-to-read description as to what this visual represents, which is shown in the following screenshot:

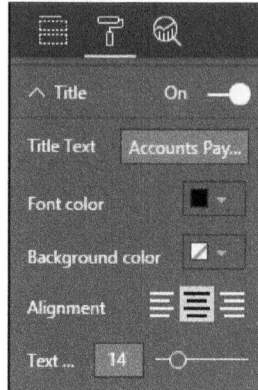

5. Slide **Category label** to **Off**. With the description of the value created in the previous step, we do not need to display the name of the field, particularly, because it offers no additional information to the visual, as you can see in this screenshot:

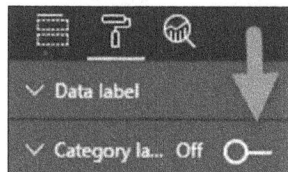

6. Finally, slide **Border** to **On**. This will provide some focus on the visual, as follows:

7. Save your `.pbix` file.

Additional formatting can be applied. I often add some background color to the visual and a darker background color to **Title**. This is entirely up to you. The following is a screenshot comparing the original visual (on the left) and the formatted visual (on the right). As you can see, the formatted visual offers much more value. Congratulations, you now have successfully created a visual.

Making a Gauge have more meaning

The gauge is another common visual used. It is important to understand that when used, the gauge will also display your value at 50%. Formatting is essential with the gauge because it is where you can specify maximums, minimums, and targets. The gas gauge in your car would be worthless if it always showed the amount of gas you have as 50%. For example, 20 gallons is 50%, one cup is 50%, and so on. Always remember to format your gauges!

Let's add a gauge now:

1. Open the Power BI file we created previously, `VendorInfo.pbix`.

2. Make sure you are viewing **Report** on the canvas. This will be the **Chart** icon in the black bar on the left side of the window.

3. In the **Visualizations** pane, select the **Gauge** icon. A blank visual will now appear on the canvas, as shown in this screenshot:

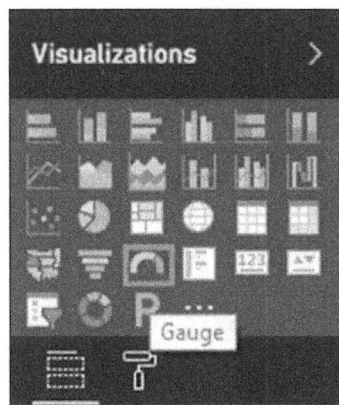

4. Make sure the blank visual is selected on the canvas. In the **Fields** pane, expand the query named **Vendors** by clicking on the arrow. Scroll down and click on **Current Balance**. See *adding a card visual* in the preceding section for a screenshot.

5. Just like when we added the card, the amount displayed is rounded and is shown as 50%, just like we discussed.

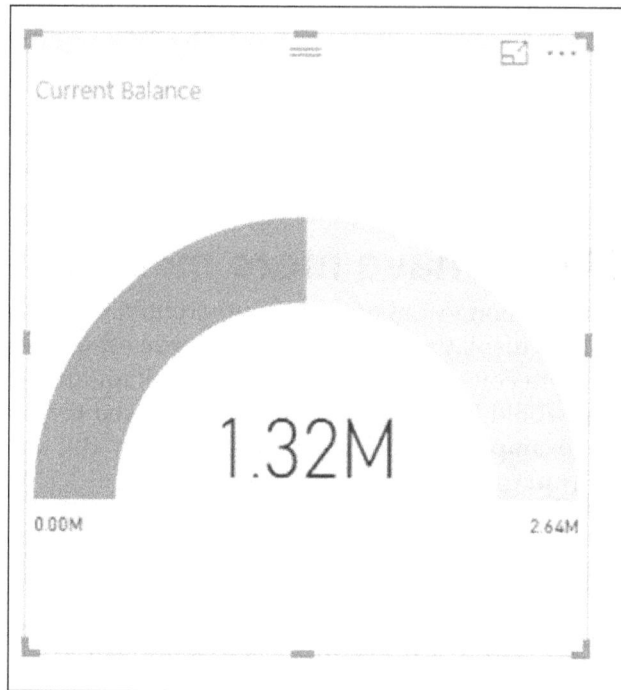

Current Balance

1.32M

0.00M   2.64M

Let's add some formatting to make this visual more valuable:

1. Make sure the Gauge visual is selected on the canvas.

2. In the **Visualizations** pane, click on the formatting option (paint/roller brush). You'll notice the visual type is highlighted for reference.

3. In the **Visualizations** pane, open **Gauge axis** by clicking on the arrow. Enter the smallest amount your AP balance would be in **Min** and the highest your AP balance would be in **Max**. Enter what your ideal AP balance would be in **Target**.

> Minimum, maximum, and target values may also come from another field in a query using the **Fields** option rather than the **Format** option.

4. In the **Visualizations** pane, open **Callout Value** by clicking on the arrow. Change **Display** from **Auto** to **None**. This will change the total amount displayed to show the full AP balance, not a rounded number.

> Using the AP balance for both the card and the gauge is a bit redundant. You may opt to remove the amount on the gauge, by turning off **Callout Value**, or by removing the card.

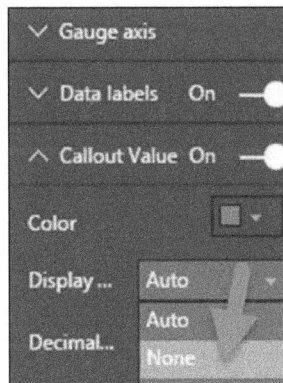

5. In the **Visualizations** pane, open **Title** by clicking on the arrow. Change the title to AP Balance, **Font color** to black, **Alignment** to center in the middle, and **Text** to **14** (you can slide the bar to increase text).

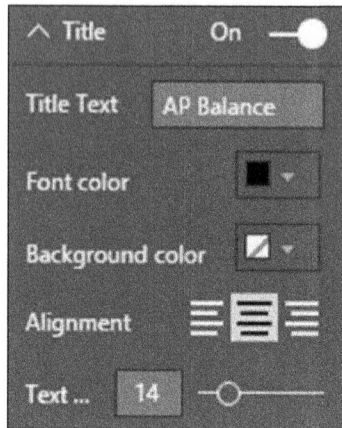

6. Finally, slide **Border** to **On**. This will provide some focus on the visual, as shown here:

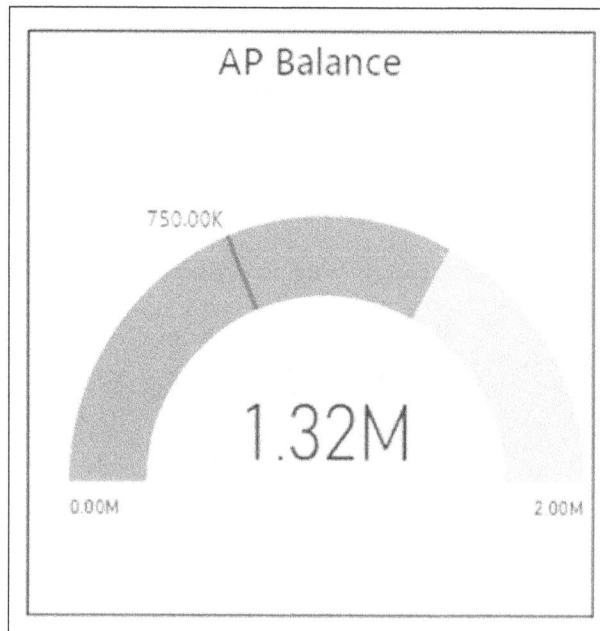

Getting down with drill down charts

Let's add a visual that is more interactive. We'll create a chart that shows all unpaid payables invoices by due date. We'll start by looking at the year and then be we will drill down, making the chart display invoices all the way down to the due date. Let's begin by following these steps:

1. Open the Power BI file we created in the last step, `VendorInfo.pbix`.

2. Make sure you are viewing **Report** on the canvas. This will be the **Chart** icon in the black bar on the left side of the window.

3. In the **Fields** pane, expand the query named **Query1** by clicking on the arrow. This is the query we created using the SQL script. Click on **Amount Unapplied**. Rather than adding the visual first, we are letting Power BI select what it deems as the best option for the data we are selecting. As we began with a number, it opened **Clustered column chart**.

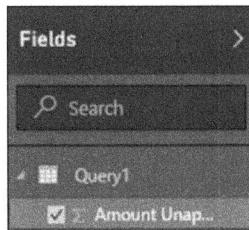

4. Right now, the visual looks extremely unimpressive. It is a single column. Let's create a column for each due date year. This is easily achieved by just clicking on **Due Date** in the **Fields** pane, as shown in the following screenshot:

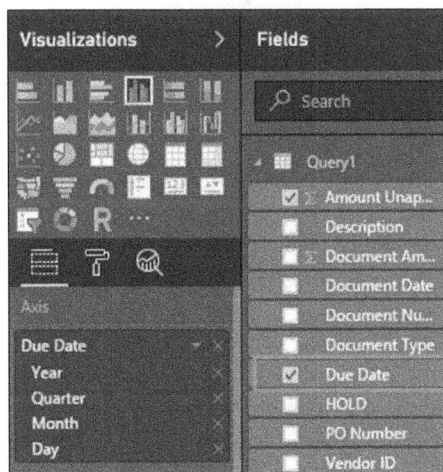

You'll notice that just by clicking on the field, Power BI was smart enough to place the **Due Date** field in **Axis** in the **Visualizations** pane. Rather than clicking on the field, you could have used the drag and drop feature of Windows to place the field in the **Axis** area.

A date hierarchy was automatically created separating out the **Year**, **Quarter**, **Month**, and **Day**. We will use this hierarchy when we drill down on the chart. You can remove any part of the hierarchy you like by clicking on **X**. For example, if you do not want to see the quarter when you drill down, just remove it from **Axis**.

This visual is including all documents, which include payments, returns, and credit memos. Let's filter out everything except invoices as that is the only kind of document we pay:

1. In the **Fields** pane, **Query1** should still be expanded. Select the **Document Type** field and drag it to the **Visual level filters** section of **Filters** in the **Visualizations** pane.

2. Leaving the **Basic Filtering** option, select only the **Invoice** option, as shown here:

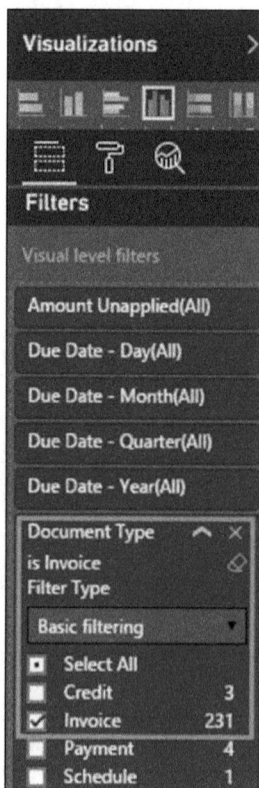

You'll notice that every field used in the visual appears in the filtering option, so it can be used to filter the data. You can also add additional filter options, as we did here. Additional filters can be added for all the visuals on this page and even for all pages in this file.

3. Grab one of the corner handles and stretch this report out to make it wider. This will help when we drill down to the day level.

4. Turn on the **Drill Down** mode by simply clicking on the down arrow in the top right corner of the visual. When on, the circle with the arrow will be highlighted, as shown in the following screenshot:

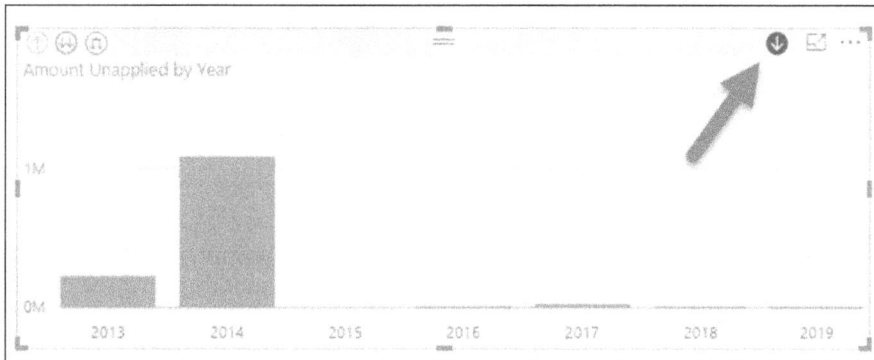

We would want to add some formatting but, basically, the visual can be used effectively as it is. Let's review how the drill down feature works:

1. Click on the column for a given year to see the outstanding invoices by quarter for that year. You'll notice that when you hover over a column, the detail for that column is displayed. The following image shows the visual before you click on the year, as you can see in this screenshot:

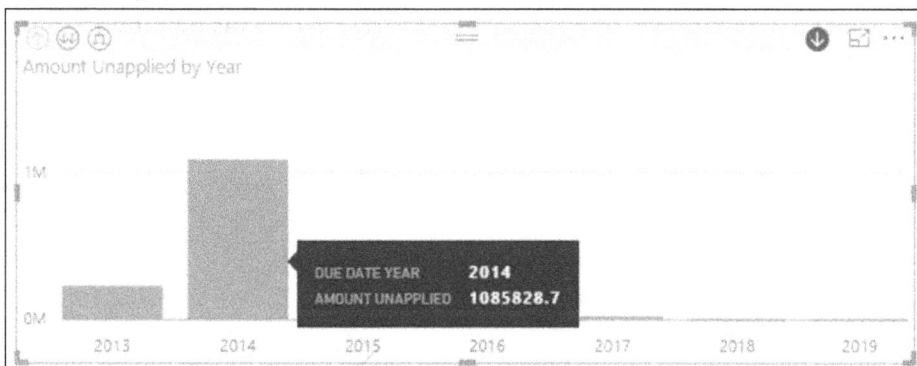

2. The quarters for the year selected are now displayed in columnar format. Again, while hovering your mouse over a given column, the details for that column are displayed. Even though the column is quarter 1, you can also see the year selected in the details, as shown in the following screenshot:

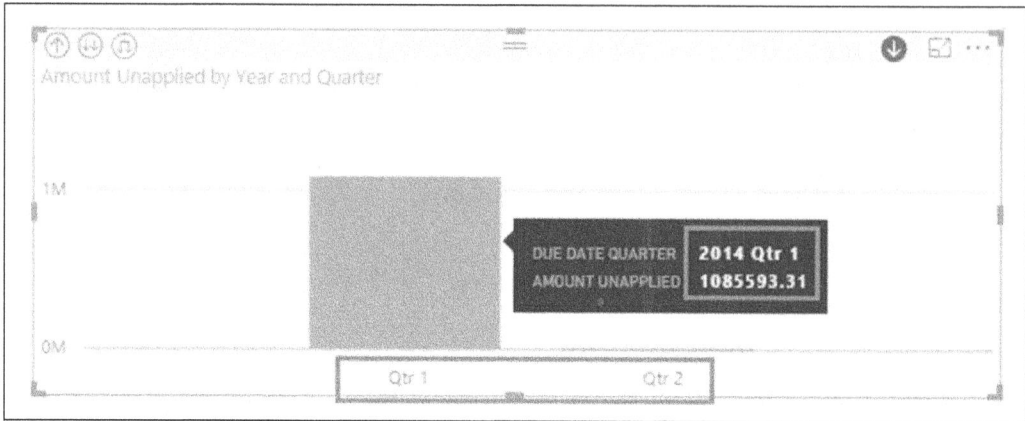

> As you probably guessed, if you click on a quarter, you'll see the months in that quarter. If you click on a month, you'll see the days of that month.

3. There are three buttons in the top-left corner of the visual. The one with the up arrow (on the left) will allow you to go back up one level. For example, if you are looking at quarters, this will take you back to years.

4. The button with the two down arrows (in the middle) allows you to go to the next level button. If you are on years, and you click it, you'll see the quarter columns that represent all years, not an individual year, like you see when you click on a single year column.

5. The final button that looks sort of like an *n* (on the right) will expand the visual down one level, but show everything. This means that if you start with year and click on this button, you'll see all year-quarter combinations that exist in the data, as depicted in this screenshot:

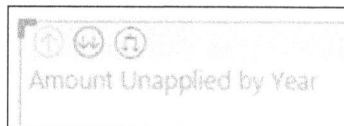

It's time to add a little formatting to make the visual look better. Let's do so by following these steps:

1. Make sure that **Clustered Column chart** with the **Drill Down** visual is selected on the canvas.

2. In the **Visualizations** pane, click on the formatting option (paint/roller brush). You'll notice the visual type is highlighted for reference.

3. In the **Visualizations** pane, slide **Border** to **On**. This will provide some focus on the visual.

4. Open **Title** by clicking on the arrow. Change **Font color** to black, **Alignment** to center in the middle, and **Text** to **14** (you can slide the bar to increase the text). As this visual is a drill down, the title will change based on the level we are viewing; so, we do not want to hardcode a title.

5. In the **Fields** pane, expand **Query1**. Click on the ellipses(**...**) for the **Amount Unapplied** field. In the pop-up menu, select **Rename**. Change the field name from **Amount Unapplied** to AP Balance. This will change the name only for the report and query. As we did not change the title name when formatting, the visual title is using **AP Balance**.

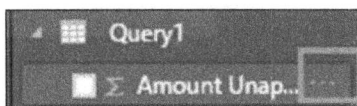

Carving out better data with a Slicer

Power BI has a slicer that works like slicers in Excel. Let's add one to the report now:

1. Open the Power BI file we created in the last step, VendorInfo.pbix.

2. Make sure you are viewing **Report** on the canvas. This will be the **Chart** icon in the black bar on the left side of the window.

3. In the **Fields** pane, expand the query named **Query1** by clicking on the arrow. This is the query we created using the SQL script. Click on **Vendor Class ID**.

4. As this is a text field, Power BI chose a **Table** view for us. Let's change it to **Slicer**. Make sure the **Table** visual is selected on the canvas.

5. Click on the **Slicer** visual in the **Visualizations** pane, as shown in this screenshot:

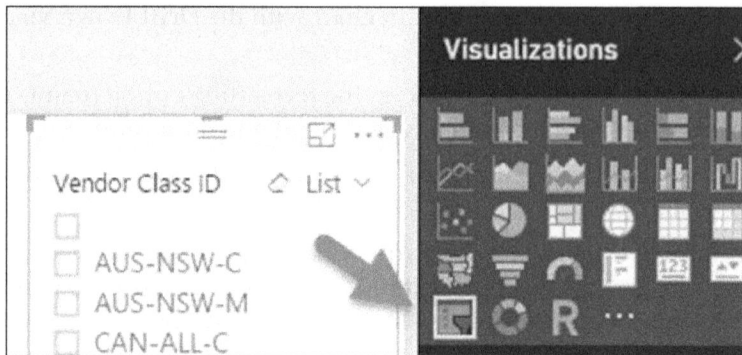

6. We added **Border** around the visual like we did in the preceding section.

7. We also formed the **Header** by increasing the **Text** size to **14** and centering it, like we did in the others. As this is an individual field, we opted to leave **Header**, which is the field name, in place of **Title**.

You'll notice that when you select one or more vendor classes, every visual on the page updates. Our report is completely interactive.

Although the visuals on our report have come from different queries, they still interact with each other. This is due to Power BI establishing a relationship between the two queries used using a feature called **Autodetect**. The **Vendor ID** field is named the same and is the same data type (Text), so Power BI assumed that the **Vendor ID** field in the open payables query is the same as the **Vendor ID** field in the **Vendor** details query. Relationships and queries can be viewed or edited in the **Relationships** on the canvas. This will be the **Organizational Chart** looking icon in the black bar on the left side of the window.

Adding final touches

There are a lot of other visuals we can add to this page, and/or even create more pages. Let's just add a title and perhaps a logo to make it more visually appealing:

1. Open the Power BI file we created in the last step, `VendorInfo.pbix`.

2. Make sure you are viewing **Report** on the canvas. This will be the **Chart** icon in the black bar on the left side of the window.

3. With **Home** selected on the menu, choose **Text Box** in the **Insert** area of the ribbon, as you can see in the following screenshot:

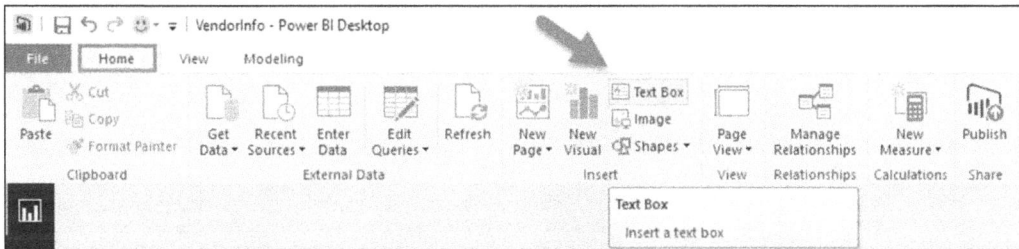

4. Before entering in a report title, change the font size to **32**. Enter AP Information, as shown in this screenshot:

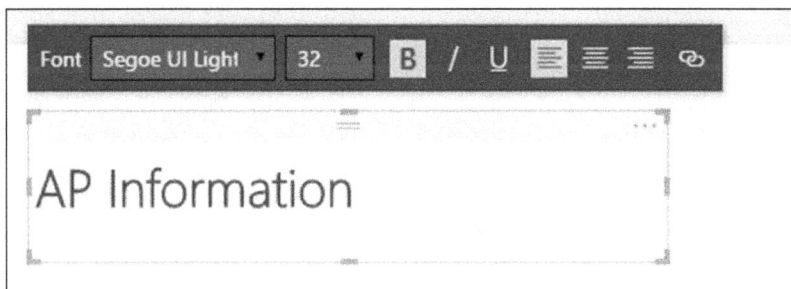

5. With **Home** selected on the menu, choose **Image** in the **Insert** area of the ribbon, as follows:

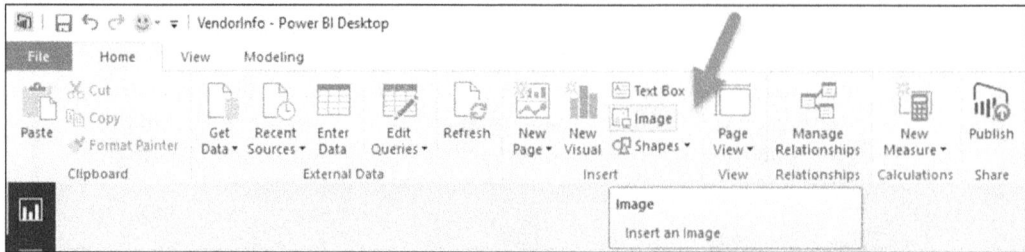

6. Find your logo (or any image) and place it on the report.
7. By selecting individual visuals (the **Text Box** and **Image** included), resize and rearrange to make your Power BI report look the way you want.

The final report is displayed as follows:

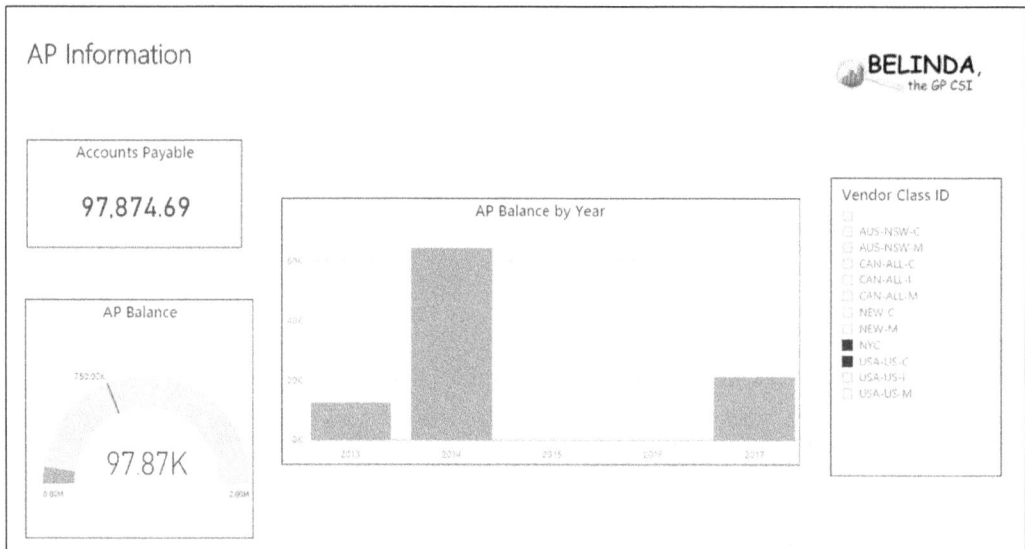

Remember to always spend time reviewing formatting options for all the new visuals added to reports. They often contain options that make the visual more valuable.

Development options - if you have a techie on staff

Custom visuals can be created if you need something beyond what you see on the **Visualizations** pane. This does involve programming or coding, so it's not something that everyone can do. If you have a developer on staff, just know that they can build custom visuals.

Fortunately, several developers have created custom visuals and made them available in a *Visual Library* for non-coding users. This library contains both standard visuals and R-powered visuals (see the next section about R).

> You can view the library at the following website: `https://app.powerbi.com/visuals/`

If you see a visual you like, click on it, and you'll have the opportunity to download both a sample (that runs in Power BI Desktop) and the visual itself. Once you have downloaded it, you can import it to the **Visualizations** pane in the Power BI Desktop by clicking on the ellipses (**...**) and choosing **Import a custom visual**, as shown in this screenshot:

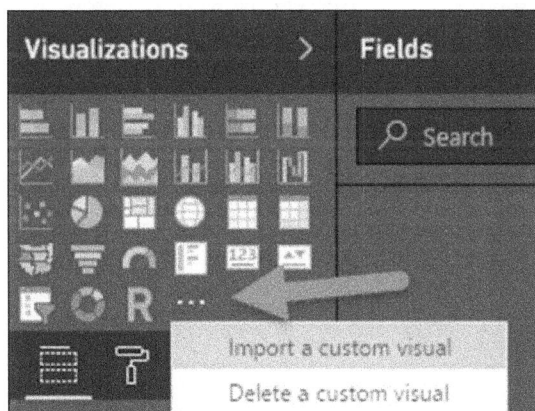

> A few important things to know about custom visual are that you'll need to import it into every Power BI desktop file you want to use it in. It gets imported into a single file, not the entire application. Also, custom visualizations do not always work when using them as embedded visuals. For example, the current version of Dynamics GP does not recognize custom visuals when using Power BI items on the **Home** page.

R - what is it and do I need it?

R is a programing language and environment that is for statistics and numbers only. It is often used by data analysts and data scientists because of its ability to support graphics. Although Power BI does support R, it does not include or install the R engine. This means that you will have to install it prior to using the R visuals.

Although R is a default option on the Power BI **Visualizations** pane, it does not work in the same method as the other options. When you add an R visual to the canvas, you'll be prompted to write your R script using an editor that opens up.

There are so many options, right out of the box, to create great visuals. Save R visuals for when you have achieved advanced status.

Summary

This was an exciting chapter. We built a super cool Power BI report using several visuals. Normally, we would add much more to this, such as a table that shows individual vendors and their balance. With the goal of providing you with an overview and getting you on the path to creating stunning dashboards, we kept it simple.

In the next chapter, we will publish this report to the Power BI Service so that we can consume the data both on the web and on our mobile devices. We'll also review options to share reports and refresh data. Isn't this fun???

11
Using the Power BI Service

Now that we've built a nice report on Accounts Payable information using the Power BI Desktop, it's time to upload what we've built into the Power BI service. Once it's in the service, we can also use it on our mobile devices.

In this chapter, we'll cover various methods of getting information into the Power BI service (web page) for consumption. Specifically, we will cover the following topics:

- Publishing to the service
- Creating a dashboard
- Q&A
- Importing an Excel report

Recap

We've spent time importing data into the Power BI Desktop using a variety of methods. At this point, we are assuming the data does not need any cleanup (or modeling). We'll be modeling our data in a future chapter. Once the report is uploaded to the Power BI service (web), we can use individual visuals on that report, and others, to create effective and informative dashboards. All of these items, reports, and dashboards can be shared with others. Some can even be refreshed automatically (capturing changes or new data).

Let's get started!

Publishing to the service

Up to this point, we were able to create reports without setting up a Microsoft Power BI account. To use the Power BI service, a Power BI account must be set up.

> You can sign up for a free account using the following URL:
> https://powerbi.microsoft.com/en-us/get-started/

We'll start populating the Power BI service using the easy-to-use feature called **Publish**. Consider the following steps:

1. Open the Power BI Desktop file we created called VendorInfo.pbix.

2. Sign into Power BI by clicking on **Sign in** at the top-right corner of your window. If your name appears instead of **Sign in**, you are already signed in. Skip ahead to step 5:

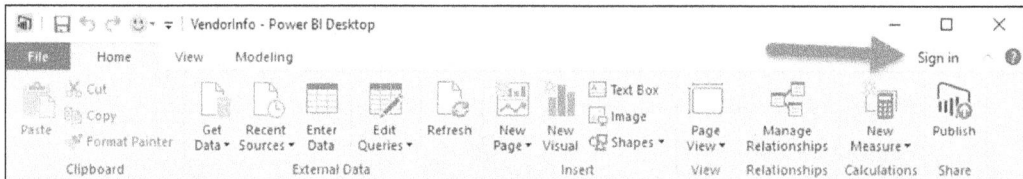

3. Enter your Power BI account e-mail in the **Power BI Desktop** window, as follows:

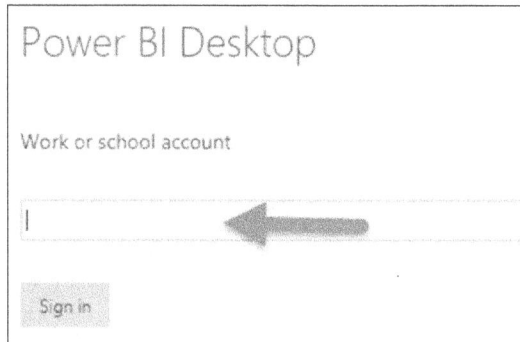

4. Enter your Power BI password in the window and click on **Sign in**:

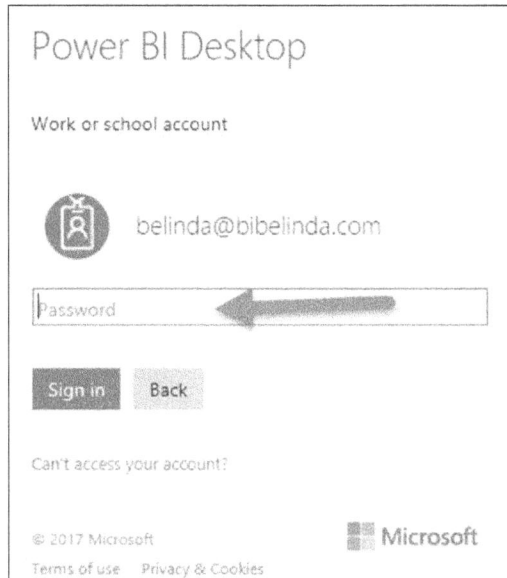

You should now see your Power BI username in the top-right corner of your Power BI Desktop application. Take a look at the following screenshot:

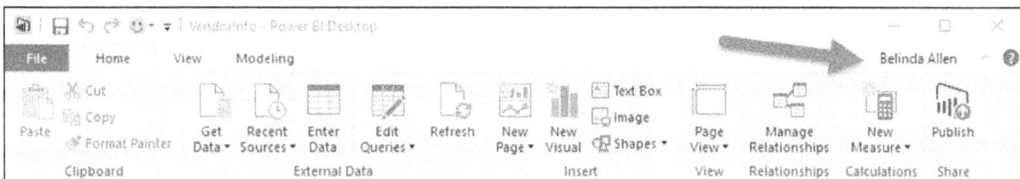

5. Click on **Publish** from the **Share** area of the **Home** ribbon:

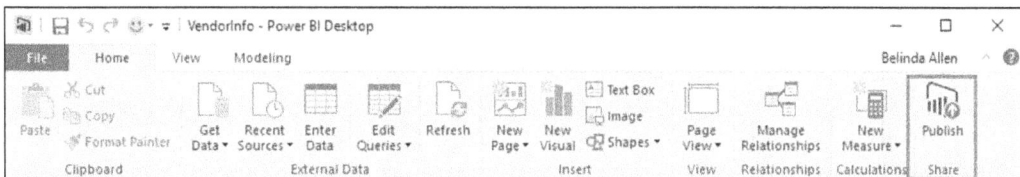

If you have the Professional (paid) Microsoft Power BI license, you will receive this additional window asking if you want to publish to your personal workspace or to an entire group setup in either Office 365 or Power BI. If you use the free version, this window does not display:

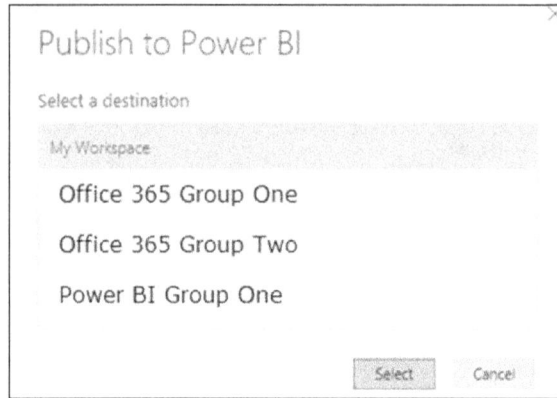

Publish to Power BI

Select a destination

My Workspace

Office 365 Group One

Office 365 Group Two

Power BI Group One

Select   Cancel

The **Publishing to Power BI** processing window will display. Consider the following screenshot:

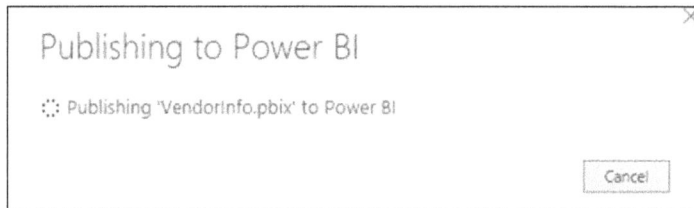

Publishing to Power BI

Publishing 'VendorInfo.pbix' to Power BI

Cancel

When publishing is complete, you'll be prompted to open the Power BI service:

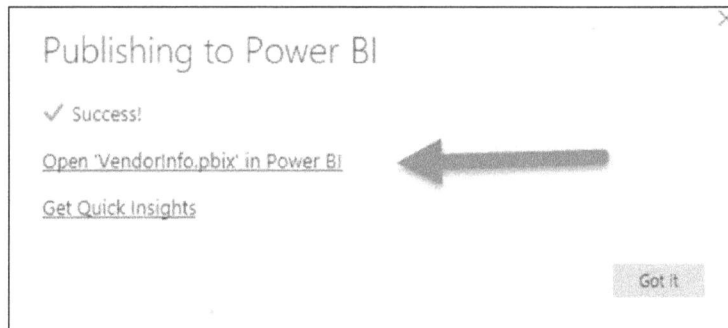

Publishing to Power BI

✓ Success!

Open 'VendorInfo.pbix' in Power BI

Get Quick Insights

Got It

[![notes icon] Upon clicking on the link, you may be prompted for your login, or you may go right to service. This will depend on your last Microsoft login in your browser.]

6. Click on **Open 'Vendorinfo.pbix'** in Power BI, and your report will display in the Power BI service:

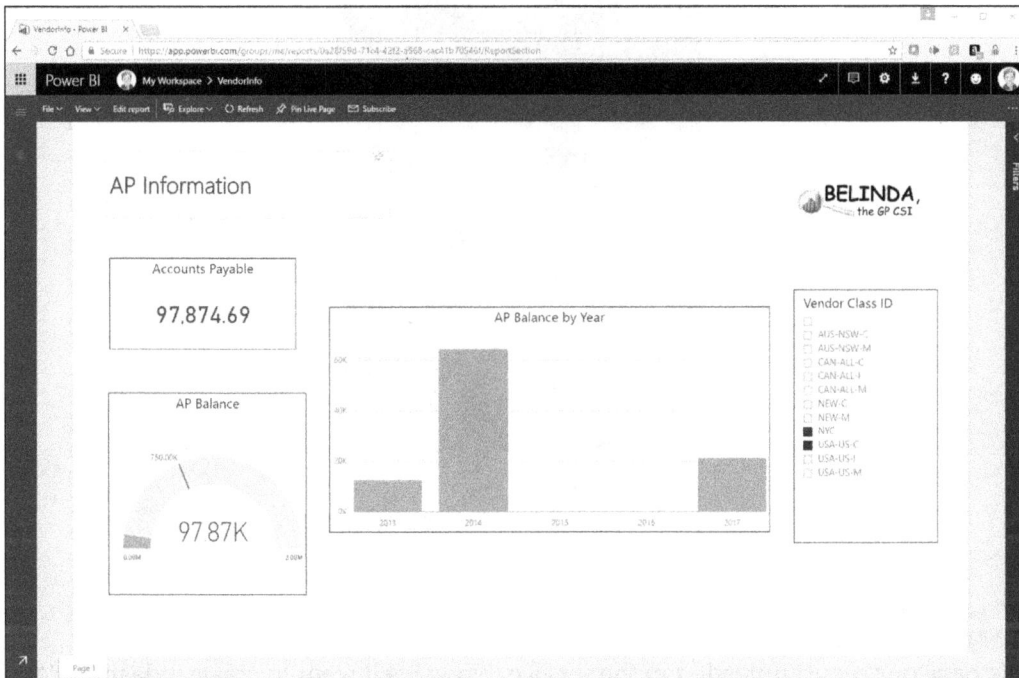

When you first publish data and/or reports to the service, a yellow asterisk will appear next to the new items, until you click on them or hover over them. You'll notice that we have VendorInfo, which was the name of our file in the Power BI Desktop as both a dataset and a report.

Datasets in Power BI is the actual data we extracted using **Get Data** in the Power BI Desktop. The data is stored inside the file, allowing us to create more visuals and ask questions of it using Q&A. **Reports** are the actual pages we placed visuals on in the Power BI Desktop. When we published our file, we published both the data and the report. Take a look at the following screenshot:

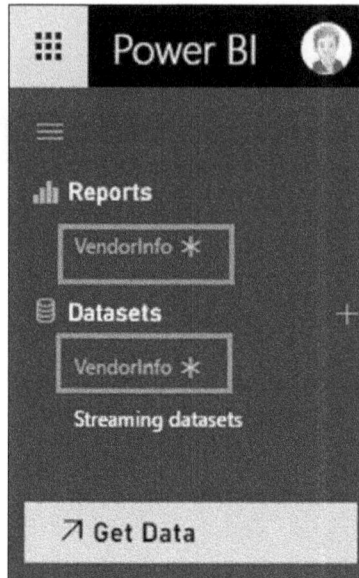

Creating a dashboard

We have our report uploaded in the service. Now, we'll want to create a dashboard. The school of thought is that you can have several reports combined from several different data sources in your service. You may want to combine these visuals together and consume bits and pieces of each report in a single view. Dashboards are just that--a single compilation of visuals from reports. You can have as many reports and dashboards as you like or need, provided you do not exceed the space allotted to you by Microsoft.

[The free version of Power BI allows you 1 gigabyte of data per user, while the paid version allows you 10 gigabytes of data per user.]

Now, let's create a dashboard from the visuals on our current payables report by following these steps:

1. Go to `www.PowerBI.com` and log in using your Power BI account, if you are not already logged in.

2. Click on the ellipsis next to `VendorInfo` under **Reports** on the Power BI navigation bar on the left:

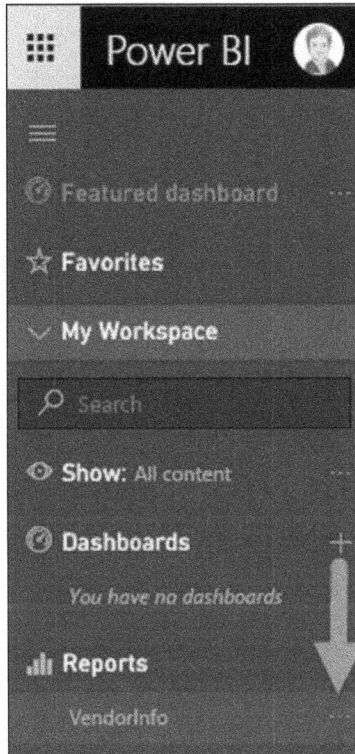

> If you do not see the navigation bar, click on the hamburger icon (three white lines on top of each other) under the yellow box (with the nine black squares) to open the navigation bar. This opens and closes the navigation bar.

3. Let's give this report a more descriptive name. Choose **RENAME**:

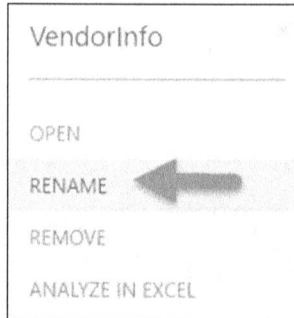

4. Change the name to AP Information and click on *Enter*:

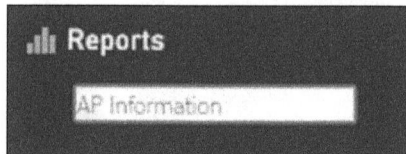

5. Click on the report we just renamed to AP Information. The report will appear on the canvas to the right.

6. Hover of one of the visuals. You'll notice that three icons will appear — a pushpin, an enlargement icon, and an ellipsis. Click on the pushpin:

7. The **Pin to dashboard** window will open, asking us if we want to add this visual to an existing dashboard or create a new dashboard. As we do not have a dashboard yet, the **New dashboard** option is selected. Enter AP Information in as the name of the new dashboard and click on Pin:

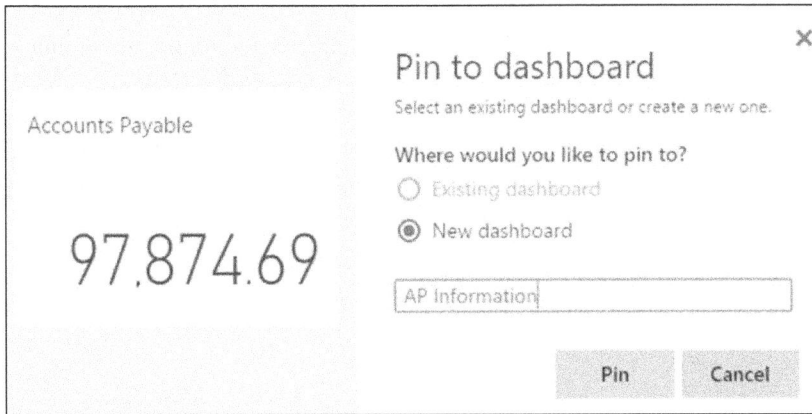

We'll now see the new `AP Information` dashboard with the yellow asterisk, which indicates that it is new, and we'll receive a message in the top-right corner of the screen that the visualization was pinned successfully. Consider the following screenshot:

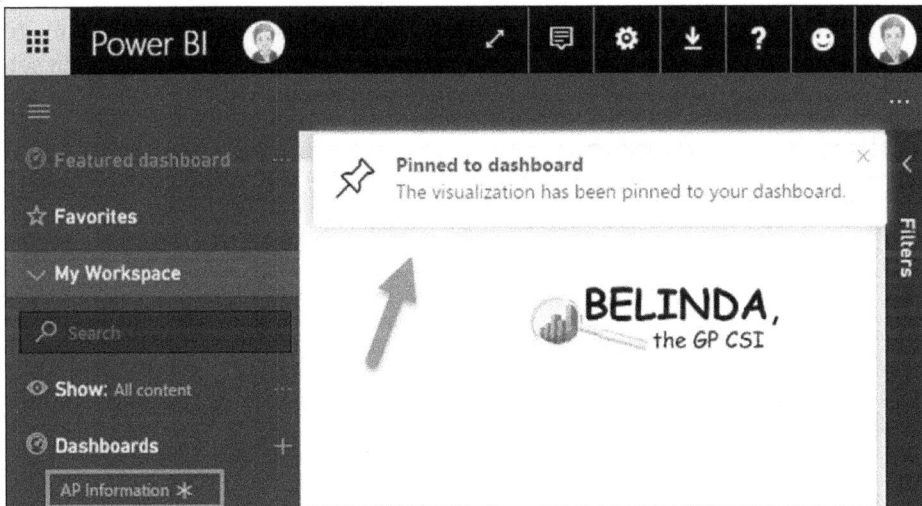

8. Lather, rinse, and repeat. Add the rest of the visuals on the `AP Information` report to this dashboard. As you pin each, this time, the **Pin to dashboard** window will default to the `AP Information` dashboard we created.

9. Do not pin the filter visual, the title, or the image (logo) to the dashboard. These do not provide value to the dashboard.

> When a visual is clicked on the dashboard, the report containing the visual will open, at which time, filters can be used.

10. Click on the `AP Information` dashboard we just created. The dashboard will appear on the canvas to the right. The following is a copy of the dashboard we just created:

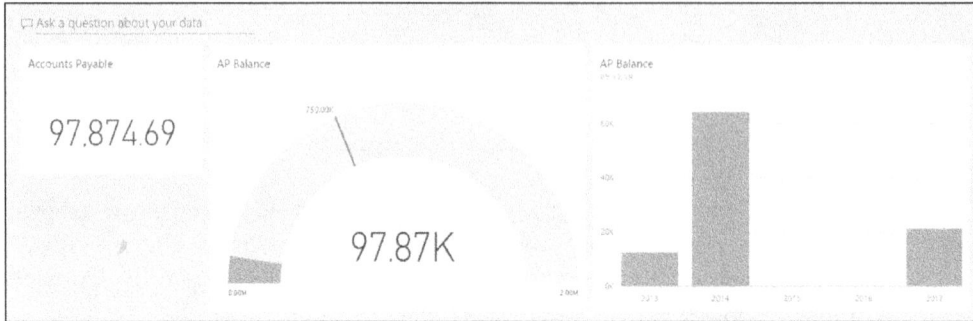

When we log in to Power BI on our iPad, which can be downloaded for free from the iTunes App Store, we will receive the following screen. We'll select **Dashboards**, then the new `AP Information` dashboard:

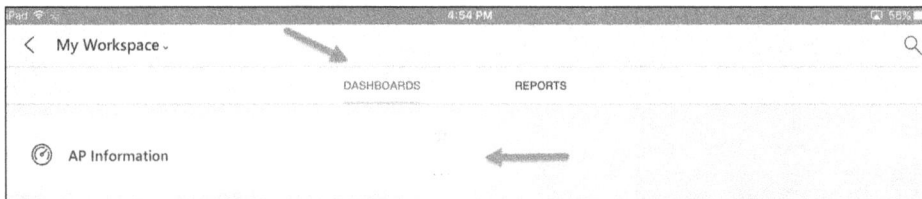

Finally, we will see that the iPad dashboard looks almost identical to the dashboard in the service:

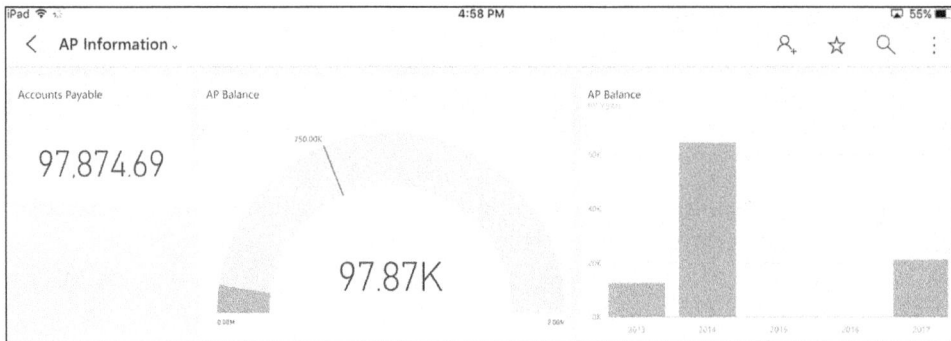

The following is the same dashboard on the iPhone:

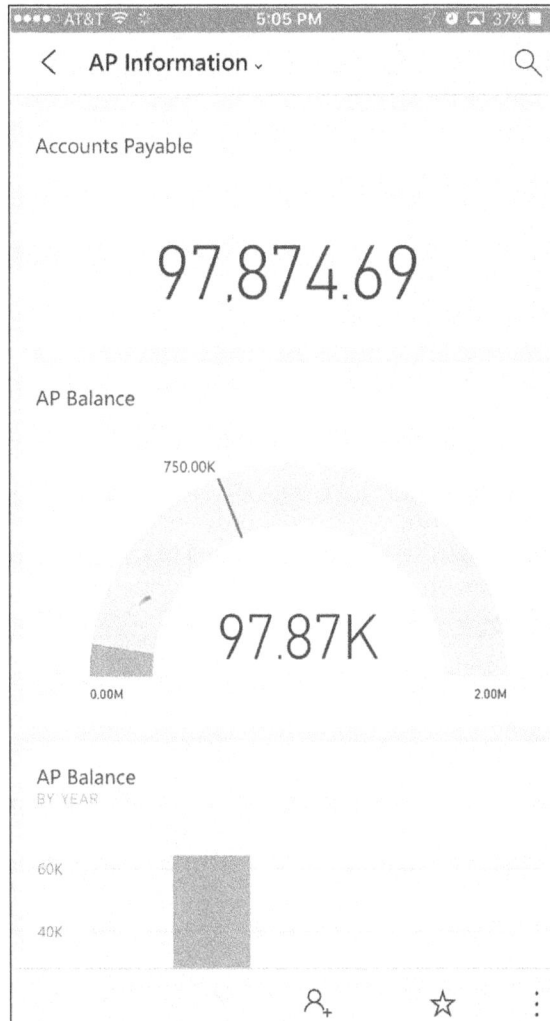

Getting to know the Q&A feature

The Q&A feature on the Power BI service allows users to ask Power BI questions in natural language about the data in the datasets. The results will be displayed in a visual, which can be pinned to the dashboard. This feature takes advantage of the technology from *Bing*, Microsoft's search engine.

The Q&A feature uses the column names as key words for the searches. This enables the designer of the reports and dashboards to customize data to include wording that is natural in your own organization. If you call your customers clients, let the column name be clients. The dashboard consumers will not always be GP users, meaning they will not think to use the word customers; they'll enter *Show Gross Margin by Client* and not *Show Gross Margin by Customer*.

Let's give it a try by performing the following steps:

1. Open the `AP Information` dashboard we created. You'll notice that in the top-right corner of the dashboard is the Ask a question about your data line. Click on that line:

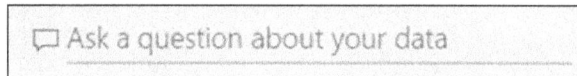

    ┌───┐
    │ ⬚ Ask a question about your data   │
    └───┘

2. In the blank line, enter `show ap balance by state`. You'll notice that as you type `ap balance` and `state`, a window appears with field names and those fields are also underlined in yellow. This means that these are actual references to columns in our dataset. Take a look at the following screenshot:

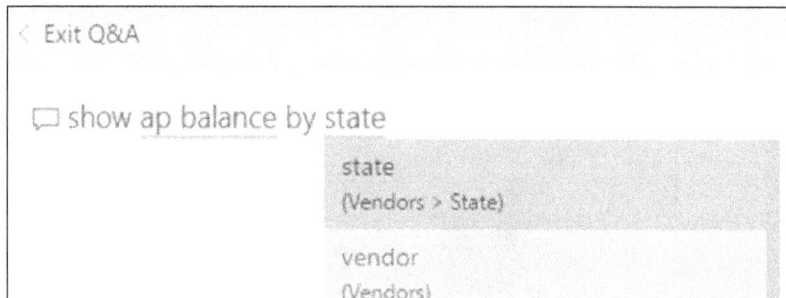

    ┌───┐
    │ ‹ Exit Q&A   │
    │   │
    │ ⬚ show ap balance by state   │
    │   ┌──────────────────┐   │
    │   │ state   │   │
    │   │ (Vendors > State)│   │
    │   │   │   │
    │   │ vendor   │   │
    │   │ (Vendors)   │   │
    └───┘

    You'll notice that the answer appears in a bar chart.

> 💡 Anything with the yellow underline in the question can be replaced by another field in the dataset to change the visualization. Changes can also be made using the **Visualizations** filters pane as well.

3. In the top-right corner of the canvas, you can click on **Pin visual** to pin this to your dashboard. Then, click on **Exit Q&A** on the top left to go back to the dashboard:

Now, our dashboard looks like the following:

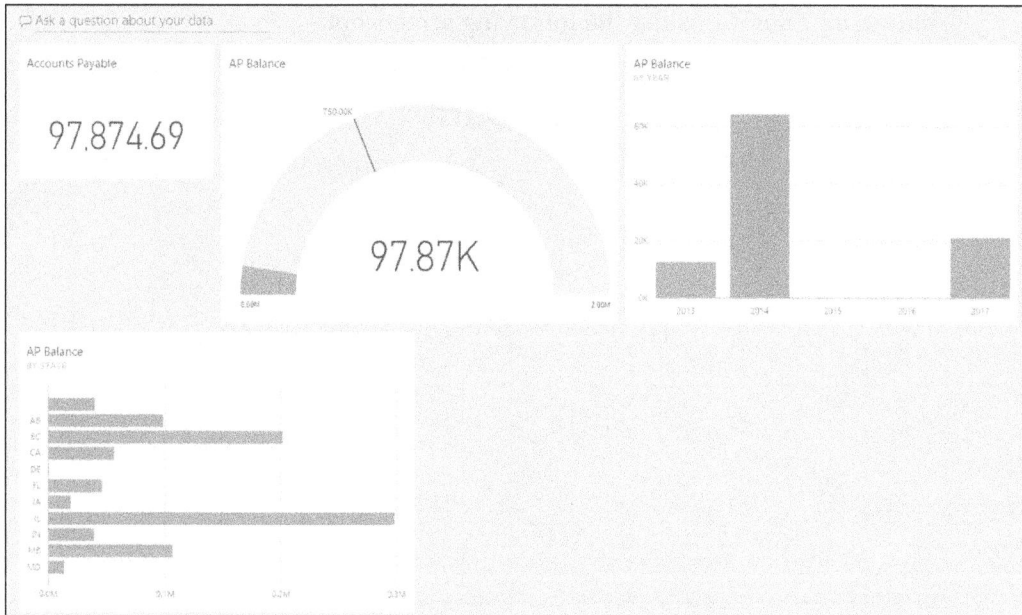

Importing an Excel report

Sometimes, the data we want to access using the Power BI service is already in an Excel report that works beautifully. Maybe, it is a financial statement we built using Jet Express for GP. Why recreate a report when all we want to do is use the Power BI service to have the report available whenever we want to reference it?

Let's add the `FinancialStatement.xlsx` report we built in *Chapter 7, Building Financial Reports in Jet Express for GP*. Perform the following steps:

1. Go to `www.PowerBI.com` and log in using your Power BI account, if you are not already logged in.

2. In the navigation pane, click on the plus sign next to **Datasets** to add or **Get Data** to the service:

3. In the **Get Data** window, under **Import or Connect to Data**, select the **Get** button for **Files**. Consider the following screenshot:

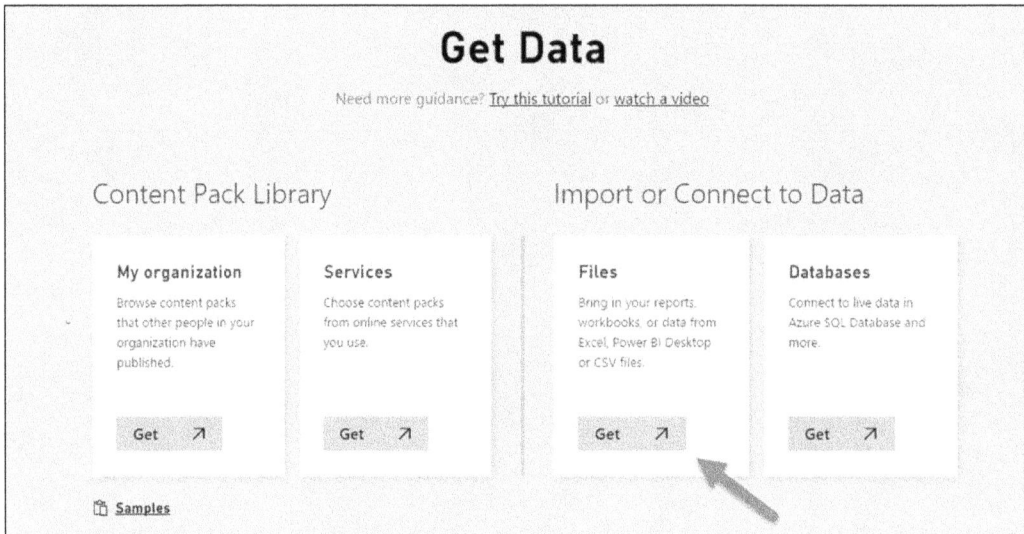

4. Click on **Local File**. Map out and find the `FinancialStatement.xlsx` file you saved in *Chapter 6, Introducing Jet Reports Express*:

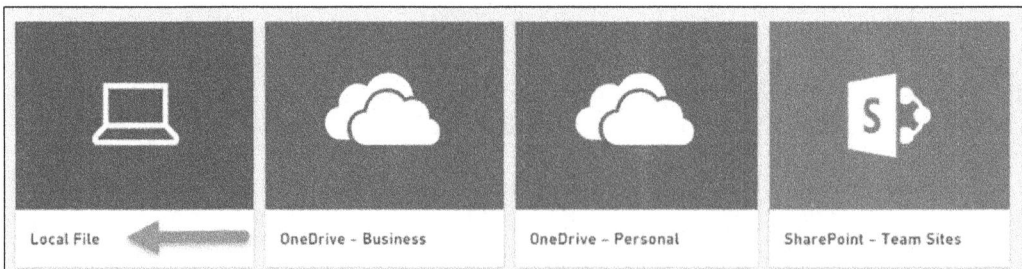

5. In the **Local File** window, select the **Upload** button:

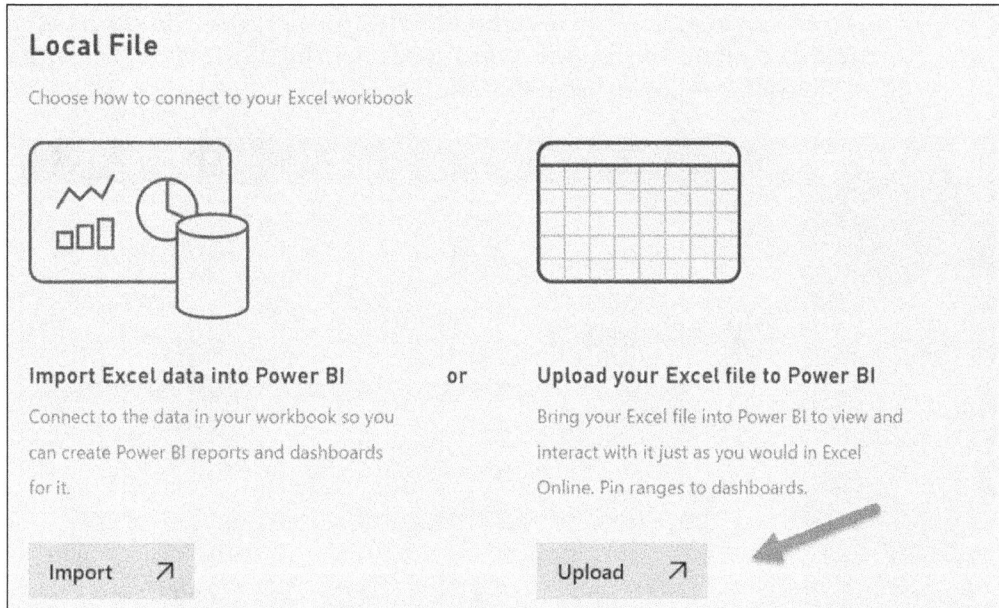

6. On the navigation pane, you'll notice a new report (with the yellow asterisk) called FinancialStatements. You may want to rename it, as it appears with no space, using the same name as the file itself. Take a look at the following screenshot:

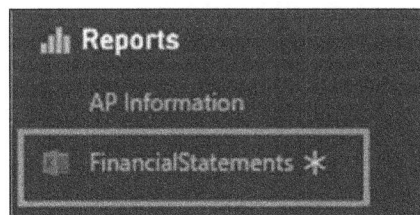

7. Click on the new report, and you'll see the report appear on the canvas. When it appears, it is actually using Microsoft Excel services or Excel Online. This allows you to review the report (not refresh), even if you do not have Excel installed on the machine on which you are using the Power BI service. Take a look at the following screenshot:

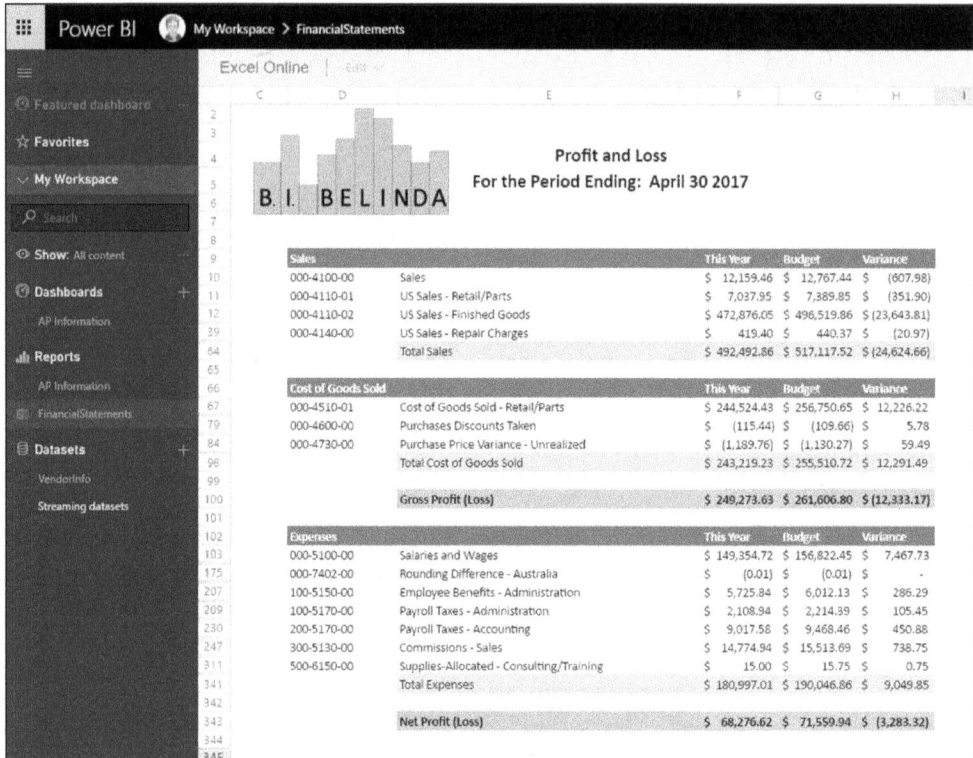

Summary

We know how cool it is to build our first dashboard, creating visuals from scratch, and seeing our efforts appear on the web service. However, know this: we've only scratched the service of what can be done in the service, and on the mobile device. There are so many more things we'd love to show, but this is a book, not an encyclopedia set (assuming that you even remember or know what that reference means). It should be enough to get you started to create and consume data in reports and dashboards using Power BI.

In the next chapter, we'll cover some basics on sharing data with coworkers. We'll also review when and how data can be refreshed directly in the Power BI service without having to republish everything.

12
Sharing and Refreshing Data and Dashboards in Power BI

So, now we have data and we have visuals, in the form of reports, and we have data and reports in the Power BI service. We are ready to share these visuals with our co-workers. There are a variety of methods of sharing these reports. The easiest, and most obvious, is just to share the Power Bi Desktop (`*.pbix`) file we create, like we do with Excel files. This certainly works, but then you might have a lot of versions out there, which also might be fine.

In this chapter, we'll cover other methods of sharing data and adding the element of refreshing dashboards as well. Refreshing becomes more important when the visuals are only in the Power BI service (web). Specifically, we will cover the following topics:

- Power BI Template
- Content packs
- Online services
- Refreshing data

Recap

We've spent time importing data into the Power BI Desktop using a variety of methods. At this point, we are assuming that the data does not need any cleanup (or modeling). We'll be modeling our data in the next chapter. We've created a simple Power BI Desktop report and published our report to the Power BI service (web), and we pinned individual visuals from that report, creating an effective and informative dashboard. All of these visuals, reports, and dashboards, can be shared with others. Some can even be refreshed automatically (capturing changes or new data).

Let's assume that your role in your company's BI methodology is to create reports and make them available to other team members. In this scenario, we will take the AP Information Power BI Desktop and information in the service that we've created and share it with other members using a variety of methods. Some of these options can be used to help you create a library of BI reports for your organization.

Power BI Template

I've already mentioned just sharing the file Power BI Desktop (*.pbix) file created as a means of sharing prebuilt reports. There are two problems with this option. One, who has the original, and if it gets changed then is it still something that is sharable? Two, there is data stored in the file so it could get quite large, eating up unnecessary hard drive (or cloud storage) space. Both of these issues can be resolved by exporting our Power BI Desktop reports to a template format (*.pbit).

Let's create a template from the AP Information Power BI Desktop file that we created:

1. Open the Power BI Desktop `VendorInfo.pbix` file that we created earlier.

2. On the menu, click on **File** | **Export** | **Power BI Template**:

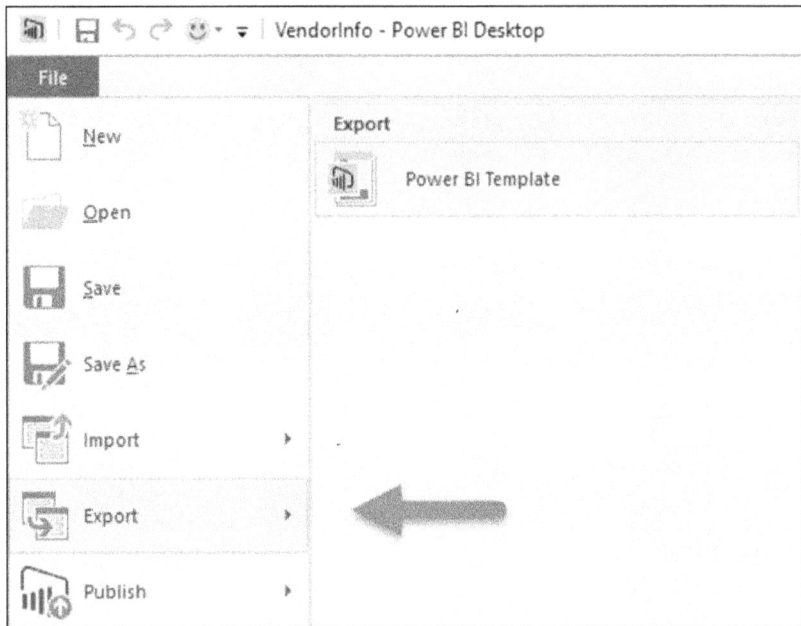

3. The **Export Template** window will open. Enter a description of the template. Click on **OK**.

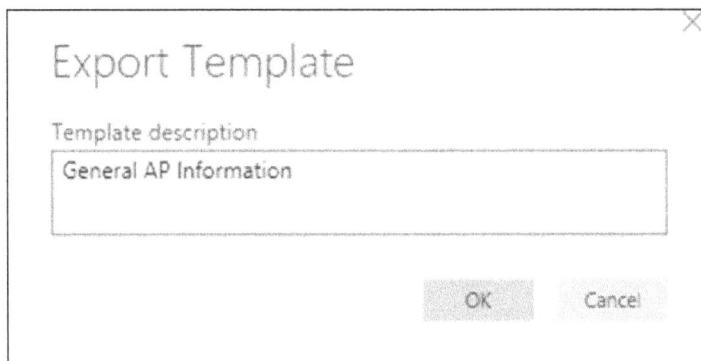

4. Save the template in a secure location. You'll notice that the template will use the same name as the Power BI Desktop report, but it will have a `.pbit` extension.

You have now created a template file based on the report we created. For users to successfully use this template, they'll need to have the same security that was used when the report was created. Also, they'll need to access the data in the same method. This means that if you get data from the local (your own network) SQL Server data, those who use the template must also be local to that same SQL Server data.

> Note that queries can be edited, changing the connection information using the Edit Queries window. By editing the connection information, templates become more flexible regarding the data they access. See the next chapter on modeling for more information on editing queries.

Now that we've exported a template, let's import it just for fun. Oh yes, we'll also import it to see how it works:

1. Open a blank Power BI Desktop file, either by relaunching or from the menu and select **File | New**. If the *Getting Started* window appears, close it by clicking on the **X** in the top-right corner.

2. In the menu, select **File | Import | Power BI Template**.

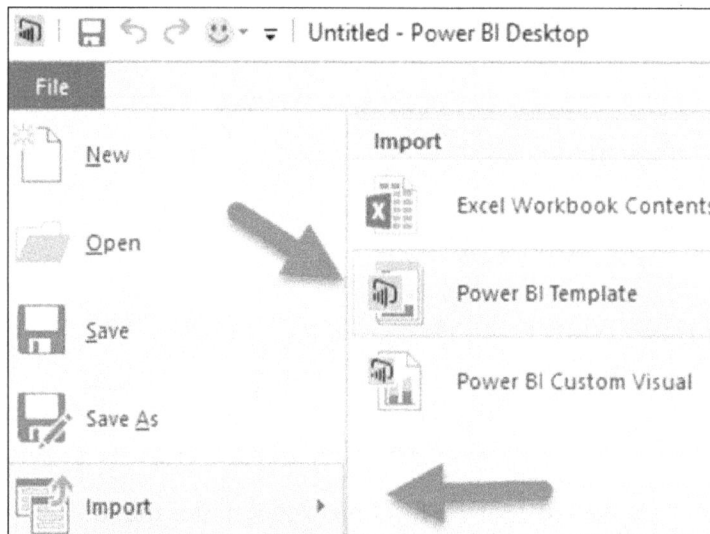

3. Find the template we created previously, VendorInfo.pbit, and click on **Open**.

   You'll see the data magically refresh and appear on your file, exactly as you had it in the original format.

Again, the major difference between the original file and a template is that the data is not saved in the template. Only the connection information, any data modeling performed, which we'll discuss in the next chapter, and any visuals/reports created are stored in the template. In this example, the size of each file is indicated in the following screenshot and, remember, this was a small dataset:

	POWER BI DESKTOP FILE SIZE	TEMPLATE FILE SIZE
VENDORINFO.*	5,674 KB	104 KB

Let's talk about data refreshing using this option of data sharing. When using the shared option of a template, in the Power BI Desktop, you can refresh by simply clicking on the **Refresh** option of the **Home** ribbon. This option will work so long as the original source is refreshable, as shown in the following screenshot:

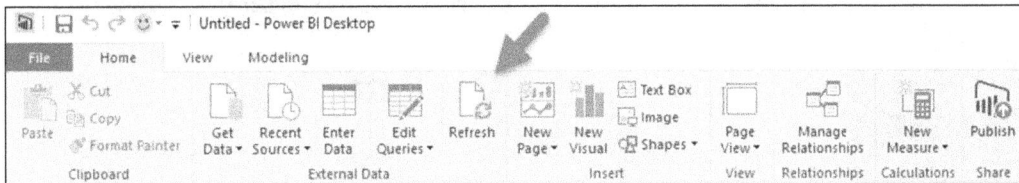

Keep in mind that if the original data source was a static, non-changing Excel file, refreshing it will get exactly the same data, resulting in no change. If you change the data in the Excel file, the refreshing will pick up the changes.

Once a template is published to Power BI service (www.PowerBI.com), refreshing will not work unless you have a data gateway installed. We'll talk about gateways later in this chapter.

Content Packs

We've just created a single Power BI Template. Imagine if we took that same idea of creating a file that had the connection information and reports established and put it all in an easy-to-access place for information sharing. That would be awesome. Actually, it is awesome. Microsoft already did it, and it's called Organizational Content Packs.

Users with the Power BI Pro (paid) license can create their own private library of Content Packs, which would become available for co-workers with a Power BI Pro account, with security enabled, of course.

> As this information is unique to our organization, and as not all of you will have a Power BI Pro account, these steps are for reading only.

We'll walk through the steps of creating an Organizational Content Pack, which are as follows:

1. Using the Power BI service, we are importing data from Excel files located on a shared `OneDrive Business` folder. On the **Power BI** pane, we will select **Get Data**, then choose to import (**Get**) from **Files**, as shown in the following screenshot:

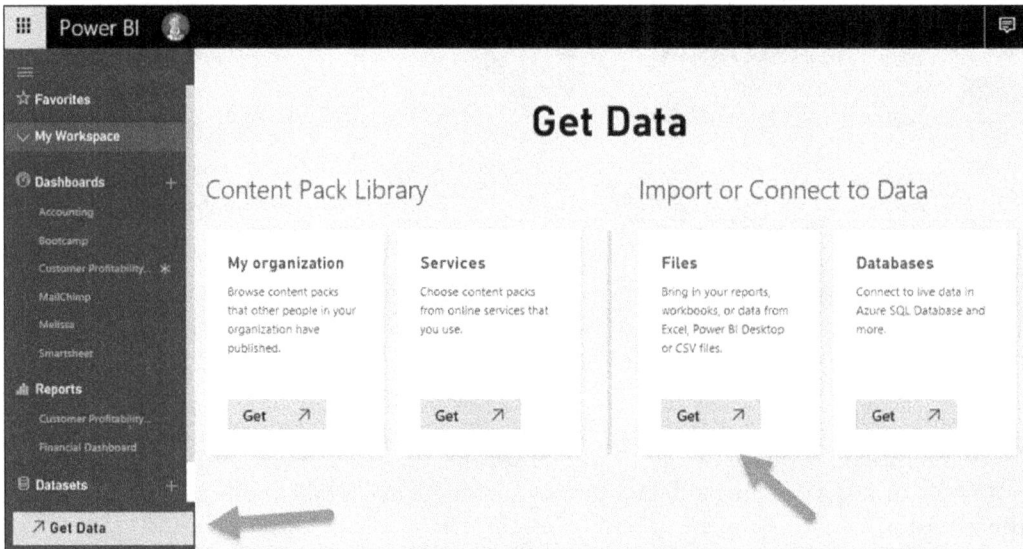

2. Then, we'll select **OneDrive - Business**:

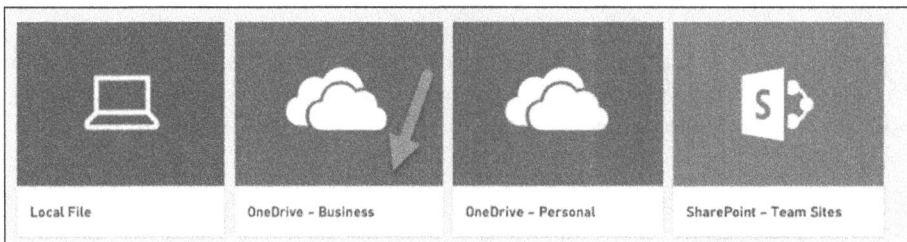

3. We will locate the file we want to bring into Power BI and click on **Connect**:

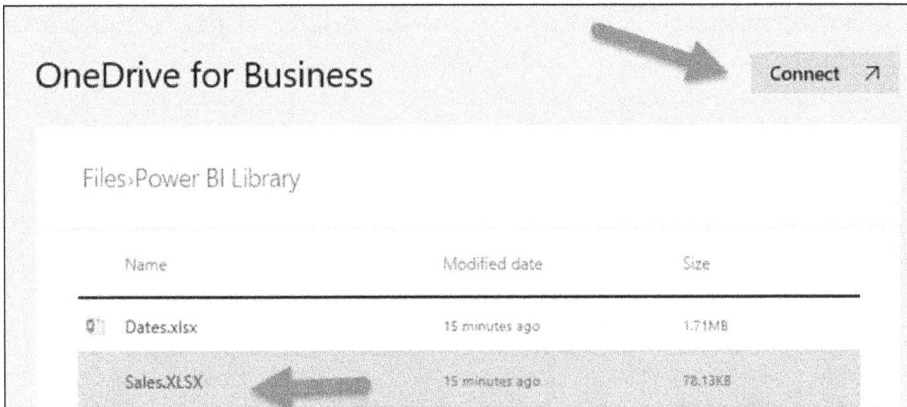

4. Then, we'll choose to *Import* the data on the file into the Power BI service as a Dataset:

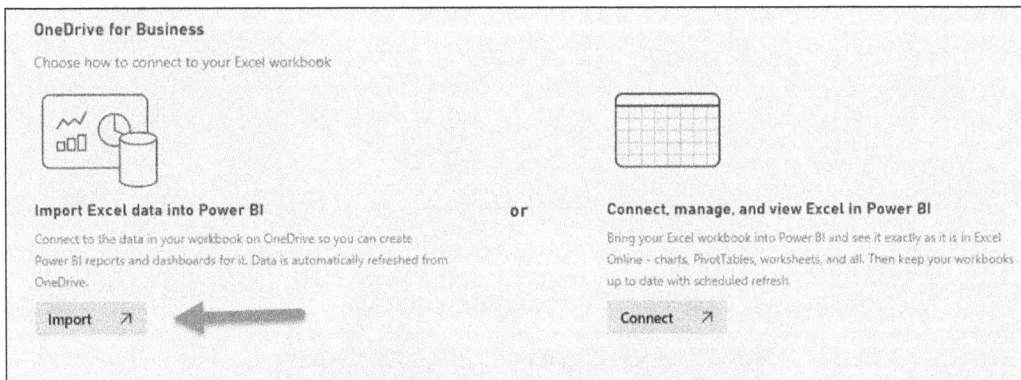

5. Next, we'll build a report. Clicking on the new Dataset will open a blank report that is connected using our newly imported set of data. We'll create visuals similar to those we set in an earlier chapter, to achieve the following dashboard:

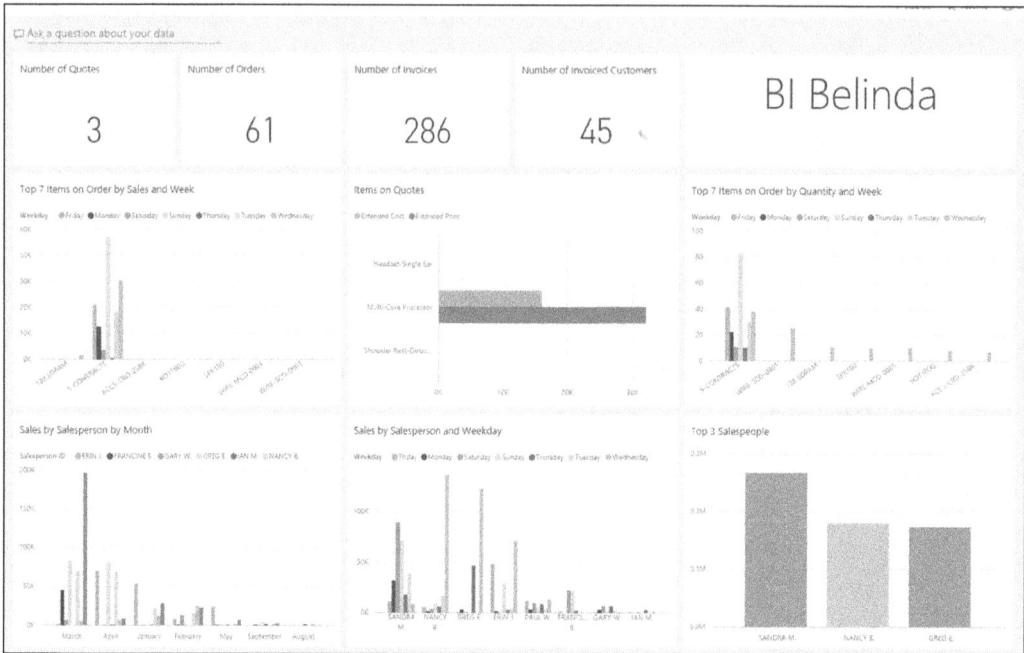

6. In the top-right corner of the Power BI service page in our browser, we will click on the gear icon, then **Create content pack**:

7. We will choose whether or not to share the new content pack with a specific group or the entire organization in the next window. Give the content pack a **Title** and **Description**. Select which items to publish with the content pack (we are choosing **Dashboard**, which will automatically select **Reports** and **Datasets**). We will also choose to upload a logo, which is optional:

Choose who will have access to this content pack:

○ Specific groups ◉ My entire organization

Title

Sales Line Data

Description

Both Open and History Sales data included in this information. Data shown by individual line items for each document type.

BELINDA,
the GP CSI

Upload an image or company logo

Image size: 45 KB or less, 4:3 aspect ratio, JPG or PNG format

Use default

Select items to publish

Dashboards	Reports	Datasets
☐ AP Information	☐ AP Information	☐ VendorInfo
☑ Sales Lines	☐ FinancialStatements	☐ GLAPAR
	☐ GLAPAR	☑ Sales
	☑ Sales Line Items	

Publish   Cancel

> If we chose the option to share with **Specific groups**, a line would appear to enter in the Office 365 group name or individual e-mail addresses.

When the content has been successfully created, a notification will appear in the top-right corner of your browser:

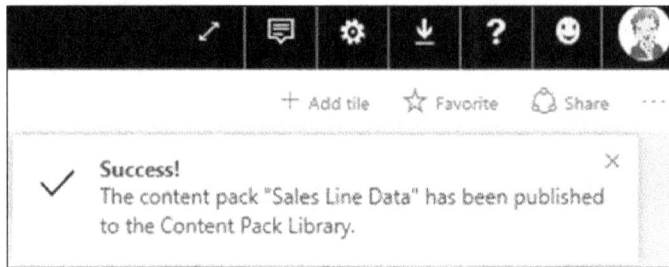

The next time any of your co-workers who have Power BI Pro choose to **Get Data** in the Power BI service, they can choose **My Organization** from **Content Pack Library** and see the new content pack we just created:

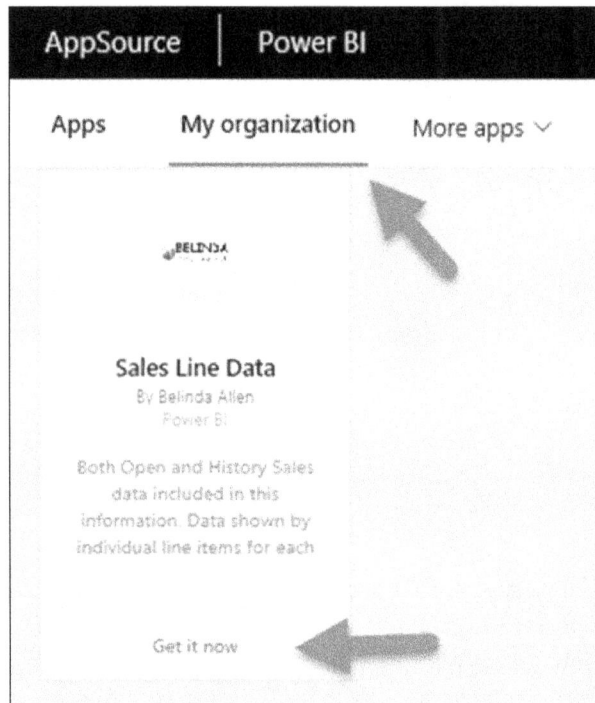

Once they click on **Get it now**, the **Dataset**, **Reports**, and **Dashboards** will be created. No manual recreating of the reports or the dashboards.

We'll discuss refreshing data in these content packs later in this chapter.

Online Services

Online Services work very much the same way as organizational content packs. They contain connection information for datasets, reports, and usually dashboards. There are, however, some major differences that are listed as follows:

- Online services connect to data that is in the cloud. This will likely be an application (or Software as a Service/Saas) to which you subscribe.

- The content (reports and dashboards) is created by the software company, not the users, although users can edit and create their own reports and dashboards after they connect to the service.

- Connecting to online services does not require Power BI Pro; anyone with a Power BI account (free or paid) can connect, provided they have an account with the application the online services connects with.

Let's walk through an example of connecting to an online service.

> As we have no way of knowing what applications the reader will use, we'll just show you how we can connect to one of our subscription applications.
>
> You should also know that Microsoft has a team in place to make sure that only certified companies publish their connections and visuals. This helps you ensure that your connection and information will be linked correctly.

Let's walk through connecting our *MailChimp* account to our Power BI:

1. We have logged into our Power BI service using our browser. On the Power BI navigation pane, we'll select **Get Data**. On the **Get Data** page, we'll select **Services** under **Content Pack Library**:

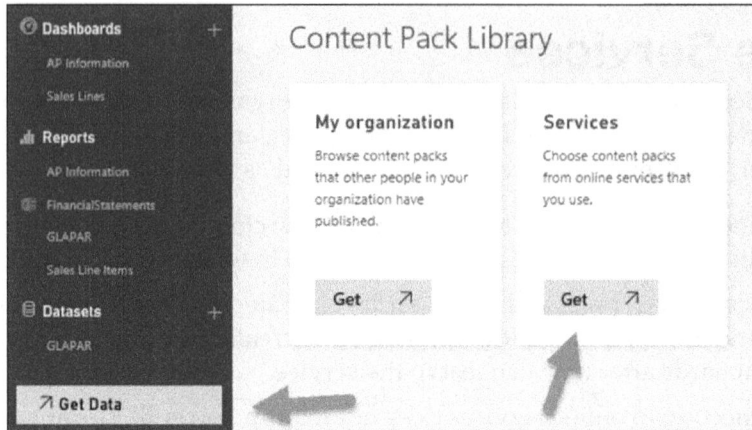

Services are listed in **Content Pack Library** because they are actually content packs that are public. Initially, these were called Content Packs, and you will likely hear someone at some point refer to them as such.

2. A list of online services appears. We will scroll to find the **MailChimp** service and choose **Get it now**:

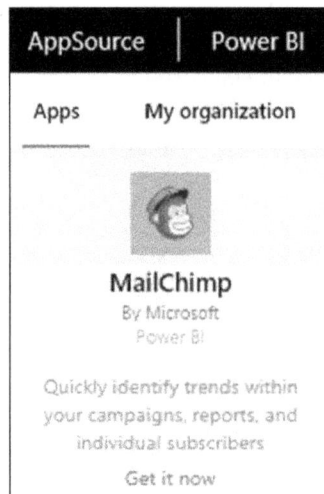

3. The **Connect to MailChimp** window appears, and we click on the **Sign in** button:

> Note that every service will have a different Connect window. Information on what authentication options, user IDs, and passwords need to be obtained by the service provider, not Microsoft.

4. The *MailChimp* log in window appears. We enter our user ID and password and click on **Log in**:

A **Dataset**, **Report**, and **Dashboard** will appear in our Power BI service, ready for us to consume the data.

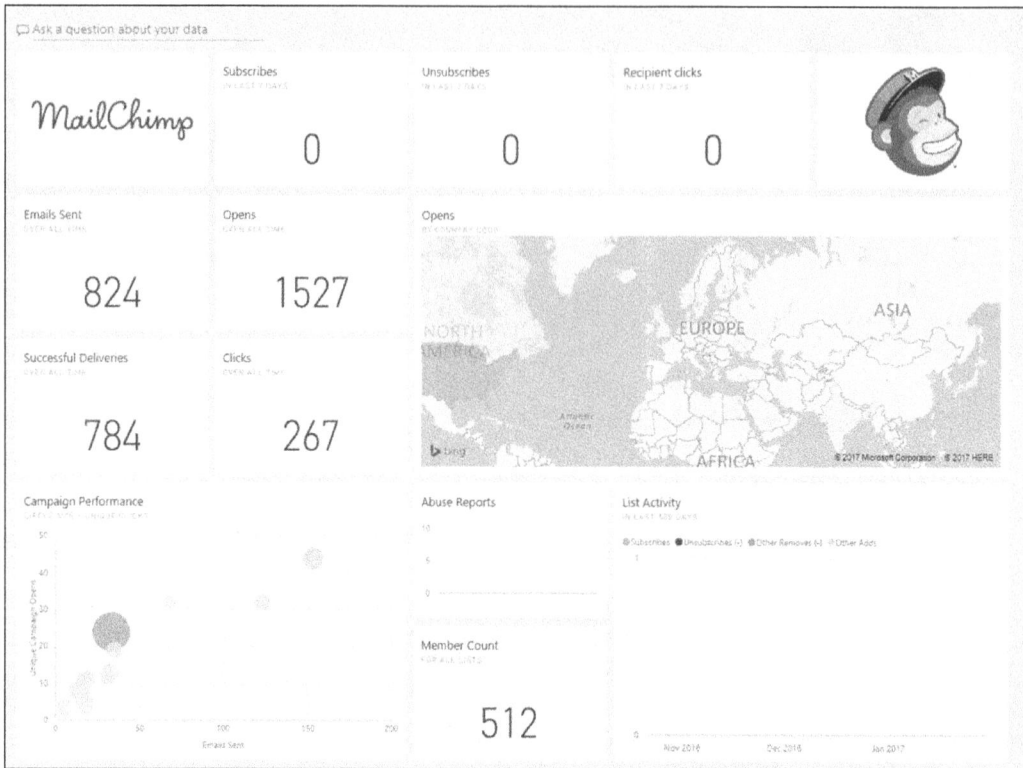

Now that this is part of our Power BI service, we can customize the reports and dashboards to fit our unique needs. As the data we are connected with is on the web already, we can refresh it easily. We'll discuss refreshing next.

Refreshing data

We've now covered three different methods to use shared data, two of which included the ability to share our work with others. Now we will need to cover how the data gets updated or refreshed. Making sure your data is up to date can be critical in making decisions. If the gas gauge in your car shows the amount of gas you had when you first got in the car, taking long road trips might result in a lot of walking to gas stations.

> It's important to understand that a Dataset in Power BI can contain connections to multiple sources. This is particularly true of data published from Power BI. We can create data connections to GP and our CRM. Two different data sources make up one dataset when published to the Power BI service.

Types of refresh

There are four types of refresh in Power BI--Package, Model/data, Tile, and Visual container. It is important to understand the difference of each of these refresh types. Let's review each now.

The first is a Package refresh. This refreshes the Power BI service with the data in the files used originally. For example, if you exported data from GP into an Excel file, the Power BI service would refresh to that Excel file (and not to the original source, GP). This is true if the file is located on your local machine, OneDrive, or even SharePoint Online.

The next type of refresh is Model/data refresh. This type of refresh will update the Power BI service with updates from the original source. In an earlier chapter, we extracted data from Facebook and from New York City's Open Data site. Refreshing data with these types of datasets would allow for the Power BI service to update with the latest data in the original source.

The next type of refresh to understand is the Tile refresh. Approximately, every 15 minutes, tiles on the dashboards will update with the latest data in the Power BI service. Clicking on the ellipse (...) in the top-right corner of the dashboard provides you with an option to refresh upon command, without interfering with the automatic refreshes.

The final type of refresh is the Visual container refresh. This is the refreshing of the visuals in a report. This happens as a byproduct of the Package and/or the Model/data refresh.

Online Services

When using online services in the Power BI service, the refreshing frequency will be set up and established by the Software company that created the service. We used *MailChimp* in our example. It is set up to refresh daily automatically, as are most services, but the refresh rate can be changed, and it can be refreshed on demand.

In the **Datasets** area of the Power BI navigation pane, click on the ellipse for the online service dataset and choose **Refresh Now**. You can also choose **Schedule Refresh** to change the frequency of the refresh:

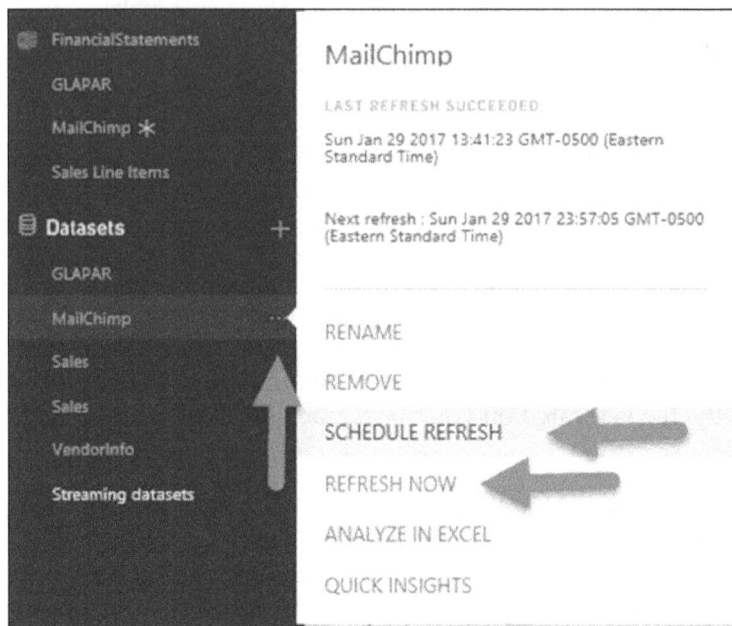

A couple of things to note—first, if you choose to refresh at a particular time using **Schedule Refresh**, the refresh will occur between the time you selected and anywhere for up to an hour after the selected time. Second, with the free version of Power BI, data can only be scheduled to refresh daily, not hourly.

Organizational Content Packs

If you use an Organizational Content in your Power BI service, you will not be able to schedule a refresh. The ability and/or frequency of refreshing are inherited by the type of dataset. The creator of content pack should consider the refreshing options when creating the content pack. For example, consider the use of a Gateway, which we'll review later in this chapter.

One-Drive and SharePoint Online

If you connect to data in a table in an Excel file on OneDrive for Business, the Power BI service will update every hour automatically. It'll update to the Excel file itself and not the original data source of that Excel file. So, if someone keeps that Excel file updated, the Power BI service will stay updated as well.

This works with OneDrive for Business because your Power BI log in will be the same as your OneDrive for Business log in. If your personal OneDrive log in is the same as your Power BI log in, this will work for OneDrive Personal as well.

This is an awesome feature but there are some exceptions. If Power Query (**Get & Transform** for Excel 2016) is used in the Excel file to query data from an on-premise source, such as SQL Server on your local network, then this hourly update will not work. You will need a Gateway, which we will review shortly, to refresh your data.

> This hourly refresh will also work with comma separated value (`*.csv`) files on OneDrive or SharePoint Online.

OData

With the release of Microsoft Dynamics GP, the new OData feature was added. I'll keep the definition of this feature to what a user would see when using it. OData is a URL or website address that connects to your data rather than a website, and, of course, is handled with a lot of security.

> You can find out more about the Dynamics GP 2016 OData Service feature at `https://community.dynamics.com/gp/b/gpteamblog/archive/2016/04/25/gp-2016-feature-of-the-day-odata-service`.
> To connect to GP or any OData feed, you would use the Power BI Desktop to connect to the data using **Get Data** | **Other** | **OData Feed**, and then publish your report to the Power BI service.

When OData is the data source, you'll need to click on the ellipse for the OData **Dataset**, then **Schedule Refresh** so you can update your log in information. The Power BI service will need to have your secure username, password, and potentially other information supplied by the software company that created the OData connection before refreshing can occur.

Gateway

A Gateway is an application that gets installed and configured, which allows for data to flow from one application to another. For example, we could set up a gateway to share data from Dynamics GP to Power BI. A single Gateway can be used for multiple users; this is called an On-Premise Gateway. You can also set up a Personal Gateway for only one user, without any configuration, although, this would allow the Gateway to work with Power BI only and not with other Microsoft tools.

You'll only be able to install one Gateway on a machine, and it cannot be a domain controller. Keep in mind, when deciding where to install the Gateway, it needs to be a machine that stays on. If you installed it on your notebook, for example, if you do not turn it on during the weekend, any daily refreshing option will generate an error.

With a Gateway installed, you can refresh the following:

- A live Analysis Servers database
- On-Premise SQL Server data, such as your GP
- Any Excel file that uses **Power Query/Get & Transform**
- Excel files with data in PowerPivot
- Many other live DirectQuery connections

We will not review how to set up a Gateway in this book. We just want you to know it exists to extend your refreshing capabilities. Just know that a Gateway will allow you the ability to refresh your Power BI service (wherever you are) with the latest information from your Microsoft GP data stored in your office.

Summary

This chapter covered a lot of information. Basically, it was a firehose delivery system. In discussing Power BI, we've connected to data and created cool reports. We published those reports to the Power BI service (or web page) and made dashboards. We even discussed how to share this data and how to refresh it. Perfect, right?

Well, we haven't yet discussed what happens if the data is not perfect. How do we make it perfect? How do we improve it for better visuals? These questions will be answered in the next chapter, when we use the Power BI Query Editor to model or clean up our data.

Using the Power Query Editor 13

So far we have extracted data into Power BI Desktop. We've created amazing visuals using our extracted data. We've even published this data to the Power BI Service, so we can consume these reports on the web an on our mobile devices. I'm sure you are wondering what is left to cover. Now we will review the basics on editing data. Data will never be perfectly presentable directly from the source. This is why understanding how to edit the data prior to making visualizations is critical. In this chapter, we will cover the following items:

- Editing data formats
- Combining and separating data
- Creating new columns of data
- Introductions to two formula languages

Recap

Oh boy, have we done a lot of Power BI work. We've extracted data, created visualizations, and reviewed how to share and refresh the data. Now, it's time to learn my favorite part: polishing the data. This is normally done between extracting the data and creating visualizations. We waited until the end to show it because creating visualizations is so easy, while editing is a little more complicated. Editing is not hard, but it is harder, and we didn't want to scare you off. The more you read, the bigger the return on investment for this book, right? Wahoo, let's go!

What is a query?

Just a brief word on what we mean when we use the term query. The basic definition of query is a question, especially, one addressed to an organization. Add in the technology element and we have a question, specifically addressed to a database, application, website, or file. In the AP Information data we've been working with in the Power BI Desktop, we've queried vendor information. We also queried the music we like on *Facebook*. We queried the Manhattan businesses with URLs from the NYC Open Data website. And, finally, we queried AP transactions from GP. Four queries, all within the same file.

We'll use the Query Editor in Power BI to clean this data up and link some of it together. This will make obtaining more meaningful visuals easier and faster. Who doesn't want easier and faster? The best part is that you can think like a user, not a developer.

Exiting Query Editor

Before we do a lot of work in the Query Editor, let's review how to exit from the Query Editor back to Power BI Desktop. It's pretty simple actually. Once you finish with your changes to the query or queries, click on **Close & Apply** in the top-left corner of the Query Editor:

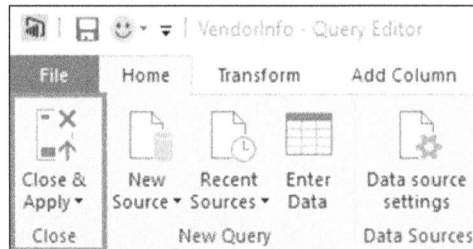

Naming queries

We have three big rules when using the Power BI Query Editor. The first rule is naming the query something that makes sense. When you have multiple queries that you've created, seeing the default names of Query1, Query2, and so on make it difficult to know which one contains the data you need to create a specific visual. If you pull from a specific table or view name, the query will already be named; although, you may still want to edit it for more detail.

Let's rename some queries now:

1. Open the Power BI Desktop file that we have been building throughout this
    section, `VendorInfo.pbix`:

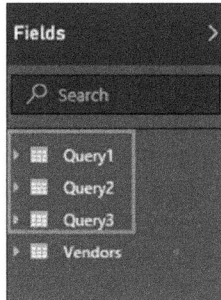

    You'll notice the query pane on the far right shows four queries. Only one
    has a name that makes sense, so let's change the others.

2. On the **External Data** portion of the **Home** tab ribbon, select **Edit Queries**
    (the icon, if you click the arrow, select **Edit Queries** from the dropdown list):

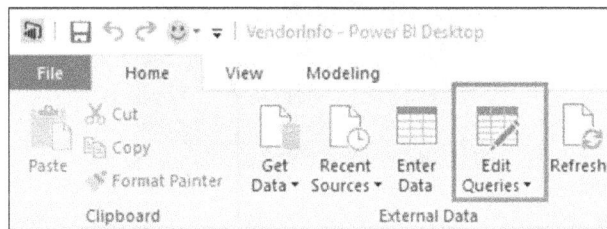

    The Query Editor will open as if it were a separate application. You will
    not be able to do anything in the Power BI Desktop until you close the
    Query Editor.

3. On the navigation pane on the left, select `Query1`. `Query1` will appear in the
    name on the **Query Settings** pane (far right). Highlight the name `Query1` and
    change it to `AP Document Details`. You'll notice the name will change in the
    Queries pane on the left after selecting *Enter*:

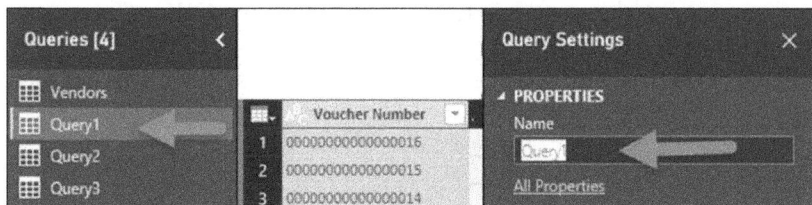

4. Rename `Query2` to `Manhattan URLs by Zip Code`.

5. Rename `Query3` to `Facebook music`.

Nice job. This will help you while creating visuals.

Using Applied Steps

When working in Query Editor, the **Query Settings** pane on the right has a section called **APPLIED STEPS**. Every change we make to the query gets recorded here. When the query is refreshed, these steps will be performed on the data, preventing us from having to rework the data every time the data updates. As we walk through some of the tasks below, we may rename the step so that we can remember what action the step performed:

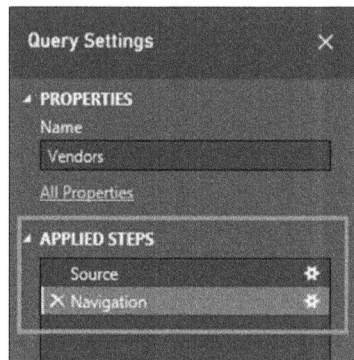

[🔦 Anytime an applied step has a gear, like the two steps in the preceding image, the gear can be clicked opening the step for editing.]

Removing unnecessary column(s)

Before we renamed the columns in the last section, we mentioned three big rules. The second rule is removing unnecessary columns. You can right-click on a column and select **Remove** to delete the column, like you do in Excel. You can even highlight the columns you want to keep and right-click and **Remove Other Columns**. We do not like this method. It's tedious and doesn't allow for easy editing using the gear in the **APPLIED STEPS**. Instead, we prefer using the **Choose Columns** option.

Let's remove all the unnecessary columns on the `Vendors` query. We'll need to make sure to keep the columns that have already been used:

1. In Query Editor, select the query `Vendors` in the **Queries** pane.

2. Select **Choose Columns** icon on the **Manage Columns** section of the **Home** tab:

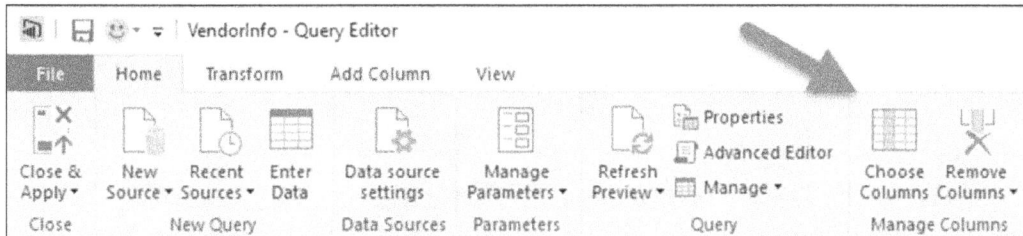

3. The **Choose Columns** window will open. Unmark (**Select All Columns**) to unmark everything, and then mark the following columns:**Vendor ID**, **Vendor Name**, **Address 1**, **Address 2**, **City**, **State**, **Zip Code**, **1099 Type**, **Current Balance**, **Hold**, and **Vendor Class ID**. Select **OK** to close the window.

4. Now, only these fields will display when building visuals. You'll also notice the applied step **Remove Other Columns** was added, with a gear, so we can edit it if we desire.

Formatting column Data Types

We have already covered two of the three big rules. The final rule is formatting the columns as text, dates, numbers, and so on. Although, Power BI does have intelligence to make a best guess, we encourage this step to make sure that the data is formatted correctly. It's possible a refresh might bring in something that might make Power BI question the type. I've seen number of formats be defined as text, preventing their use in column and bar charts. It's worth the time to perform this one-time action.

Let's do this step for the `Vendors` query:

1. In Query Editor, select the query `Vendors` in the **Queries** pane.

2. Highlight the first column, **Vendor ID**. Select the drop-down list for **Data Type** in the **Transform** area of the ribbon on the **Home** tab. Select **Text** from the list:

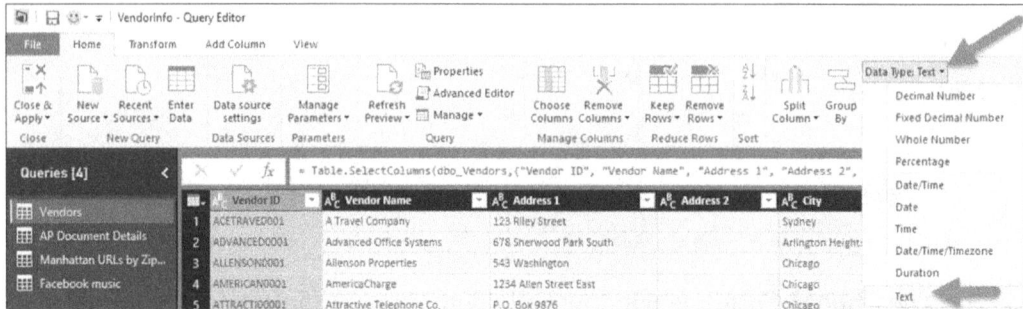

[
 💡 Even if the Data Type is already text, it's worth the time to define the column type up front; rather than potentially letting a refresh down the road cause Power BI to set the type to general. When the data is not formatted with the right type, visuals on your reports may not work.
]

3. Repeat the previous step for all columns except **Current Balance**. If you like, you can select all the remaining columns and change them with one action by holding down the *Ctrl* key while you select each column.

4. For the **Current Balance** column, follow the same steps, but select **Decimal Number** as **Data Type**.

[
 💡 Changing the data type can also be achieved by right -clicking after the column is selected and then choose **Change Type**, then the appropriate data type.
]

What is the M language?

This section is just a FYI kind of section. We've started watching the work we are doing in the Query Editor begin appearing in the applied steps. As we continue working in this chapter, we'll be reviewing and editing the applied steps. As we perform a task that gets recorded as a step, we are actually updating the **Power Query Formula Language** known as **M**. M is a bit of an informal name, and it stands for mashup, because we are mashing up data.

The probability is that you'll never need to do anything with the M expression. However, to be on the safe side, let me show you where it is located.

> If you choose to follow along, be aware that one small change can break your data and/or your reports.

1. Select **Advanced Editor** from the **Advanced** area of the **View** ribbon in the Query Editor, as shown in the following screenshot:

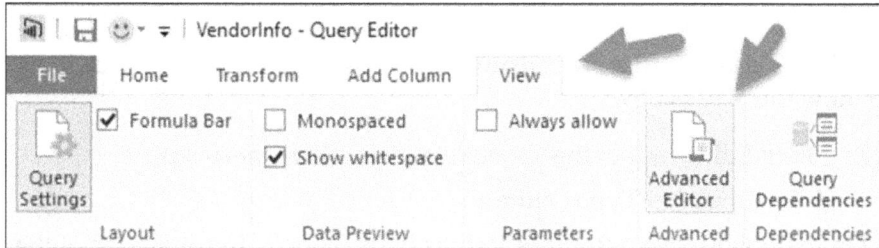

2. **Advanced Editor** will open with the M expression in an editable box:

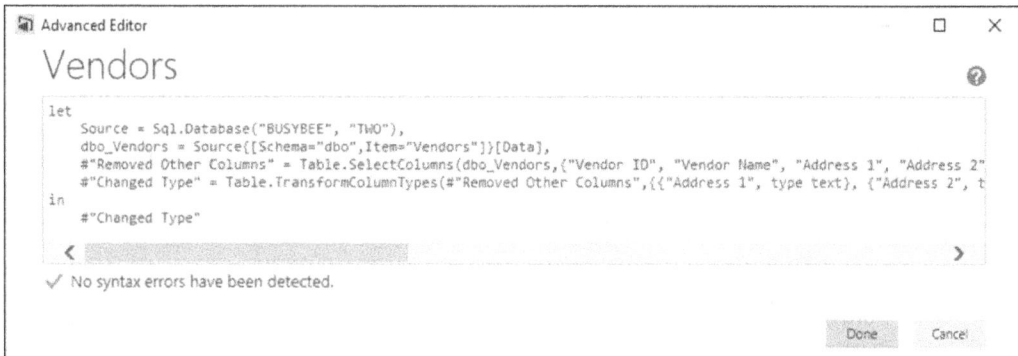

> The expression can be copied and placed in a blank query connection on another file, replicating all of the work performed by the connection and in the Query Editor.

3. Click on **Done** to close the window.

Using Replace Values

If we asked you if your data was clean and organized, you would probably say yes. However, data usually always has issues. For example, in a field for **State**, some users could enter NY and some could enter New York, along with a lot of other variations that include N.Y., N. York, and more. If the state of New York is spelled out in just these four ways, that is four separate entities as far as your computer is concerned. Your machine does not have the capacity to interpret the meaning, only exactly what is entered, even though you may occasionally think the computer hates you.

One of the tools that Power BI Query Editor has that helps with this kind of situation is the **Replace Values** feature. This feature is similar to **Find** and **Replace** in Excel. Let's see how this works now:

1. In Query Editor, select the Vendors query in the **Queries** pane.

2. Highlight the **1099 Type** column.

3. On the ribbon, select **Replace Values** in the **Any Column** section of the **Transform** menu:

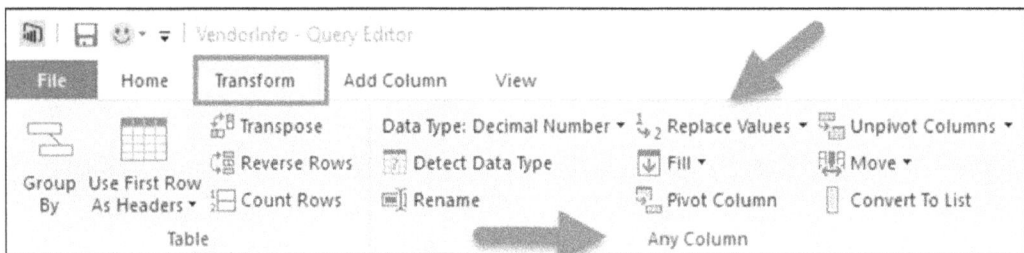

4. In the **Replace Values** window, enter Not a 1099 Vendor (as it appears in the column) in the **Value to Find** field. Enter n/a in the **Replace With** field. Click on **OK**:

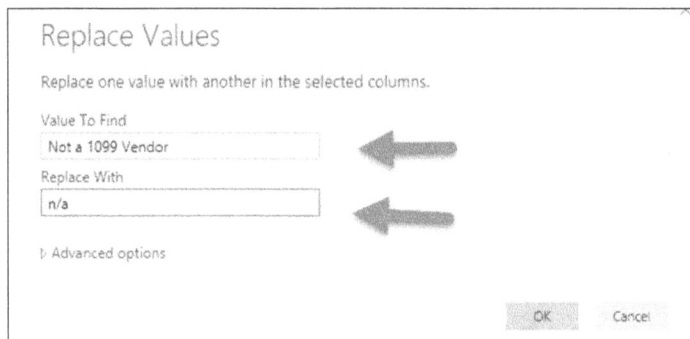

You'll notice that the data in the column has been updated.

We often use this feature to make the quarter (1, 2, 3, and 4) appear as Q1, Q2, Q3, and Q4.

Transforming data

Sometimes, the data is in the field correctly, but it is not capitalized the way you want or there are blank spaces at the end of the field. This will happen more than you would expect. Power BI can handle these situations as well.

Trim a little off the top, the right, the left, and so on

In a database, a single field will have a maximum allowable length. Occasionally, all data in those fields will be the maximum length, even when spaces are used to fill the empty spots. Imagine you have a **Vendor ID** field with a maximum allowable length of 16 characters, which is the case in Microsoft Dynamics GP. In some tables, **Vendor ID ABC001**, which is actually six characters, will fill the entire space so 10 blank spaces are at the end. Normally, these blank spaces are not an issue; although, it will take longer to extract the data because it has to pull each blank space as well. If it were just a matter of data extraction, we probably wouldn't even address this issue in this introduction section. The bigger problem occurs when we try to connect two queries together. If one just has **ABC001** and the other has **ABC001** followed by 10 spaces, Power BI will not be able to recognize that these are the same vendor. We'll address this using the **Trim** feature. Let's do this now:

1. In Query Editor, select the Vendors query in the **Queries** pane.
2. Highlight the **Vendor ID** column, then right-click on **Transform** from the pop-up menu, then choose **Trim**:

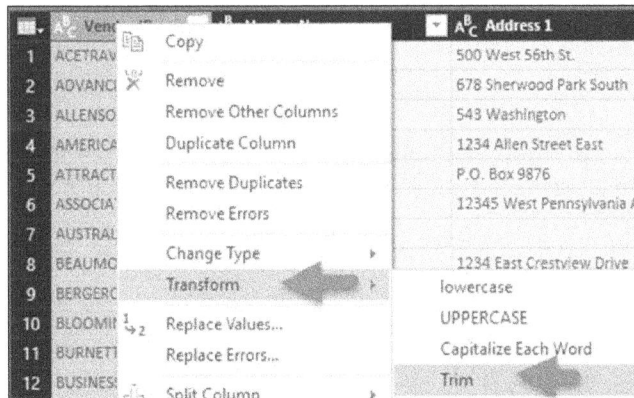

All blank spaces at the beginning and the end of the data in this field will be removed.

3. In Query Editor, select the `AP Document Details` query in the **Queries** pane.

4. Highlight the **Vendor ID** column, then right-click and choose **Transform** from the pop-up menu, then choose **Trim**.

We have now made sure there are no trailing spaces after the Vendor IDs, so they should be able to match up properly. We'll be combining these two queries later.

Formatting with Case

For the sake of aesthetics, or even joining two queries together, you may find the need to alter the case of the data in the query. Fortunately, for all of us, this is a feature built in to Power BI. We've noticed that the AP documents we've extracted from GP have no specific pattern of case for descriptions. It appears that some users enter both upper and lowercase, while others use just upper or just lower. Let's make this consistent now:

1. In Query Editor, select the `AP Document Details` query in the **Queries** pane.

2. Highlight the **Description** column, then right-click and choose **Transform** from the pop-up menu, and then choose **UPPERCASE**:

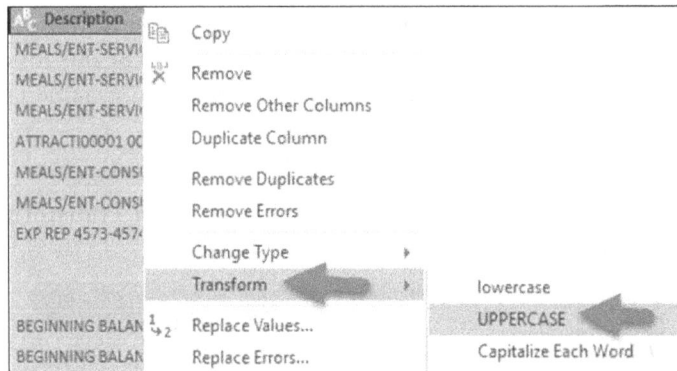

- Normally, we prefer to **Capitalize Each Word**, but in the case of GP, sometimes, **Description** is populated with **Customer ID** (for example, Refund Checks), which should stay in uppercase.

Working with dates and times

As Dynamics GP uses SQL Server for the database, and SQL Server tracks dates with the time, GP dates have a time attached to them. As cool as this may sound, GP doesn't use the time portion, so the time is always defaulted to midnight (12 AM).

> There are a few places where time is tracked (for example, the advanced purchase order feature of purchase order approvals). In these rare exceptions, GP will use one **Date/Time** field for the approval date and a separate **Date/Time** field for the approval time.

When a record has a date on it, such as an AP invoice, it's probable that we'll want to see data grouped by elements of that date (for example, years, quarters, months, weeks, and/or days). A due date for an AP invoice is an excellent example of this. We usually like to see our AP invoices grouped by 30-day ranges of the due date, resulting in what we call aging buckets.

The Query Editor in Power BI makes working with dates and times a child's play. Let's edit some date fields, while adding some additional fields that we can use to group data:

1. In Query Editor, select the `AP Document Details` query in the **Queries** pane.

2. Highlight the **Document Date** column, then right-click and choose **Change Type** from the pop-up menu, and then choose **Date**:

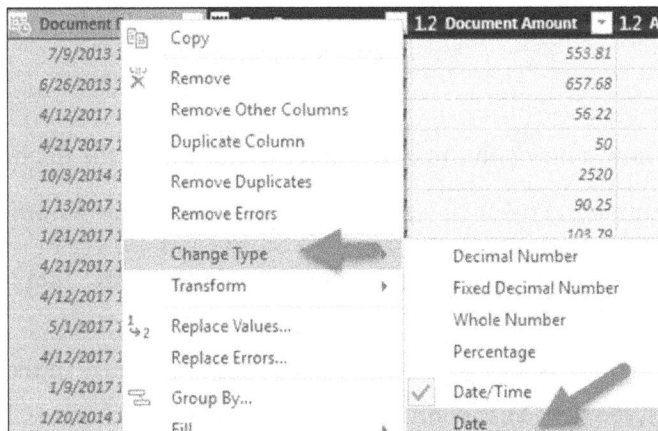

We could have also changed the data type from the **Transform** section of the ribbon using the **Home** tab after selecting the column.

Since Power BI recognized this column as **Date/Time** data, a checkmark appears by that type (prior to changing it). You can see that we have a large variety of options, including the option to display this field using only the time. This would be how you extract the time element rather than the date.

Now that we've edited the way the data displays, let's use this data to create some additional columns:

1. In Query Editor, select the AP Document Details query in the **Queries** pane.

2. Highlight the **Document Date** column. Choose **Add Column** from the menu. You'll see the **Date** option **From Date & Time** area is lit up, while the other two options are not. As the column we selected is a date, only the date options will work.

3. Select **Date**, then **Year**, and **Year** again. This will create a column that displays the document date year:

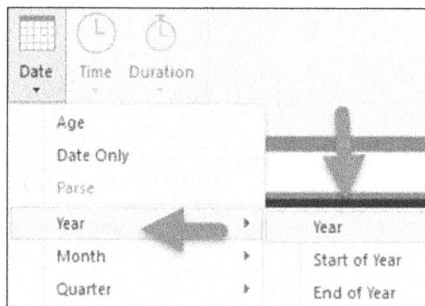

4. There is now a new column at the end for the year of the document date.

As the year is a number, Power BI will default this data type as a number. Although this is not really a problem, if we use this field on a visual, Power BI will probably try to sum the years rather than group by the years. Let's set the data type as text to prevent this from happening:

1. In Query Editor, select the AP Document Details query in the **Queries** pane.

2. Highlight the new **Year** column, then right-click and choose **Change Type** from the pop-up menu, then choose **Text**.

For any **Date** field, we can create a new column (or display the existing date column) in any of the following formats:

- **Year**
- **Start of Year**
- **End of Year**
- **Month** (displays as a number)
- **Start of Month**
- **End of Month**
- **Days in Month**
- **Month Name** (displays as text; we use this one a lot)
- **Quarter**
- **Start of Quarter**
- **End of Quarter**
- **Week of Year** (displays as a number)
- **Week of Month** (displays as a number)
- **Start of Week**
- **End of Week**
- **Day** (actual date of the month)
- **Day of Week** (displays as a number)
- **Day of Year** (displays as a number)
- **Start of Day**
- **End of Day**
- **Name of Day** (displays as text; we use this one a lot too)

Another date format we use a lot is **Age**. This will display the number of days, hours, minutes, and seconds between a date field and whatever day and time it is right now. This is great to analyze due dates. Let's add a column to display the number of days an invoice is past due:

1. In Query Editor, select the AP Document Details query in the **Queries** pane.
2. Highlight the new **due Date** column, then right-click and choose **Change Type** from the pop-up menu, then choose **Date**.

3. Choose **Add Column** from the menu. Select the **Date** option **From Date & Time**, and then select **Age**. This will create a column, AgeFromDate, that shows the difference between the **Due Date** column and right now in **days:hours:minutes:seconds**.

4. We will only need to see the number of days in this new column, so let's change the data time from a time type to a whole number. Highlight the AgeFromDate column, then right-click and choose **Change Type** from the pop-up menu, then choose **Whole Number**.

5. As we have two dates in this query, the name AgedFromDate doesn't tell us which date is being aged, so let's rename it. Double-click on the column name. When the entire name is highlighted, replace the column name to **Days Past Due**. We'll be using this column in a **Data Analysis Expressions (DAX)** formula later in this chapter.

> Note that there are similar options for time. We can use any of these options to create new columns or transform existing columns.
>
> If you have data with the date and time fields both active, and you want them in separate columns, the easiest method of doing this is to highlight the column and use the **Add Column** option like we did for the year above, but select a time element instead. Then, you can change the data type of the original column to just show the date.

Merging columns

There will be occasions where you'll want to combine columns together to form a new column. Although it may be advantageous for the data to be separated in a database, it's not always the way we want to see our data in reports. A good example of this in GP is employee and salespeople information. There is a field for the first name and a separate field for the last name in the database. While reporting, we want a single field that uses the whole name, which leaves us with the task of merging these two columns (or fields) together. Using the data, we've already extracted, let's combine the city, state, and zip code for our vendors into a single field:

1. In Query Editor, select the Vendors query in the **Queries** pane.

2. Let's keep the original separated columns by creating a duplicate of each one, then merging the duplicated columns. Highlight the new **City** column, then right-click and choose **Duplicate Column** from the pop-up menu:

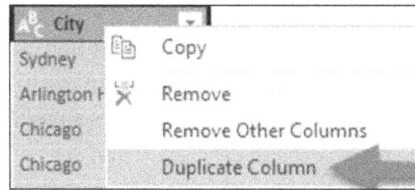

3. Highlight the new **State** column, then right-click and choose **Duplicate Column** from the pop-up menu.

4. Highlight the new **Zip Code** column, then right-click and choose **Duplicate Column** from the pop-up menu.

> Our new columns retain the old column names by adding a dash and the word copy at the end. This keeps the column names unique. In Power BI, each column name in a single query must be unique. As we'll be merging the columns together, these names will disappear when the column is merged so that there is no need to rename them at this stage.

Let's make sure that we have no blank spaces at the end of our fields. To do this well, we'll use the Trim feature we already discussed:

1. Let's select all three new fields. Highlight the new column, **City – Copy**, then hold the *Ctrl* key down and highlight the **State – Copy** column and the **Zip Code – Copy** column. All three columns should now be selected.

2. Right-click on the three selected columns, choose **Transform**, then **Trim**. Now, all three columns should be free from blank spaces at the beginning and the end of each data field.

Let's merge the city and state columns together first:

1. Highlight the new column, **City – Copy**, and the **State – Copy** column. Select **Merge Columns** from the **Text Column** area of the ribbon on the **Transform** tab. Alternately, you may also right -click and choose **Merge Columns**:

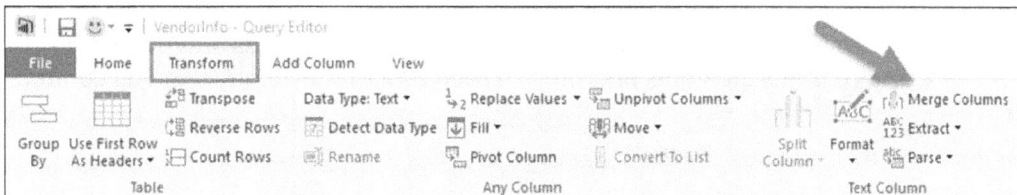

2. The **Merge Columns** window will open. City and states are usually separated by a comma followed by a space, which is how we will separate these columns here. Click on the **Separator** drop-down list. You'll notice that there is not an option for comma-space, so we'll use **--Custom--**. Click on **--Custom--**:

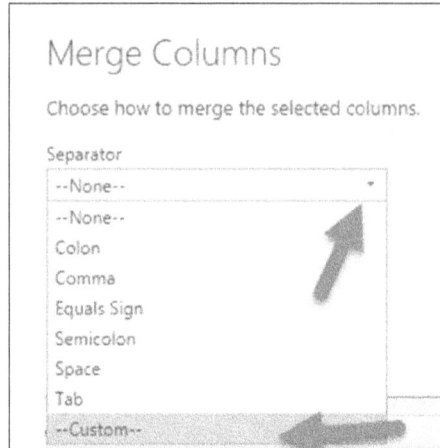

3. A blank field will open under the **Separator** field. Enter a comma, then a space. We can leave the new column name as Merged as we'll be merging this column with the zip code next and that's where we will create a new column name:

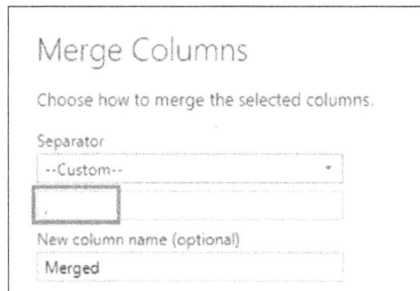

4. Click on **OK**. Now you'll see that the **City – Copy** columns and the **State – Copy** columns are gone, and they've been replaced by a new Merged column.

Merged		Zip Code - Copy
Sydney, NSW		2086
Arlington Heights, IL		60004-2922

Now, let's add the zip code to our new column and rename it. Then, it'll be ready for use!

1. Highlight the new `Merged` column and the **Zip Code - Copy** column. Select **Merge Columns** from the **Text Column** area of the ribbon on the **Transform** tab.

2. The **Merge Columns** window will open. City and states are usually separated by two spaces from the zip code, which is how we will separate these columns here. Click on the **Separator** drop-down list. You'll notice that there is not an option for two spaces, so we'll use **--Custom--**. Click on **--Custom--**.

3. A blank field will open under the **Separator** field. Enter two spaces. Let's change **New Column name** to `Address`:

4. You should now see a single field for the address:

Splitting columns

Previously, when discussing why you would want to merge columns, we talked about employee and salespeople names. Now, let's talk about how we would handle it if we had the full name of someone (for example, employee, salesperson, contact, and more), and you wanted a column with just the last name. Power BI Query Editor has the ability to separate the data in a single column.

In our `Vendors` query with which we've been working, we have a column for **Vendor Class ID**. In the sample data from GP, Vendor Classes have the country identified first, and then it uses two other codes that are all separated by commas. Let's assume that we want a separate column for each of the three segments in this sample Vendor Class data. Let's perform this action now:

1. In Query Editor, select the `Vendors` query in the **Queries** pane.

2. Highlight the **Vendor Class ID** column. It's possible that we may want the class ID intact for some instances and broken down for others. Let's make a duplicate and keep the original column. Right-click on the column and choose **Duplicate Column**:

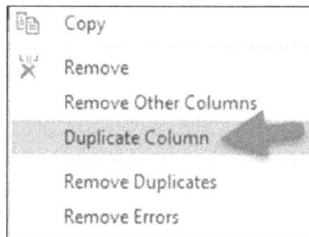

3. A new column named `Vendor Class ID - Copy` is now the last column in our query. Highlight this new column. Select **Split Column** from the **Transform** area of the ribbon on the **Home** menu. Then choose **By Delimiter**:

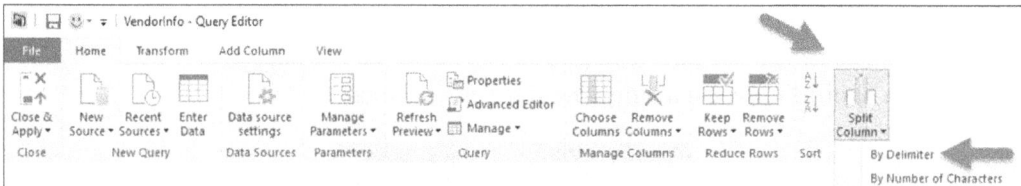

Separating columns, we can tell Power BI to separate based on a specified number of characters (for example, after the first three characters, the last three characters or every three characters.) We can also have Power BI separated by something else (for example, a space, a tab, a colon, and much more) called a **delimiter**. The delimiter can also be separated by the first occurrence, the last occurrence, or every occurrence in.

4.   The **Split Column by Delimiter** window will open. Open the drop-down list for the **Select or enter delimiter** field. One of our **Vendor Class ID** fields is **USA-US-M**, and we want to separate this by the dash, which is not one of our options, so we'll choose **--Custom--**:

5.   A new blank field will open under the **Select or enter delimiter** field for you to enter what you want to use to denote when the field should be separated. We'll enter a dash (-). Make sure the **At each occurrence of the delimiter** option is marked. Click on **OK**:

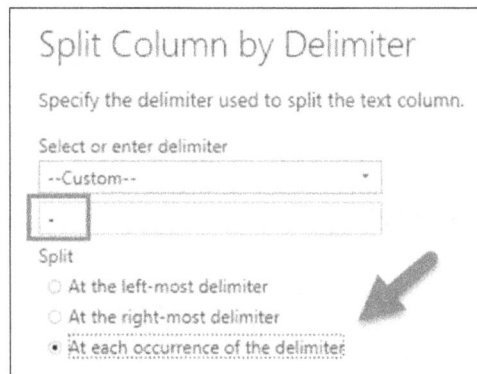

6.   Now we have three columns for the separated three sections of the class ID. Rename each column to Class Part 1, Class Part 2, and Class Part 3 respectively.

7. You may also notice that some fields in columns two and three have a null value. This is due to our splitting an empty column. Let's replace the values, like we did previously, replacing the null with nothing:

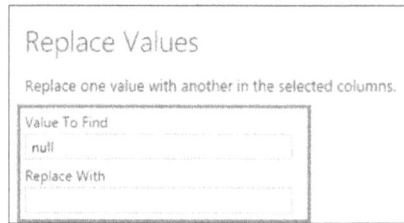

Replace Values

Replace one value with another in the selected columns.

Value To Find

null

Replace With

> It's important to note that when splitting a column with a delimiter, the delimiter will be removed. In the preceding example, we separated it with the dashes. The dashes are removed as part of the separating.

Merging queries

One of the most powerful (pun intended) benefits of Power BI is the ability to bring data in from multiple data sources. Frequently, these disparate data sources can be combined together as a single data source for easier visual creation.

Although our Vendors query and our AP Document Details query come from the same SQL Server database, we'll merge them together as a single query. This is not an uncommon practice. Occasionally, you'll likely find yourself in a position where you want to join separate tables or views within GP together into a single query. Let's add the vendor class and the address (from the Vendors query) to the AP Document Details query:

1. In Query Editor, select the AP Document Details query in the **Queries** pane. Although we can create an entirely new query by merging the two columns together, we'll just add the new column that we want from the Vendors query in the AP Document Details query.

2. Select the words **Merge Queries** from the **Combine** area of the ribbon from the **Home** tab. If you click on the arrow, you'll have a drop-down list that will allow you to create a new query from the merged queries. If you get this drop-down list, select **Merge Queries**:

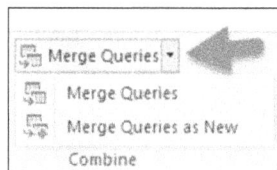

Merge Queries ▾

Merge Queries

Merge Queries as New

Combine

3. The **Merge** window will open with the `AP Document Details` query in the section at the top. Select the drop-down list for the bottom section and select the `Vendors` query.

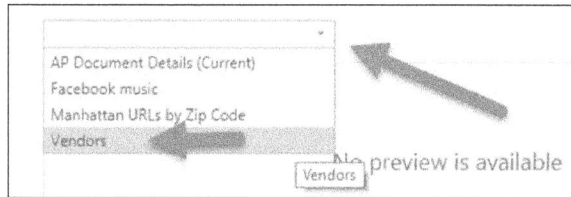

4. In the **Merge** window, highlight **Vendor ID** in both the **AP Document Details** area at the top and the **Vendors** area at the bottom. This is how we define that when the vendor from one query equals the vendor from the second query, they belong together. As vendors have a unique ID, we only need to link (or join) these two queries together by this **Vendor ID** field:

> If the joining is done incorrectly, the results will be useless, even if data exists. So, if you are not sure about how to join, consult your partner or your IT team.

5. Leave **Join Kind** to the **Left Outer (all from the first, matching from the second)** option as it is. If we have vendors with no outstanding invoices, their details will not show. Click on **OK**.

Technically, the queries are now merged, but we will need to expand the new fields that we want to add. Let's do that now:

1. There is a single new column at the end of the AP Document Details query that represents all of the columns from the merged Vendors query. The column name is NewColumn and there is a double-headed arrow next to the column name. All rows in that column have the word **Table** in a different color than the rest of the fields. Click on the double-headed arrow:

2. A pop-up window will appear with all of the columns from the Vendor query. Make sure **Expand** is selected. Unmark **Select All Columns** then mark **Address 1** (the street address), **Vendor Class ID**, and **Address** (the field we created that shows city, state, and zip):

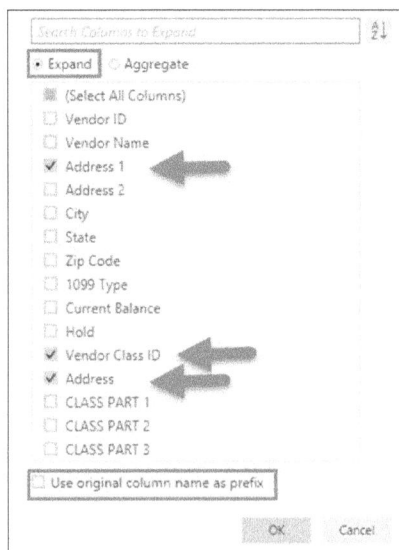

> If we started with the Vendor query, we could have used Aggregate instead of expand for the AP Document Details query. We would then be able to add the number of outstanding invoices to the vendor data.

3. Unmark **Use original column name as prefix** and click on **OK**.

You'll now see your new columns at the end of the **AP Document Details** window. You can use them as if they were there from the start.

Imagine combining CRM data, marketing database data, industry data, and more to your GP data. It's done the same way. You not only can imagine it; you can do it now!

Appending queries

On occasions, you may choose to append queries rather than merge them. Here's another example that will explain the difference. You have a list of customers in GP and a list of prospects in CRM. You want to combine them into a single query with **Customer ID** and **Prospect ID** in the same column; with **Customer Name** and **Prospect Name** in the same column, and so on. This is appending, and Power BI can handle this easily as well.

Let's share a few screenshots with you, rather than walking you through it step by step:

1. First, we will perform **Get Data** for both data sources.
2. We'll need to make sure the columns are in the exact same order (**ID**, **Name**, **Address**, and more) with the exact same column names.
3. Make sure the columns in both queries formatted the same; for example, the **ID** column is formatted as text for both.
4. Highlight one of the columns in the Query Editor and select **Append Queries** from the **Combine** area of the ribbon from the **Home** tab.

5. If appending **Two tables** together, select the second table and click on **OK**:

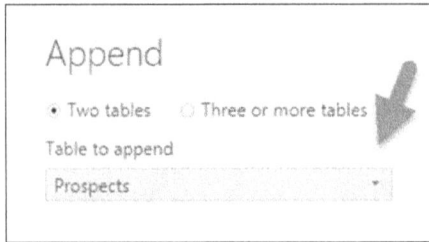

Append

○ Two tables   ○ Three or more tables

Table to append

Prospects

6. If appending **Three or more tables** together, select the additional tables, click on **Add**, and then click on **OK**:

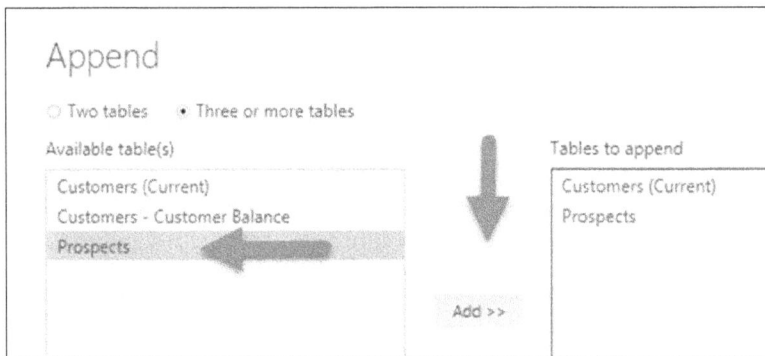

Append

○ Two tables   ● Three or more tables

Available table(s)

Customers (Current)

Customers - Customer Balance

Prospects

Tables to append

Customers (Current)

Prospects

Add >>

Now you have one query with both sets of data displayed as if it were one data source all along.

You can create a brand new query rather than adding to an existing query by clicking on the arrow next to **Append Queries** from the ribbon, then selecting **Append Queries as New**.

If you have two columns with different names, they will not append, they will each retain their own column. For example, if I had **Customer ID** in one query and **Prospect ID** in the other, these would stay separate columns. If I change the name of each column prior to appending to simply **ID**, then they will create one column for both.

Summarizing with Group By

When creating visualizations in Power BI, data can be aggregated (summarized, counted, averaged, and more). There are circumstances where the data needs to be aggregated prior to being used on visualizations, perhaps so it can be merged or appended to another query. When this circumstance arises, we can use the Power BI **Group By** feature in the Query Editor. Let's do that now by creating a list where each vendor is listed once, along with the total amount due and the number of invoices that are outstanding:

1. As we've used the `AP Document Details` query for visualization, we do not want to aggregate that query. Instead, we'll duplicate the `AP Document Detail` query and use the duplicate. In the **Queries** pane on the left (sometimes referred to in Microsoft literature as a blade), right-click on the `AP Document Details` query:

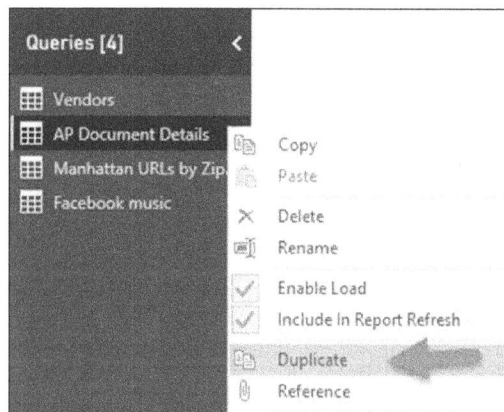

2. Select **Duplicate** from the pop-up menu. A new query will appear called **AP Document Details (2)**.

3. Right-click on **AP Document Details (2)** in the **Queries** pane and select **Rename** from the pop-up menu. Rename the query to `AP Document Summary`. Now we have a new query that we can aggregate.

4. Highlight AP Document Summary in the **Queries** pane. Click on **Transform** on the menu. Select **Group By** in the **Table** area of the ribbon:

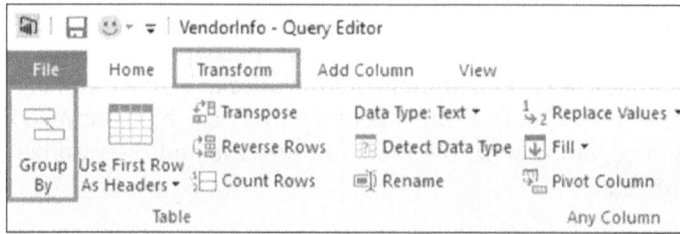

5. The **Group By** window will open. This is where we decide which columns we'll make unique to the rows and which columns we'll aggregate. In the **Group by** drop-down list, select **Vendor ID**. Then click on the **Add grouping** button to add another field to group:

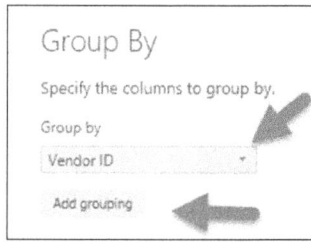

6. In the new **Group by** drop-down list, select **Vendor Name**.

7. In the bottom section of the **Group by** window, change **New column name** from **Count** to Number of Open Documents. Click on the **Add aggregation** button, as shown in the following screenshot, to add another column:

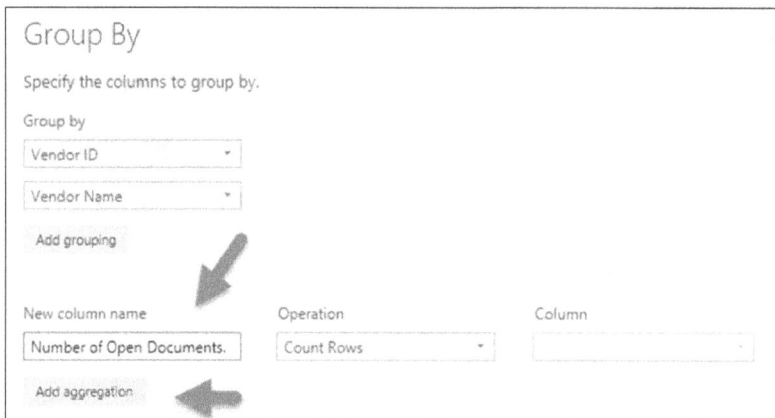

8. In the new fields created by the **Add aggregate** button, change **Operation** from **Count Rows** to **Sum** using the drop-down list. Change **Column** from **Voucher Number** to **Document Amount** using the drop-down list. In **New column name**, enter Amount Due. Click on **OK**:

New column name	Operation	Column
Number of Open Documents.	Count Rows	
Amount Due	Sum	Document Amount

Add aggregation

You have now changed a detail query into a summary query. This query can be used as is, or merged/appended with another query.

Formulating with DAX

There is another method of adding columns and even calculations that occur during the refresh that do not take up data space. It's called DAX, which stands for Data Analysis Expressions. DAX is actually a set of functions, operators, and even constants. The best part of DAX is that it closely resembles Excel formulas, which makes it easier to wrap your head around. DAX is also used in other applications, for example, SQL Server, Excel Power Pivot, and more.

In our AP Document Details query, we've already created a column that tells us the days past due for each document. Let's use DAX to create a column that uses that date to make an Aging Bucket, for example, **Current, 0-30 Days Past Due**, and more, so we can create a visual of our Accounts Payable aged by due date:

1. If you are in the Query Editor, **Close & Apply** to get back to the Power BI Desk. In the **Fields** pane, hover your mouse over the AP Document Details query and the ellipsis will appear (**...**). Click on the ellipsis to open a pop-up menu. Select **New column** from the pop-up menu:

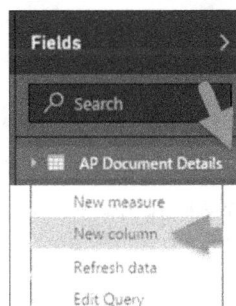

2. You'll now have an additional field in this query in the **Fields** pane. You'll also see the formula bar start to create a DAX formula at the top:

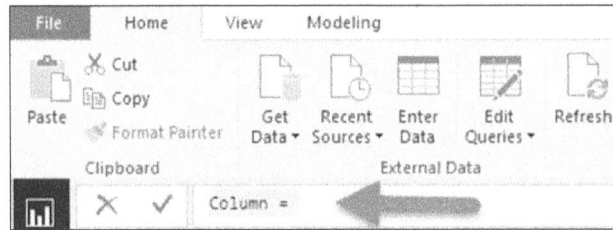

3. Click on the **Column** word in the formula bar and enter the name `Aging Bucket`. Click to the right of the equal (**=**) sign and type the word `if`. The formula wizard will try to assist you by providing information:

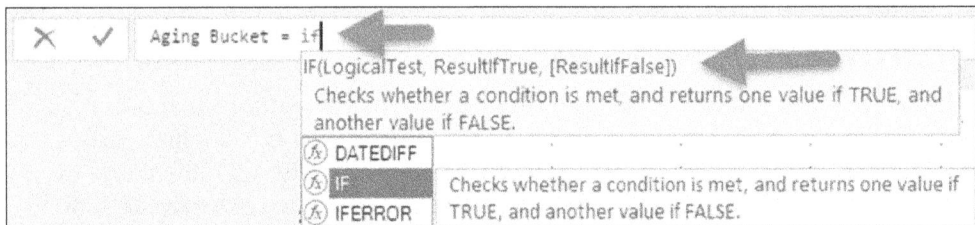

4. Knowing what we want to see and using the information for the formula that popped up, our formula should be written as follows:

```
=if(Days Past Due <1, It's current, otherwise it's past due)
```

5. Enter a start parenthesis after the word `if`, then type the word `Days`, which is the start of the field we want to add. You'll see that the only result left in the wizard is our field from the query, **AP Document Details [Days Past Due]**. Click on the *Tab* key on your keyboard to select the field, or you can type the whole thing in:

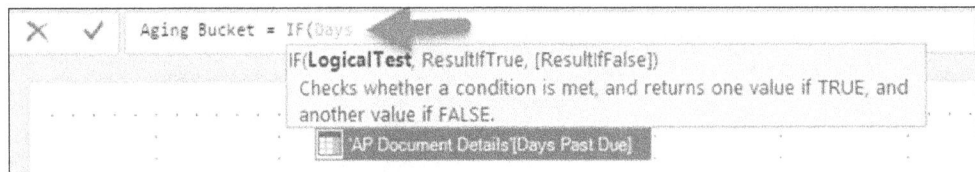

6. To complete the formula, we'll define when the **Days Past Due** is less than 1 day, it is current otherwise it's over 90 days past due, then end parenthesis. Type it like this:

```
< 1, "Current", "Over 90 Days")
```

7. Click on the checkmark to accept the formula. Your formula should look like the this:

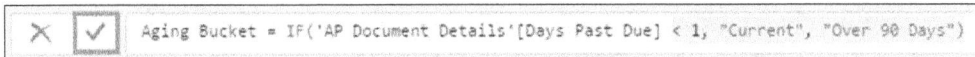

```
×   ✓   Aging Bucket = IF('AP Document Details'[Days Past Due] < 1, "Current", "Over 90 Days")
```

> We will fill in the two aging buckets in the middle using a concept called **nesting**, so we will start with the beginning and end for simplicity. The order of the formula is important to work. Is it less than 1? No, it's greater than 1. Is it less than 30? No, it's greater than 30. Is it less than 60? No, it's greater than 60. Is it less than 90? No, it's greater than 90. Use a logical order to establish ranges.

8. You'll now notice that your new calculated column has been renamed in the **Fields** pane to `Aging Buckets`. Click on the new column in the **Fields** pane to ensure that the formula is the focus in the formula pane.

9. Highlight the entire formula except the equal sign, and copy it to your clipboard using *Ctrl + C*. The following is the portion you'll copy:

```
IF('AP Document Details'[Days Past Due] < 1, "Current", "Over
90 Days")
```

10. In the formula field, erase `"Over 90 Days"` and paste (*Ctrl + V*) in the formula in your clipboard. Change the second `<1` to `<31` and change the second `"Current"` to `"0-30 Days"` that will make your formula then look like the following piece of code:

```
Aging Bucket = = IF('AP Document Details'[Days Past Due] < 1,
"Current", IF('AP Document Details'[Days Past Due] < 31, "0-30
Days", "Over 90 Days"))
```

11. Our formula now accounts for everything under 31 days past due. In the formula field, erase `"Over 90 Days"` and paste (*Ctrl + V*) in the formula in your clipboard. Change the second `<1` to `<61` and change the second `"Current"` to `"31-60 Days"` that will make your formula then look like the following piece of code:

```
Aging Bucket = IF('AP DOCUMENT DETAILS'[DAYS PAST DUE] < 1,
"CURRENT", IF('AP DOCUMENT DETAILS'[DAYS PAST DUE] < 31, "0-
30 DAYS", IF('AP DOCUMENT DETAILS'[DAYS PAST DUE] < 61, "31-60
Days", "OVER 90 DAYS")))
```

12. Let's do this one final time. In the formula field, erase `"Over 90 Days"` and paste (*Ctrl + V*) in the formula in your clipboard. Change the second `<1` to `<91` and change the second `"Current"` to `"61-90 Days"` that will make your formula then look like the following piece of code:

```
Aging Bucket = IF('AP Document Details'[Days Past Due] < 1,
"Current", IF('AP Document Details'[Days Past Due] < 31, "0-
30 Days", IF('AP Document Details'[Days Past Due] < 61, "31-
60 Days", IF('AP Document Details'[Days Past Due] < 91, "61-90
Days", "Over 90 Days"))))
```

13. Click on the checkmark to save the formula:

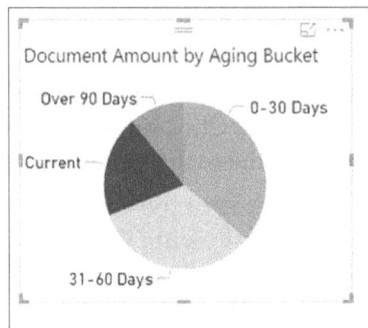

Document Amount by Aging Bucket

Over 90 Days · 0-30 Days

Current

31-60 Days

We quickly created a pie chart that shows our outstanding payables by these new buckets. This is just one example of how DAX can be used to improve your Power BI experience.

Summary

There are so many formulas, calculations, transformations, and more that can be used in Power BI to model (or improve) your data for more efficient and effective reporting. We could only scratch the surface with a few items in this chapter. Hopefully, it's enough to peak your interest in becoming a business intelligence champion for your organization.

The next chapter is the last chapter. It's where we threw together a few items in Excel, Jet Express for GP, and Power BI that we think are cool that just didn't fit into our outline for other chapters. It's a bonus chapter that is just for fun. We hope you enjoy it!

14
Bonus Chapter

The foundation of what we wanted to cover for dashboards and reporting for GP data has been covered. That being said, there are still tons of things we wish we could include but we didn't think you'd be up to purchasing an encyclopedia; assuming, of course, you are old enough to know why we think that's funny.

In this chapter, we want to give you a couple of extra cool features you might find advantageous to use. We'll just throw out two additional topics for each of the following tools:

- Excel 2016
- Jet Express for GP
- Microsoft Power BI

Recap

We've already covered the foundations for Excel, Jet Express, and Power BI. We've built some reports and dashboards as well. We've extracted data for a variety of sources, not just Microsoft Dynamics GP. In this final chapter, let's just have some fun!

Excel 2016

In keeping with the reporting theme of this book, we want to share two methods of sharing your Excel 2016 reports if you have an Office 365 subscription. Report distribution is as important as the report itself. The first will be via an instant message for one-on-one (or more) sharing; and the second is for presenting your report, live to a group or just one person. What good is a report if nobody reads it? Does it make a sound like the proverbial tree falling in the woods?

Sharing Excel reports via IM

Some of our reports are created on the fly, meaning something right away based on a unique request. Let's assume that a department head asked us for a financial statement, and we want to share it immediately and be available for a small dialogue. **Instant Messaging (IM)** is a great distribution option for this scenario. Distributing the report via IM, we will not only share the report, but we will imply that it possible for recipients send a message if they have a question or comment. Let's do this now:

1. Open the report in Excel 2016 that you want to share. We will open the `FinancialStatement.xlsx` file we created in *Chapter 7, Building Financial Reports in Jet Express for GP*.

2. Select **File** from the Excel menu. Select **Share** and then **Send by Instant Message**. Click on the address book icon to select who should receive this IM. The report name will become the subject, which will become the name of the IM conversation. Optionally, include a message for the recipients and click on **Send IM**:

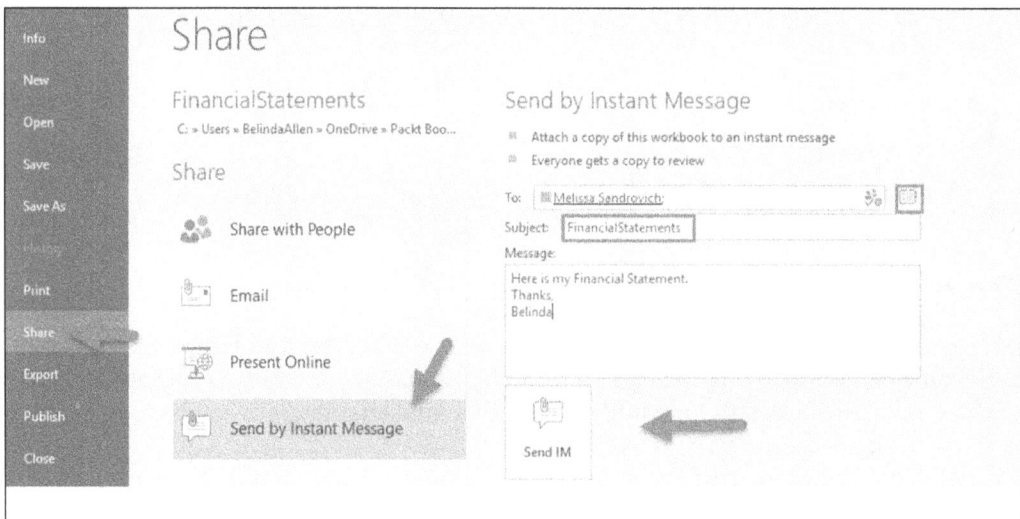

3. *Skype for Business* will create your IM session, and you can begin a chat dialogue with your recipients:

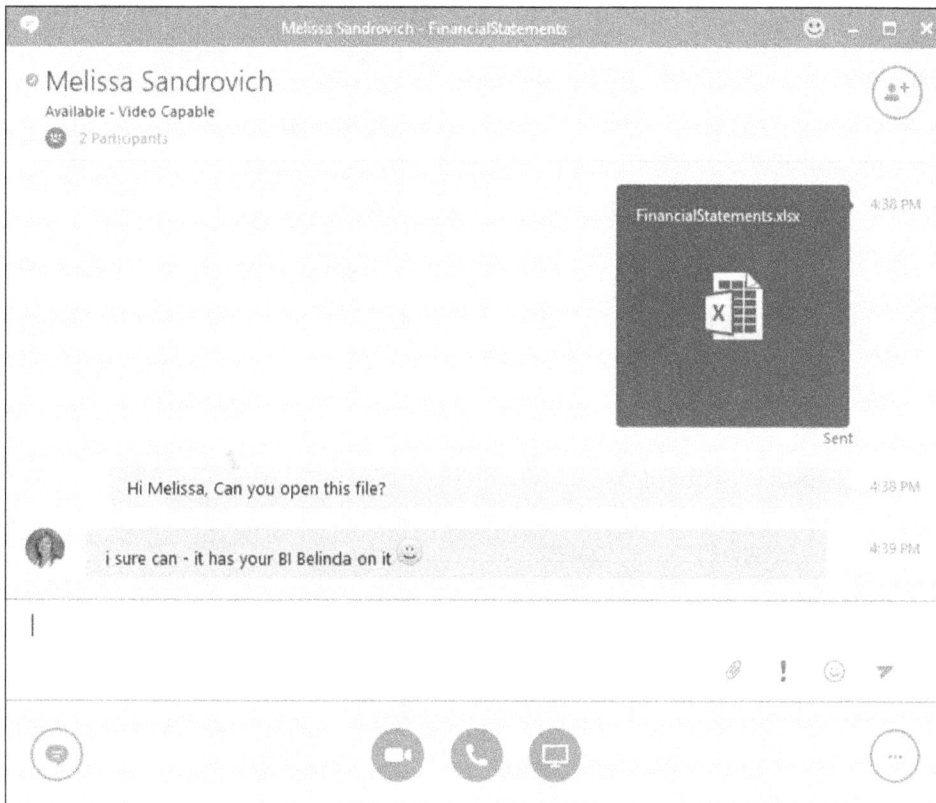

Sharing Excel reports via live presentation

Similar to the method we used to share the Excel report in an instant message, we can generate a *Skype for Business* meeting to show our report as a presentation:

1. Open the report in Excel 2016 that you want to share. We will open the `FinancialStatement.xlsx` file we created in *Chapter 7, Building Financial Reports in Jet Express for GP*.

2. Select **File** from the Excel menu. Select **Share** and then **Present Online**. Click on **Present**:

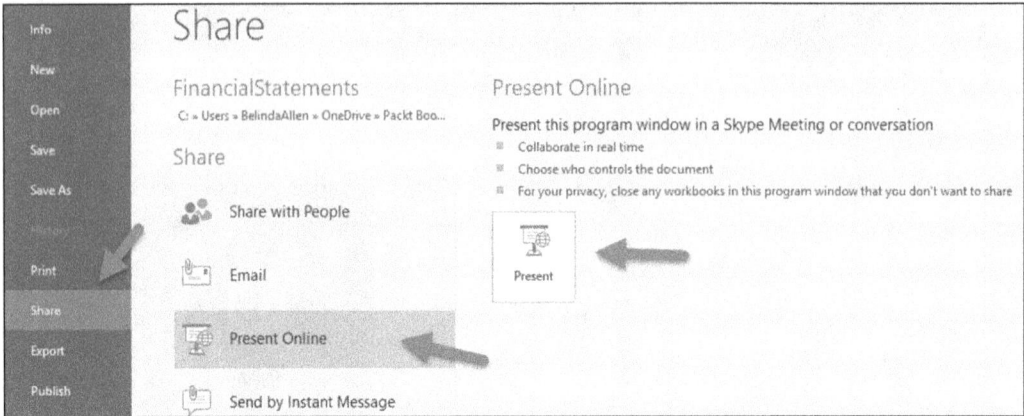

3. The **Share Workbook Window** will open. Select **Start a new Skype Meeting** and click on **OK**:

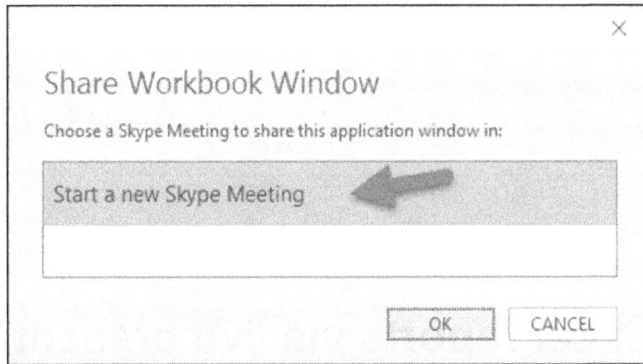

4. A *Skype for Business* meeting will open, and you'll be prompted for how you want to be connected for audio in the **Join Meeting Audio** window. Make the selection that is appropriate for your computer. We have a microphone and speaker, so we **Use Skype for Business** for audio. Click on **OK**:

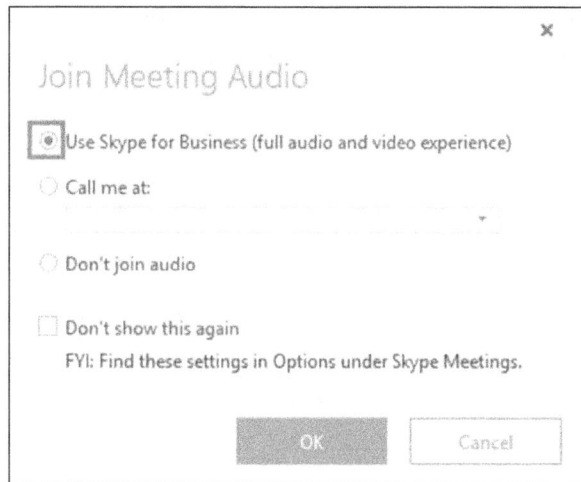

5. You are now presenting your Excel report. From this point, it's all you and *Skype for Business*:

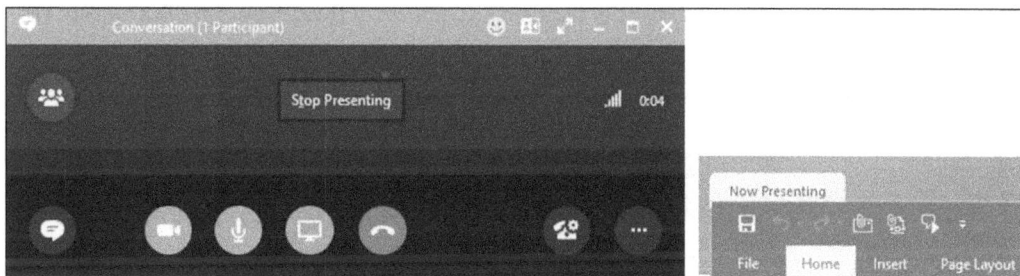

Jet Express for GP

There are two additional features we'd like to share regarding the GL function for building any financial statements using Jet Express for GP. One feature can eliminate a potential problem, while the second adds cool functionality to refreshing reports. Let's dig into these now.

Eliminating values that should be zero

Occasionally, when referencing categories or accounts that have no transactions and, therefore, a zero balance, Jet may display an amount because it doesn't know what to do if no transactions exist. This is easy to correct and/or prevent.

In the following example, we have built a report that displays the account number, account description, and the amount for two account categories. The first category is **Cash** and the second is **Deferred Revenue/Expense** accounts. Although there are some accounts assigned to the **Deferred Revenue/Expense** categories, these accounts have never been used; yet, a balance displays on the report. Let's correct this now:

Account	Description	Amount
000-1100-00	Cash - Operating Account	$ 570,104.47
000-1101-00	Cash in Bank - Canada	$ 8,957.84
000-1190-00	Cash Suspense	$ -
	Deferred Revenue / Expense	$ 266,259.75

We'll show you how to correct this now:

1. When using the **GL** function to add amounts in the **Jet Function Wizard**, we'll edit the **Account** line. Place your cursor before the cell reference (where the corresponding account is located). Click on **Allow Special Characters** on the ribbon. Alternately, you can add "@@"& before your cell reference:

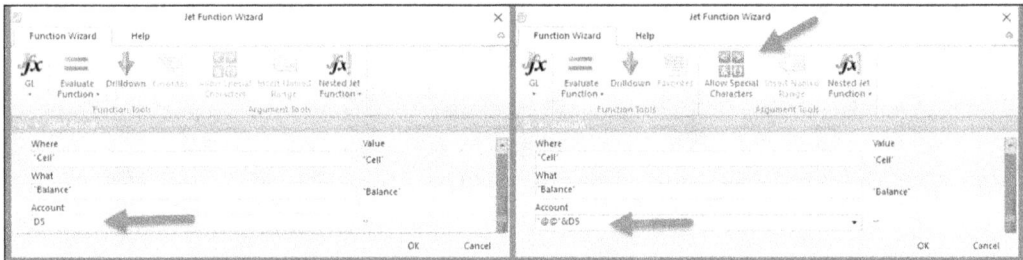

2. After refreshing, you'll see the amount has been corrected to zero. Easy-peasy!

Account	Description	Amount
000-1100-00	Cash - Operating Account	$ 570,104.47
000-1101-00	Cash in Bank - Canada	$ 8,957.84
000-1190-00	Cash Suspense	$ -
	Deferred Revenue / Expense	$ -

Refreshing with an option window

When we created our `FinancialStatement.xlsx` file report in *Chapter 7, Building Financial Reports in Jet Express for GP*, we built it in a manner that the user would have to edit the date field on the report when refreshing for a different period. The user experience is much improved if a pop-up window appears asking *Report on which period?* A pop-up window will also reduce the potential to edit the report in a way that breaks it. In *Chapter 6, Introducing Jet Reports Express*, a pop-up window was created automatically as part of the Table Builder functionality when we built our **General Ledger Trial Balance**.

Let's add this pop-up window to our report now:

1. Open the report in Excel 2016 that you want to share. We will open the `FinancialStatement.xlsx` file we created in *Chapter 7, Building Financial Reports in Jet Express for GP*.

2. At the bottom of the Excel report, click on the plus sign to add a new worksheet or page. Rename the new worksheet to `Options`:

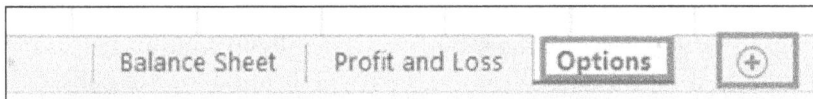

Balance Sheet	Profit and Loss	Options	⊕

3. In cell A1 of the new `Options` worksheet, enter `Auto+Hide+Hidesheet+Values` so this worksheet will not display or show when looking at the Excel report in the Jet Report mode.

4. In cell C1, enter `Title` and in cell D1, enter `Value`:

◢	A	B	C	D
1	Auto+Hide+Hidesheet+Values		Title	Value
2				

5. In cell A5, enter `Option`. In cell C4, enter `Report Options`. In cell C5, enter `Report on which period?` In cell D5, enter `4/30/17`:

◢	A	B	C	D
1	Auto+Hide+Hidesheet+Values		Title	Value
2				
3				
4			Report Options	
5	Option		Report on which period?	4/30/2017

6. At the bottom of Excel, click on the **Profit and Loss** tab to open the worksheet that contains the P&L report. Cell A4 is where we were manually entering the reporting date. Let's change this cell to reference the date cell (D5) on the new `Options` worksheet. The formula would be =*Options!D5*, or you could click in the address field, type =, and then click on the **Options** worksheet and then cell C5:

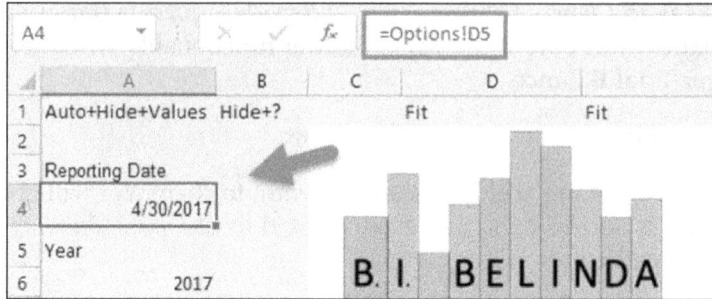

7. At the bottom of Excel, click on the **Balance Sheet** tab to open the worksheet that contains the Balance Sheet report. We built this one differently, referencing the year and the month individually in column **E**. Click on cell E6 to edit the year cell first. We'll use the Excel formula for Year and point to cell D5 on the **Options** tab. We'll do the same for the month:

   ° **Balance Sheet** page | cell E6 | formula: =*YEAR(Options!D5)*

   ° **Balance Sheet** page | cell E7 | formula: =*MONTH(Options!D5)*

8. Now, when you use the **Refresh** button on the **Jet** menu to refresh the report, a pop-up window will display, asking you **Report on which period?** You can edit the **Value**, which is the reporting date, and the reports will display using this new date after you click on **Run**.

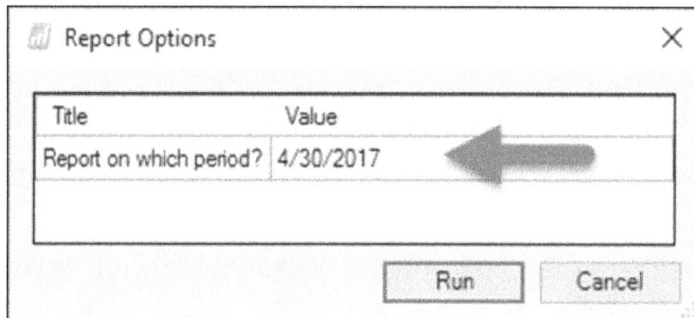

Microsoft Power BI

There are so many cool things to show in Microsoft Power BI that we debated what to show in the bonus chapter for a long time. Finally, we settled on creating a visual that uses a map as the foundation and creating visuals when our data source is a series of files.

The former is pretty self-explanatory. We'll create a map that displays our customer balances by the location of the customer itself. The latter is a great solution when data is fed to us through a series of files, such as from a point of sale system. A point of sale system would provide us with a report every day. These reports can be placed in a folder, and we can read all the files from the folder as if they were one data source. Although it may seem that this is a less common scenario, at some point in the future, you'll need it and be glad that you know about it.

Map of customer balances

As we already mentioned, our goal in this section is to walk you through creating a visual of a map that displays the customer balances by their location. There are two visual mapping options in Power BI, a Map and a Filled Map. The Map visual shows a particular point on the map, while Filled Maps shows data as geospatial, like a heat map. To make your first map experience easier, we'll use the regular Map visual. Let's get started:

1. To use maps, we will need location information. Let's create a new Power BI Desktop file, connect to our SQL Database like we did in *Chapter 9, Getting Data in Power BI,* and connect to the view **Customers**. When connecting, click on **Edit** rather than **Load**. This will open the query up in the Query Editor. If you click on **Load**, it's fine, you'll just need to click on **Edit Queries** to open the Query Editor.

2. Click on **Choose Columns** from the **Manage Columns** portion of the ribbon from the **Home** tab.

3. In the **Choose Columns** window, unselect **(Select all Columns)** and then reselect the following columns--**Customer Number, Customer Name, Address 1, Address 2, City, State, Zip, Country, Customer Balance, Customer Class,** and **Salesperson ID**. Click on **OK**.

4. Set the **Data Type** to all columns except **Customer Balance** as **Text**. Set the **Data Type** for **Customer Balance** as **Decimal Number**.

5. Click on **Close & Apply** to exit the Query Editor and begin building our map visual.

6. In the **Visualization** pane, click on the map icon. It's the one of the globe. The one that looks like the United States is the filled map visual. Take a look at the following screenshot:

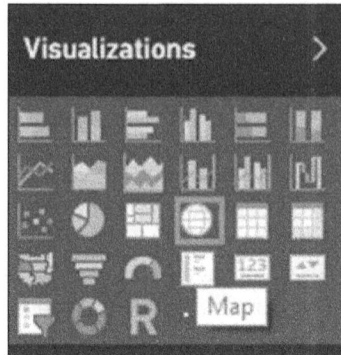

7. The empty visual will appear on the canvas. As this is the only visual we will build on this page, let's grab the corner handle and stretch it out so it covers the page, making a big map.

8. Keep this visual selected and let's begin to populate it. Grab the **City**, **State**, **Zip**, and **Country** fields one at a time and drag them to the **Location** area of the **Visualization** pane:

9. As of now, the map is displaying each location of where customer balances are located. Let's edit the map so we can see a larger circle for locations with the largest balances. Drag **Customer Balance** from the **Fields** pane into the **Size** field on the **Visualization** pane:

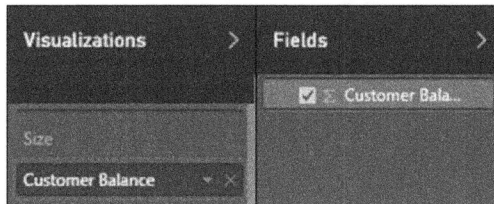

10. As a final touch, let's alter the visual to include Salesperson. Drag **Salesperson ID** from the **Fields** pane into the **Legend** field on the **Visualization** pane:

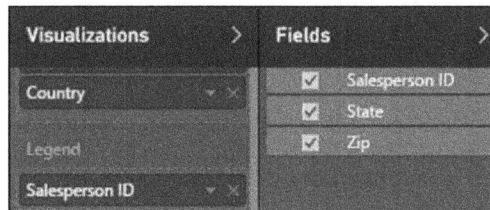

11. The map visual is now completed. You'll notice that you can zoom in and out with your mouse. The map itself has drill-down functionality at the top as well:

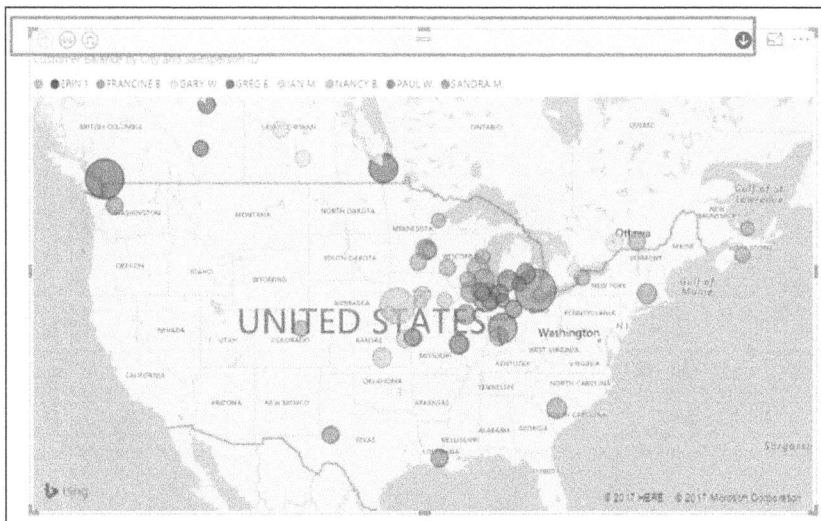

Maps are not only fun to build, but they can offer some pretty cool insight to your data as well, without asking for directions!

Getting data from a folder

At some point, you'll be in a situation where the data you want in your report is coming to you in pieces (for example, weekly, monthly, and so on), and you want to be able to combine it all together and create a single reporting unit. The easiest way to achieve this is to have a dedicated folder for all of these individual files. We can then report using the folder, rather than each file individually.

> When using this folder approach, each file must be formatted exactly the same way, with the same column names, number of columns, and file type.
>
> Now that you have MinGW and MSYS, there's no need to be jealous of those with a Linux installation anymore, since they implement in your system the most important parts of a Linux development environment.

Let's show you how we use this feature now. We'll break it into steps, so if you have similar data of your own, you can follow along, otherwise, you can just reference to this section later when you need it.

1. In the Power BI Desktop, we'll choose **Get Data** from the **Home** ribbon. We'll then choose **File** and **Folder**. Then, we'll click on **Connect**:

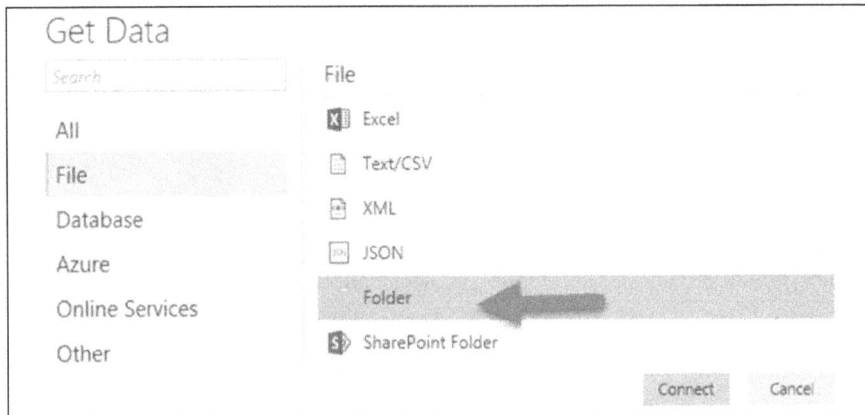

2. The **Folder** window will open. Use the **Browse...** button to find the path of the folder that contains your files. Click on **OK**:

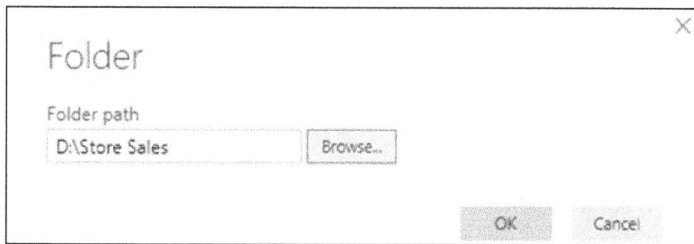

3. The data preview window will open. As we are looking at a folder, we'll see a list of the files, and not the data in the files. Click on **Edit**:

4. The Query Editor will open, displaying the list of files:

5. We'll right-click on the first column, **Content**, and choose **Remove Other Columns**. We want the content from the file. You'll see it also has a two down arrows icon that indicates there is more data available by the drill-down on these fields:

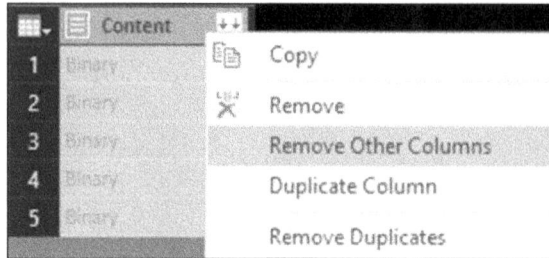

6. With **Content** being the only column remaining, we'll click on the two down arrows icon on that column. A new window will appear that reviews the data (or content) of each file. We'll leave the default options and click on **OK**:

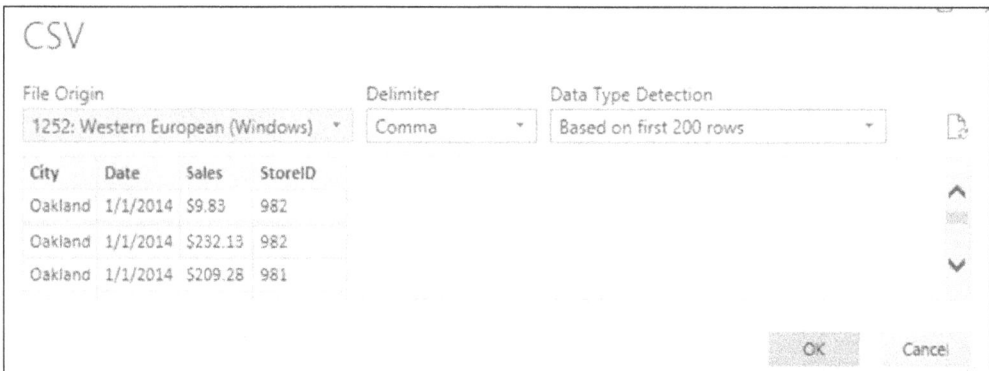

Steps 4, 5 and 6 could be avoided by clicking on **Combine & Edit** in step 3, but we wanted you to see what was actually happening.

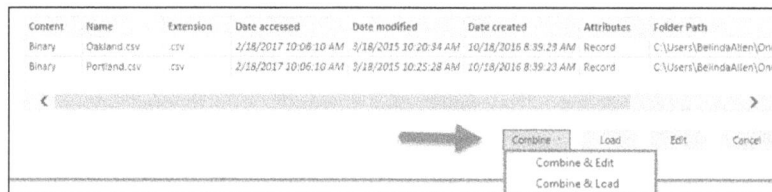

7. We ensure that the **Data Type** is set to **Text** for the **City** and **StoreID** columns, **Date** for the **Date** column and **Decimal Number** of the **Sales** column.

8. Each individual file in the folder contains header information (that is **City**, **Date**, **$ Sales**, and **StoreID**). By combining these files together, for all files after the first file, the headers have become part of the dataset. We will need to remove these subsequent headers from the data. We can simply use the filter function for the first column to remove all cities that are named **City**.

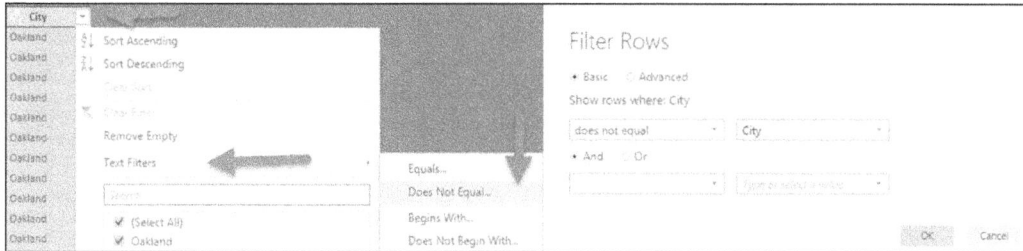

> This is why making sure the column names are exactly the same is important. It keeps the column names out of the data.

9. We will **Close & Apply**. Build our visuals using our new dataset. In this example, the following visual is made up of five separate *.csv files that act as one:

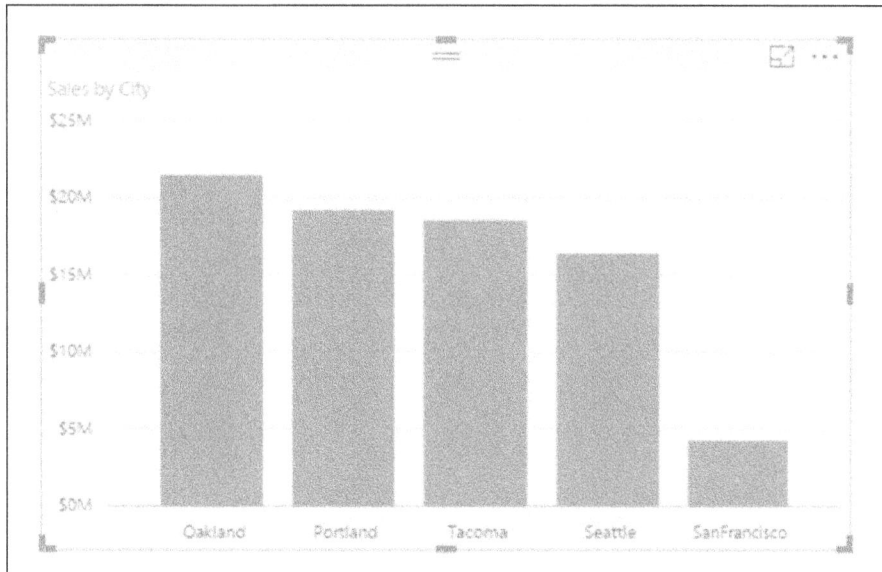

Summary

This brings us to the end of our bonus chapter, and our book. There is so much powerful information available to us using these tools. Tools you have and tools that are free for you to use.

Our world moves faster and faster every day. We need tools that can help provide us with accurate information faster and faster so we can make good and informed decisions. We are confident that these tools can help you do that.

Thanks for spending time with us, investing in yourself and your business.

Index

A

Accounts Payable (AP) 228
Analysis Cubes 31
Analysis Cubes for Excel (ACE) 31-33
Applied Steps
  using 284
Autodetect 243

B

Balance Brought Forward (BBF) 169
balance sheet
  building 164-177
bar chart
  building, with trend line 95-98
Business Intelligence (BI) 33

C

Client Access License (CAL) 34
Color Scales 102
column
  Data Types, formatting 285, 286
  merging 294-297
  removing 284
  splitting 297-300
Columns 53
conditional formatting 74
connected pivot tables
  creating, from inside Excel 67
connected pivot tables, creating
  receivables pivot table, adding 69-71
  sales pivot table, building 67-69

content packs
  about 218
  Online Services 218-221
  Organizational 222
Corporate Performance
        Management (CPM) 33
custom visuals
  creating 245

D

dashboard
  about 124
  building 74, 75
  creating 252-257
  design, creating 139
  preparations 75, 76
  reference 140
data
  Case, formatting 290
  connecting, in Dynamics GP 208
  Direct SQL Connect 208, 210-212
  Excel reports, used in Power BI 204-208
  obtaining, from files 204
  obtaining, from folders 223
  Open Data Protocol (OData) 215-217
  refreshing 140
  SQL statement 212-215
  transforming 289
  trimming 289, 290
Data Analysis Expressions (DAX)
  about 294
  formulating 307-310

www.ingramcontent.com/pod-product-compliance
Lightning Source LLC
Chambersburg PA
CBHW080909220326
41598CB00034B/5520